CORNELIUS VANDERBILT.

THE CRUISE

OF THE

STEAM YACHT NORTH STAR;

A NARRATIVE OF THE

Excursion of Mr. Vanderbilt's Party

TO

ENGLAND, RUSSIA, DENMARK, FRANCE, SPAIN, ITALY, MALTA,
TURKEY, MADEIRA, ETC.

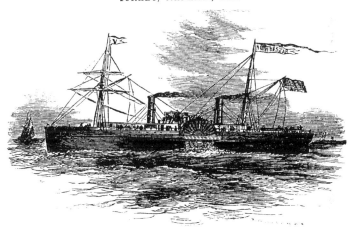

BY THE

REV. JOHN OVERTON CHOULES, D. D.,

AUTHOR OF THE "HISTORY OF MISSIONS," "YOUNG AMERICANS ABROAD," ETC.

BOSTON:
GOULD AND LINCOLN.
NEW YORK:
EVANS AND DICKERSON.
1854.

Entered according to Act of Congress, in the year 1854, by
GOULD & LINCOLN,
In the Clerk's Office of the District Court of the District of Massachusetts

Stereotyped by
HOBART & ROBBINS,
NEW ENGLAND TYPE AND STEREOTYPE FOUNDRY,
BOSTON.

Printed by Geo. C. Rand, No. 3 Cornhill.

To

GEORGE PEABODY, ESQ.,

THE

HONORED AND PATRIOTIC REPRESENTATIVE OF AMERICAN PRINCIPLES

IN LONDON,

This Narrative of a Steam Yacht Excursion in Europe,

MADE BY

AN AMERICAN MERCHANT,

Is Inscribed with great Respect,

BY HIS OBLIGED FRIEND,

J. O. CHOULES.

PREFACE.

I HAD the opportunity afforded me, by an indulgent congregation, to spend the summer of 1851 in Europe; and, on my return, I published a small volume (on which I was aided by three young friends and pupils, who were the companions of my tour), entitled "Young Americans Abroad, or Vacation in Europe." This had a favorable reception by the public, and has passed into a fourth edition and been reprinted in London. I had no idea that I should again revisit the Old World; or, at least, supposed that many years would elapse ere such a gratification could be enjoyed.

Last February my valued friend, Mr. Vanderbilt, informed me that he proposed in May to take his family on a voyage to the principal seaports of Europe, in a steam yacht then building for that purpose; and he most kindly invited me to be his guest. I saw no way by which I could accept his generous proposition consistently with the duties which I owed to my church and congregation; but, with a spirit of liberality and affection which I can never forget, they urged my acceptance of so fine an occasion to visit portions of the world rarely accessible to American tourists, and I concluded to join the party. My friends generally suggested that the excursion would afford sufficient interest to warrant a record. My excellent publishers, Messrs. Gould and Lincoln, at once claimed a volume; and, finding that my fellow-voyagers wished for a memorial of our four happy months spent in the North Star, I have consented to chronicle the movements of the most agreeable association of my life. I know that books of Travels have multiplied of late with fearful rapidity; but still the vast amount of readers in our country creates a steady demand for such publications.

A book of travels that contains reliable and interesting information has a good tendency. I remember with pleasure my own boyish gratification in reading Mavor's fine collection of voyages and travels; that set of books gave a turn to my future life, and a large share of my happiness may be traced back to the influences produced on my mind by the perusal of such works. It is a great thing to excite the intellect of a lad in a right direction. When I was about nine years of age, I used to pass many delicious hours in a cobbler's stall, not eight feet square, listening to his stories about the American revolutionary war, and the wars of the English and French in Canada. I made my earliest acquaintance with Lake George, Ticonderoga and Niagara Falls, by the side of the old man's lapstone, whilst he told me how fields were won; and Cobbler Hunt's stories about Indians and lakes, beavers and buffaloes, swans and flamingoes, had much to do with creating a desire to know more of the scenes of his exploits and adventures. This world is full of beauty, and it teems with wonders; and I never see a fresh portion of God's earth, but I feel some respect for the old gentleman's opinion, who, on going from Maine to Albany for the first time that he had left his native state, declared, on his return, that the world was more extensive than he had supposed. There is much to see wherever we turn, if our eyes are opened. All men have their own peculiar taste; and in a party of three or four visiting a foreign city, each member of it will see things in a different point of light. I believe that few persons have enjoyed so fine an opportunity to visit the coast of Europe as we had who formed the North Star party; and I hope that a plain narrative of the excursion, which has excited so much interest at home and abroad, may prove useful and entertaining. Those of our countrymen who were in Europe this summer are well aware that the presence of the steam yacht in foreign ports was to them the occasion of justifiable pride; while to foreigners she was the fruitful theme of admiration and reflection.

JOHN OVERTON CHOULES.

NEWPORT, R. I., *Jan.* 9, 1854.

Contents.

CHAPTER I.

ORIGIN OF THE YACHT VOYAGE — VARIOUS IDEAS AS TO ITS OBJECT — MR. VANDERBILT'S EXACT ARRANGEMENT — DESCRIPTION OF NORTH STAR — HER INTERNAL ARRANGEMENTS — FURNITURE, ETC. — COMMANDER ASA ELDRIDGE, ESQ. — OFFICERS AND CREW, ... 17

CHAPTER II.

READY TO SAIL — ALL ON BOARD 19 MAY — YACHT RUNS ON A REEF — NAVY-YARD AND DRY DOCK — REPAIRS SOON MADE — DEPARTURE 20 MAY — PILOT LEFT YACHT — MUSTER-ROLL OF THE PARTY — FAMILY WORSHIP — EMOTIONS OF VOYAGERS — SAFETY, NOT SPEED, THE RULE — STRIKE OF FIREMEN — GREEN HANDS — DIVINE SERVICE — LAND-BIRD — CONCERTS — GREAT RUN OF THREE HUNDRED AND FORTY-FOUR MILES — COMFORT AND LUXURY OF VOYAGE — MR. VANDERBILT'S COURTESY — PILOT — CHANNEL, ... 25

CHAPTER III.

SOUTHAMPTON — SCENERY — HISTORICAL ASSOCIATIONS — STEAM PACKET COMPANIES — HIGH-STREET — AMERICAN VICE-CONSUL, MR. COX — DOCKS — STEAMERS — REV. THOMAS ADKINS — ARRIVE IN LONDON — QUEEN'S DRAWING-ROOM — OBJECTS OF CURIOSITY, ETC. — HYDE PARK — KENSINGTON GARDENS — REGENT'S PARK — VISITS TO WESTMINSTER AND OTHER PUBLIC PLACES — WINDSOR — HAMPTON COURT — BRISTOL — CLIFTON AND VICINAGE — TINTERN — HENBURY AND COTTAGES — LOCAL SCENERY — BERKELEY CASTLE — GLOUCESTER — CHELTENHAM — ENGLISH COUNTRY SCENERY, ... 33

CHAPTER IV.

HON. AND REV. BAPTIST NOEL — MR. GEORGE PEABODY — OPERA — DINNER AT RICHMOND — HON. STEPHEN A. DOUGLAS — RECEPTION-NIGHT AT HON. J. R. INGERSOLL'S, THE AMERICAN MINISTER — THE LORD MAYOR'S SOIRÉE — MR. DEPUTY BENOCH — THOMAS PRICE, LL.D. — TOOVEY'S BOOKSTORE — DEPUTATION FROM SOUTHAMPTON — TONE OF ENGLISH FEELING TOWARDS THE UNITED STATES — AN ENGLISH TRAVELLER — STREET AMUSEMENTS — SCENE IN AN OMNIBUS, ... 46

CHAPTER V.

INTEREST EXCITED BY ARRIVAL OF THE NORTH STAR — LONDON DAILY NEWS — DULWICH GALLERY — MR. THOMAS COLLEY GRATTAN — A QUICK TRIP TO LEIPSIC — OUR RETURN TO SOUTHAMPTON — VISIT TO NETLEY ABBEY — HISTORICAL NOTICE — SCENERY — REV. DR. KREBBS — EXCURSIONS — REV. ALEXANDER MACLAREN — SERVICES OF THE SABBATH, 57

CHAPTER VI.

JUNE 13, THE BANQUET AT SOUTHAMPTON — CARD OF INVITATION — APPEARANCE OF TOWN — VICTORIA ROOMS — MAYOR — DINNER — ACCOUNT OF PROCEEDINGS AND SPEECHES IN THE HAMPSHIRE INDEPENDENT — EXCURSION OF THE NORTH STAR, WITH THE MAYOR AND INVITED GUESTS, ROUND THE ISLE OF WIGHT — DINNER ON BOARD — ACCOUNT TAKEN FROM THE HAMPSHIRE INDEPENDENT, ... 69

CHAPTER VII.

VOYAGE — COAST OF NORWAY — KRONBORG CASTLE AND ELSINORE — SHIPS IN THE SOUND — COPENHAGEN — BORNHOLM AND OLAND ISLANDS — DR. LINSLY — MIRAGE — DAGO ISLAND — STEAMER NEPTUNE — CRONSTADT — FORTIFICATIONS — DOCKS — SHIPPING — PUBLIC BUILDINGS — CHOLERA — PETERHOFF — WOODS — VAUXHALL HOTEL — MARLY AND MONTPLAISIR — PETER THE GREAT — HIS HOUSE — FURNITURE — COTTAGE OF CATHERINE — A RIDE THROUGH THE GROUNDS — WATER-WORKS, ETC. — PETERHOFF IMPERIAL PALACE — IMPERIAL YACHT, AND GRAND DUKE CONSTANTINE — ADMIRAL GLASSENOFF — MR. MULLER — MINIATURE PALACE — COSSACKS, ... 108

CHAPTER VIII.

SMALL STEAMER — DRESS OF OFFICERS — VIEW OF ST. PETERSBURG — QUEER PROCESSION — HOTELS — POLITENESS — MR. ROPES, U. S. CONSUL — SUMMER ISLANDS — PETER THE GREAT'S FIRST HOUSE — THE CITY — ADMIRALTY — STATUE OF PETER — NEFFSKY PERSPECTIVE — SERFS — VIEW OF CITY BY MOONLIGHT — WINTER PALACE AND ITS DEPARTMENTS — REGALIA — THE HERMITAGE — PAINTINGS OF DIFFERENT SCHOOLS — THE LOGGIE — PETER'S MUSEUM — PRECIOUS STONES — HOROLOGE — WREATHS AND LAURELS FROM CHERSONESUS — MARBLE PALACE — ALEXANDER PILLAR — MR. EVANS — MONASTERY OF ALEXANDER NEFFSKY — ENGLISH CHURCH — KESAU CATHEDRAL — ITS INTERIOR AND SERVICE — ISAAC CHURCH, ... 121

CHAPTER IX.

MAJOR THOMPSON BROWN — DROSKYS — WEDDING — GOSTINNOI DVOR — STREETS — MILITARY — FAREWELL TO ST. PETERSBURG — RETURN TO THE YACHT — VISITORS — REGATTA — CRONSTADT — MR. WILKINS — DANGEROUS POSITION — VISIT FROM GRAND DUCHESS OF OLDENBURGH AND FAMILY — STEAMBOAT PARTY AND IMPERIAL BAND — THE EMPEROR — QUEEN DOWAGER OF HOLLAND — NARROW ESCAPE, ... 141

CHAPTER X.

VOYAGE — COPENHAGEN — THORWALDSEN'S MUSEUM — FRUEKIRKE — THORWALDSEN'S CHRIST AND HIS APOSTLES — THE SCULPTOR — ROSENBERGH PALACE — ITS RICH COLLECTIONS OF ART — COINS AND MEDALS — PARK — STATUARY — COUNTRY — EXCHANGE — GALLERIES — AMALIENBORG PLADS — SONG OF THE WATCHMAN, ... 149

CHAPTER XI.

OFF FOR HAVRE — SCENERY OF THE SOUND — ISLE OF HUEN — TYCHO BRAHÉ — NORWAY AND SWEDEN — GODWIN SANDS LIGHT-SHIP — DOVER AND WALMER CASTLES — HAVRE — STEAMER FRANKLIN — MR. VESEY, U. S. CONSUL — THE TOWN — HISTORICAL INCIDENTS — INGOUVILLE — LEAVE FOR PARIS — ROUEN, POISSY, ETC., ... 158

CHAPTER XII.

HOTELS — HON. S. G. GOODRICH — AMERICAN CLERGY IN EUROPE — REVIEW — REV. ROBERT LOVETT AND HIS CHAPEL — CONFERENCE OF AMERICANS — METHODIST CHAPEL — LOUVRE — JARDIN DES PLANTES — PALAIS DE JUSTICE — FLOWER-MARKET — HOTEL DE CLUGNY — ENGLISH FRIENDS — VERSAILLES — GARDEN OF THE TUILLERIES AND CHAMPS-ELYSÉES — PONT NEUF AND OLD PARTS OF PARIS — HOTEL DE VILLE — CHURCHES — ROYAL LIBRARY — GOBELINS — ST. DENIS — NEUILLY — CHAPELLE ST. FERDINAND — CHAPELLE EXPIATOIRE — FONTAINEBLEAU, ... 165

CHAPTER XIII.

REV. J. R. PEAKE — NAPOLEON'S TOMB IN THE HOTEL DES INVALIDES — LOUIS PHILIPPE — DESCRIPTION OF THE CRYPT — GALLERY, ETC. — MOSAICS — CARYATIDES — SARCOPHAGUS — RELIQUARY — ALTAR AND BALDAQUIN — GUIDE — CLIMATE OF PARIS — OVERTURES MADE TO MR. VANDERBILT — WOODMAN AND FORR — RAILROAD TO ROUEN — HISTORIC NOTICE — POPULATION OF ROUEN — CATHEDRAL — INTERIOR — MONUMENTS — RICHARD CŒUR DE LION, ETC. — ABBEY OF ST. OUEN — PALACE OF JUSTICE — JOAN OF ARC — CORNEILLE — ENGLISH CHURCH — VISITORS, ... 186

CHAPTER XIV.

VOYAGE RESUMED — BAY OF BISCAY — VIGO BAY — LOSS OF ROBERT OGDEN FLINT — ROCK OF LISBON — CAPE ST. VINCENT — TRAFALGAR — TARIFA — COAST OF AFRICA — ROCK OF GIBRALTAR — MALAGA — QUARANTINE — WATERING — VISITORS FROM SHORE — FUNERAL SERMON — CATHEDRAL — BEGGARS IN THE STREETS — A PRETTY BOY AND A STRONG RESEMBLANCE — JOSE CUBERO — PRIEST WITH BELL AND BOX — BULL RING — REV. CHARLES BRERETON — BISHOP OF BARCELONA — CALECHES AND DRIVERS — RIDE TO MR. DELIUS' VILLA AND VINEYARDS — ALAMEDA — MULETEERS — MR. CONSUL SMITH — HARBOR OF MALAGA, ... 199

CONTENTS. XIII

CHAPTER XV.

OFF FOR LEGHORN — CARTHAGENA — IVICA — MAJORCA — MINORCA — CORSICA — SCENERY — GORGONA — LEGHORN — HOTEL ST. MARCO — FREE PORT — OPERA — SCOTCH FREE CHURCH — SERVICE ON SABBATH — STREETS ADMIRABLY PAVED — EVENING SERVICE — THE PARSONAGE-HOUSE — GOSPEL IN ITALY, ... 211

CHAPTER XVI.

ARRIVE AT FLORENCE — HOTEL D'ITALIE — RIDE — CITY AND STREETS, ETC. — PITTI PALACE — PICTURES — CANOVA'S VENUS — DUKE'S APARTMENTS — MUSEUM — POWERS AND HART — POWERS' STUDIO AND HIS WORK — HART'S STUDIO — BUSTS OF AMERICANS — STATUE OF HENRY CLAY — UFFIZII GALLERY — STATUARY — TRIBUNE — VENUS DE MEDICI — KNIFE-GRINDER, ETC. — TITIAN'S VENUSES — RAPHAEL'S PICTURES, ETC. — NIOBE — RUBENS — POWELL'S DE SOTO, ETC. — CATHEDRAL — CAMPANILE — BAPTISTERY — SANTO CROCE — CHAPEL OF THE MEDICI — ST. LORENZO — SACRISTY — MICHAEL ANGELO'S DAY AND NIGHT — PALAZZO VECCHIO — DUCAL PIAZZA — STATUARY, ... 218

CHAPTER XVII.

SANTA MARIA NOVELLA — PAINTINGS — SPEZIERIA — RESIDENCE OF MICHAEL ANGELO — CHURCH OF THE ANNUNCIATION — THE CASCINE — SCENERY — MOUNTAINS — THE BRIDGES — FRIENDS IN FLORENCE — OLIVER CROMWELL'S PORTRAIT — IMPRESSIONS OF FLORENCE — LEAVE FOR PISA — THE CITY — LEANING TOWER — CATHEDRAL — CAMPO SANTO — THE BAPTISTERY — SANTA MARIA DELLA SPINA — THE CAMELS — LEGHORN — GOVERNMENT ALARMED AT OUR YACHT — VISITORS, ETC., ... 233

CHAPTER XVIII.

LEAVE LEGHORN FOR CIVITA VECCHIA — HARBOR — DIFFICULTIES ON OUR WAY — DISAPPOINTMENT — VOYAGE RESUMED — SEE ST. PETER'S AFAR OFF — ISCHIA — PROCEDA — BAIA, ETC. — BRIDGE OF CALIGULA — NAPLES — THE BAY — RENEWED DISAPPOINTMENT — SWIMMERS — LADY MORGAN — VESUVIUS, ETC. — CAPRI AND SUNSET — STROMBOLI AND ÆTNA — CAPE FARO, OR PELORUS — SCYLLA — EARTHQUAKE OF 1783 — MESSINA — SCENERY OF THE STRAITS — RHEGIUM — MOUNT ÆTNA — SYRACUSE — CAPE PASSARO — MALTA, ... 244

CHAPTER XIX.

HARBOR — ARABS — ALLOWED TO LAND — VISIT FROM MR. CONSUL WINTHROP — DIVERS — HISTORICAL NOTICE — VALETTA — THE RACES — MALTESE BOATS — INVITATION FROM THE GOVERNOR TO TAKE DINNER — INVITATIONS FROM THE OFFICERS OF THE GARRISON — VISIT TO SIR WILLIAM REID — GOVERNOR'S PALACE — MR. WINTHROP'S RESIDENCE — MSS. OF ITALIAN OPERAS — CAPTAIN THOMAS GRAVES, R.N. — CITTA VECCHIA — SHOPS — THE GOVERNOR AND SUITE VISIT THE YACHT — ST. JOHN'S CHURCH — WALLS OF THE CITADEL — COUNTRY PEOPLE — COSTUME — FORTS ANGELO, RICASOLI, MANOEL, TIGNÈ AND ST. ELMO — TURKISH SIEGE IN 1565 — DEPART FOR CONSTANTINOPLE, ... 256

CHAPTER XX.

MOREA — CERIGO — CAPE COLONNA — TENEDOS — PLAINS OF TROY — ENGLISH AND FRENCH FLEETS — SIGÆUM — HELLESPONT — DARDANELLES — CASTLES OF EUROPE AND ASIA — PROPONTIS, OR SEA OF MARMORA — FIRST VIEW OF STAMBOUL — SCENERY — ANCHORAGE OFF PERA — MR. BROWN AND OTHER VISITORS — VISIT TO PERA, GALATA AND TOPHANA — SULTAN'S NEW PALACE — GULLS — SULTAN'S FIRMAN — SERAGLIO — ATMEIDAN, OR HIPPODROME — SUBLIME PORTE — LIBRARY — ANCIENT ARMOR — MOSQUE OF ST. SOPHIA — HISTORICAL NOTICE, ETC., ... 275

CHAPTER XXI.

MOSQUE OF ACHMET — MUZZEIN'S CALL — COSTUMES OF THE JANISSARIES — REV. MR. BENJAMIN — TOMB OF SULTAN MAHMOUD — BAZAARS — SHOPPING — VISIT TO THE ENGLISH YACHT SYLPHIDE — TURKISH VISITORS — AMERICAN MISSIONARIES — EXCURSION TO SCUTARI — HOWLING DERVISHES — CEMETERY — WEDDING — BULGURLU — SCENERY — CHALCEDON — A KIOSK — HOUSE IN WHICH THE LATE SULTAN DIED — SOLDIERS COMING IN FROM ASIA — DARK RIDE — SAIL TO BEBEK — AFFECTING INCIDENT — VILLAGE OF BEBEK — MISSION PREMISES — EDUCATION OF BOYS IN MECHANICAL ARTS — PERSECUTION — MR. HAMLIN — ARMENIAN PRIEST — THE FAMILY CIRCLE — "LIGHT ON THE DARK RIVER" — MISS LOVELL — MR. MINASIAN, ... 289

CHAPTER XXII.

SULTAN GOING TO MOSQUE — CAIQUES — A STEAMBOAT CHARTERED — EXCURSION UP THE BOSPHORUS — EUROPEAN BANK — TURKISH AND EGYPTIAN FLEET — SYMPLEGADES — BLACK SEA — ASIATIC COAST — LAND AT KANDALI — RETURN TO YACHT — DEPARTURE FROM CONSTANTINOPLE — VOYAGE TO GIBRALTAR — ARRIVAL AT THE ROCK — APPEARANCE OF ROCK AND TOWN — THE METHODIST CHAPEL — REV. W. H. BIDWELL — STREETS AND MARKETS — SHOPS AND GOODS — EXCURSION TO THE ROCK — ENGLISH OFFICERS — ST. GEORGE'S HALL — ST. MICHAEL'S CAVE — MONKEYS — DINNER AT MR. SPRAGUE'S — HISTORICAL NOTICES — SMUGGLERS SHOT — PROFFERED HOSPITALITIES — EXCURSION TO THE CORK WOODS — "CHARLEY," THE MOORISH MERCHANT — DINNER WITH THE FORTY-FOURTH REGIMENT — VISITORS TO THE YACHT, ... 304

CHAPTER XXIII.

LEAVE GIBRALTAR — TANGIER — SAIL FOR MADEIRA — PORTO SANTO — MADEIRA — FUNCHAL, AND ITS ASPECT — LANDING IN THE SURF — HISTORIC NOTICE — LEGEND OF MACHIM — OBSERVATIONS ON FUNCHAL — CATHOLIC INTOLERANCE — MANNERS OF PEOPLE — EXCURSION TO THE CHURCH OF OUR LADY OF THE MOUNT — SCENERY — A MIRACLE — MR. GEORGE BROWN — BEGGARS — ARTICLES FOR SALE — YATES' HOTEL — HIS STUDY — CLIMATE — SIR JAMES CLARK AND LEIGH HUNT — POPULATION — BOARDING-HOUSES — MODES OF TRAVEL — SHOPS — THE BOY-BEGGARS — BLAST OF THE VINEYARDS — THE VINE — WINES OF THE ISLAND — FRUITS AND VEGETABLES — TREES AND FLOWERS — BIRDS — FISH — DEPARTURE, 325

CHAPTER XXIV.

LEAVE FUNCHAL — APPEARANCE OF THE ISLAND — SKIRT THE SHORE — ROUGH WEATHER — LIVE STOCK — A WRECK DISCOVERED — FLYING-FISH — SANDY HOOK — SALUTATIONS ON ARRIVAL — SUMMARY OF THE VOYAGE — OUR OBLIGATIONS TO MR. AND MRS. VANDERBILT — CAPTAIN ELDRIDGE AND HIS OFFICERS — THE VOYAGE A SOURCE OF PRIDE TO THE COUNTRY, ... 346

List of Illustrations.

———◆———

LIKENESS OF CORNELIUS VANDERBILT, ... FRONTISPIECE.
STEAM YACHT NORTH STAR, ... TITLE-PAGE.
LIKENESS OF CAPTAIN ASA ELDRIDGE, ... P. 22
ST. VINCENT ROCKS, CLIFTON, ... 40
HENBURY COTTAGES, ... 42, 45
ST. PETERSBURG, FROM THE ENGLISH QUAY, ... 126
GRAND ENTRANCE TO THE CRYPT, AND VIEW OF NAPOLEON'S TOMB, 189
MOSAICS ON PASSAGE-FLOOR LEADING TO THE TOMB, ... 190
ROUEN, ... 193
LEGHORN, ... 212
PALAZZO VECCHIO, FLORENCE, ... 230
VALETTA, FROM SLIEMA, ... 258
MALTESE COUNTRY MAN AND WOMAN, ... 269
CONSTANTINOPLE, ... 280
GIBRALTAR, FROM THE SPANISH SIDE, ... 311
FUNCHAL, FROM THE SEA, ... 327

CHAPTER I.

ORIGIN OF THE YACHT VOYAGE — VARIOUS IDEAS AS TO ITS OBJECT — MR. VANDERBILT'S EXACT ARRANGEMENT — DESCRIPTION OF NORTH STAR — HER INTERNAL ARRANGEMENTS — FURNITURE, ETC. — COMMANDER ASA ELDRIDGE, ESQ. — OFFICERS AND CREW.

EARLY in the spring of the present year, the attention of the country was directed to an item in the daily papers of New York, containing information that Mr. Vanderbilt was constructing a steam-ship of large dimensions, which he intended as a yacht for the accommodation of his family and some invited friends in a voyage to the principal sea-ports in Europe. The announcement of this project excited a deep interest in the public mind, and the excursion became a prominent subject of conversation.

Mr. Vanderbilt was known to his countrymen as a thoroughly practical man, whose energy and perseverance, combined with strong intellect and high commercial integrity, had given him immense wealth; all his undertakings had been crowned with signal success, and his great enterprise in opening a communication with the Pacific by the Nicaragua route had made him a reputation in Europe; and a general expectation existed that he would carry out his plan in a manner that would redound to the honor of the country. Various opinions were entertained as to his ultimate designs. Many imagined that Mr Vanderbilt proposed to effect some great mercantile operation, — he was to sell his ship to this monarch, or that government, — or, he was to take contracts for the supply of war steamers; all sorts of speculations were entertained by that generally misinformed character, — *the public*. In February I was sitting with Mr. Vanderbilt in his library, when he gave me the first information I had received of his intentions, and he kindly invited me and my wife to accompany him to Europe in the month of May. The ship was then on the stocks, but he named the very day on which he should sail, and gave me the details of his proposed route, and from which few deviations were afterwards made. Mr. V. expressly informed me that his sole object was to gratify his family and afford himself an opportunity to see the coast of Europe, which he could do in no other way; and he observed that, after more than thirty years' devotion to business, in all which period he had known no rest from labor, he felt that he had a right to a complete holiday.

The following description of the yacht appeared in the *Illustrated News*, published in New York, April 9, 1853, and I select it for my present purpose, as it is, I believe, strictly correct:

"MR. VANDERBILT'S STEAM YACHT.

"The latest enterprise in the way of steam vessels, with which Mr. Vanderbilt has had any connection, is the construction of a yacht, for private purposes, to be propelled by steam. This vessel is called the 'North Star,' and was lately launched at New York. She is to leave on a cruise to the east about the middle of May. Mr. Vanderbilt goes out in her, with some thirty or forty ladies and gentlemen, his friends. We believe he intends to land first at Southampton, then go round to London. From there the trip is to be extended, first up the Baltic to St. Petersburg, and then return, and go up the Mediterranean, calling at Gibraltar, Naples, Malta and Athens, visiting Constantinople and Alexandria. What will the wealthy noblemen of England — the proprietors of sailing yachts of fifty and a hundred tons — say to a citizen of the United States appearing in their waters with a steamship yacht of twenty-five hundred tons burthen; a vessel large enough to carry the armament of a British seventy-

DESCRIPTION OF NORTH STAR. 19

four? We have shown our transatlantic cousins one sample of yachting, about which we do not care to boast. Dropping the past, we are sure the English nobility and gentry will give the gallant 'commodore' a reception commensurate with his rank as a merchant prince, — one who goes abroad in a style not inferior to their own youthful sovereigns. We predict a sensation, at the appearance of this vessel in Europe, second to that of no arrival they have ever had from any quarter of the globe.

"The North Star has been built under the immediate supervision of her owner, whose principal object has been to combine beauty of model with strength and durability; and, although connoisseurs in naval architecture bespeak for her a speed equal to any of our sea steamers, yet it has not been so much the design of her owner to produce the fastest vessel afloat, as a noble specimen of American mechanical skill. Her boilers and the principal part of her engines are on board, and she will in a few weeks be ready to sail for Southampton.

"To her builder, Mr. Simonson, too much praise cannot be awarded for the care and skill he has displayed in the construction of this noble ship; which, apart from the beauty of her model, is probably the strongest fastened vessel of her tonnage afloat. She is 260 feet on the keel, 270 feet on the spar deck, 38 breadth of beam, 13 feet from floor timber to lower deck beams, 7 feet 8 inches between decks, 7 feet 6 inches between main and spar decks, making her whole depth 28 feet 6 inches. Her keel, of white oak, is 15 inches sided by 14 inches wide, stem and stern posts of the same material, with double aprons, and inner posts of live oak, bolted through with $1\frac{3}{8}$ copper bolts, deadwoods of white oak and 13 inches through, fastened with $1\frac{1}{2}$ inch copper bolts, in the most substantial manner. The floor timbers are sided 12 inches, and moulded 13 inches, being placed close together, and bolted through sideways with $1\frac{1}{2}$ inch bolts. The main kelsons, of which there are five rows extending the entire length of the ship, are of white oak, sided 15 inches by 32 inches deep, the first tier being fastened by two copper bolts 1¼ inches in diameter, through every floor timber, the upper tiers secured to the lower one with large iron bolts. The bed upon which the engine rests is composed of four rows of kelsons, 2 feet 2 inches by 5 feet deep, secured by iron screw bolts driven from the bottom before the vessel was planked. The outside planking of white oak, 3½ inches thick, increasing to 5 inches, is secured with copper bolts and locust trenails, there being 32,000 of the latter driven through and wedged upon both sides. There are six bilge streaks on the inside of the ship, covering the floor heads and futtocks 12 by 14 inches, fastened to the timbers with iron bolts, and bolted edge-lays between every frame.

"The ceiling is of six-inch yellow pine, and bolted in the same manner as the bilge streak, forming one substantial mass of timber 14 feet in depth. The lower deck clamps, on which the beams rest, are 7 inches thick, thoroughly fastened with iron bolts driven from the outside, and riveted on the inside.

"There are 45 deck beams in the lower deck, with carlines between, sided 15 inches and moulded 14 inches, with lodging and bosom knees of white oak, and a large hanging knee on each end. The water ways on top of the lower deck are composed of three pieces, extending the whole length of the ship, thoroughly bolted, — making this deck sufficiently strong to stand any reasonable strain. The clamps to support the main deck are of yellow pine, 6 inches thick and 14 inches wide, of two widths. This deck is securely kneed, in the same manner as the lower one. The stanchions, which extend from the floor timbers to the lower deck beams, have a large bolt passing through them, and are continued on to the upper decks, thus connecting the deck with the bottom of the ship. The lower and main deck plank are of white pine, 3 by 5 inches; the upper or spar deck extending the entire length of the ship.

"Her machinery is from the Allaire works. She will be propelled by two lever beam engines: cylinders, 60 inches; length

HER INTERNAL ARRANGEMENTS.

of stroke, 10 feet; diameter of wheels, 34 feet. Her boilers, of which she has four, are 24 feet long, 10 feet diameter, 11½ feet front, 11 feet high, with single return flues.

"Her cabins and interior arrangements combine all that is required to insure comfort and elegance.

"The *Staten Islander* of the 20th of May, speaking of the yacht, stated that 'the main saloon is splendidly fitted up with all that can tend to gratify the eye and minister to luxurious ease. The state-rooms, which lead from it on either side, are fitted up in the first style of the upholsterer's art. The furniture throughout blends in one harmonious whole; there are none of those glaring contrasts which are too often met with, and offend the eye and taste by their incongruities. This saloon is of beautiful satin-wood, with just sufficient rosewood to relieve it, the work of which was executed by Mr. Charles Simonson. The cabinet furniture and upholstery were furnished from the extensive establishment of Messrs. J. & J. W. Weeks. The furniture of the main saloon is of rosewood, carved in the splendid style of Louis XV., covered with a new and elegant material of figured velvet plush, with a green ground filled with bouquets of flowers. It consists of two sofas, four couches, six arm-chairs. Connected with this saloon are ten state-rooms, superbly fitted up, each with a French *armour le gles*, beautifully enamelled in white, with a large glass door — size of plate, forty by sixty-four inches. The berths are furnished with elegant silk lambricans and lace curtains. Each room is fitted up with a different color, namely, green and gold, crimson and gold, orange, &c. The toilet furniture matches with the hangings and fittings, by being of the same colors, and presents a picture of completeness not often met with. The saloon and state-rooms are kept at a pleasant temperature by one of Van Horn's steam heaters, which occupies the centre of the cabin. It is a beautiful specimen of bronze trellis-work, with marble top, and has richly burnished gilding. The tapestry carpet is one of gorgeous pattern. Forward of saloon is a magnificent dining-saloon. This is fitted up in a style entirely new to sea-going vessels. The walls are covered with a preparation of ligneous marble, polished to a degree of mirror-like brightness that marble is incapable of receiving. The panels are of Naples granite, the style of Breschia jasper, and the surface of yellow Pyrenees marble. The ceiling of this room is in panels painted white, with scroll-work of purple, light-green and gold, surrounding medallion paintings of Columbus, Webster, Clay, Calhoun, Washington, Franklin and others, together with various emblematic conceptions. All the table furniture is of the most gorgeous description. The china is of ruby and gold finish, and the silver ware of the finest kind. The entire interior furnishing has been done with the single idea of producing the very best effect possible, and every article shows elaborate design and workmanship, which reflects much credit on American taste and skill.'

A fine entrance saloon, leading from the deck, conducts, by an elegantly adorned staircase, to the main saloon. This reception saloon has a circular sofa capable of seating some twenty persons, and is covered with crimson plush. Over the stairway is a good painting of Mr. Vanderbilt's summer villa at Staten Island, which was placed there, without his knowledge, by the polite attention of his artist friend.

The command of the steamer was given by her proprietor to Asa Eldridge, Esq., a gentleman who had established a high nautical reputation as a commander in the India, Liverpool, and California trade. The first officer was Mr. Cope, of Virginia; the second, Mr. Petersen, a native of Sweden; the chief engineer was Mr. Germaine, of New York; the steward, Mr. Larner, formerly of the Cunard line; the purser, Mr. John Keefe, the well-known caterer of good things at the café near the Racket Club, in Broadway.

Several of the hands who shipped for the cruise were young men of the best families in the country, who were attracted by the prospect of visiting so many celebrated cities and places in a short summer passage.

CHAPTER II.

READY TO SAIL — ALL ON BOARD 19 MAY — YACHT RUNS ON A REEF — NAVY-YARD AND DRY DOCK — REPAIRS SOON MADE — DEPARTURE 20 MAY — PILOT LEFT YACHT — MUSTER-ROLL OF THE PARTY — FAMILY WORSHIP — EMOTIONS OF VOYAGERS — SAFETY, NOT SPEED, THE RULE — STRIKE OF FIREMEN — GREEN HANDS — DIVINE SERVICE — LAND-BIRD — CONCERTS — GREAT RUN OF THREE HUNDRED AND FORTY-FOUR MILES — COMFORT AND LUXURY OF VOYAGE — MR. VANDERBILT'S COURTESY — PILOT — CHANNEL.

ALL preliminary arrangements having been made, and the "North Star" having made a satisfactory trip to Sandy Hook, — the only trial to which she was subjected, — the party assembled on board for our departure, May 19th, at the wharf belonging to the Allaire works, near the foot of Corlears-street. A party of our friends, consisting of between four and five hundred persons, was on board the yacht, who were to accompany us to the Hook, and return in the Francis Skiddy, which, as a mark of respect to Mr. Vanderbilt, had been loaned for the occasion by her owner, J. McCullough, Esq. At half past ten A. M. the wheels were in motion, but in three minutes after, the force of the ebb-tide operating upon the yacht, which had no steerage-way, she struck hard and fast upon the reef which lies at the pier. Here we were placed in what an old gentleman on board termed "a located position." The Huguenot steamer came to our assistance, and in a few hours we entered the Dry Dock, at the Government Navy-yard, where we received all necessary aid, afforded in the kindest manner by Commodore Smith, the chief of the Bureau of the Dock and Navy-yard, and Captain Boorman, the commandant of the Navy-yard. It ought to be stated, that as soon as the accident occurred a telegraphic message was sent to the Secretary of State and the Navy Department;* and an order was promptly responded that we should be received at the Dry Dock, which, fortunately, was unoccupied at the time. The Dry Dock is a most splendid work of art; and by the force of the powerful steam-engine it was soon emptied, and the North Star was exposed to the examination of the ship-carpenters. It was found that the damage was very slight; she had only lost a part of her shoe, and roughed her copper in a few places. Everything was made right in a short time, and the anxiety of the party, which had been considerable, lest a delay should prove inevitable, was at once relieved; and, at seven minutes to eight o'clock P. M., on the 20th of May, we left the gates amid the cheering of our kind friends who lined the dock; and, as we steamed down the river, we fired salutes and received them from various ships, and at the Battery, where a large party had gathered to give us a farewell greeting. As the North Star passed by Staten Island, and just opposite to the residence of Mr. Vanderbilt's mother, rockets were let off, and guns fired from the yacht. The night was fine, and the moon, shining in a cloudless sky, gave us a charming view of one of the sweetest islands of the world. At half-past nine o'clock we were outside the Hook, and all in fine spirits, as the pilot, Mr. John Martineau, left the ship. Just before leaving, he was called into the cabin and received the present of a purse of gold, which was intended to show that no blame was attached to him by Mr. Vanderbilt on account of the disaster at leaving the dock on the previous day. The presentation was made by Mr. H. F. Clark.

Perhaps this may be the proper time to record the muster-roll of the party, which consisted of the following persons:

Mr. and Mrs. Cornelius Vanderbilt,
Mrs. James Cross,
Miss Kate Vanderbilt,

FAMILY WORSHIP. 27

Master George W. Vanderbilt,
Mr. and Mrs. W. H. Vanderbilt,
Mr. and Mrs. D. B. Allen,
Mr. and Mrs. George Osgood,
Mr. and Mrs. W. K. Thorn,
Miss Louisa Thorn,
Mr. and Mrs. Daniel Torrance,
Mr. and Mrs. H. F. Clark,
Mr. and Mrs. N. B. Labau,
Dr. and Mrs. Linsly,
Rev. Dr. and Mrs. Choules,
Mrs. Asa Eldridge.

Soon after leaving Sandy Hook, Mr Vanderbilt requested me to conduct family worship on board the ship throughout the voyage, and to appoint such an hour as I thought most suitable. It was accordingly agreed that prayers should be attended every evening at nine o'clock, and that grace should be said at all the meals on board ship. It affords me great pleasure to record that nearly all the party regularly attended throughout the voyage, as well as at the Sabbath-day services, when a sermon was preached at eleven o'clock. It is a happy thing for the voyager who for the first time looks back upon the receding shores of his beloved land, that, amid the disquietudes that fill his imagination and the natural forebodings of terror, connected, probably, with actual suffering, he has the prospect of revelling amid the cherished day-dreams of his boyhood; he anticipates an association with the glorious homes of England, the battle-fields of freedom, the classic plains of Italy and Greece, and the storied shores of the Mediterranean. I have noticed, on several passages over the Atlantic, that a thoughtful and contemplative mood is the characteristic feature of the voyager for the first two or three days; his mind appears to fall back upon his history, and, apart from the excitement of life's usual tide, the man *remembers the way by which he has been led.* A great change is felt to have been made in a few short hours. The different pursuits of life in which all have been occupied are broken off. A period of calm repose is afforded; a thing so new and untried by most of our party, — business men, for whose ardor the days are too short and the nights are too long.

The next day after leaving New York, the day was all that we could desire; not a cloud was visible, the sun shone most gloriously, and it seemed happiness to exist. At twelve o'clock, it was announced that we had made one hundred and seventy-six miles since eight o'clock the previous evening. This was regarded as satisfactory for the first day, because we were under moderate steam. Mr. Vanderbilt distinctly informed us that his plan was to insure safety for the prosecution of the whole voyage, which would probably be one of nearly twenty thousand miles, and that the attainment of great speed was no object of his ambition. Of the power and capacity of the North Star he had no doubt; but, with such objects to effect as he proposed, he felt unwilling to make any rash attempts at unusual rapidity.

It is worth stating that, in making up the complement of firemen for the voyage, Mr. Germaine had selected a company of picked men, whose abilities he knew from former service. But, an hour before the yacht was to commence her voyage, this department of the ship's company saw fit to strike for wages, supposing that such a measure, at so critical a juncture, would meet with a sure compliance. But the calculation was made without the host, and in total ignorance of the man with whom they had to do. True to his principles of action in all his business affairs, Mr. Vanderbilt refused to be coërced by the seeming necessity of the case; he would not listen for a moment to demands so urged, and in one hour selected such firemen as could be collected; and many of them were green hands, and ill-adapted to give efficient service in their most important department, where skill and adroitness are necessary qualifications, and can only be the result of experience. Several of the seamen, too, were fresh from the rural occupations of life. One youth was ordered to strike two bells, and, after a tardy movement, he reported that he could only find one bell! Several whales were seen not far from the ship, and their gambols amused those who had never before seen Leviathan at home.

On the 22d, our party was all in usual health, with the exception of three of the ladies, who suffered from the new acquaintance formed with the ocean, although the sea was as smooth as the North river. At eleven o'clock divine service was performed in the saloon, and attended by many of the officers and crew of the ship. In view of the long period of intimate association we were likely to spend on board the yacht, the text selected for the occasion was one of a practical character, — Proverbs 16 : 32. " He that is slow to anger is better than the mighty, and he that ruleth his spirit than he that taketh a city." The singing was fine, and the accompaniment of the piano very acceptable. The log of the ship this day recorded two hundred and seventy-two miles.

The 23d was a bright, fine day, and the run of the yacht two hundred and seventy-eight miles, — the wind abaft, and a little more sea on, causing her to roll. We passed the ship Sharon, of Bath; we gave her three hearty cheers, and she returned the compliment by lowering her flag.

24*th*. — Our run was two hundred and sixty miles. At seven minutes past seven A. M., we stopped one hour to key up. All day amused by vast schools of porpoises playing close around us, and nearly touching our wheels.

25*th*. — Two hundred and seventy miles. In the night we crossed the banks of Newfoundland; the day was slightly foggy, the sea like a mirror, with a perceptible ground-swell. In the morning, between two and three, we passed and spoke the Mary Crocker, of Bath, from Liverpool, bound to Philadelphia; we glided close by her stern. Soon after daylight, a small land-bird flew on board; it appeared quite exhausted. Poor thing! it had lost its way, and here it was almost mid-ocean. We fed it with crumbs and seed, and it seemed nearly disposed to form an acquaintance with our canary-bird. A recent traveller, in recording a similar event, says, very beautifully, of a stray bird, "Is it not an epitome of man when he breaks the golden chords of that harmony which bind him to his God?"

The extreme tranquillity of the ocean prevented us from feeling that we were at sea. The pleasant weather kept us much on deck, and we found constant employment in gazing upon the lights and shades of the ever-rolling waves. Our evenings were spent very agreeably in listening to music from the ladies. We had a fine piano, and several of the party possessed vocal powers of a high order. I have rarely enjoyed a concert on shore as much as some of our entertainments at sea. One gentleman of the party possessed fine taste in Italian music, and several others had good voices, and our concerts would have been respectable on shore; but at sea they were marvellously well received by a gratified audience. The ladies were always in voice, and many a song I heard on the ocean-wave will long dwell upon the ear of memory. The sailors, too, were decidedly fond of negro melody. One of them, who answered to the euphonious name of "Pogee," was, I think, quite equal to the Christy Minstrels. Every evening, he made plenty of amusement for all hands; and many a merry group have I seen gathered round him to listen to "Jordan am a hard road to trabel, I believe."

26th. — The ship's run was two hundred and eighty-five miles. Exchanged signals with the ship Charlotte Harrison. Her decks crowded with emigrants. Day overcast.

27th. — No observation by sun. The calculation of the log was two hundred and sixty-five miles. This day our bird left us. Saw several vessels.

28th — We made three hundred miles, and had a fine breeze. The day charming.

29th.—Sunday. Our ship's reckoning was three hundred and thirty-seven miles. After a thick night, the sun rose clear. Attended divine service.

This was a great day's work. Our average revolutions fourteen and one-half. No doubt exists that we could have made three hundred and sixty miles, had the effort been put forth. The Baltic, on a trip from Liverpool to New York, once made three hundred and thirty-six miles; but the difference of time in her favor was twenty-eight and one-half minutes, making her running-time twenty-four hours, twenty-eight minutes, thirty seconds. Whereas we were going east, and so lost twenty-eight and one-half minutes on our twenty-four hours. Giving the North Star the benefit of this calculation, and our twenty-four hours affords a run of three hundred and forty-four miles. It will astonish many to learn that the consumption of coal this day was only forty-two tons, by the engineer's register.

In relation to the style of living on board the steamer, I may say that, with all our knowledge of the splendid accommodations of the ship when we commenced our voyage, yet I think none of the party expected the luxurious fare with which we were provided. I hazard no contradiction from any of my messmates, when I say that on our voyage from New York to Southampton our table was equal to that of any hotel in America, and the desserts rivalled in richness and variety anything that I have witnessed in the Astor, Metropolitan or St. Nicholas. It would be wrong if I omitted to express my admiration of Mr. Vanderbilt's kindness and bearing in the supervision of all our affairs. Naturally anxious for the success of his undertaking, he was cautious, prudent and self-reliant. Often did I wish that more than the members of our privileged company could have seen him day by day, kind and attentive to his officers, polite and liberal to his guests. Mr. Vanderbilt I had long known to be possessed of great qualities, a mighty grasp of intellect, and capabilities of the highest order. Yet, till I entered upon this voyage, I did not adequately appreciate his knowledge of men, his fine tact, his intuitive perception of the fitting, and his dignified self-control; and I felt glad that such a man, self-made as he is, should be seen by the accidental sons of nobility and fortune in the Old World.

Tuesday, June 1, at ten minutes past six, New York time, we took a pilot on board — making our voyage from pilot to pilot ten days, eight hours, forty minutes. The fellow proved to be careless and ignorant, and he managed to place the yacht on a bank of soft mud, not far from the Needles. At the flood tide we got off, and anchored in the night, at Southampton-water. Our passage up the British Channel was delightful, giving us fine views of the English coast, including Cornwall, Devonshire and Dorsetshire. The opening up of the Bill of Portland was a noble piece of scenery, and all our party spent the day on deck; and as the day was fine, though breezy, we enjoyed every moment. The passage, as we passed the Needles, was deeply interesting; we obtained a fine view of the stupendous cliffs which overhang them, and admired their isolated situation and exceedingly picturesque form. These huge rocks, as well as the awful cliffs, seem to be composed of a pearly-colored chalk.

CHAPTER III.

SOUTHAMPTON — SCENERY — HISTORICAL ASSOCIATIONS — STEAM PACKET COMPANIES — HIGH-STREET — AMERICAN VICE-CONSUL, MR. COX — DOCKS — STEAMERS — REV. THOMAS ADKINS — ARRIVE IN LONDON — QUEEN'S DRAWING-ROOM — OBJECTS OF CURIOSITY, ETC. — HYDE PARK — KENSINGTON GARDENS — REGENT'S PARK — VISITS TO WESTMINSTER AND OTHER PUBLIC PLACES — WINDSOR — HAMPTON COURT — BRISTOL — CLIFTON AND VICINAGE — TINTERN — HENBURY AND COTTAGES — LOCAL SCENERY — BERKELEY CASTLE — GLOUCESTER — CHELTENHAM — ENGLISH COUNTRY SCENERY.

It was one of England's most joyous, brilliant mornings, when we woke up and gazed out upon as richly cultivated a landscape as the southern coast of Britain can present. Directly before us lay the ancient town of Southampton, which is situated upon a promontory, formed by the confluence of the small rivers Test and Itchen. A gradual ascent leads towards the north. The tide flows to some distance above the town, and the noble estuary, known as the Southampton-water, extends several miles below, and affords convenient anchorage to shipping at all states of the tide, while the charming Isle of Wight constitutes an immense breakwater, and protects it from the rage of ocean storms. The salubrity of this region has established its reputation as a watering-place; and the climate being so mild and dry, it has been a popular resort for invalids afflicted with pulmonic affections. Very numerous instances of benefit to those who have suffered from bronchial irritation are reported. It is a matter of notoriety that all epidemics have assumed a milder form in this vicinity than in most other places. Dr. Granville, in his capital work on the Spas of England, awards high commendation to this town as a resort for the weak, and speaks of its gravelly soil and its fine dry walks. The approach to Southampton from the water presents a pleasing landscape. The churches, towers and spires on the central point, with the rivers on either side winding into the distant, obscure gray, and the fine woodlands of the New Forest, with the beautiful villas off to the left, and the noble ruins of Netley Abbey at the right, combine to delight the eye; and on few spots can a weary voyager land in Great Britain with more pleasurable emotions than at this venerable town. It was here that Dr. Watts was born, and, gazing upon the fair prospect beyond the water in front of the town, he wrote the well-known and exquisite stanza —

> "Sweet fields beyond the swelling flood
> Stand dressed in living green."

It was on this very beach that Canute rebuked his sycophantic courtiers, as the advancing tide approached the Danish monarch. From this port the army of Henry V. sailed to France when he attempted the conquest of that country. And a still more important historical event is associated with Southampton, and one that must ever make it an interesting place to New England men; it was from this town that our Pilgrim Fathers sailed in the Mayflower, when they commenced the voyage of destiny, to found a commonwealth which is now exerting an influence all over the globe. I should mention that all around are to be traced the remains of Roman works; close by was their great Camp Clausentum. For many years Southampton was a remarkably still, quiet place; but it has undergone a vast change in a few years, by the construction of railroads and docks. The steam packet companies, Oriental, West India and South-western, have selected this as their port for passage to the Mediterranean, West India and American ports; and a busy sight it is to see the arrival and departure of the immense steamers. We found several fine hotels; one, styled the New York Hotel, had the star-spangled banner displayed for our special accommodation. Some of our gentlemen, who repaired to it for a lunch on shore, were not very favorably impressed with it. Radley's Hotel, near the railroad, and I think the Dolphin, are well-kept houses.

I hardly know a town that can show a more beautiful main street than Southampton, except it be Oxford. The High-street opens from the quay, and under various names it winds in a gently-sweeping line for one mile and a half, and is of a very handsome width. The variety of style and color of material in the buildings affords an exhibition of outline, light and color, that I think is seldom equalled. The shops are very elegant, and the streets are kept exceedingly clean. In the absence of Mr. McCroskey, the United States consul, we were visited by his obliging and polite representative, Mr. Cox, and Mr. Hillier, his kind assistant; and by his advice the North Star hauled into the docks for the purpose of coaling. We were much gratified by an inspection of the docks, pierhead and quays, which are admirably constructed, and look as if designed to last for all time. The buildings around the quays are in fine taste; and we observed one in particular, a handsome erection of the Italian style, belonging to the Royal Yacht Club. From the officers of this club we received a polite invitation to visit their house and use their rooms. The Plata, a large steamer of twenty-eight hundred tons, was lying next to the North Star. She had just returned from the West Indies or Brazil, and had lost several persons by yellow fever. Close by us were the Oronoka, a fine steamer, just ready for sea, and the Indus. All these were first-class steamers. Here, too, was the old Great Western, so familiar to New Yorkers, undergoing repairs, which seemed really necessary. A steam frigate came into the dock to receive a part of a regiment bound to a foreign port. The soldiers, as they marched along the dock, looked like fine fellows, and many of them had their wives to embark with them. Thirty years had passed away since I had visited this town, and I almost dreaded to call on my former acquaintances, lest I should feel how the march of time had left its footsteps and impressions. I called on the Rev. Thomas Adkins, the Independent minister, who settled over his congregation in 1810. I well remembered his manly form and his noble bearing, and, as I approached his residence, I told the ladies that Mr. Adkins used to be regarded as one of the noblest-looking men in England. We found him at home, and I was delighted and astonished to perceive how very gently age had touched his princely form. He certainly was the finest-looking man I saw in England, of his age; and our ladies thought him one of the most splendid men they had ever seen. Mr. Adkins and his wife visited us on board the yacht, and we passed a very pleasant hour in conversation respecting friends of other days, most of whom are removed from the present state. Mr. Adkins has a large congregation, and his townsmen are justly proud of his talents and finished character as a Christian gentleman. The church under the pastoral care of this gentleman dates its origin to the important year 1688. We saw less of my venerable friend than we should have done, as he was just on the eve of setting out on his summer excursion to France. In the evening, a party from the ship rode through the town and round its environs. I do not believe that the ladies will soon forget the delight which they experienced from their first sight of the cottages and villas of the suburban region of Southampton. The next morning, June 2, we took the train to London, at eleven o'clock A. M. We had a good view of Winchester and its noble cathedral; and some of the party visited the grand old city, and partook of the hospitalities of Mr. Alderman Andrews, whose name is so endeared to Americans. We arrived at London at two o'clock. As it happened to be a Queen's Drawing-room that day, we found the city in a high state of excitement, and the hotels thronged. Seldom have I known so much difficulty in obtaining accommodation; and, as our party was a large one, it was no easy matter to find quarters for all in one hotel. I was anxious to get in at my old favorite house, the Golden Cross, Charing Cross, nearly opposite to Northumberland

House; but Mr. Gardiner was unable to take even half our number. We at last established ourselves at St. James's Hotel, in Jermyn-street, and found good accommodations. Two or three noblemen reside in this hotel; and one, Lord Blayney, has made it his city residence for many years. Our friends, who were in London for the first time, were greatly delighted with the extraordinary display of equipage occasioned by the Drawing-room. Every street was thronged with carriages waiting for their turn to take up the company at the Palace. The coachmen and footmen all had immense bouquets in their bosoms, and the splendid liveries and powdered heads and white wigs of the drivers were novelties to most of the North Star party. I was anxious to know what would be the first object of curiosity to the ladies, and not a little surprised to find that the Thames Tunnel was voted for as our primary visit. The morning was devoted to it, and a visit to the Tower, the Monument, and St. Paul's Cathedral. This last edifice was so lumbered up with scaffolding erected for the great gathering of the school-boys, held on the 1st of June, that we had but a very poor view of the noble sanctuary. By the way, after visiting almost every celebrated religious temple of Europe, I am satisfied that St. Paul's Cathedral is kept in the worst condition of any that I have seen. Its statuary has on it the thick dust of long, long years; and the general internal appearance of the church is discreditable to the nation. My impressions in reference to this cathedral are gathered from frequent previous visits, and have nothing to do with its condition at this time.

After dinner we rode to Hyde Park, and there we were amused with a spectacle that can be witnessed nowhere else. Hundreds, and I may say thousands, were taking their accustomed rides, and we had a good opportunity to see the ladies, gentlemen, horses and carriages, of London and England. The horses we thought, on the whole, not what we had expected, but there were some very noble animals; the ladies appeared to great advantage, but we thought that the gentlemen certainly might improve in horsemanship.

London is indeed to be envied for the possession of her parks; they are her gems, her crowning glory, in my esteem. Three hundred and forty-nine acres, and close to the brick and mortar, and noise and turmoil, of this great Babel! This park has a great entrance from Piccadilly, by fine arched gateways, with a lodge, and several other approaches from Oxford-street, Bayswater, Kensington and Knightsbridge. The park is laid out with noble walks, and spacious drives, in which only private carriages are admissible. From April to July, between five and seven P. M., the scene presented is very gay and attractive. A road called Rotten Row is kept exclusively for the use of equestrians; it is nearly two miles long, and is covered with fine loose gravel. In the park is the beautiful sheet of water known as the Serpentine, and at its junction with Kensington Gardens is an elegant stone bridge. The Serpentine extends over, I think, not less than fifty acres, and early in the morning it affords fine bathing to hundreds of the citizens of London. The noble old trees of this park are worthy objects of admiration. I like to stand on the high ground near the Edgeware road, and catch glimpses of the river through the forest trees, while off to the south are seen the Surrey Hills, and church-spires and antique towers on all sides, and fine mansions peeping from the trees. Here, too, are often witnessed the reviews of the troops stationed in the metropolis. I spoke of Kensington Gardens: these are a continuation of Hyde Park, and embrace three hundred acres. In 1550, all these six hundred and forty-nine acres were a royal enclosure, and stocked with game, and Majesty hunted for pastime. It was appropriated in 1851 to a nobler end; and here was the most important popular gathering that England ever witnessed, at the Great Exhibition. Our rides through the Regent's Park, which contains four hundred and fifty acres, afforded us much enjoyment. The villas and terraces which have been built during the last fifteen years are exquisite specimens of architecture. Here are the Zoological Gardens and the Coliseum. No foreigner should fail to visit this noble park; and here I think he will gain his best estimate of the beauty and elegance of English city life, as it is enjoyed by the opulent. The long walk, with its four lines of elm-trees, is a remarkable avenue.

We made very interesting visits to Westminster Abbey, the new Houses of Parliament, Bank of England, Royal Exchange, British Museum, Buckingham Palace, and other great objects of curiosity in London; and excursions were made to Hampton Court, Windsor Castle, Richmond, &c.

Several members of the party left London for other places. Some went to Liverpool, and others to Bristol, Clifton, Bath, Gloucester and Cheltenham. I cannot omit mention of a rapid visit which I made to my native city, and where I had the good fortune to arrive just in time to join a large family party at dinner, enabling me to meet those with whom I must otherwise have left England without enjoying an interview. Bristol is a glorious old city; it is full of history; not a street, a church, a hill (and, like Rome, it has seven hills), but is identified with other days, and days of note. It boasts of Roman settlement; figured largely in the wars of the barons; was the birthplace of Sebastian Cabot; was a great bone of contention between Royalists and Parliamentarians; was the scene of poor Naylor's judicial tortures, and Judge Jeffries' cruelties; the home of Chatterton, Southey, Coleridge, Cottle, Hannah More, Robert Hall, Richard Reynolds, William Thorp, Dr. Ryland, Bird, the artist, Bayley, the sculptor; was represented in Parliament by Edmund Burke; was burned and sacked by the rioters in 1831; and is the abode of more Christian charities than any other city I know, excepting Boston and New York. Here is the great boast of the west of England,—the unrivalled parish church of St. Mary Redcliffe. This venerable pile is undergoing a thorough renovation. It contains the monument and grave of Admiral Penn, father of the founder of Pennsylvania. In the evening — our only one — we took a carriage to visit Clifton, on the banks of the Avon, with its unequalled scenery

ST. VINCENT'S ROCKS, ON THE AVON.

of St. Vincent's Rocks, the Down, Hotwells, Henbury and Blaise Hamlet. I have no knowledge of any spot on earth that can furnish a ride of such beauty in five hours. From the hill at Kingsweston we looked down upon the winding Avon, saw its junction with the " Severn swift," gazed upon the Welsh Hills, Bristol Channel, and took a look over at the mouth of the Wye and Wynd Cliffe, close by which is Tintern Abbey, the shrine of beauty at which my boyish devoirs were often paid. Tintern is the grandest ecclesiastical ruin in Europe, and Mr. Webster regarded it as alone sufficient to recompense a traveller for crossing the ocean to pay it a visit. I never heard the great man more eloquent than one day, after his return from Europe, when he conversed upon the abbey and its vicinage. The Wye had filled the sportsman's eye, and the beauties of the works of religion and art had animated his mind. I remember he expressed the wish that he could have had gathered round him, when he stood at Tintern, all he loved. Henbury, about four miles from Bristol, is one of England's most beautiful villages; it looks full of peace, contentment, elegance and virtue. Here is Blaise Castle, the residence of John Scandret Harford, a man of large fortune, fine literary taste, and great eloquence, and, what is more and better than all, a Christian man. In many respects he resembles our own Everett. From his domain the eye drinks in scenes of paradisiac beauty. In the distance are ridge upon ridge of mountain ranges off in Monmouthshire, bold and green, then dimly blue. In the village, the munificence of this gentleman has laid out ten cottages of great taste, known as Blaise Hamlet, and which are the residences of ladies of decayed fortune; such another group of sweet rural homes England cannot show. O, the happy hours of my boyhood that I have passed in this village, on the Avon's banks! and what tea-drinkings have I had in these cottages, and in the arbors which surround them! I really believe that, either from the impressions which I received in childhood in this glorious region, or from some peculiar organization, I have felt so much delight in rambling abroad among scenes of beauty, sublimity, and historical interest. Nor do I regret a wayside wandering I have ever made. I am sure that Wordsworth spoke like a prophet when he said,

"And not unrecompensed the man shall roam,
Who, to converse with Nature, quits his home."

Why, there are hundreds of nooks and dells, ingles and hillsides, lanes and orchardings, streams and lakes, mountains and cataracts, mapped into my very soul; and often do I get their latitudes and longitudes in solitary hours and in night seasons. I do not repent me that these witching charms have led me off from the turnpike road of life as by a magic spell. Yes, long years ago, when I have listened to the thrush and blackbird in this same village, I have blessed the man who helped to make the region have so much of heaven in its pathways. I feel young again as I walk through woods and vales where I learned to be what I am.

These cottages are all different in style, and either of them would form an admirable lodge for a gentleman's estate. The sketches of a few are shown in the accompanying illustrations,

HENBURY COTTAGES

and I took the pains and expense to obtain drafts of the ground plans of all of them, with a plot of the group entire. O, that some of our wealthy men would adorn the neighborhood of our cities with so much of beauty and the sweet charity of life! From Bristol we took our route through Gloucestershire, for Cheltenham. The county of Gloucestershire is renowned for its scenery, and nowhere can the traveller find so much manufacturing interest united with more perfect rural beauty than he meets with in the rail-car between Bristol and Gloucester. The factory and its operatives are planted on the edges of hills, under the wings of woods, amid honeysuckles, laburnums, gilliflowers, and jessamines; all around are running brooks and singing birds and busy bees. And what roads and lanes of beauty! — and then the exquisite mingling up of gorse, and bloom, and heath, and fern! Talk of cottages! — come and see the laboring man's cottage on these hill-sides. There are flowers all round his door, ivy trailing to the gable-ridges, fruit-trees right and left, and one side of the house is pretty sure to have a pear-tree trained all over it. No man understands the thousand beauties of Great Britain who does not wander through her inland counties, and tramp through the unnumbered old roads *that lead to nowhere.*

We passed by Berkeley's flinty towers, where England's king died at the command of his cruel queen, Isabella, the she-wolf of France. This castle will well repay a visit from the tourist. I am familiar with it, and know few places more deserving notice. The private chapel is one of the oldest in the kingdom, and in the mansion are capital pictures by Jansen, Holbein, Lely, and Vandyke; while few collections can show better specimens of Claude Lorraine, Salvator Rosa, Ostade Wouvermans, Peter Keefs, Both, and Leonardi da Vinci. Those who are pleased with old furniture will have a treat in this castle. One cabinet of oak is thought to be unsurpassed; and here, too, are the sofa, chairs and bedstead, which were the cabin furniture of Sir Francis Drake in his famous voyage round the world. Close to the church-yard stands Chantry Cottage, the residence of the immortal Jenner.

Gloucester is a staid, respectable little city; and, like all cathedral towns, contains a decent share of pompous complacency. A recent increase of business has come to this place by railroad communication and enlargement of her access to the ocean, by which it has become a port of entry. This city has a pleasant site on the east bank of the Severn, and has four fine streets, which proceed from the centre of the town. The cathedral is a noble edifice, and was originally the convent church of a Benedictine abbey, which was erected in the early part of the eleventh century. The choir of this church is, perhaps, the finest specimen of the florid style of architecture in the kingdom. The building is rich in monuments; and among the more recent ones are those to the memory of Jenner, who introduced vaccination as an antidote to the sad malady of the small-pox, and Robert Raikes, who founded Sunday-schools. Gloucester took a decided stand against Charles I. in the civil wars; and Charles II., on his restoration, ordered the walls of the city to be demolished.

Cheltenham is a modern place. It has grown up in the present century, and presents more of the appearance of progress and improvement than most English towns. Its newness reminds one of an American town or city. It is renowned for its medicinal springs, and, like our Saratoga, is much resorted to by the fashionable. Our object in visiting Cheltenham was to pay our respects to a family from whom, in 1836, we had received great kindness and attention; and our short tarry was a very delightful one, enabling us to recall days of pleasure which we often think of in our western home.

The ride from Cheltenham to Swindon, where we took the Great Western Railroad, is through a lovely piece of country. We were delighted with the snugness and comfort of the dwellings of the gentry; and all the cottages, excepting of the very poorest class, presented something attractive. We noticed high-fenced fields all fringed with noble trees; houses buried up in shrubberies and clumps of forest wood; beautiful cattle browsing in rich pasturage; and all this often in the smallest space, so that a glance of the eye takes in the entire picture. The constant green of England is to me the great charm of her natural scenery; it is like the smile on woman's face, giving expression to every change of feature. I am sure that these exquisite snuggeries must exert a favorable influence upon the domestic qualities and much of the simplicity of English character may be traced to the prevailing love of rural life. You may travel all over Europe, and find no such homes as are everywhere to be met with in England. You have a sense of tranquillity, and the spots are favorable to thought. I love the pleasures of city life, and I know that art, science, intellect, literature, are in a great metropolis, — it is the royal exchange for the human mind. I appreciate libraries and lectures, collections, galleries and museums; but still, when I enjoy the shade of venerable elms in a fine old farm-house, on the banks of a river which almost washes its walls, and gaze out on the garniture of hill and vales, I am conscious of pleasure which London or New York cannot afford. What we sadly want, in our happy and glorious country, is to circumscribe the beautiful, and learn the knack of creating rural scenery on a small scale in our sequestered villas and cottages.

HENBURY COTTAGES.

CHAPTER IV.

HON. AND REV BAPTIST NOEL — MR. GEORGE PEABODY — OPERA — DINNER AT RICHMOND — HON. STEPHEN A. DOUGLAS — RECEPTION-NIGHT AT HON. J. R. INGERSOLL'S, THE AMERICAN MINISTER — THE LORD MAYOR'S SOIRÉE — MR. DEPUTY BENOCH — THOMAS PRICE, LL.D. — TOOVEY'S BOOKSTORE — DEPUTATION FROM SOUTHAMPTON — TONE OF ENGLISH FEELING TOWARDS THE UNITED STATES — AN ENGLISH TRAVELLER — STREET AMUSEMENTS — SCENE IN AN OMNIBUS.

ON our first Sunday morning in London, a party was formed to hear the Hon. and Rev. Baptist Noel, brother to the Earl of Gainsborough. Mr. Noel was formerly chaplain to the queen; but, a few years ago, he became a dissenter. He preaches in a very plain meeting-house, formerly occupied by the Rev. John Harrington Evans, also a Baptist dissenter from the national establishment. The place of worship will accommodate about one thousand persons, when the galleries are filled. The congregation is large. We found every seat filled, and benches in the aisles. Mr. Noel is about fifty-four years of age, and looks much younger. He is a fine figure, and has a resemblance to the engraving of Bishop Heber. The singing was congregational, without any organ; all present seemed to unite, and the effect was excellent. The tunes were such as every one recognized. I remember that *Oswestry* and *Helmsley* were used that morning. We were much gratified with the prayer offered. It was uttered slowly; the petitions were very minute and definite; and there was a decided avoidance of anything like set phrases.

The text was in the fifth chapter of the first Epistle to the Thessalonians, from first to the fifth verse: "But of the times and seasons, brethren, ye have no need that I write unto you,"

&c. The congregation seemed furnished with Bibles, and every one appeared to turn to the text. The discourse was expository; and not often have I listened to such a noble specimen of lecturing from the desk. I have heard this preacher when he was far more eloquent, but never when he appeared to finer advantage as a religious instructor.

We left St. John's Chapel much pleased with its distinguished minister, and we should all like to listen again to his solemn teachings.

One of the first persons to call upon Mr. Vanderbilt and his family in London was our distinguished fellow-citizen, Mr. George Peabody, whose generous hospitality to his countrymen has rendered him so well known to hundreds who have visited the metropolis. Possessed of ample means, this gentleman delights in paying attentions to all who come to him with proper claims upon his notice. Probably no American resident in England has done as much as Mr. Peabody in bringing the best men of England and America together, and thus cementing a strong national friendly feeling. The celebration of the fourth of July, 1854, by Mr. Peabody, when he entertained a thousand guests, and had among them the Duke of Wellington, and many others of the peerage, was a measure that, a few years ago, would hardly have been anticipated; and, indeed, cautious folks dissuaded the large-hearted man from attempting it. Mr. P. proffered Mr. and Mrs. Vanderbilt and ladies the use of his boxes that evening at the opera, and as long as they remained in town. The following notice of the opera was furnished me by the kindness of one of the gentlemen of our party, who was present:

"OPERA IN LONDON.

" Meyerbeer's great opera, 'Les Huguenots,' was represented at Covent Garden. It was the height of the season; a large and fashionable assemblage filled the house; England's favorite,

Queen Victoria, and Prince Albert, were there, and many of the fairest and noblest of the land; yet we were disappointed. The spectacle was not so gorgeous and brilliant as we had expected on a court-night, — neither in the first *coup d'œil*, the beauty of the ladies, nor the elegance of their toilet. The theatre is vast, and handsomely decorated; but the boxes, being very deep, and partitioned off all the way up, conceal half the occupants, and present an air of heaviness. The queen and her suite occupied three double boxes, on the left side of the stage. She came in shortly after the overture was played. There was no ostentation in her manner, and no recognition by the audience of the presence of majesty. The royal fauteuil, placed in the centre of the box, did not seem to please her; and, declining the proffered aid of the lords-in-waiting, she, with perfect nonchalance, rose, and drew another chair from the back to the front, and seated herself. The queen is very robust and youthful-looking. She wore a rich white dress, exceedingly *decolté*, covered with point lace, and one ornament of great value — a magnificent pearl — on the stomacher. She wore no diadem, or insignia.

"Prince Albert is a tall, stout-looking man, light-haired, and partially bald. His appearance was anything but aristocratic, notwithstanding he exhibited a large star on his left breast, and a wide crimson silk riband over a white waistcoat. The queen and her royal consort were very quiet, and attentive to the performance. They left, shortly before it terminated, with as little ceremony as they had entered.

"We searched scrutinizingly among the noble circles to discover something in form or feature marking the stamp of hereditary nobility; but in vain. There were some exceptions, though not numerous enough to characterize the mass; and we concluded that, divested of their rank and privileges, they were only common clay, after all.

"The opera was glorious. The whole 'get up' was grand, far surpassing anything ever seen in America; — the scenery well painted, and admirably illustrative of the times represented; the stage business thoroughly managed; a powerful and efficient chorus; a numerous and exquisitely-trained orchestra, led by the famous Costa, and the principal rôles sung and acted by Grisi, Mario, Castellan, Formes and Belletti. Some of us, who had heard Grisi a dozen years before, remarked that her voice had measurably lost its freshness and volume, while her figure had gained in stoutness. But the irresistible attractions of her sublime declamation, her impassioned acting, and the enchanting tenderness of her smile, remained with undiminished power. Mario has the loveliest voice ever heard in man, at the same time virile and sonorous. He is still in the prime of his remarkable manly beauty, and still, without compeer, the first tenor in the world. Castellan has not improved since she visited America. Her singing is flexible and brilliant, cold and unsympathetic. Formes — now that Lablache's once Titan powers are on the wane — stands at the head of all bassos. His voice is very remarkable, — the most powerful in the low notes, and the deepest, known; it moves, as it were, in solid squares. Belletti, Jenny Lind's favorite singer, took the part of San Bris. For him it was an ungracious rôle, and he did not show to advantage. It was mainly recitative. We missed those beautiful cantabile airs which, in the concert-room, made him the unrivalled baritone. The opera in London is a wonderful performance; the audiences there are more appreciative than in the New World, and the *tout ensemble* produces an effect impossible to conceive from any description."

Four of our party accepted an invitation to dine with Mr. Peabody at Richmond, to meet Mr. Senator Douglas, who, like ourselves, was taking a tour of observation. No one who has read much respecting England can fail to know that Richmond has long been renowned for its exquisite scenery. It was called by the Saxons the "*Shene*," or beautiful. Thomson, the poet of the Seasons, wrote many of his sweetest descriptions while staying in this place; and his immortal poem is almost a panorama of the scenery for ten miles around. On the hill the spectator obtains a view of the most impressive panorama of English landscape which the country affords. I would advise all travellers, who can afford the time, to devote a day or two to this vicinity. In Richmond Park there are the pleasantest walks, and oaks which might awaken the devotion of a Druid; and the American tourist is reminded of the oak-opening in Michigan. The traveller will not fail to be charmed with Kingston, Ditton, Hampton Court, and Bushy Park. The dinner was an elegant repast, and we met at table a number of our countrymen whom it was a pleasure to meet; — among others, Gen. Cooper, of New York, — who, with his family, have made a very extended European tour, — Captain Folsom, &c. Mr. Douglas made a very sensible and eloquent reply-speech; and I think that all who were present were much gratified with his practical, enlightened and patriotic views. Our minister at the Court of London — the Hon. Joseph R. Ingersoll — held a levee during our stay in town, to which Mr. Vanderbilt and his friends received an invitation. The attendance was large, and the party a very fashionable one. The display of diamonds was very brilliant. General attention was directed to Mr. Vanderbilt, who was quite the man of the occasion; and all seemed desirous to obtain an introduction to one whose excursion was the great topic of newspaper correspondence and general conversation. Mr. Ingersoll was very courteous, and, with his accomplished niece, Miss Wilcox, seemed desirous to render us every facility to make our visit in London agreeable. At this entertainment many of the nobility expressed an earnest wish that Mr. Vanderbilt would bring his yacht round to the Thames, and enable the fashionable world — then, of course, in London — to visit the North Star. Mr. V. would have been glad to gratify these requests; but he had no desire to take a step which might appear like ostentation, and, moreover, he feared that the steamer would probably meet with obstructions in the river.

On the 8th of June Mr. and Mrs. Vanderbilt, and several members of their family, attended a soirée, at the Mansion House, to which we had been politely invited by the Lord Mayor. This was a favorable occasion to observe the splendor of a London civic entertainment. The magnificent apartments are worthy of England's metropolis. We were courteously received by the chief magistrate and the Lady Mayoress.

The Lord Mayor, this year, is the Right Honorable Thomas Challis, a wealthy merchant in hides, and a member of Parliament. This gentleman is a distinguished dissenter, and belongs to the body of Christians known as "The Connection of the late Countess of Huntingdon." His lordship is the treasurer of the college at Cheshunt, where the clergy of this denomination receive their theological training. On this occasion there were, probably, some twelve or fifteen hundred persons present, including the Archbishop of Canterbury and seven other prelates, several members of the British cabinet, and a large number of the peerage. The party embraced many distinguished literary men, and Mr. Carlyle had many attentions shown him. The ball-room over the great Egyptian hall was filled with a unique collection of educational apparatus; and this had been placed here for the examination of the party, many of whom were delegates from all parts of the kingdom, attending a great educational meeting. A more interesting spectacle than was here afforded can hardly be imagined; and, with such means and appliances as we saw, the schools of Great Britain must be in a prosperous condition. Maps, charts, globes and philosophical apparatus, were everywhere to be seen; and the access to the room was crowded quite as densely as that leading to the place for refreshment. Among other distinguished visitors, I noticed Miss Greenfield, the "Black Swan," who was attended by a colored gentleman

It would be wrong to omit mention of our obligations to Mr. Deputy Benoch, whose polite attentions will be long remembered by many of the North Star party. This gentleman was exceedingly kind in pointing out the notables assembled.

I felt pained at the necessity imposed upon me to be apparently neglectful of many dear and valued friends in London and its neighborhood; but a stay limited to ten or twelve days, and many of which were entirely due to those of the party who were in London for the first time, precluded the possibility of calling on many whom I longed to see.

We visited the Rev. Dr. Cox, of Hackney, — so well known in America from his visit, in company with Dr. Hoby, in 1835. We found the venerable man in usual health, and little supposed that his death was so near an event. On our arrival at New York, we learned that he died September 5th.

We had the pleasure to spend some delightful hours with Thomas Price, LL.D., the distinguished editor of the *Eclectic Review*, one of the ablest English periodicals, and which always has in its support the ablest pens of the liberal party. In this review appeared the best productions of the late John Foster. I made several agreeable lounges at the great bookstores of London, and was especially delighted with the glorious collection of old books at Mr. Toovey's, 42 Piccadilly. This vast library is peculiarly rich in works illustrative of English history, and I never met with so many of the county historians as are here gathered together. If any man wants to see the finest possible specimens of binding, let him call at Toovey's, where he will find the work of Lewis, Payne, Duseuil, Derome, Montague, Kalthœber, and all the best binders of past times. On one occasion, I met with three distinguished bibliopolists at this shop, — Lord Hastings, Sir David Dundass, and Mr. Henry Foss. These gentlemen all spoke of the large collections of books, of high character, which are constantly exported to order from the United States, and raising the prices of old standard works as a consequence. It was gratifying to hear their remarks in relation to our United States ministers to the court of London. It was observed that no country had ever sent such a number of great men as the United States, — Adams, Jay, Pinkney, King, Gallatin, J. Q. Adams, Rush, Bancroft, Everett and Ingersoll, were regarded as first-class men; whilst Stevenson and Abbot Lawrence have left an enviable reputation as gentlemen of the true old English school. It gave us much pleasure to meet with a large number of our fellow-citizens, from different states in the Union, while we were in London; and they all appeared happy to pay their respects to one so well known at home as Mr. Vanderbilt. I found my old friend, the Hon. J. T. Van Allen, late U. S. Chargé d'Affaires at Equador, still enjoying the best English society, and as happy as I left him in 1851.

While we were in this place, a deputation from Southampton waited on Mr. Vanderbilt, consisting of the mayor of the town and several members of the corporation; the object of their visit was to present an invitation to Mr. V. and his party to partake of a public entertainment proffered by the principal merchants and tradesmen of that borough. This kind expression of public sentiment would have been respectfully declined; but it was found that such arrangements had already been made, that it would be wrong to disappoint the wishes of the good people of the town.

I wish to offer some remarks upon the tone of feeling which I found prevalent in England, with those persons in whose society I happened to pass my time, in relation to the United States. There is a very general sentiment and pride entertained by the country at our wonderful success and advancement in the scale of nations, arising from the fact that we are of English origin. An Englishman loves to think that those who speak his language, and have the laws of his land, and the religion of his fathers, should have in less than eighty years become a government reckoning twenty-five millions. He is pleased to hear of our extensive resources as regards variety of climate; and you can seldom talk with any person in England who has not a relative, dear friend, or former neighbor, now settled in the Union. If the United States should ever be placed in a critical position, and her interests be at stake, England would rise up, with the voice as of one man, and fly to our aid. The liberty of speech is quite as well understood in England as with us, and as freely indulged; nothing social, religious, political, escapes their scrutiny and discussion; the popular mind has been directed to great subjects, and important results have been effected by public opinion. There is a disposition to regard all reforms as possible; and the great subject of slavery is one that has taken hold of the public mind far more than it has ever interested the government. Hence all classes talk of slavery in America as a thing that can be reached, — ay, and easily. This arises from total unacquaintedness with the political relations of our country, and the state of parties in our political world. Only let an intelligent Englishman reside in the States a year or two, or travel through it, and he is almost sure to correct his opinions, and moderate his censures, upon this vexed point. We are far too sensitive about foreign sentiment respecting our habits, manners and institutions. Perhaps we are too exacting; we are certainly foolishly impatient under criticism, and this is encouraged by a few heady, reckless men who have the control of newspapers, and who, by thoughtless and even wicked articles, strive to kindle up a bad feeling between the two countries, who have more in common between them of momentous interest than any other two nations on the globe. I have never known a sensible American, who visited England, who did not leave it with increased respect for English character; and I am sure that all sensible, educated Englishmen who visit our shores find enough to praise; and they would say, "If we must change England for another land, let our homes be in America!"

The influence of America upon Great Britain is felt more and more every year. Our intercourse must be very intimate. Not only will England need our cotton; she wants our wool (which she believes will soon be the best in the world), our wheat, our corn, our beef, pork, hams, cheese and butter; and, if we provide these things for her market, we must become a great manufacturing people as well, and still we shall be the best customer for her exports. The severest censures I heard upon our country came from men of great wisdom, and benevolence, and practical good sense; and I confess that I think their remarks have much force, and that there is too much occasion for their utterance. They express a fear that there is not in our country a sufficient pride in labor; that we are already regarding it with aversion, and that luxury is likely to be our bane. We do want more nationality, more patriotism; and the people are far too prone to value that which has crossed the ocean to that which is fabricated at their own doors. A very wise and thinking man, who had gone through our country, told me in England that the most justifiable object of pride he saw in America, to an American, was Lowell. The remark was also made by this gentleman, that in his visit he was grieved to find the children of men who had grown rich by labor regarding all employment as dishonorable. Certainly our large cities do afford sad instances of a purse-proud spirit; and the only hope is, that when wealth is lavished, expended, the next generation must go to work again; but the contagion of example, and the want of virtuous and wise training, will first bring a sad harvest of crime, folly and misery, to society.

Few things amused our party more than the out-door, street exhibitions in London. In Jermyn-street, directly in front of our hotel, every afternoon a set of men in semi-mountebank and Highland costumes went through all sorts of fêtes, rivalling the Ravel family. The party consisted of three or four, and sometimes five. The street was regarded as their legitimate board, and cloths were laid down and the antics played off without any hindrance from the police, who frequently looked on. The eyes of the performers were often directed to the windows of our hotel and one opposite; and I fancy the returns were tolerably satisfactory, as they came day by day. The Happy Family, too, proved a constant source of interest; while Punch and Judy proved as omnipotent in attraction as they were in the beginning, and ever will be.

Mr. Vanderbilt and some of the gentlemen attended the Ascot races; and, in going over from Windsor, they occupied seats in an omnibus, and the subject of conversation happened to be the American steam yacht at Southampton. One of the persons present said that he had been to see her, and gave a pretty glowing account of the North Star. He spoke of her elegance and accommodations at full length, and then ended by remarking that the commodore was a wide-awake man; that he had twelve sons on board, and made them work the ship; and that he saw seven or eight of them rowing the barge ashore. Mr. V. and his son, sitting next to the speaker, smiled and laid low.

CHAPTER V.

INTEREST EXCITED BY ARRIVAL OF THE NORTH STAR — LONDON DAILY NEWS — DULWICH GALLERY — MR. THOMAS COLLEY GRATTAN — A QUICK TRIP TO LEIPSIC — OUR RETURN TO SOUTHAMPTON — VISIT TO NETLEY ABBEY — HISTORICAL NOTICE — SCENERY — REV. DR. KREBBS — EXCURSIONS — REV. ALEXANDER MACLAREN — SERVICES OF THE SABBATH,

THE arrival of the North Star in England was an event which called out the attention of the public press all over the kingdom; and the London daily papers contained numerous descriptions of the ship, and various articles upon her proprietor and his undertaking. Some of them were amusing enough. The following article appeared in the London *Daily News*, June 4:

"A WORD ABOUT MR. VANDERBILT'S YACHT.

"An American merchant has just arrived in London, on a pleasure trip. He has come by train from Southampton, and left his private yacht behind him in dock at that port. This yacht is a monster steamer. Her saloon is described as larger and more magnificent than that of any ocean steamer afloat, and is said to surpass in splendor the Queen's yacht. The walls of the dining-room are clothed with a new material, resembling polished marble and malachite. The building of the vessel alone cost one hundred thousand pounds. The expense of keeping it up is three hundred pounds a week. Listening to the details of the grandeur of this new floating palace, it seems natural to think upon the riches of her owner, and to associate him with the Cosmo de Medicis, the Andrea Fuggers, the Jaques Cœurs, the Richard Whittingtons, of the past; but this is wrong. Mr.

Vanderbilt is a sign of the times. The mediæval merchants just named stood out in bold relief from the great society of their day. Mr. Vanderbilt is a legitimate product of his country, — the Medicis, Fuggers, and others were exceptional cases in theirs. They were fortunate monopolists, who, by means of capital and crushing privileges, sucked up the wealth of the community. They were not a healthy growth, but a kind of enormous wen on the body politic. It took Florence nearly fifteen centuries to produce one Cosmo, and she never brought forth another. America was not known four centuries ago; yet she turns out her Vanderbilts, small and large, every year. America, which was only discovered by a countryman of Cosmo running against it by mistake on his way to the Indies, is the great arena in which the individual energies of man, uncramped by oppressive social institutions, or absurd social traditions, have full play, and arrive at gigantic development. It is the tendency of American institutions to foster the general welfare, and to permit the unchecked powers of the highly gifted to occupy a place in the general framework of society which they can obtain nowhere else. The great feature to be noticed in America is that all its citizens have full permission to run the race in which Mr. Vanderbilt has gained such immense prizes. In other countries, on the contrary, they are trammelled by a thousand restrictions. Look, for instance, at the land to which the discoverer of America was hastening, as he thought, when he ran against the New World. Look at India. The whole wealth of the country is absorbed, and the development of its industry is checked, by a government that hangs like an incubus over it, and paralyzes its free motion. Its capacities for wealth are enormous, but no one makes use of them. Its population is stationary or degenerating. It can with difficulty pay up the revenue which its masters exact from it. It is becoming bankrupt, and will be perhaps chargeable to the mother country. Its hundred millions of inhabitants vegetate in poverty, their ideas limited to the narrowest of all spheres. While hundreds of thousands of emigrants are pouring annually into America, and becoming absorbed into the population of that country, adding to its wealth and their own, India is a sealed territory to nearly all except those who have friends in Leadenhall-street or Cannon-row. What can man do in a country like India, but vegetate among the oppressed, or live the life of a Sybarite among the oppressors? Is it wonderful that at the first sound of the railway whistle the Lotos-eating lords of the land should rush away up the country, far away from a sound which everywhere is connected with energy, wealth, activity, freedom and progress?

"But it will be said — why is the greatness of America to be unnaturally magnified by being compared with India? Why not compare it with England, where there are free institutions, immense manufactures and commerce, and where there is no more impediment to a man's becoming a Vanderbilt than in America? Walk into the Royal Exchange in the afternoon just before four o'clock, and you could be shown numbers of men who could do — if they thought it worth the while — everything that Vanderbilt has done, twice over. Look at Liverpool. Look at Manchester. Are not men of colossal fortunes to be found there? Is there anything in the air or the institutions of these towns to prevent men becoming possessors of incomes that are reckoned by tens of thousands? Possibly not: but there is something in the air or the institutions of the country of which these towns are a fraction that prevents these men living as becomes the creators of stupendous fortunes by their own industry. Your men of rank here — your makers of millions for themselves, and tens of millions for the country — too often spend their time, their intellect, their labor, in order that they may be able to take rank among a class of men who occupy their present position in virtue of what was done for them by some broad-shouldered adventurer, who, fortunately for them, lived eight hundred years ago in Normandy. Those who ought to be the Vanderbilts of

England would shrink from employing their wealth in the magnificent manner adopted by their American friend. They would dread the effect of making any unusual display, which would surely subject them to the reproach of being millionaires and parvenus. Here is the great difference between the two countries. In England a man is too apt to be ashamed of having made his own fortune, unless he has done so in one of the few roads which the aristocracy condescend to travel by — the bar, the church, or the army. And, if he is vulgar enough not to be ashamed of himself, his wife and children make amends, by sedulously avoiding everything which can put other people in mind of their origin. It was thought something superhumanly heroic in Sir Robert Peel to confess that he was the son of a cotton-spinner, although everybody knew it. Persons who have perused the biography of Mr. Pendennis will remember how the gifted and hard-working father of that gentleman looked back on his long and useful career in the medical profession as a thing to be especially forgotten, and never thought himself a true man till he was enabled to stand in gaiters, like a true landed proprietor, at the gate of his miniature domain of Fair-oaks. The ancestral Pendennis of the medical profession is the type of English society.

"Does the reader see what looms through these parallels? We wish to point out, as we have pointed out before, the essential weakness, the vicious condition, of English society. In precisely the same manner (although in an infinitely greater degree) as the English army is damaged by the 'cold shade of aristocracy,' so are English society and the English nation vitiated by the aristocratic prejudices that run through it. Between the cobbler who patches a shoe, and the merchant who imports the leather to make it, there are some three or four grades, the members of each of which would scorn to associate with those of the grade below. The merchant himself hopes that he or his children may walk at last amongst the lords of the land, and, as a step to this, he takes care to have his children educated where they shall lose all traces of the impressions that may have been made upon them by those who dwell in his own circle, and where they may acquire the habits and customs of the world to which he fondly hopes they may aspire.

"It is time that the *millionaire* should cease to be ashamed of having made his own fortune. It is time that *parvenu* should be looked on as a word of honor. It is time that the middle classes should take the place which is their own, in the world which they have made. The middle classes have made the modern world. The Montmorencis, the Howards, the Percys, made the past world, — and they had their reward. Let them give place to better men. It is not the strong arm which now founds nations, or makes them great. The work has been taken out of the hands of the mighty in war, and given to those who are strong in council, — to the lords of the elements, to the tamers of the great forces of nature. These must take their position. They must assert it, and scorn to put up with the faded distinctions that formed the glory of the ruling classes centuries back. There are men who feel this now. There are not wanting, even in this country, men who know their own dignity too well to think that it can be increased by being transplanted to another circle of society. We want the Vanderbilts of England to feel what they are, and to show it. We don't ask each of them to build a monster yacht. We do ask that they would assert the greatness of their own position. We do require that they shall do everything, by providing amply for education, to elevate the class to which they belong, and put it upon the level to which it is entitled. The middle classes of England are the creators of its wealth, and the source of its power. Let them take example from America, and not shrink from acting as if they knew this. If they could be brought to let their children become as distinguished for high mental and moral cultivation, by an improved system of education, as they themselves are for their great practical knowledge, the classes which now virtually make the greatness of the country would become its actual rulers, and the only obstacles to its indefinite progress would be removed."

The state of the weather is in England a never-failing topic of conversation among her population. This arises from its frequent changes. During our visit in London of ten or twelve days, we had no reason to complain; it was charming, and all the fine region about the city was seen to the best advantage. I could not be in London without a hasty visit to Dulwich, to take a look at my old favorite pictures, in a gallery which in early days seemed marvellous, and, now that I have seen other larger ones, still delights me; for it contains less rubbish and mediocrity than almost any gallery I can mention. My admiration is always ready when I gaze at Rembrandt's Jacob's Dream, and the Martyrdom of St. Sebastian, reputed to be a Guido. I pretend to no connoisseurship in painting, but I know that I am pleased with a good picture; and I think I am never more alive to thought, nor more disposed to affection, than when returning from a capital collection of paintings.

I cannot omit to speak of the pleasure which we experienced in meeting with our friend Mr. Thomas Colley Grattan, who was formerly Her Majesty's consul at Boston. This gentleman, so well known by his charming works of fiction and his admirable social qualities, is now resident in London, enjoying the finest health, and, as usual, the object of warm attachment to his numerous friends. The services which this gentleman rendered to his country during the period in which he represented her in Massachusetts were most important; and to his kindness and humanity many a stranger in a strange land has been indebted for substantial, valuable aid, and judicious advice. England never had a more valuable representative in our country than Mr. Grattan.

I fear that the ladies would hardly forgive me if I should not say that they experienced much enjoyment in a visit to Madame Tussaud's great Museum of notables in wax. Indeed, this is a wonderfully curious place, and it grows better worth a visit every year. Here is the noble old warrior, the late Warden of the Cinque Ports, sleeping that rest which knows no awakening till the last great trumpet sound. Here, too, is Napoleon's campcarriage; and a most comfortable one it is too; it was captured at Waterloo. I cannot mention a hundredth part of the groups and individuals here to be seen. The Royal Princes of England look like pretty children. We were pleased with Shakspeare in his youth, bluff Harry and his six wives. Madame Tussaud is herself represented as in sleep, her bosom gently heaving at intervals, and an old man at the end of the couch looking on with great attention through his spectacles, slightly moving his head, as if in a meditative mood; a woman, brushing by the old man's coat, turned round to apologize! Here, too, was a superb Mosaic table offered for sale. On its surface was Napoleon and his twelve marshals. Some of the young folks visited the Chamber of Horrors. But we see too much of horror in every-day life to feel any great enjoyment in a retrospect of the terrible in a vast aggregate; and so let this go by.

I ought to mention that while we were in London Mr. Allen left us to take a hasty run to Leipsic, where he had a son in one of the best schools of that city. He had not seen his boy for three or four years, and parental affection, aided by rail-cars and steamboats, carried him to Germany and back in four days; and we had the pleasure to welcome his son as a new member of our party, at least till our return from Russia to Copenhagen, when he would return to his studies. The presence of Mr. William V. Allen was not only a great addition to the happiness of his parents, but was felt to be a pleasure by all on board. A right-minded youth, sensible and accomplished, he was always agreeable, and disposed to gratify his friends and acquaintances;

and his perfect knowledge of the German language often proved useful to us in many ways whilst we were at the North.

On our return to Southampton, we at once addressed ourselves to excursions to Netley Abbey and the Isle of Wight. The abbey is the great lion of the neighborhood; and, like most of the ecclesiastical ruins of England, it remains a witness to the taste of its founders, who rarely neglected to select sites of extraordinary beauty for conventual purposes. The road is short, but pleasant. It leads over a fine wooden bridge, by the old Roman Clausentum. Noble residences and charming lodge cottages are in sight, and fine views are obtained of Southampton and its water. Before reaching the ruins, we passed the pretty village of Weston, of which delightful spot Miss Mitford has written so sweetly:

> "We might as soon describe a dream,
> As tell where falls each golden beam;
> As soon might reckon up the sand,
> Sweet Weston, on thy sea-beat strand,
>   As count each beauty there.
> Hills which the purple heath-bell shield,
> Forest and village, lawn and field,
> Ocean and earth, with all they yield
>   Of glorious or of fair."

The Netley Hotel is a pretty Elizabethan erection, and from this point the first view is obtained of the abbey. Although the vicinity of Southampton is not characterized by any very bold or romantic scenery, having neither crag nor rocky mountains, yet it is full of quiet beauty, and has for ages attracted the invader, pirate and merchant. At a very early period it captivated the religious of the Catholic Church, and here they selected a home for worship and retreat. Romans, Norwegian sea-kings and Danes, all settled down at Southampton; and Canute made it his great sea-port, and the city of Winchester, close by, was his capital. A monastery was established on the west bank of the Itchen, one mile and a half from Southampton, in 1124, by a body of Black Canons. At the beginning of the 13th century, some Cistercian monks came from France and settled in the New Forest, half-way between Calshot and Hurst Point. Their convent they called Beaulieu. They erected a superb abbey, as we may judge from the few remaining relics. This body sent forth a colony, who reared the walls of Netley Abbey.

The Cistercians, to whom Netley Abbey belonged, owed their origin to the Abbey of Citeaux, in Burgundy, and the order there commenced in 1098. Its spread and prosperity may be chiefly ascribed to the great energy of its third abbot, Stephen Harding. All Cistercian abbeys were dedicated to the Virgin Mary. Henry III. is sometimes regarded as the founder of Netley, and the date ascribed to its erection is 1239. At the dissolution of monasteries by Henry VIII., this body consisted of the abbot and twelve monks.

The location is on the bank of Southampton-water, and three miles below the town, and nearly opposite the New Forest. It was formerly surrounded by terraces and fish-ponds, and the property was enclosed by a moat and wall, parts of which we found remaining. The style of architecture was the early English at the period of its change to Gothic. All the principal arches are pointed, and the semi-circular arch is only used for strength and in small gateways. Netley is a fine specimen of the early transition style, and its leading feature was the use of the mullion, and slight tracery at the head of the windows. The abbey was built of stone from Purbeck, in Dorsetshire, and Caen, in Normandy. The dimensions of the abbey are two hundred and eleven feet in length, fifty-seven wide, one hundred and sixty at the transepts, and from ground to the top of the gables eighty feet. The impression produced on entrance is one of deep awe and reverence. The side walls present a long perspective of thick ivy, and the gray tops form a noble contrast of color. On the ground are ruins of the groined roof and various remains of the formed domestic apartments — for at the dissolution the building was secularized. I have no time to describe the exquisite beauty of the aisles, the south transept, which is in better preservation than any other portion of the edifice; nor can I do more than mention the east aisle of this transept, which constitutes the LADYE CHAPEL.

The chancel is a spot where I could linger long, and fancy the solemn processions to the choir and altar during the three centuries in which, I doubt not, earnest and devout worship marked the services of good men, who, having sung the song of the mass on earth, are now singing the song of Moses and the Lamb in heaven. I do not believe that, in abjuring the errors of an idolatrous and apostate community, we are justified in denying that she has had the truly good and pious in her communion. A multitude, I love to think, have, in dark ages, made their way home to Zion with songs, and the ministrations of monks and friars may have been means of grace and imparted hopes of glory. All this I can cordially believe, whilst I regard the existence of Popery as one of the deadliest curses to the race, and anticipate its overthrow as the loveliest vision which the fulfilment of God's promises to his church is about to unfold, in answer to the prayers of the saints on earth and the redeemed in heaven.

The east window was greatly admired by all our party. Amid its mutilations, the great mullion and the circumference remain; and, festooned as it is with ivy, it fastens the eye of the beholder. I have never seen more glorious masses of ivy, nor as many wall-flowers, as at Netley. Yet, I am forced to say, that this abbey will not bear comparison, for local beauty and architectural grandeur, with my favorite Tintern.

As we were making the inspection of these venerable ruins, a large party drove up to the gateway, and we were all of us delighted to meet with our excellent friend, the Rev. Dr. Krebbs, of New York, who, with his party, had that morning landed at

Portsmouth from a packet-ship; and, with true American go-ahead energy, here they were, the same day, sight-seeing; having taken the rail to Southampton, and commenced doing up England by a visit to Netley. Dr. Krebbs was in the pursuit of health; and it was a very pleasant thing for him to meet in the abbey with his own family doctor, "the beloved physician," Dr. Linsly. Here I may observe that our good doctor met in London with several of his patients, and rarely have I seen more cordial greetings than were exchanged. A warmer heart, full of sympathy for all the sorrows of the afflicted, never beat in human breast than in this excellent man, who, I imagine, must have been sadly missed by his numerous friends.

Several of our friends made an excursion to the Isle of Wight, visiting Cowes, Ryde, and Osborne House, the marine villa of Queen Victoria.

Others of us spent the day at Southampton, attending divine service. When in London, I had been strongly advised to hear the Rev. Alexander Maclaren, who was spoken of as an excellent preacher. I therefore determined to attend his meeting-house in the morning. It is known as Portland Chapel, and is a small and plain building, and very unlike what a Baptist church would be in such a town in America. The congregation was plain, and the house not quite full. Mr. Maclaren took his text from the 25th Psalm, 14th verse: "The secret of the Lord is with them that fear him," &c. I hardly know how to express my admiration of this discourse, or of the manner in which the entire service was conducted. I have heard Hall, and Chalmers, and Jay, Hamilton, Cummings, Noel, and other great preachers in England; but I do not remember that I ever listened to a more impressive sermon. Mr. Maclaren is a Scotchman, of prepossessing appearance, and his manners in the pulpit are natural and dignified. I have certainly heard nothing in England that is at all equal to this gentleman's oratory; and then, aside from the attraction of manner, the reasoning was close and the peroration as pathetic and earnest as I can imagine to be possible. Dr. Krebbs fully coincided in my estimate of the service.

After service, I was invited to officiate in the evening; but I felt too desirous to enjoy another gratification in listening to such instructions. The members of our party, too, were very anxious to attend again upon the service; and, with quite an addition to our number, we were among the evening worshippers. I now found the chapel crowded, and it was with much difficulty that we were scattered round. The congregation, too, was of a very superior class of hearers to that I had seen in the morning; and I felt sure that there were representatives from various congregations in the town. An American, who has never been in England, cannot understand the light in which Congregationalists, Presbyterians, Baptists and Methodists, are regarded by the established church and its adherents. Talents, social worth, even wealth, seem to be regarded as nothing unless they are placed upon the altar of uniformity. The sermon of the evening was founded upon Psalms 8: 5, — "Lord, what is man," &c. The audience seemed to me held in a state of almost breathless silence and attention. The hold of the preacher on his hearers appeared to be like that of a prophet who had brought a message from "the Holy One." The imagery was grand, and was in the lips of a master in Israel; and we all felt the force of the preacher's subject, — *The Dignity of Man.* But, when he described man's apostasy and ruin, no one could fail to experience the emotions of Job, who exclaimed, "I abhor myself in dust and ashes." We all of us retired from that humble sanctuary expressing the earnest wish that such a preacher might have a more fitting sphere for labor. And yet I know not that this is right. In the great gathering-day, I doubt whether any preacher of the gospel will feel that in this world his field of occupation was too limited; while thousands will lament the extent of their responsibility, and will mourn over their omissions and short-comings in duty.

CHAPTER VI.

JUNE 13, THE BANQUET AT SOUTHAMPTON — CARD OF INVITATION — APPEARANCE OF TOWN — VICTORIA ROOMS — MAYOR — DINNER — ACCOUNT OF PROCEEDINGS AND SPEECHES IN THE HAMPSHIRE INDEPENDENT — EXCURSION OF THE NORTH STAR, WITH THE MAYOR AND INVITED GUESTS, ROUND THE ISLE OF WIGHT — DINNER ON BOARD — ACCOUNT TAKEN FROM THE HAMPSHIRE INDEPENDENT.

I STATED, in my notice of our days in London, that a deputation from Southampton had proffered Mr. Vanderbilt an invitation to an entertainment given by the citizens, and that the honor was accepted. On our arrival at Southampton, we found the streets placarded with notices of a public entertainment at the Victoria Rooms; and a very superbly-engraved card, in gilt letters, with a fine likeness of the North Star in the centre, surrounded by gilt flags and the arms of Southampton, was addressed to each member of the party. As a memorial of the voyage, I annex the card of invitation which I received on the occasion:

THE MAYOR,
MERCHANTS AND TRADERS OF SOUTHAMPTON,
Request the pleasure of the Rev. DR. and MRS. CHOULES' company at a
DEJEUNER, on MONDAY, 13 June, 1853, at the Royal Victoria
Assembly Rooms, in honor of the visit of
COMMODORE VANDERBILT,
In his splendid Steam Yacht North Star.
At 3 o'clock.

Monday, the 13th of June, was a most delightful day; and when we came on deck we found the flags of the shipping in dock all gayly waving to the breeze, and noticed banners from the hotels and public buildings, while the church-bells were ringing merry peals of cheer and gladness. Everything denoted mirth and holiday, and our feelings were somewhat peculiar when we felt that all this was a matter in which we were personally concerned, and was intended for the honor of our ship, her owner, and our country.

At two o'clock P. M., carriages were on the dock, which had been most politely sent by the committee of arrangements, to convey the party to the Royal Victoria Rooms, the scene of civic hospitality. The streets were full of spectators, and bells were pealing out sweet melody, as English parish bells alone can do it. On arriving at the Rooms, we were courteously received by the gentlemen in waiting, and were escorted through a fairy scene of winding stairs, all covered with evergreens and flags, into the saloon of reception, where we were presented to Mr. Lankester, the Mayor, who wore his gold chain of office, and by him were introduced to the Lady Mayoress, and a large number of ladies and gentlemen. The room was spacious, and opened upon a terrace affording a charming view of the water; and I noticed several venerable trees, and some small pieces of artillery, which were more for adornment than use; a pretty fountain off to the left was an ornament to the terrace.

At three o'clock the Mayor announced that dinner was ready, and led Mrs. Vanderbilt to the room, followed by Mr. Vanderbilt and the Lady Mayoress, and the rest of the company. The scene that opened upon our view was exceedingly striking, and we all thought that we had never beheld a dining-room so elegantly decorated. The flags of England and the United States were beautifully entwined, and the entire arrangements of the room were as elegant as possible. The tables were superbly arranged, and presented a fine display of plate, whilst the entertainment itself was of the richest character. The presence of nearly a hundred ladies gave a charm to the occasion, and afforded us additional pleasure.

I think I cannot do better than insert in this place the account of the banquet as recorded in the *Hampshire Independent* of Saturday, June 18,—a very excellent liberal paper, edited by my valued and eloquent friend, Mr. Falvey. I regard the description as very truthful and graphic.

It may not be inappropriate here to remark, that whilst Mr. Vanderbilt has long been known to his fellow-countrymen by the title of Commodore Vanderbilt,—a compliment paid him as the veteran head of the steam navigation of the northern states,— yet *he* on no occasion used the appellation, or wished it employed. I allude to this, because the common use of the title in this narrative of the English press prevents my altering the phraseology. If anything, during the whole excursion to Europe, impressed me strongly as it regarded Mr. Vanderbilt's deportment, it was his uniform modest and dignified reserve, and avoidance of all pretence to ostentatious show and public notice. Often did he decline attentions which were pressed upon him at various points of our progress, and very frequently to the great disappointment of those who greatly wished to do him honor, and show their regard for his country.

"THE AMERICAN STEAM YACHT NORTH STAR.—PUBLIC BANQUET TO COMMODORE VANDERBILT.

"The banquet to Commodore Vanderbilt, by the merchants and traders of Southampton, in acknowledgment of the compliment paid to this port as the high road between England and New York, in selecting it for his visit, and of the great courtesy shown to the public by throwing open his splendid yacht for general inspection, came off at the Victoria Rooms on Monday, with an *éclat* which has never been surpassed by any previous entertainment of the kind that has taken place in this town. Of all the fraternal gatherings which have, of late years, characterized our port, none have gone beyond this one, either in point of interest, or the excellent and satisfactory manner in which the whole of the arrangements were carried out. The banquet took place at the Victoria Rooms, and, notwithstanding the short time necessarily allowed for preparation, about two hundred persons, inclusive of the distinguished party of American guests, assembled on the occasion.

"The decoration of the room was assigned to Mr. Triggs, and most ably did he perform his task. Flags of all nations, in which the English and American colors, of course, were prominently displayed, hung round the room, which, added to the excellent effect produced by the peculiar ornamentation of the orchestra, and the graceful intermingling of wreaths and bouquets of flowers, a large floral star being suspended from the centre of the ceiling, rendered the appearance of the room, as soon as the doors were thrown open to the company, that of a large fairy bower. Indeed, we never saw the Victoria Rooms so beautifully decorated on any previous occasion. A handsome collection of green and hot-house plants and flowering shrubs was gratuitously supplied by Mr. William Rogers, sen., from his old-established nursery at Red Lodge and his floricultural establishment in the High-street, which were arranged by Mr. Sawyer, and had a most agreeable effect in connection with the other decorations of the room.

"The lower room was set apart as a reception room, wherein the guests and visitors generally were received, on their arrival, by the Mayor and Mayoress; and we need hardly say that Commodore Vanderbilt and his family received a hearty welcome on their arrival. The day being beautifully fine, the company promenaded the grounds till the banquet was announced to be ready, which, together with a suspension of lines of flags between the trees and the balconies, and the performances of a capital brass band which was stationed on the green, drew crowds of spectators along the western shore road, which runs in front of the grounds, by whom the gay and exhilarating scene appeared to be much enjoyed. In the banqueting-room a full and highly efficient quadrille band, under the direction of Mr. F. Targett, occupied the orchestra; and a party of vocalists from London, consisting of Mr. Ransford, Mr. Ransford, jun., and Miss Ransford, lent their powerful aid to the general harmony of the festive gathering.

"The Mayor of the borough (J. Lankester, Esq.) presided with great ability, supported, right and left, by the American guests, who comprised Commodore Vanderbilt and lady, D. B. Allen, Esq., and lady, G. A. Osgood, Esq., and lady, W. K. Thorne, Esq., and lady, Horace Clark, Esq., and lady, Dr. Linsly and lady, N. B. Labau, Esq., and lady, D. Torrence, Esq., and lady, W. H. Vanderbilt, Esq., Jun., and lady, Master G. W. Vanderbilt, Miss Vanderbilt, Miss Thorne, Mr. W. Allen, Capt. A. Eldridge and lady, Rev. Dr. Choules and lady, and Mrs Cross. Amongst those present we also noticed Mr. Deputy Bennoch (from London), the Mayoress, Mr. Alderman Andrews and lady, Mrs. Croskey, the Rev. J. W. Wyld, Mr. Alderman Palk and lady, Mr. Alderman Allen, Mr. Alderman Tucker, Mr. Alderman Bienvenu, Mr. Sheriff Aldridge; Councillors Blatch, Graham, Copeland, Scovell, Borrett, Degee, Buchan, Davies, Brinton; Capt. Peacock, Mr., Mrs. and Miss Mayes, Mr. and Mrs. Pegler, Mr. and Mrs. H. J. Buchan, Mr. Falvey, Mr. and Mrs. T. P. Payne, Mr. W. Lankester, the Messrs. Sharps, Mr. and Miss Randal, Miss Sharp, and many other of the leading tradesmen of the town and their ladies.

"The following letters were received in reply to invitations to attend the banquet:

"'*Legation of the United States, London,* 11*th June,* 1853.

"'MY DEAR SIR: I have just received the very kind invitation of the Mayor and Stewards, so obligingly forwarded by you, to be present at a *dejeuner* to be given by the Mayor, merchants, and traders of Southampton, to Commodore Vanderbilt and family, on Monday next.

"'I regret exceedingly that an important engagement, made many days since, for Monday, must deprive me of the honor of being present on this interesting occasion; and I regret this the more, as H. E. Mr. Ingersoll being also engaged, the American Legation must be unrepresented.

"'Having been the recipient, on more than one occasion, of the hospitality of your excellent Mayor and Corporation, I can readily anticipate how much enjoyment your guests will receive on this occasion.

"'I beg you to present my respects to his worship the Mayor, and accept for yourself the sentiments of kind regard with which
"'I have the honor to be, dear sir,
"'Your obliged and obedient servant,
"'T. B. LAWRENCE.
"'CHARLES E. DEACON, Esq.'

"'45 *Portland-place, London, June* 11*th,* 1853.
"'Mr. Ingersoll has the honor to acknowledge the receipt of the kind invitation of the Mayor, merchants and traders of Southampton, to a *dejeuner,* on Monday, the 13th of June, to receive Commodore Vanderbilt and family; and he particularly laments that engagements, previously formed, will prevent him from having the pleasure of joining the agreeable and distinguished party.'

"'*London, June* 11*th,* 1853.
"'Mr. Peabody sincerely regrets that having invited a large party to dinner at Blackwall on Monday, the 13th he will be deprived of the pleasure of waiting on the Mayor, merchants, and traders of Southampton on that day, according to their kind invitation.'

LETTERS OF APOLOGY. 75

"' *June* 13*th*, 1853.

"'MY DEAR SIR: May I request you to communicate to Mr. Mayor, and the other gentlemen who have done me the honor to invite me to the fête to be given in honor of your American guests, my great regret that pressing and important business prevents the possibility of my attending.

"'I am, faithfully yours,
"'A. E. COCKBURN.
"'C. E. DEACON, Esq.'

"'23 *Portman-square, London*, 11*th June*, 1853.

"'MY DEAR SIR: I very much regret that it will be quite out of my power to avail myself of the invitation with which your Mayor has honored me for Monday next, to welcome Commodore Vanderbilt and family. I shall be in Committee all day, and in the evening have to watch a motion in connection with a railway company affecting the interests of my constituents.

"'I shall feel obliged to your worthy Mayor if he will kindly say as much on my part to the commodore, and assure him that I really feel vexed that I cannot be present to welcome so distinguished a fellow-laborer in steam navigation, but that I still hope the opportunity may occur before he leaves Europe.

"'Very truly yours,
"'B. M. WILLCOX.
"'C. E. DEACON, Esq.'

"'*Mansion House, June* 11*th*, 1853.

"'MR. MAYOR: I am requested by the Lord Mayor to say that he fears his engagements will render it impossible for him to comply with your kind invitation; but that, if it should be possible for him to leave town at the time, it will afford him great pleasure to do so.

"'I am, sir, your very obedient servant,
"'C. R. EDMONDS.
"'THE MAYOR OF SOUTHAMPTON.'

"'61 *Cornhill*, 11*th June*, 1853.

"' Mr. Sheriff and Alderman Carter presents his compliments and hopes the pleasure of meeting the Mayor of Southampton on Monday next, the 13th inst.

"' CHARLES E. DEACON, Esq., &c. &c. &c.'

"The *déjeuner* and dessert was served by Mr. Gibbs, whose catering gave much satisfaction to the company. The wines were of first-rate quality, the champagne and hock being supplied by Mr. F. Perkins, and the remainder of the wines by Messrs. Maber and Parker. Indeed, every department was done full justice to by the gentlemen to whom they were respectively assigned.

"Grace before meat was offered by the Rev. J. W. Wyld, and at the close the grace, 'For these and all thy mercies' was chanted by the Messrs. Ransford in beautiful style.

"The first toast given by the chairman was the health of the Queen, which was drank most enthusiastically, and followed by the band playing the National Anthem, the air of which was beautifully sung by Miss Ransford, the whole company standing and joining in the chorus.

"The chairman next gave the health of Prince Albert — the beloved consort of Her Majesty, the patron of the arts and sciences, and the warm advocate of the comfort and happiness of the whole community. Drank with loud applause.

"Glee — 'Where art thou, beam of light!'

"The chairman, in proposing the next toast, said that, in the exercise of their undoubted prerogative, the American nation had chosen a form of government different from our own, which had worked in an unparalleled degree, in the history of the world, for the welfare of that country. (Hear, hear.) They had established a republic, instead of a monarchy, with a president chosen every four years; and under her successive presidents they had advanced to that state of unexampled prosperity which they now enjoy. (Hear, and cheers.) They had selected men of wisdom and talent, equal to the exigencies of the times, to fill that high and honorable office; and he gave them, with much pleasure, the health of 'The present President of the United States of America.'

"This toast was received with loud and long-continued cheering, and the whole company rose and stood during the performance by the band of 'Hail Columbia;'—a mark of respect to the ruling head of the American nation with which Commodore Vanderbilt and his friends were much pleased.

"Mr. Alderman Laishley rose to propose the next toast. He said he most sincerely and heartily congratulated the Mayor on his being honored with an opportunity, during his tenure of office, of entertaining as his guest so distinguished and worthy a representative of the American people. He rejoiced that these occasions of mutual good feeling and fellowship arose, from time to time. The people of Southampton had not forgotten, nor would they soon forget, when, for the first time in the history of their ancient town, there floated on our waters that noble specimen of the naval force of the United States, the St. Lawrence, in 1848, commanded by one of her most gallant sons, whose dignified bearing, whose courtesy and kindness, as well as that of the officers under his command, and the orderly conduct of the crew, made an impression, not only on the corporation, but also on the inhabitants of the town at large, which neither time nor distance would be able to efface. (Loud cheers.) And then there was the recollection of the second visit of that noble ship to our port on her mission of peace, bearing the contributions of that enterprising people to the World's Exhibition. True, compared with the show and the tinsel of some of those exhibited by the old states of Europe, they were apparently modest and unpretending, and at first rather excited a smile that they should have travelled so far only to go back again; but, as day succeeded day, and weeks and months elapsed, they excited the attention of the practical and philanthropic, the ingenious and inventive,— and what was the result? Why, that amidst that world of competitors they carried off some of the highest prizes, and the most distinguished honors. And, for this most obvious reason, that, while much that was glittering and dazzling was well adapted for the few, *those* were the very things which were everywhere wanting to promote and increase the comfort and well-being of the many. (Much cheering.) Nor could they allow such an occasion as that to pass by without a renewed expression of their admiration of the gallant commander of that ship — on that occasion Captain Sands — and the distinguished officers under his command; long might they live in the enjoyment of every good, an honor to their country, and a blessing to the world! For the visits of that noble vessel to this port they were indebted to the exertions and good opinion of a gentleman whom they all highly esteemed, and whose absence that evening was deeply regretted; he meant Mr. Croskey, the United States consul, who had so long and so honorably represented that government at this port. (Applause.) And, now they were most unexpectedly and happily favored by the visit of one of the most enterprising, successful, generous, and large-hearted men of that extraordinary people,— one who, having, as he was informed, embarked a large amount both of capital and skill in the vastly-growing commercial interests of his country, had lived to see his public spirit, his gigantic intellect, his scientific attainments, rewarded with a success rarely, if ever, surpassed in that or in any other country. (Cheers.) The people of Southampton might indeed well be proud of the distinction thus conferred upon them. He (Mr. Laishley) could well imagine how intense the interest felt by the gallant commodore and his amiable family, as they rounded the old Castle of Calshot, to find themselves steaming up that very river in a yacht, the magnificence of which was perhaps unequalled in the world, down which, in 1620, the Pilgrim Fathers, their honored ancestors, started in their frail bark of one hundred and eighty tons burden, for their distant and unknown destination. (Hear, hear.) Talk about warriors and diplomatists; these were the men, wherever they were found, who were nobly and successfully contributing to make the world one country and man one family (loud cheers),— men, upon whom Providence having smiled, had not only the power to get wealth, but the heart to diffuse it. It was by colossal intellects such as these that the pathway of the great deep was rendered not only safe and easy, but attractive and inviting too; and that, not only to the hardy sons of the soil, the muscle and sinew of the human race, but to the gentleman, the scholar, the man of literature and science — nay, to ladies, too, of education and station, and even of these some of the most fragile, and sensitive, and delicate, as they saw that evening, inducing them, without hesitation or apprehension, to visit lands the most distant, and people often the furthest removed from all their habits.

"Bad sailor as he was, a look at that magnificent vessel, so snugly berthed within their docks, would almost lead him to imagine that a voyage in her, at any time, and to any part of the world, would be nothing else than an occasion of pleasure, a very holiday festivity, on the spacious deck of which the voyager might breathe the pure air as freely, and, no doubt, often as plentifully, too, as he pleased, or unite with his fellow-travellers in recreation and amusement — by day beholding the wonders of the deep, and by night admiring the garniture of the heavens. (Applause.) In the superb saloon — a compartment which would not discredit the palace of Britain's queen — he might converse with authors of every age, and partake of the luxuries of every clime, assured, whether engaged in the one or the other, that, under the direction of the gallant commodore, his officers and crew, he was being safely wafted to his desired haven. It was only to gaze for a moment or two upon that noble specimen of marine architecture, to see, and to feel, too, that, as to the age in which they lived, it was, as to the discoveries of science and the inventions of art, the product, the flower, the cream, of all the ages past and gone. 'Nobody,' said the illustrious Prince Albert, some time since, 'can doubt for a moment that we are living at a period of wonderful transition, tending to that great end to which all history points — the realization of the unity of the human race.' Why, all that was wanting was, that men of all nations and kindreds should thus meet together, see each other, and talk together, to know, and to feel, too, that they were children of the same common Father — a world of brothers, intended to be drawn together by mutual interests and sympathies, instead of being divided and dissevered by mutual jealousies and antipathies. (Loud and prolonged cheering.) Who could estimate the effect which in a few years must be produced on the intellectual, the moral, the religious and the social condition of the world, by the rapidly increasing intercourse of the sons of man? By these means it would be that both the geographical and political barriers which from age to age had separated nation from nation — barriers which had rendered them, not only strangers, but enemies to each other — were being daily broken down and demolished. National prejudices and antipathies were everywhere giving way, as opposed alike to the best interests of man, and to all the institutions of the Almighty. How terse and how truthful were the remarks of one of the earlier Presidents of the American Union — he believed it was Mr. Jefferson: — 'We, the Americans,' he said, 'ought, above all things, to cultivate the most friendly alliance and brotherhood with Great Britain, because she can do us more harm than any other nation; and she ought, above all things, to cultivate the same friendly feeling towards us, because we can do her more good than any other people.' Hence, how important that, in accordance with the toast he had the honor to propose, all the deliberations of her Majesty's ministers and the statesmen of England and America should tend to promote the welfare of mankind and the civilization of the world! But these gratifying reünions, these friendly greetings, this social, happy intercourse, of the people of different and distant nations, would tend far more to cement and render permanent and enduring the bonds of universal brotherhood, than all the diplomacy of the one country or the other. (Hear, hear.) The toast he had to propose for their acceptance was — 'Her Majesty's Ministers, and the Statesmen of England and America : May all their deliberations tend to promote the welfare of mankind, and the civilization of the world.'

" 'Rode's Air,' with variations, was then sung by Miss Ransford, and loudly applauded.

" The Mayor said he now came to *the* toast of the day (applause), and, as usual, Mr. Laishley had so taken the wind out of his sails that he had left him little to say. But he remembered that he had at that moment sitting at his right hand one of the merchant princes of America (hear, hear), — a gentleman who owed his position entirely to his own industry, perseverance, and extensive knowledge of mankind. He had ever been an enemy to all monopoly, and that was the foundation of his great success. (Applause.) His aim had always been to abolish all monopolies, and so he had created the important position which he now occupied in America. And, then, look at his family! (Loud cheers.) He was not, like many of our anchorites, contented with amassing a large sum of money, but he had brought up a large and interesting family. (Hear, and cheers.) Commodore Vanderbilt was the largest steamboat proprietor in the United States; and now, as a sort of frame to the picture, he had brought his splendid steam yacht into the Southampton waters, to show them what the Americans could do in the art of steam-ship building. (Loud applause.) He (the Mayor) was not going, on that occasion, to talk about the port of Southampton, but he could not help thinking that the commodore had shown singular good sense in bringing his yacht to this port. (Laughter and cheers.) The position of Commodore Vanderbilt in America was equal to that of any of the ducal houses in Great Britain. (Hear, hear.) He was the proprietor of large building establishments, and employed more men than any other person in America. There must, then, be something in such a man (loud cheers), and he hoped that his career would be followed up for many years yet to come. The example he set showed to persons in this and other countries what might be done by industry, energy and perseverance, without being born to inherit fortune and wealth. (Applause.) He gave them, as a toast — 'Commodore Vanderbilt: May every happiness accrue to himself and family during his interesting voyage, and every success attend all his spirited enterprises.' The toast was drank with enthusiastic applause, renewed again and again.

"Band — 'The Star-Spangled Banner.'

"Commodore Vanderbilt (whose rising was the signal for renewed rounds of cheering) said: — Ladies and gentlemen, I am glad to see you. It affords me sincere pleasure to make your acquaintance. It shows that we are all one people (hear, hear), and I hope that, by the power of steam, our common countries will be so bound together that no earthly power can separate us. (Loud applause.) Since we landed in your beautiful town, we have made a hasty race over part of Her Majesty's dominions; and, were I able to express the gratification we have experienced in passing through the country and your town, and the interest we feel in all your citizens that we have had the happiness to meet, I am fearful you would construe it into an attempt to make a speech. But I must refer that task to my friend Mr. Clark, who will address you much better than I can possibly do.

"The Mayor jocularly remarked that no one could question the right of the worthy Commodore to call on a gentleman to whom he had given one of his daughters to act as his substitute, and he was sure the company would listen with pleasure to Mr. Clark one of the Commodore's sons-in-law. (Applause.)

"Mr. Clark received a hearty welcome, and, when the applause had subsided, spoke as follows : — Ladies and gentlemen, I rise in obedience to the call made upon me by the gentleman whom you are pleased this day to honor. As a member of his family, as an individual privileged with this opportunity of meeting the gentlemen and ladies of England, I should have been glad to have remained in silence, gratified with your magnificent hospitality. But, when I recollect that the honorable gentleman from whom you have just heard a few words sustains to us one of the most sacred relations on earth (hear, hear), — that we have received from his hearth those who are the partners of our lives (hear), — that he, like your own illustrious admiral, expects every man on whom he calls to do his duty (great cheering), — when I remember these things, and the obligations we owe to him and to you for the honor you have done him, I feel that it would be out of place in me to refuse to respond to his call. We came from our homes in the far west, neither hoping nor expecting to receive such princely honors as those which you have conferred upon us. Commodore Vanderbilt constructed a steam yacht in accordance with his tastes, and at considerable expense, and invited us to visit, with him, this glorious land — the birth-place of our fathers. (Loud cheers.) If it has so happened, or shall so happen, that you find in this yacht anything to merit or receive your approbation, — about her construction anything tending to advance the general improvement of the age, and the growing commerce of the world, — Mr. Vanderbilt is already amply compensated. (Hear, and cheers.) His paramount object, in this visit, was our improvement and our pleasure, and to that he has amply contributed; and the reception which he and his family have received on the occasion has been all that we could have asked, and much more than we could have anticipated. We left our homes in the far west, after taking farewell, for a season, of all our domestic pleasures and ties there left behind us, — a few days of unalloyed pleasure, passed in contemplation of the works of the Great Creator on his broadest and most glorious field, — a few nights of calm repose, undisturbed by danger or fear, — and, lo! your magnificent shores burst upon our view. (Much cheering.) We had heard of your generous hospitality, which we are now enjoying. We had heard of your beautiful river, of the charming landscape scenery which surrounds you, and of your port, which offers its great advantages to the commerce of the world. (Hear, and cheers.) We had been told of your salubrious climate, and the unexampled growth of your city. We were, therefore, prepared for what we have seen. But when we arrived on a fine sunny morning, — when your beautiful river first opened to our view, — we little thought, till we so soon experienced it, that we should so truly find ourselves at home. Everything around us here looks like home. (Loud cheers.) Perhaps you have never visited New York, though but a short distance across the Atlantic. In its natural position it bears a strong resemblance to the great and ancient city in which I now stand, and from whose inhabitants we have received such kind and generous-hearted attention. The city of New York stands at the confluence of two vast and mighty rivers, whilst directly in front, to guard its commerce from the storms of the ocean, lies Staten Island, which your honored guest has enriched by his enterprise, and adorned by his taste. (Great cheering.) There lies New York, offering its noble harbor to the whole world, with one hand grasping the east, and another the west. Thus, also, do you lie at the confluence of two rivers, and in front, not our Staten Island, but your most beautiful isle, — the Isle of Wight, — to shield your commerce from the storms of the ocean, and to furnish you with the flowers of early spring. Have we not, I ask, a right to feel ourselves at home? (Enthusiastic cheering.) We have not been treated as strangers, and we do not feel ourselves to be strangers. (Hear, hear.) We have one common origin. We speak one common language. We are all engaged in one common cause — the improvement of mankind. The English is our mother tongue; our ears are attuned to its melodies, and we know no other. (Renewed applause.) Those who suppose that we are a different race forget that we are all one and the same people, and but one and the same. Your great names are our great names. Your past history is our past history. Your glorious future is our hope and our pride. We sprang from you. We are happy thus, as if returning home, to greet you (immense cheering), — to visit England, the renowned empire of which it has been well and truly said 'that her morning drum-beat, keeping time with the hours, encircles the earth in one continuous strain of the martial airs of England.' We are proud of the ancestry from whom we claim our descent. We have stood on the soil which holds the sacred remains of Milton and Shakspeare. (Applause.) We have stood in the halls which once echoed with the eloquence of a Chatham, a Fox, a Pitt, and a Burke. (Continued applause.) Their fame is ours, as well as yours. All that you can say — all that the great Anglo-Saxon race who inhabit England can say — is that their ancestors were the countrymen of those men; and so were mine. (Hear, and cheers.) It was little over two hundred years ago that the Mayflower, with her precious freight of noble men, left your beautiful harbor for the stern and rock-bound coast of New England, and from the loins of one of those men he who now addresses you has descended. (Hear, hear.) How are we reminded of our home by everything we now see about us in England! You doubtless all remember that, after the Mayflower left your port, she was compelled to put into Plymouth to be refitted. Starting again, they named the place of their landing in America Plymouth. Within two hundred miles of that sacred spot now stand Newport, Southampton and Northampton — three of the most beautiful of our American towns. In view of all this, and of the welcome as generous as is this you have given us, I did not feel myself at liberty to refuse the call of my friend and father-in-law. (Applause.) We have now stood in England, and we are proud of you. We glory in your prosperity and advancement as in that of a parent. And it is right that this feeling should be mutual. Is this the first occasion in human history when a son feels proud of his father, and the father has still the same right to be proud of his son? (Cheers.) Where is the

English heart that does not glory in the prosperity of his child? And I tell you there is no true American heart which does not glory in the prosperity of his father. (Great cheering.) We have, I again repeat, stood in England; we have seen your institutions; we have beheld and examined, as far as the short time we have been here would permit, your noble and illustrious charities; and we have not failed to observe the universal good order and contentment which pervade your people. We have inspected your works of art. We have not failed to notice that everything around you is prospering, and that the only signs of decay are to be found in those old structures which you are so proud to preserve, and which attest the glory and antiquity of your country. (Loud cheers.) From the time of landing on your shores till this hour, we have felt one universal thrill of admiration, which will not subside till we again reach our homes in the western world. We have been struck by the permanency and solidity of your structures, and, whatever may be the opinions of a few amongst you and us, who will dare to revile England and her institutions, we say it is utterly impossible for anything but admiration to be the general and abiding feeling. The convulsions of nature may, in the long ages of the future, overwhelm this island; but, so long as the world remains, so long will England's usefulness be felt, and her power and glory be known and acknowledged. (Applause.) Your respected chairman has been pleased to say that we Americans have chosen a form of government entirely different from your own; but in that opinion I take the liberty of telling him he is mistaken. There is a great similarity between our respective forms of government. Some of the most conservative of our forms are taken from yours. Ours is based on the power of the people, and yours is the same in theory and in practice. We have a government of checks and balances; and so have you, for what your Parliament adopts must be sanctioned by the queen before it has the effect of law, and the sceptre of your queen is powerless without the will of your Lords and Commons. Ladies and gentlemen, come and visit us. (Loud cheers.) A few pleasant days, and a few pleasant nights, will land you on our shores. Visit and examine our institutions; see how the rich protect the poor, and the poor respect the rights and property of the rich. Examine our laws, and you will find the Magna Charta of your own King John incorporated in every State of the Union — your far-famed Bill of Rights grafted on our statute-books. (Loud and prolonged cheering.) You will feel thoroughly at home. We will greet you as friends, and, if you see us at home, you will find the sure indicia of our English origin, and you will all come to the conclusion that we have no right to boast of any superiority over you, and you of none over us. (Renewed applause.) There is no set of institutions so perfect that the one cannot derive aid and improvement from the other. (Hear.) I have intruded much longer upon your time and patience than I had intended, but your kindness has sustained me. Amongst the blessings of Providence still in store for us, I do most sincerely hope that we may be able to cultivate still further the acquaintance which, under such favorable auspices, we have now been able to make with you. — The honorable gentleman sat down amidst the most enthusiastic acclamations.

"Mr. S. Payne briefly proposed, as the next toast, 'Mrs. Vanderbilt and the Ladies,' which was drank with all the honors.

"Band — 'Here's a health to all good lasses.'

"Duet, Mr. and Miss Ransford — 'Tell me, gentle stranger.' — *Parry*.

"The Mayor, here took the opportunity of announcing that Commodore Vanderbilt, with the generosity that marked his career, had placed his magnificent yacht at his disposal on the following day (Tuesday), for an excursion, to which all those present at the banquet would be admitted by tickets, which could be obtained at the town clerk's office between half-past nine and half-past ten on Tuesday morning. The yacht would start at eleven. This announcement was received with much cheering.

"Mr. Vanderbilt, jun., offered his thanks for the reception they had given to the toast, and set the room in a roar of laughter by expressing a hope that, as the bump of cautiousness had always distinguished his father, they would allow the son to exhibit it also, by saying nothing more, especially as this was his maiden speech. He proposed the health of 'The Ladies of England: Noble specimens of God's handiwork.' The toast having been duly honored,

"Mr. Deacon (the town clerk) acknowledged the compliment, and said that the ladies of England were delighted with that opportunity of greeting the ladies of America.

"The Mayor said the next toast was not a political one, and therefore he hoped it would be drank by all. He had received a telegraphic despatch from Sir Alexander Cockburn, regretting his inability to be present. He proposed 'The Members for the Borough.' Drank with much applause.

"Mr. Falvey said it was his pleasing duty to propose for their acceptance the next toast; and, in doing so, he would take that opportunity of remarking that, from the able speech they had heard that day from Mr. Clark, and from others that had been delivered during the visit of the St. Lawrence to Southampton, it was very evident that the people of America, amid their other excellent qualities, had not neglected the cultivation of the art of oratory. (Cheers.) They had satisfactorily demonstrated that it was a popular error to suppose that men who could discourse most eloquently were not men of action; because, both in the Congress of the United States, and even on ordinary festive occasions, the practical go-ahead character of our American brothers by no means caused the divine art that enabled Demosthenes to hurl defiance at King Philip, or Cicero to denounce the crimes of Verres, to be neglected. (Hear, hear.) It was said, of old, that the wise men came from the east; but, however that might be, they could affirm with truth in our own day that the practical and enterprising men came from the west; and, although they in Southampton were not so far north as to make the large and rapid fortunes that some persons did in that part of the country, they were sufficiently south to have their hearts partake in some measure of the character of their genial climate, and leap, as it were, with friendly and fraternal greetings to welcome their guests from the other side of the Atlantic. (Cheers.) The toast which he had to propose made a special reference to Washington and Franklin, — two of the great founders of the mighty republic of the west; and it would not be out of place to mention, on that interesting occasion, when they were honored by the presence of so many ladies, that it was to a fond mother's teachings the illustrious warrior and statesman of America was indebted for that ardent love of truth and those lessons of patriotism that, throughout the whole of his useful life, formed the leading characteristics of his mind. (Cheers.) As the mariner of old, before the discovery of the compass, looked anxiously up to the north star for safety and for hope in steering his way through the ocean, so George Washington, amid painful and difficult trials, in contending for a time with factious intrigues, and even conspiring generals, looked only to the honor, the glory, and the independence of his native land, as the one great object of his existence. With such an example to guide them, in addition to their own industry and intelligence, and with the old spirit of the Anglo-Saxon race, the future of America would be even greater than its past; and he said this not in the way of paying a cold and formal compliment to Commodore Vanderbilt and his family, but because the genius and power of his great country was felt and acknowledged in every part of the globe. (Cheers.) He begged to propose, with all his heart, the toast that had been placed in his hands, and to apply to the two nations of the one common origin the words of an American authoress:

> 'Then pray we for our country, that England long may be
> The holy and the happy, and the gloriously free.
> Who blesseth her is blessed — then peace be in her walls,
> And joy in all her palaces, her cottages, and halls.'

Mr. Farvey concluded by proposing — 'The Sons of America: May they ever be found worthy of their illustrious predecessors, Washington and Franklin; and may the genius and virtue of their many distinguished citizens continue to guide the onward progress of that great and flourishing people.'

"Scotch Ballad, by Miss Ransford, — 'Of a' the airts the win' can blaw,' — which was rapturously applauded, and a repetition called for and accepted.

"Major Labau (another of Commodore Vanderbilt's sons-in-law), in a very eloquent address, responded to the toast.

"Mr. Mayor, Ladies and Gentlemen: There are times when such is the intensity of the human feelings that the heart throbs, the bosom heaves, the nerves are relaxed, and the tongue almost refuses to perform its office. Such a time is the present, and such are my feelings. Standing for the first time on England's soil, and partaking of her numerous bounties, emotions strange and new agitate my soul.

"As you, sir, have observed, — and I thank you for the thought, — there departed from your hospitable port, some two hundred years ago, a frail bark freighted with Pilgrim Fathers. Like Noah's weary dove, she went forth, and pursued her way o'er the trackless ocean. By the providence of God, a resting-place was found in the western world. I need not now depict the sufferings and trials of those fathers; nor need I tell of their landing in a wilderness, the dangers they incurred, the perils they encountered. All is as familiar as your household history; and in recounting these things I should only tell you that which you yourselves do know. Suffice it to say, that a colony was founded; infant as it was, it grew apace. As years rolled on it waxed stronger and stronger, until it reached the proportions of a man, and now stands forth the 'Giant of the West.'

"That giant, your progeny, now sends us, his children, upon a visit to our grandmother, glorious Old England! Ay, glorious Old England! next to mine own land I love her sea-girt isle. I love and venerate her flag, which has ever floated high above the din of battle, and under which a Wellington and a Nelson have fought and conquered. I love to wander through the rich fields of her intellect, and cull from thence the gems of a Cowper, a Dryden, a Shakspeare, and a Milton. I love to wander 'mid the stars of heaven, and read their names and characters by the aid of a Newton and a Herschel. (Cheers.)

"But why, let me ask, are we here? Why are our national banners entwined together for the decoration of this hall? Here is a result; what, then, is the cause? Mankind are too apt to take things as they are. They know results, without caring for causes. We are content to look upon and admire the running stream, without caring to go back and ascertain by what hidden mystery the bubbling water is sent up from the bosom of the earth. Thought is our only medium of knowledge, whatever its sphere or its degree. All begins and ends with thought. Why, then, are we here? Has etiquette dictated this banquet? Has it originated in fashion, which makes the heart cold and calculating, causing men to live not for what they are, but for what they seem to be? No, sir. The banquet is dictated by other causes, by higher feelings, and nobler motives. Are we not the same people? Do we not speak the same mother tongue, bow obedience to the same principles of law, and kneel in worship before the altar of the same great God? Sympathy draws us to each other; unity of interest binds us together; and one common cause leads us to travel side by side the rugged paths of life. Our countries are both engaged in the advancement of civilization and science. Both labor for the amelioration of the condition of man; for the freedom of the serf; for the freedom of the ignorant. Both strive to rend asunder the chains upon the conscience, the intellect, the pursuits, and the persons of men. Both raise up the fallen, encourage the weak and tottering, and extend powerful protection to those unfortunates whom the vultures of despotism would cover and devour. Ay, here, as in America, may the political offender find an asylum and refuge, upon a soil from which the despots of Europed are not, cannot tear him! (Great applause.)

"Like assimilates with like. England and America are engaged in generous rivalry, each glorying in the success of the other. Ocean steam-navigation brings us nearer to your shores, and is fast tending to make the Atlantic to us a Pacific Ocean. (Cheers.)

"Well may we mingle around the festive board in the sincerity of friendship and brotherly love. These 'merrie meetings' make us better acquainted with each other. Here, divested of care, the toils and troubles of life, we shine forth the natural, not the artificial man. Indulging in these thoughts, I have almost forgotten the purpose for which I arose. As an humble citizen of America, I respond to the sentiment, 'The Sons of America: May they emulate the example of their illustrious WASHINGTON and FRANKLIN.'

"Such a sentiment, coming from English hearts, pronounced by the lips of British freemen, and receiving the enthusiastic reception which Englishmen can give to that which is heartfelt and sincere, comes with great force. We thank you for your generous wish. And, though we cannot boast of possessing in their perfectness the godlike virtues of a Washington, or the plain, straight-forward simplicity and integrity of a Franklin, yet do we all unite in preserving that halo of glory which their names and deeds have thrown around our country. Through them have we assumed our high place in the political region, and, like the milky-way, whiten along our allotted portion of the hemisphere. It shall be our duty first to preserve inviolate that union which the blood of our sires has cemented together. We will protect it from the grasp of a foreign foe, as well as protect it from the suicidal hands of domestic fanaticism. We strive to maintain national faith and honor, pure and intact. In this, at least, shall we live worthy of a Washington. We strive to promote art and science, and drive forever from our fair land ignorance and superstition. In this shall we live worthy of him who, Promethean-like, drew down to earth the fires of heaven, and made the forked lightning subservient to his genius.

"Having done this, we extend to England the right hand of fellowship, and promise to stand with her in all good and great works in the defence of liberty, and in the maintenance of the religion of our fathers. It does not require the vision of a seer to perceive that the time will come when England and America must form a close alliance. The mariner sees in the cloud no larger than his hand danger and tempest. Such clouds are now seen in the political horizon. As men having at heart the good of our country and the cause of human kind, it behooves us to watch and guard. There is yet to be fought the great battle of nations; whether it be as against the onward crushing march of despotism on the one hand, or the wild, roaming and ungovernable passions of men let loose for the destruction of their kind on the other. How, when, or where it shall come, no man knoweth; and yet each and all of us feel, in the solemn stillness which pervades the earth, that the elements are gathering for fearful strife. Heaven's breezes bear upon their wings the groans of Europe's down-trodden millions. Autocrat diplomacy, which has for its object the plunder of the weak, is weaving around the governments of Europe a net-work intricate and dangerous. It is the modern Delilah, through whose instrumentality the institutions of liberty are to be shorn of their strength, and delivered over into the hands of the Philistines. In that hour of strife, and the night of horror which precedes it, let England and America be found together standing firm as adamant. Let England, sitting proudly upon the bosom of the waters, receive upon her white cliffs the wild waves of popular commotion, to hurl them back into the angry flood from whence they sprang. Ay, let our banners be entwined together, and defended by the dauntless hearts of Englishmen and Americans, whose battle-cry shall be, 'For God, the religion of our fathers, liberty and freedom.'

"Gentlemen, I have already trespassed too long upon your patience. Allow me, however, ere I close, to thank you in behalf of my respected father-in-law, and of our party, for your kindness and hospitality. We have been the recipients of your kindness, and we are sensible that we owe it not to any peculiar merit of our own, but to the fact that we are American citizens. As such, and as strangers, we came among you, and you send us hence your firm, fast friends. Upon this shoal of time have we met, and in the fulfilment of our destiny must again separate. Soon a mighty ocean shall roll between us. But distance shall not efface from our thoughts the recollection of your kindness, nor destroy the emotion of love and respect we shall entertain for you. In after years we shall think of this hour, and shall regard it as an oasis in the desert of life's pilgrimage, around which memory shall love to lie lingering,

'Like Adam near lost Paradise.'

" In conclusion I give you this sentiment:

"The Lion of England and the Eagle of America: May they hunt the foe together; and that which the keen sight and fierce talons of the one shall hunt out and take hold of, shall be utterly destroyed by the mighty strength of the other.' (Cheers.)

"Mr. Alderman Andrews, in proposing the next toast, said that during the last few years there had been so many manifestations of the union and good feeling subsisting between the people of England and America — between New York and Southampton — that they seemed to be, indeed, one people and one family. (Hear, hear.) The St. Lawrence visited them as a war frigate, and they welcomed Captain Paulding and his officers as members of one common family. Time rolled on, and the St. Lawrence visited their port again, when the American people sent over in her a large freight to the Great Industrial Exhibition of 1851, and the same hospitable reception was awarded to Captain Sands and his staff of officers. And now they had another opportunity, in the visit, on a trip of pleasure, of the splendid steam yacht North Star, the property of a noble-minded man, who had brought with him his interesting family. (Applause.) The qualities of this noble vessel had been spoken of by the whole of the press, and the conduct of the worthy commodore, his family, Captain Eldridge, and the officers, was deserving of all praise. Never had they experienced more courtesy and generosity than from all on board this fine yacht. He had to propose 'Success to the North Star, her commander, officers, and crew.' — The toast was drank, with loud and long-continued cheering.

"Song, Mr. Ransford, — 'Old Simon the Cellarer.'

"Capt. Eldridge said he was much obliged to them for the honor they had done to the toast, especially for the way in which it had been received. It went down as though it was good. (Laughter and cheers.) It was always gratifying to a man, and especially on such an occasion, to have his health drank so unanimously, with such kind feeling. He was glad to say that he felt no embarrassment — he felt quite at home. (Hear, hear.) The reception they had experienced was a source of gratitude to himself, and his officers and crew, most of whom, he was proud to say, were the sons of gentlemen. (Hear, and cheers.) This was the first time he had visited Southampton; and he was much pleased with the port, the entrance of the docks, and the excellent accommodation afforded (loud cheers), — at the courtesy they had experienced, and the police and all other regulations appertaining to the docks. (Hear.) The visit of the North Star had created some interest, and he thought it was justly due. It was a noble and glorious enterprise, and he felt proud of the ship and the position he held in her. The commodore had conferred an honor upon him in giving him the command, and he thanked him for it. He was proud of him as a man, and also of his sons and daughters, — he loved them all. Every captain was proud of his own ship, and he had no wish to be particular in this respect. (Laughter and cheers.) He thanked Mr. Andrews for the courtesy, kindness and hospitality, he had received at his house; and he thanked them all for the honor that had been conferred on the gallant commodore and his party. The North Star was opened to the public last week, and he then hoisted the English flag by the side of the American, and so he hoped the two flags would long continue. (Loud cheers.) England and America, if separated, may get into difficulties, but, united together, they will whip the world. (Loud cheering.)

"The Rev. J. W. Wyld, in proposing the next toast, said it had been remarked by a speaker, — one of their brethren from America, who had preceded him, — that we were prone to take up with things as they offered themselves to us, without inquiring into them, — to wander by the stream, without caring to seek out its source. Such a remark was naturally suggestive of the fact that the significance of an incident or event was materially connected, in our judgment, with the aspect under which it was viewed. Thus was it in reference to the present festivity, and the circumstances which had given rise to it. He could imagine many a listless spectator looking on the North Star yacht, now lying by the quay of our docks, without attaching any meaning to the simple circumstance that she *was* lying there. He could likewise imagine some one of those good-natured people, to be found in society, whose pleasure seems to consist in calling in question the seasonableness of the pleasures which every one else enjoys (hear, hear), — he could imagine some one of those good-natured people inquiring, 'Why so much ado about a gentleman and his family coming to port in their own vessel?' 'Is this a matter to be noticed by demonstrations of joy and public feasting?' 'What is there in such an incident to originate a banquet under the auspices of the Mayor and the principal merchants and traders of the town?' Such inquiries as these he was fully prepared to meet. (Hear, hear.) In his humble opinion, the arrival of Commodore Vanderbilt was associated with much that was highly significant, and which gave not only the foundation of reason and propriety to their present proceedings, as being a friendly welcome, but also as having a beneficial bearing on the national relationships of two great countries for the future. (Applause.) It was significant of the advanced state of the world at this time, to behold a gentleman freighting a vessel with those who were nearest and dearest to him on earth, and confidently setting out to traverse the greater half of the globe, and pay his respects to the chief civilized nations. (Cheers.) It was significant of the advanced state of science and art; for, without the knowledge of the aid which there could be summoned to afford him, the practicability of his carrying out his purpose within a given time, and thus making a tour of recreation thousands of miles away from home a limited episode in the gigantic activities which employed him in his own country, would never have found a place in his thoughts. It was significant, also, of the advancement of commerce; for it was a man whose wealth had been amassed in commerce that was enabled thus, in his own vessel, to transport himself at pleasure to distant shores. (Hear.) He desired, therefore, plainly to assure those who were guests on this occasion, that they who had invited them to this entertainment could give a reason for such invitation; that they knew what they were doing; that this festivity was not a mere ceremonial of etiquette (hear, hear, and loud cheers), — not the form into which a momentary impulse of courtesy had shaped itself; — but a deliberate expression of sincere feeling, — a real English-hearted welcome. (Renewed cheering.) He had seen it stated that their chief guest, Commodore Vanderbilt, was a 'self-made' man. He could not understand, however, in what the peculiar force of this descriptive epithet consisted. It was a description which, in his humble judgment, belonged, as a matter of course, to all men of honorable celebrity. Divine Providence did not, at the first hand, so to speak, make men great, or honorable, or useful. This was, in a measure, left to be the work of their own prudence, industry and integrity. There were materials placed within their reach by Providence, out of which they might elaborate to themselves a station and a name amongst their fellow-men; and, if these were judiciously and opportunely employed by them, they became great. (Hear.) Similar advantages and similar opportunities might be granted to two men of similar abilities; but the one, neglecting these advantages and opportunities, and being unfaithful to his own inward monitions, passed through life unknown, and at length descended to the grave unmissed, unhonored and unsung; whilst the other, duly improving every advantage, wisely using every opportunity, and loyally heeding every dictate of an enlightened judgment within him, became a man whom a nation might be proud to call its own, and whom the admiration of the world would be ready to honor. (Applause.) In welcoming, then, such a ' self-made ' man amongst them to-day, they were also testifying their homage to the great cause of commerce, with which his greatness was identified; and, in doing this, their proceedings might be viewed as further including an unfeigned regard for the cause of civilization in general; for commerce was the offspring of peace, and in proportion as peace prevailed commerce was favored, and in proportion as commerce was favored the mutual intercourse of mankind was promoted; and in proportion as the mutual intercourse of mankind was promoted, good understandings, friendship, and true brotherhood amongst the individuals of our race, were fostered. (Applause.) He had heard of a Scottish farmer, who, in the course of one of his morning rambles, beheld, through the mist that covered the valley along which he was proceeding, a figure approaching him, like that of a giant, brandishing a club wherewith to smite down every living creature that might come in his way. Startled at this strange appearance, the farmer for a moment paused ; but, seeing the monster continuing to advance, he felt his native valor instinctively urge him onward to the encounter. As, however, he continued to come nearer to the figure, and the figure came nearer to him, and the mist between them both began to clear away, the farmer beheld the form of the stranger reduced from the proportions of a giant to those of an ordinary man, and his terrible club turned into a moderately-sized walking-stick ; and when at the last he actually came up to the said figure, he became apprized of the fact that, so far from its being a giant, or even a stranger, it was his own brother. Thus had it often happened in the history of human society. Men beheld each other at a distance, and through the mists of prejudice and ignorance, as strangers and monsters ; but, as they came nearer to one another, and the mists which had distorted their figures in the eyes of one another cleared away, they found themselves to be brethren to one another. (Loud cheers.) It was only because men were reciprocally unacquainted that misunderstandings and dislikes, hatred and all kinds of erroneous estimates, were mutually promoted. Repetitions of such a scene as the present were amongst the best modes of dispelling foolish and false feelings between man and man, and truly contributing to insure the peace of the world, and consequently the interests of commerce. He believed, indeed, that there might arise occasions when war was a righteous duty. (Hear, hear.) He spoke this guardedly, and consistently, in his judgment, with his being a minister of peace. He held that there might be times when it was incumbent on every good citizen, every true lover of his country, to buckle on the weapons of fight at the bidding of the chief magistrate, and hold himself in readiness to be disposed of as being set for the defence of his fatherland. (Hear, hear.) Yet he would observe that such a view as this regarded war as a horrid necessity only, on the supposition that every other method for vindicating right and justice had been adopted. But, alas ! how generally had wars been fomented by the ambition and avarice of princes and rulers. Wars, as they had appeared on the page of history, had been the arguments of madmen, or the reckless staking of the welfare of thousands to serve the folly of one or a few. It was not the interest of the people of one country to quarrel with those of another, whatever might be the designing aims of their rulers. (Loud cheers.) Nor would they ever quarrel, if left to follow out the development of the commercial spirit. It was this spirit, he believed, which had, in times past, invariably been the reverse of blessedness to every community. He could not resist the impression that many of those who, in ancient times, were most renowned, were men of commerce, and not men of war. Abraham and the other patriarchs, it was well known, were large sheep-owners. And, for his own part, he doubted not that, if we could get at the right explanation of many traditions that have come down to us from the first ages of the world, your traders, your men of business, would be found holding the chief and most important positions. What should hinder us from getting at the most satisfactory explanation of the story of Jason and his 'golden fleece,' by assuming that this Jason was one of the 'go-ahead' men of his time, and, having freighted his vessel with a cargo of what might have been the Manchester goods of that era, he returned home with a sheep's skin full of gold as the result of the sales he had effected? It was just such meetings as the present that tended to make the commercial spirit between England and America the bond of peace. The influence of such a meeting could not be calculated. It would not be limited to the personal feeling of those who had honored them as their guests that day; it would have a wider range of extension, and the cordial greeting here given to one of the principal merchant princes of America would become known throughout his country, and, as often as referred to, would be productive of the most desirable and kindly of feelings. The hope had been expressed that the eagle of America and the lion of England would always be found hunting together. Yes, he trusted that they would thus hunt, in company and harmony, for the purpose of removing all meaner birds and beasts of prey from the face of the earth, and for the clearing away of everything that was destructive to the world's civilization. The interests of England and America were the same. There was a family tie between John Bull and his son Jonathan, and the peace which was essential to its preservation was bound up in their commercial relationships. This, then, was the sentiment of the toast he was intrusted to propose — 'England and America: May peace and commerce long unite them.' The reverend gentleman was loudly cheered on resuming his seat.

"The Rev. Dr. Choules, in rising to acknowledge the toast, was much applauded. He said:

"I suppose that I have been called upon to respond to this toast on account of my relation to England and the United States. I am a native of England, but have been a resident in the American Union for thirty years. I love the land of my birth, and I glory in the country of my choice. No man lives who longs more than I do to see these great and glorious lands united in the bands of cordial, brotherly attachment, and I am glad to know that all good men in both of them participate in this desire; and, if it were not for the denaturalized efforts of a few corrupt leaders of the press, and a handful of partisan demagogues, the feeling would be almost universal in Great Britain and America. Our happy country has much to enlist the warm affections of her citizens. Sir, America has a history of which we may be proud. Her founders were not children suckled by a she-wolf in the woods, — they were no fugitives from a ruined Troy; but they were a rare race of men, reared up for a rare purpose. They sought what England did not *then* afford; and they found the object of their pilgrimage,

'A faith's pure shrine,
Freedom to worship God.'

"Now, every nation on earth is turning to America the look of imploring pity; long, long may she be the lighthouse of the world, — the evangelist of the nations! (Hear, and cheers.) As soon as our citizens land in England, they feel at home, thoroughly at home! We love to call England 'the old country,' 'mother country,' and 'land of our fathers.' What sort of a land should we now possess if we had a Spanish origin, a French descent? Let the distracted states of South and Central America furnish the solution. (Hear, hear.) Americans claim an equal interest, as Mr. Clark has eloquently told you, in your Milton, Bacon, Newton, Burke, and Boyle; these and Shakspeare are quite as much ours as they are yours. These intellectual treasures belong to us as much as they do to the lords of the British soil. This patrimony is *ours;* and our sons have had their patriotism animated by careful study of the acts and sufferings and speeches of your Hampdens, Russells, Vanes and Sydneys. Land of our fathers, and the home of a civilization such as our world cannot parallel! far distant be the day when Americans shall cease to feel devotion at the shrine of thy mighty dead, and gather fresh inspiration from their genius, learning and virtues! (Loud cheers.)

"When we land in your venerable town, sir, we, too, have local associations of the tenderest character. We cannot forget that hence sailed the Mayflower and her precious freight. On board that ark was written the first constitution that insured to man the enjoyment of equal laws and full liberty of conscience. Probably many who saw that ship depart regarded it as a matter of small moment; only the departure of a few weary men and women panting for a land of freedom, where they could worship God free from oppression and persecution. These men had small means, and wore plain habiliments. Thus it is in the providence of God, who often connects ultimate grandeur with apparent original insignificance. Newton, you know, ascended to the loftiest heights of science by the acquisition of the alphabet; the

Saviour of the world was once the occupant of a stable; and the foundations of our holy religion were laid by a few poor fishermen. Yes, I think it probable that men, standing on your beautiful shores, gazed and smiled at the Mayflower as she departed from your waters; but they were looking at men who were to found an empire of freedom, and who, soon after landing in a long-boat from their weather-beaten bark, kindled up a beacon fire which will yet enlighten the world, and carried with them a leaven which has yet to leaven the whole mass of suffering humanity. (Hear, and cheers.)

"When we land in Southampton, we cannot forget your illustrious Watts, whose songs have charmed and taught our childhood, animated the devotions of our fathers' sanctuaries, and placed notes of triumph in the lips of myriads as they have gone through the valley of the shadow of death. The true interest of Britain and the United States is to cultivate a brotherly regard; our interests are identical. (Yes, yes.)

"If Americans visit England, and Englishmen visit the United States, interchanging civilities and hospitalities, as we are now doing, no premier nor government of either country can ever set these great nations at war, — a game which rulers cannot play at when the people are wise and virtuous. (Applause.)

"I beg leave, sir, to propose 'The health of that venerable lady, Mrs. Vanderbilt, the mother of your honored guest.'

"This toast was warmly responded to by the company.

"Commodore Vanderbilt said he had been accustomed, all his life, to go direct to a point; and he would therefore, without preface, propose 'The Mayor and Corporation of Southampton.' Drank, with loud cheers.

"Glee, by the Ransford family — 'Sportive little trifler,' — *Bishop*.

"The Mayor briefly replied, remarking that the Mayor and Corporation had arduous duties to perform, but such seasons as this amply repaid them for all their troubles and difficulties.

"Mr. Mayes, in a few eulogistic remarks on that gentleman's character and conduct since his residence in Southampton, proposed the health of 'Mr. Croskey, Consul of the United States of America; and prosperity to the Ocean Steam Navigation Company of New York.' The toast was warmly received, and acknowledged, in a few words, by the Mayor, on behalf of Mr. Croskey.

"The toasts of 'The Town Clerk' and 'The Press' were subsequently drank and responded to, and the company separated, looking forward with agreeable anticipations to a pleasant excursion on the morrow."

"EXCURSION ROUND THE ISLE OF WIGHT AND TO SPITHEAD.

[Taken from *New Hampshire Independent*.]

"On Tuesday morning, about four hundred persons, consisting of the Mayor and Mayoress, many members of the corporate body, the principal merchants and tradesmen of the town, a goodly party of ladies, &c., availed themselves of the kind offer of Commodore Vanderbilt to take a trip in the North Star; and, accordingly, about half-past eleven o'clock, the gallant vessel steamed away from the dock-head, an excellent band on board playing the national anthem, and the national colors of England and America proudly floating in the breeze from the mast-heads. Several hundreds of persons had assembled on the docks to witness her departure. The invitation-cards notified a trip to Spithead, to view the Duke of Wellington, the magnificent new screw three-decker, and the other ships of the squadron lying at Spithead; but, after passing Calshot Castle, the party on board were delighted to find that the bow of the North Star was turned to the westward, and that a trip round the Isle of Wight had been resolved on. The weather was fine, and the Solent and the Channel were perfectly calm. The magnitude of the yacht and the smoothness of the sea prevented much motion being felt during the whole of the voyage. The afternoon being beautifully fine and clear, the lovely and majestic scenery, for which the back of the Wight is so justly celebrated, was much enjoyed by all on board, especially by the American ladies and gentlemen, and a more delightful trip was never made. In passing Ventnor, flags were run up the several flag-posts on shore, in compliment to the North Star, which was returned on board by dipping colors, and firing a succession of salutes. About four o'clock the North Star got to Spithead, and steamed twice through the fleet, thus affording the company an opportunity of seeing the Duke of Wellington, and the other ships of the squadron moored there. The fleet comprises the Duke of Wellington, 131; Ajax, 60; Blenheim, 60; Hogue, 58; Edinburgh, 58; Sidon, 22; and Odin, 16. On nearing the first-named magnificent and stupendous ship, the North Star fired a royal salute, the whole company on board cheering, and the band playing 'God save the Queen.' This demonstration was replied to from the Duke of Wellington by cheering, on the part of the crew, who manned the rigging for the purpose, and dipping the ensign. The guns were not, however, returned, — naval etiquette preventing a salute in honor of a private and non-official personage. The sight at Spithead was a very imposing one, and, combined with the inspection of the lovely natural wonders ranging the coast, from the Needles on the west to the Culver Cliffs on the east, rendered this one of the most interesting and pleasant excursions ever made in this part of the world.

"After leaving Spithead, the gallant yacht steered for Southampton; and, during her progress up the Southampton river, the company assembled in the saloon, where they were briefly addressed by the Mayor. His worship acknowledged, on behalf of the people of Southampton, the great compliment that Commodore Vanderbilt had conferred on them by visiting their port, and the kindness and courtesy of himself and family in throwing open to the public his yacht, — an object worthy of much curiosity; and, after dwelling on the advantages which an interchange of civilities amongst individuals belonging to two of the greatest nations of the world must produce, he proposed three cheers for Commodore Vanderbilt and his family. This call was right heartily responded to by the company, whose cheers rung through the ship for several minutes. Major Labau, on behalf of the commodore, thanked the Mayor and inhabitants of Southampton for the cordiality with which they had been received, reiterating the kindly and fraternal sentiments which characterized the speeches delivered at the banquet on the preceding day, and which cannot but be productive of good feeling and amity between the nations. The company were subsequently addressed, in obedience to calls made upon them, by the Rev. A. McLaren and F. Cooper, Esq., by which time the yacht had reached the entrance of the Southampton docks, where the excursionists took leave of their American friends, amidst the warmest expressions of affectionate regard and esteem.

"During the whole of the day the greatest attention and courtesy was shown by the Americans to their numerous guests. The whole of the ship was thrown open to the visitors, and refreshments of every kind were served in the most lavish abundance. Although the number of persons on board (including the commodore and his family, the crew, &c.) could not have been much under five hundred, yet the great size of the ship, the splendid fittings and roomy arrangements of the cabin and saloons, and the convenient and extensive promenade afforded on the spar deck (nearly three hundred feet long), and other portions of the vessel, caused the party to appear by no means a large one. After dinner, the young folks repaired to the gun-deck, and had a joyous time in waltzing, with excellent music from the band. Among the visitors on this excursion were W. H. Wills, Esq., of Bristol, and the Rev. Mr. Gunn, of Warminster, who came on purpose to visit the yacht.

"The North Star goes through the water most beautifully, and with great speed, the machinery working with exquisite smoothness. The two large sway-beams, working on deck at a great elevation, and communicating the driving-power to the ponderous cranks below, are a novel feature in this country, and give the ship a curious appearance from the distance.

"The North Star ran alongside the dock-head about half-past six o'clock, and the band played the national anthems of England and America whilst the company were landing."

"DEPARTURE OF THE NORTH STAR.

"Immediately the English guests were all landed, the North Star put about, and bade a final adieu to Southampton, starting for the German Ocean. It is understood that she will proceed up the Baltic and the Neva, and from thence Commodore Vanderbilt will visit the shores of the Mediterranean.

"Commodore Vanderbilt has left behind him agreeable reminiscences of his kindness and courtesy from the moment of his arrival. It is calculated that at least ten thousand persons have inspected the North Star at Southampton.* The yacht will not again call here, as she is to touch at Havre on her way from the Baltic trip to the Mediterranean."

* A large party of visitors was on board at Southampton, who came from Scotland direct to visit the North Star.

CHAPTER VII.

VOYAGE — COAST OF NORWAY — KRONBORG CASTLE AND ELSINORE — SHIPS IN THE SOUND — COPENHAGEN — BORNHOLM AND OLAND ISLANDS — DR. LINSLY — MIRAGE — DAGO ISLAND — STEAMER NEPTUNE — CRONSTADT — FORTIFICATIONS — DOCKS — SHIPPING — PUBLIC BUILDINGS — CHOLERA — PETERHOFF — WOODS — VAUXHALL HOTEL — MARLY AND MONPLAISIR — PETER THE GREAT — HIS HOUSE — FURNITURE — COTTAGE OF CATHERINE — A RIDE THROUGH THE GROUNDS — WATER-WORKS, ETC. — PETERHOFF IMPERIAL PALACE — IMPERIAL YACHT, AND GRAND DUKE CONSTANTINE — ADMIRAL GLASSENAPP — MR. MULLER — MINIATURE PALACE — COSSACKS.

JUNE 14. — Immediately after landing our friends at Southampton, we steamed off, at about eight o'clock P. M., for St. Petersburg, making use of only two boilers, and consuming only twenty-five tons coal. The intense fog, which sprang up and continued for the next two days, deprived us of much enjoyment, and on the 15th and 16th we were unable to take observations. The 17th was a delightful, balmy day, and the sea continued, as it had been from leaving England, like a sea of glass. On the morning of the 18th we were all on deck at sunrise, enjoying a most charming view of the coast of Sweden and Denmark, as we were sailing through the narrow passes of the Skager Rack and the Cattegat. This is the anniversary of the battle of Waterloo, and controversy runs sharp between the admirers of Wellington and the emperor. Alison's history is in great demand, and, of course, is criticized pretty freely. A recent attempt in New York to bolster up every act and opinion of the great man is also quoted as an indication of public opinion. A more unscrupulous vindication was never written in France; and, in many respects, it beats the emperor's own bulletins. That Napoleon was a great man, — that he was, in many respects, a benefactor to France, — no one will deny; but that his restless ambition was a scourge to Europe, is apparent; and the wisdom of the courts of Europe could devise no safety for themselves short of his overthrow. We were all enchanted with the prospect that opened upon us as we made Elsinore, and obtained a sight of Kronborg Castle, which is beautifully situated on the narrowest part of the sound, opposite the Swedish seaport of Helsinborg, about three miles distant. This noble fortress was built by Frederick II. at the close of the sixteenth century, and is regarded as one of the noblest castles of northern Europe. It is built in the Gothic style, and has several lofty towers and turrets. The design of the fortress was made by the great astronomer, Tycho Brahé. It was in this prison that Queen Caroline Matilda was so long confined, on account of her supposed criminal intercourse with Count Struensee. At this place is laid the scene of the great play of Shakspeare; but it is all the merest fiction, as we have no proof to show that Denmark ever had a Hamlet for its sovereign. Elsinore is a pretty town, with fine environs; its present population is about ten thousand. It is calculated that about eighteen thousand ships pass through the sound annually, and here it is that the tax is paid on their cargoes. This tax was reduced in 1842, and again in 1846. In 1847 the number of vessels which passed Elsinore was twenty-one thousand five hundred and twenty-six, and in 1850 there were more than seven thousand British ships.

When we entered the sound we were presented with a most extraordinary spectacle; a calm had prevailed for a few days, and a vast collection of ships and vessels of all descriptions had gathered together; and now we found between Elsinore and Copenhagen, at a moderate estimate, I think, not less than one thousand, all under way. At one point Mr. Vanderbilt, Captain Eldridge, and other members of the party, reckoned two hundred and fifty-three sail in sight at once, and all, I think, within a circle of two and a half miles. Many of these were large ships, and several hoisted the stars and stripes. I think the distance from Elsinore to the capital is about twenty-five miles; and our entire passage was one of great beauty. The Swedish shore was very fine, and on the Danish coast we noticed several most enchanting spots. Here and there were old castles, and several fine woods. It was pleasant to observe the churches, all of which looked in good condition. At half-past eleven we stopped our steamer off Copenhagen, and a party landed to obtain supplies of milk, eggs, butter and poultry. Our friends returned from the city after a delay of four or five hours, but they brought a good account of the place, and very excellent supplies. The best-made butter that we saw on our whole voyage was that which came on board at Copenhagen. Here, too, we obtained fine fish from the fishing-boats that were near us and returning home. At quarter past four P. M., we were off for Russia.

Sunday, 19th June, was as beautiful a day as we could desire. The Baltic was as smooth as the Hudson, and we were not sensible of any motion excepting the rapid progress of our yacht. And now we were experiencing the novel pleasure of the long days which are known in this season in the high latitudes, and the marvellous stories of which we had read in our youth. It certainly was strange to find the *night* only lasting for about two and a half hours. This was the case on the night after leaving Copenhagen; and the most of it I passed on deck, in agreeable chat with Captain Eldridge, whose fund of knowledge, acquired by extensive travel and nautical experience, combined with great shrewdness of observation, always afforded us entertainment. After passing the grounds of Copenhagen, and taking our departure from the light-ship, we steered for the light-ship outside Falsterbo light-ship, stationed off the reef of the same name; and, on rounding this, we steered directly for Bornholm. In the evening we passed Bornholm, and I am quite sure that no one on board the North Star will ever forget the magnificence of the night.

MIRAGE — DAGO ISLAND. 111

It certainly was the most glorious nocturnal season that I ever witnessed, — cloudless, and so light that only one or two stars were visible, and the moon shone in a milder lustre than we had ever before seen. Bornholm is an island belonging to Denmark, about twenty miles in length, and ten or twelve wide. The shores are lofty, and present a bold, rocky appearance, and all around it are dangerous reefs. Ronne is the chief town, on the west side. At the north point of the island is a light-house built on a mountain, called, I think, Steilebergh, and our chart gives it an elevation of two hundred and eighty feet above the surface of the sea. About fifteen miles east of Bornholm is a large group of rocks, called Eartholms; on one of these there is a castle called Christiansoe, and in this place is a small but safe harbor. Our course now lay direct for Oland Island, and we made the South-head light-house; thence sailed for Gottland Island, and, coasting which, we made Ostergarns Island and light-house, and then sailed for Dago Island. Our good friend, Dr. Linsly, was now a sad sufferer. In travelling from Liverpool to London he was attacked with a pain in the neck; it kept increasing, and had now become a severe old-fashioned carbuncle, of large size. His sufferings were very painful, and it was in vain that I prescribed the lancet, which he acknowledged was the regular and proper thing in such cases provided; but he squirmed at the fitting remedy, and, doctor-like, refused to take his own medicine. Soon after dinner our attention was directed to nine large ships-of-war; they appeared with all sail set, and not more than ten or twelve miles off, but as we approached they vanished. After sailing for three hours and making forty miles, we came upon the Russian fleet, consisting of nine ships-of-the-line, that were taking their usual summer cruise, and then found that we had witnessed a remarkable case of mirage.

June 20, at nine A. M., we passed the light on Dago Island, at the entrance to the Gulf of Finland, and before noon were in sight of Nickmans Shoal, the spot where the British steamer, the

Neptune, was lost in May; her masts and chimney are still standing. We now passed by off Revel, and had a good view of its towers and shipping, light-houses and innumerable buoy flags. We next steered to pass Kokskar light, and then direct for the north side of Hoogland, making Rothscar light on our passage. We now headed for the Sommers light, and, passing which, we sailed between the Neva tower and the flags and beacons on the Stone ground, directing our course for the Tolbeacon light, from whence about twelve miles carried us to the island upon which Cronstadt is situated.

21*st*, *Tuesday.*—This is the longest day, and the sun did not set till nearly ten o'clock, and then rose again before two, and all the interval was one continued bright twilight, so that we could read the small type of the *Courier and Enquirer* and *Herald* on deck with great ease. At half-past twelve a bright halo indicates the proximity of the sun to the horizon during his absence. All were on deck to witness the sun rise, and I do not think that we shall soon forget the novelty of twenty-four hours of day-light in one day. At ten o'clock we stopped opposite the guard-ship. Officers came on board, examined our passports, took a list of our names, objects, &c. We were then permitted to anchor off Cronstadt, and at eleven we were all settled down off this great fortress and naval dépôt. Here we were again boarded by officials, and after a few moments' explanation they retired, and the captain went on shore and made a representation to the governor of our objects and the character of the excursion. He was politely received, and orders were at once given for our landing when we pleased.

Cronstadt is a strongly-fortified garrison, and is the great safeguard of the metropolis. The population in the summer, when all is lively in the docks and navy-yard, is about thirty thousand, but in the winter not more than twelve thousand. This is the great dépôt of the northern fleet of the empire. In the dock appropriated to the ships-of-war I should think forty might be accommodated; and when we arrived there were twelve ships-of-the-line all undergoing repairs and receiving outfit, while in the river, directly around the North Star, were several noble steamers belonging to the government, and we at once recognized the Kamtschatka, built for the Czar in New York a few years ago. An immense harbor for merchantmen attracted our notice. It will receive, I should think, seven or eight hundred, and certainly not less than five hundred were in it during our visit; among these were several of our own country. I noticed the Peterhoff, of Boston, the Sewell, of the same port, and other eastern ships. The fortifications are of vast strength, and it seems as if no ship could pass the rocky islet and its auxiliary forts with safety, if its passage was disputed. The water is quite shallow, and the law is exceedingly severe against placing any obstruction in the access to the Neva. No ballast or waste is allowed to be thrown overboard off the town. We found the town without any particular charm; but the arsenal, and navy-yard, with its ships, impressed us most favorably. The navy is as fine-looking as could be desired, and no American would feel mortified if he saw such vessels carrying the banner of his country. As we lay at anchor, we were much gratified to watch the incessant transit of steam and tow boats up and down from St. Petersburg to Cronstadt. The scene was one of great interest. I differ entirely from the guide-books as to the beauty of the shore on the passage to the capital; so far from being tame, I regard the prospect off to the right as very fine. From the deck of the North Star I saw distinctly the rays of the setting sun play on the dome of the churches and the golden spire of the admiralty, although we were at a distance of about eighteen miles.

Our friends visited, in Cronstadt, the Marine Cadet Building, and the Naval Hospital. These are very spacious edifices, and are both conducted admirably. They are under the eye of the emperor, who frequently drops in to make an *unexpected* visitation. The hospital is regarded as a model institution. The streets are so wide, and the people in them so few and far between, that we instantly felt that the place looked solitary. It was here that we learned that the cholera was in St. Petersburg, and that not a few cases existed in Cronstadt. And here I may observe, that, for a day before our arrival, and all the next day, there was scarcely a person on board our ship who had not, in some degree, the premonitory symptoms of this awful scourge of the nations.

Our friends now divided into parties. Some took a steamer to Oranienbaum, — a little town, near to Peterhoff, — to which place they proceeded by droskys, the ride being one of about five miles.

Mr. Vanderbilt chartered a small steamer, and his family went direct to Peterhoff, and he remained on board. We landed at the emperor's wharf, at which we found the royal yacht lying, with her steam up. She was a very splendid boat, of fine model, and as gay as blue paint and gilt ornament could make her. Her bow was very fine, and adorned with a golden eagle and an imperial crown. The sentries were about to dispute our landing at this place, when one of the officers, who had visited the yacht the day before, stepped up, ordered us to land, and politely assisted the ladies, and then gave us direction to the hotel at Peterhoff. Peterhoff is the summer residence of the Russian court; and I do not wonder that each successive emperor makes it his favorite abode. Our walk, for half a mile, lay through the most charming wood; and the deep shades had been most evidently the care of men who had great taste, and well understood wood-craft. How our lost Downing would have rejoiced in this place! We passed by noble oaks, and wanted to stop and admire them at once, without waiting for a regular survey of the place; and perhaps it was an inward premonition that we were on what Russians regard as holy ground, for in a short time we found that one or two of these glorious monarchs of the wood were planted by the hands of that wonderful man Peter the Great.

On getting out of the wood, we entered a village of great beauty and elegance, and soon found ourselves comfortably ensconced in a hotel known as Vauxhall, and which made quite an appearance. The first thing was to obtain rooms, and this is the most important thing in a Russian tavern. The rooms were most exquisitely neat,— cleanliness itself; the furniture good, but scarce; beds all single; and the charge was made for beds rather than rooms. A sofa, fitted up with sheets, paid as well as a bed. After disposing of our entire party, the next thing was to get a lunch; and this was done very satisfactorily, as we were all hungry. The provisions were excellent, and, as we found everywhere in Russia, entirely in the style of the French cuisine.

After our refreshment, we started on a tour of inspection. I have visited most of the great palaces of England and France, and other countries in Europe, but I have seen no locality for a palace that pleases me more than Peterhoff, — at least, for a residence in summer. Its position is good; it is at the mouth of the Neva, and commands a fine view of Cronstadt, from which it is, perhaps, ten miles distant. Our first sight was the residence of Peter the Great; it is not far removed from the old palace. Marly is beautifully surrounded by trees, and the house is quite small, and not very unlike a Dutch farm-house. Its interior is quite like some old houses that I remember on the North river. In this snuggery Peter died. We saw the bed on which he breathed his last; the bed-clothes are all preserved, as when he occupied the chamber. On the pillow are his caps and night-clothes, and his *robe de chambre* lying on the coverlet of the bed. Nothing can be more simple than all the furniture. The rooms are small; and you can fancy that the old people who live in the cottage have just stepped out. In the room adjoining the small chamber are his slippers, boots and sedan-chair, and other articles of personal dress. In a small corner-cupboard are his camp equipage, as plain as tin, iron and brass, can be. The walls of the kitchen are covered with blue Dutch tiles. Nothing indicates that royalty ever resided here, but some *good* Flemish pictures, and a few elegant Japanese cabinets and beautiful stands. His escritoire remains as he last used it. A long, narrow saloon, which is really a covered gallery, has many portraits; and here the emperor used to walk, and receive his visitors. The dining-room was a small apartment, with a circular oak table, and the panels of fine Japanese work; the lower wainscoting of old black oak. From a noble terrace, paved with marble, Peter could gaze upon his infant navy, lying off at Cronstadt. The rocks of the sea-shore come quite up to the balustrades of the terrace, and greatly add to the scenery. The Empress Elizabeth used to retire from the pomp of royalty at this quiet spot, and is said to have cooked her own dinners. We then went to visit the cottage of Catherine, the interior of which is excessively rich; and its mirrors, and wonderful collection of china and glass, entirely captivated our ladies. In no place have I seen such magnificent specimens of Dresden porcelain as in this gem of a palace; and the gorgeousness of some of the apartments struck us peculiarly, after the contrast we had witnessed in the humble apartments of the great monarch. We now set off in carriages, to ride round the pleasure-grounds, and see the charming villas and gardens connected with the present abode of royalty. The verdure of the sward, and the foliage of the woods, and the gay flowers of the thousand garden beds and borders, transcend all that I have known of beauty in the country-life of any part of the world; and, when we think that all this enchanting display has sprung up in six weeks, — for no longer ago it was absolute winter, and thick snow covered the face of the earth, — we feel that we are indeed in a land of wonders, and it is with an appreciating understanding of the mystery involved, that we exclaim, of the Great Author of all that is fair and excellent, "*Thou renewest the face of the earth.*"

PETERHOFF—ORNAMENTS OF PALACE-GARDENS.

The gardens are very extensive,—the drives enclose thirty miles; and fish-ponds, temples, villas, &c., are too numerous to allude to in detail. The bathing-house of the imperial family is a most admirable building; and from a chaste marble structure you walk down into a large sheet of water, surrounded by a dense foliage of lofty trees. The vast amount of water at command enables the imperial owner to rival, if not surpass, the celebrated water-works at Versailles. Every possible surprise awaits the wanderer through these grounds. You are standing to admire some beautiful tree; the guide has touched a spring, and every branch, and every twig, and every leaf, is turned into crystal; and a fountain rises from that tree, which is metallic, although the spectator supposed it to be veritably a production of the forest. While passing over exquisite bridges from island to island, and in boats drawn by stationary ropes, we observed the imperial gondolas, which are much used by the royal family.

On one of these islets we were pleased with what seemed to be a beautiful temple; and, ordering the driver to stop, we alighted from the carriages, and soon reached it on a movable platform, propelled by two men drawing on ropes on either side of it. Never was there a more blissful retreat than this peaceful spot. The temple was a lovely miniature villa. Statuary decked the outer niches of the walls. The entrance was through a long passage, roofed with ivy; a high wall was covered with the same, so trained as to allow medallions and marble entaglios on the wall to appear as within a frame. Here was a fountain, in the centre of a large basin, flowers rare and fragrant, and some most precious groups of statuary, forming a *coup d'œil* at once fairy-like and enchanting. Opening on the fountain was a fine spacious summer-room, furnished with a rich divan piled up with cushions. In front of it stood a small, low table, supporting a reclining Cleopatra, the poisonous asp upon her arm, and her left hand rested on her heart. Here, too, was a beautiful mosaic table. The next room was peculiarly tasteful, and full of comfort. The table, writing-desk, statuary, all looked as though the most fastidious taste had directed the position of each object. The garden of this islet was radiant with roses, azaleas, fuchsias, carnations.

The palace is a large building, painted yellow, and picked off with white. It has no very great architectural merits; but the chapel, which stands at one end, has a gorgeous dome, which reflects every ray of light from its gilt surface. We were shown through the palace with every attention, and were much gratified with the regal display of objects of art. The malachite, porcelain and statuary, were exquisitely beautiful; and there were several good paintings. In one large apartment there are more than three hundred portraits of the prettiest girls in Russia, executed for Catherine II.; and very pretty some of them are, too, in their national costumes. From the royal residence down to the bank of the Neva is a series of terraces, and one continued series of waterfalls, lakes and fountains. The basins, Neptunes, Tritons and cascades, must be seen, for no written description will do them any justice. Again and again did we drive round this fairy spot; and we left it never again expecting to see so much that is beautiful in the arrangement of gardens and grounds.

When we returned to Vauxhall, to dinner, we found Mr. Vanderbilt, and learned from him that the royal yacht, which we had seen at the wharf with her steam on, had made a trip to the North Star, and brought as a visitor to him the Grand Duke Constantine, the second son of the emperor, and the High Admiral of the Russian navy; and, on his return to Peterhoff, he brought Mr. Vanderbilt in his yacht, and sent round one of the emperor's carriages, with the royal livery, to take Mr. and Mrs. V. round the place. The duke made quite a long visit on board the North Star, inspected every part of the ship with much interest, and requested permission to have some officers of the topographical corps allowed to come on board, to take drafts of the ship, her cabins, engines, &c. This was cheerfully acceded to. These gentlemen came, another day, with their portfolios, and made capital views of the machinery, &c. With the duke was a gentleman, named Muller, who is on terms of some intimacy with him, and from whom we continued to receive very polite and useful attentions while we remained in Russia. After dinner we went to the parade-ground, in front of the palace, as it was expected that the emperor would be present when the band performed their evening music. While promenading I had the pleasure to meet Admiral Glassenapp, who had visited our yacht the day of our arrival, and with whom I had gone through our steamer. He was very polite, gave me every explanation as to the troops, and, pointing to a window, told me that the emperor was in that room, and was so engaged that he would not appear on the ground. He had that day given audience of leave-taking to our minister, Mr. Brown, who was recalled by the new administration. Admiral Glassenapp is a very intelligent man, about forty or forty-five years of age, and has the command of the Naval Cadets, who are now in three frigates, lying off in the Neva, just opposite the palace. The admiral speaks English tolerably well, and very much reminds me of General Totten, of the United States' Engineers, as I remember him when he resided at Newport. Just as we were talking, the band struck up a very solemn air; all hats were off instantly, and a death-like silence, for a few moments, pervaded the vast assemblage. It was the evening prayer, and is observed by the military with great solemnity. I have not often observed a more devotional observance than that which I was so happy as to witness on this occasion. In the evening we were all much fatigued; but our friend Mr. Muller insisted that I should ride a mile or two, to see the new splendid Tea House, which has lately been built for the heir apparent, who has just married. A pleasant ride brought us to this most elegant establishment. The Tea House is a miniature palace. It is a large, splendid mansion, but small for a regal residence. Here everything surpasses, in exquisiteness of furniture and splendor, any palace I have seen in Europe. The rooms are quite of moderate dimensions, but the style of finish is beyond my previous ideas of domestic architectural beauty. The pictures, statuary, hangings, are all as beautiful as the art of Europe can furnish. The portraits of the emperor and empress, Alexander, and other members of the royal family, were in the best style of the art. I shall never forget the staircases, the bath-rooms, and the library. The bed-rooms, and every part of the establishment, were thrown open to our inspection; and the ladies who were with us regarded this as the great treat of the day. Other things we had seen were of days gone by, but this was the splendor of the present age; and perhaps no palace in the world is superior to this bijou in its completeness of arrangement. The timepieces of this palace are of vast value. The gardens are fine; and nature has done much for the grounds, as off to the right is a deep ravine, with fine walks and artificial terraces. Here, as at Peterhoff, I noticed the best specimens of gilly-flowers that I ever saw, whole beds of white double-flowers, and some of the deepest scarlet. Roses were just beginning to appear; but the wild ones were in profusion. We were all amused at seeing the nurse-maids, on the parade-ground, with the infants under their care. Some of these servants had head-dresses which would have been worth looking at in Barnum's Museum. We noticed about a dozen Cossacks of the Don. They were stern-looking men, of large proportions, with head-dress of a peculiar cast. They carried long spears. Admiral Glassenapp informed me that a few of the Cossacks and Circassians are always near the person of the Czar, and that it is intended as a compliment to these valuable portions of the army.

CHAPTER VIII.

SMALL STEAMER — DRESS OF OFFICERS — VIEW OF ST. PETERSBURG — QUEER PROCESSION — HOTELS — POLITENESS — MR. ROPES, U. S. CONSUL — SUMMER ISLANDS — PETER THE GREAT'S FIRST HOUSE — THE CITY — ADMIRALTY — STATUE OF PETER — NEFFSKY PERSPECTIVE — SERFS — VIEW OF CITY BY MOONLIGHT — WINTER PALACE AND ITS DEPARTMENTS — REGALIA — THE HERMITAGE — PAINTINGS OF DIFFERENT SCHOOLS — THE LOGGIE — PETER'S MUSEUM — PRECIOUS STONES — HOROLOGE — WREATHS AND LAURELS FROM CHERSONESUS — MARBLE PALACE — ALEXANDER PILLAR — MR. EVANS — MONASTERY OF ALEXANDER NEFFSKY — ENGLISH CHURCH — KESAN CATHEDRAL — ITS INTERIOR AND SERVICE — ISAAC CHURCH.

We left Peterhoff in the morning boat for St. Petersburg, but several of the party retained their rooms, and went to and fro daily; but I felt anxious to see as much as possible of the city in our brief stay, and therefore reluctantly left what I shall ever regard as one of the most attractive spots I ever visited. The charms of Peterhoff are not its palace and its imperial residents, but the glorious exhibition which is laid open to the admirer of nature.

On getting on board the small steamer, we found a crowded deck. Very many of the passengers were officers; they all wore the dark gray or blue cloak reaching to the very heels, and the standing collar fitting close up to the ears. This, in such hot weather as we were then enduring, struck me as remarkable; but I afterwards learned that, such is the strictness observed in the army inspection, that not a spot or particle of dust is overlooked; and that to protect the person, this immense cloak is part and parcel of every Russian officer. Most surely, all I saw wore them. A very queer appearance, too, do these cloaks present upon the shoulders of their occupants, because the immense epaulettes extend from the shoulders, and give a square form to the upper part of the cloak. I saw several fine-looking boys, from ten to fifteen or sixteen years of age, who were military cadets; they all wore the same order of cloaks, and some of the little fellows, who had green uniforms, were made to look ridiculous by large cocked hats.

The appearance of the great city excited our interest, and we were all gazing at its golden domes and minarets, so entirely unlike any city we had yet seen. The public buildings and the English quay are in themselves astonishing structures, and produce a most favorable impression on the voyager before he lands. We had no difficulty at the custom-house; our permits from the governor of Cronstadt seemed an "open sesame" in our case, and we and our baggage passed without any trouble or delay. I do wish that our friends could have seen that North Star party on the noble quay! There we were, as devoid of all ability to talk Russian as the serf drosky-drivers were to talk English. Our friend, Mr. Muller, was soon at our elbow, and a little army of droskys was laid under conscription. I think the procession that left that quay was as ludicrous as any in which I ever had been called to figure. My luck secured me an elegant post-chaise, and a glass coach conveyed Mr. and Mrs. Vanderbilt; but the rest of the party were bestowed upon the great vehicle of the land, — the ever-present drosky. Such laughing as we had, as we galloped over the great bridge, at our friends, sitting side-ways and other ways on those hard benches, covered with blue cloth, and resting upon apologies for springs, and running on four wheels! An immense baggage-wagon, filled with our luggage, brought up the rear, and really looked as if we were about to become actual settlers, instead of mere transient sojourners. We first drove to the Hotel des Princes, to which we had been strongly advised. Here we were most politely received by a young gentleman, who informed us that the hotel was too full to receive so large a party; but he insisted on our all coming in till some of the gentlemen could make suitable arrangements. We were shown into a superb parlor, and immediately the waiters spread a table, and placed on it bread, butter, anchovies, caviare, claret, sherry, brandy, ice, and cakes in variety. This excellent lunch was very seasonable, as it was now twelve o'clock, and the day intensely hot, — quite equal to our usual summer heat in New York. Soon after we had refreshed ourselves, our friend returned, and we found that everything was prepared for our reception at Demmouth's, by the side of the Moika canal. On calling for our bill, the gentleman who had first received us declined making any charge, and we found it impossible to put our lunch to any other account than the polite attention of the French proprietor, Monsieur Auguste. Three gentlemen and their ladies remained at this hotel, and had as elegant accommodations as could be found, I think, in Europe. We were all of us soon comfortably domiciled at our quarters; and I may say that I think the hotels of St. Petersburg have been slandered as to the cleanliness of their apartments. Most certainly, at neither of the two establishments we tried had we any reason to complain, but rather were disposed to think them exceedingly comfortable.

It would be wrong not to speak of the kindness which we met from our consul, Mr. Ropes, and his excellent partner and brother-in-law, Mr. Prince. Of these gentlemen I shall have more to say. Mr. Brown, the United States minister, left Petersburg the day we arrived; but he had, I believe, a short interview with Mr. Vanderbilt, as' he was on the eve of departure. It was now that we found the kind services of Mr. Muller of great value, and he was indefatigable in his efforts to aid our movements in and around the city.

Soon after taking possession of our hotel, we ordered carriages, and, after riding through the great streets of this wonderful metropolis of the north, we went to see the Summer Islands. If the map is consulted, it will show that in the delta of the Neva there are many small islands. Some of these are still desert spots, or covered with brushwood and small trees, affording covert to wolves and bears; but several of the islets near to the city have been reclaimed and placed under the highest class of cultivation, and, by the aid of bridges, are united. These islands are the favorite resort of the nobility and wealthy men of St. Petersburg, and innumerable houses and villas have sprung up. Our ride was one of at least ten miles, and we passed the splendid palace of Count Orloff, on the river bank, and through a village of cottages which much resembled the rural abodes of Switzerland. Yellagin Island is a charming spot, and here is the emperor's datscha, a very comfortable-looking country-house. A prettier view than is enjoyed from this spot cannot be desired. The eye rests with pleasure on the gay parterres of extensive and well-cultivated gardens, on the noble river, and on the golden spires, domes and minarets, of the city and its innumerable palatial buildings. The avenues of these wooded islands are most extraordinary pathways, and are cut through dense forests of birch and pine wood. Some of the private houses are models of comfort and coseyness, and I fancied that enjoyment and happiness were no strangers in this delightful region. Many of the buildings were apparently mere pine-board erections, and of a very extemporaneous character. I understand that every one who has the means is in the habit of migrating to these truly elysian fields and charming islands in the summer months. The small retail dealers have their little cottages, and visit their families on Sundays and holidays. The constant improvements going on in this city must be made during the brief summer, and the dust and dirt, combined with occasional excessive heat, afford sufficient inducement to flit, as the Scotch call a removal, from town to country.

The estates of the Counts Nesselrode and Strogonoff are very extensive, and the houses and parks are rich in statuary. Everything I saw would have been a source of admiration on the banks of the Seine, or the shores of the Arno, and was very far beyond anything I expected to meet on the Neva. I ought to say that nearly all the habitats of any mark on these islands had fine green and hot houses attached. We were conducted to a spacious establishment, where the gardens were large, and the orchestra and ball-room opened upon them. This place had a mineral spring. We had an excellent dinner furnished at a short notice, but there did not seem to be much company about. Later in the evening, no doubt, we should have seen more persons. The price of dinner was fourteen rubles for thirteen persons, inclusive of good claret. Our earliest visit in the city was made to the original cottage residence of its founder. This is a spot I had longed to see. I wanted to sit down in a room where a man had dwelt, and thought, and acted, who had done so much to leave his mark upon the age in which he lived. It is a very small affair, and contains but three apartments. The furthest one was his bedroom, the next his chapel, and one off to the right was his room for company. We saw many articles that belonged to the great man, kept under glass cases; and pictures, maps, plans and charts, are on the walls, as when he resided here. One map of the city is of his own draft. The chapel is occupied by a priest, and daily service is observed; it was going on when we visited it, and the audience consisted of some six or eight woful-looking devotees, all upon their knees, or with their foreheads on the ground. Beads and trinkets were offered for sale to us, and all round the door we were beset with monks and nuns from the country, as we were told, begging for their conventual institutions; and a sad, dirty-looking set they were. The entire building, which was originally a log cottage, has been surrounded with a plank covering, by the order of the late Emperor Alexander. Here, too, we saw a large boat which Peter constructed, I suppose, after his initiation into boat and ship-building in Holland. Not far from this spot we saw the first church which was erected in St. Petersburg.

The city is principally situated on the south bank of the Neva, and comprehends several islands; and, as much of it was originally a mere marsh, it has had to undergo a thorough drainage, which has rendered large canals indispensable. These are constructed of the most massive materials, and have a fine appearance. The date of the city is from 1703; and in one century and a half all this magnificent metropolis has been called into existence by a people supposed to be semi-barbarous; and yet it transcends, in many respects, every other capital of Europe. I quite agree with the lamented Stephens, who stated in his travels, "I do not believe that Rome, when Adrian reared the mighty Colosseum, and the Palace of the Cæsars covered the Capitoline Hill, exhibited such a range of noble structures as now exists in the Admiralty Quarter." The admiralty itself is the central point, on one side fronting the Neva, and on the other a large open square, and has a façade of marble, with ranges of columns a quarter of a mile in length. A beautiful golden spire shoots up from the centre, towering above every other object, and seen from every part of the city glittering in the sun; and three principal streets, each two miles in length, radiate from this point. In front is a range of Boulevards, ornamented with trees, and an open square, at one extremity of which stands the great church of St. Isaac. This square extends to a great distance, and on it are the Winter Palace, Hermitage, and other splendid erections.

In walking along this square, the admiralty is off to the left. The Neva runs in front of the grand façade. Here, too, near by the Isaac church, is the far-famed statue of Peter the Great. This is a glorious creation, and is regarded as the *chef-d'œuvre* of Falconet.

The pedestal is a natural block of granite, just as taken from the quarry. Peter is seated on horseback; one hand is pointing

ST. PETERSBURG.—FROM THE ENGLISH QUAY.

STATUE OF PETER THE GREAT.

significantly, the horse paws the air with his fore-legs, whilst the hinder are trampling upon a serpent. The weight of the statue is poised on the tail of the horse, which is fastened on the stone. The inscription on the pedestal is,

PETRO PRIMO,
CATHERINA SECUNDA.

I thought with pride of our own Mills, who has succeeded so nobly in his equestrian statue of Jackson, and in which the horse is self-poised.

The great street of the city — the Broadway — is the Neffsky Perspective, named after Alexander Neffsky, the patron saint of St. Petersburg. I think this and the other two streets, radiating from the admiralty, are two hundred feet wide. The channel-gutter is in the middle of the street, and on each side of it are wooden pavements broad enough to allow two carriages or wagons to cross each other. The pavements are wide and well made. Many of the shops and stores on this Perspective are fine, and have very much the appearance of similar establishments in New York, London or Paris.

I know not how it is, but I never before felt so solitary in a large city. There are few persons in the streets, and certainly seven out of ten we meet are serfs; and all the drosky-drivers are wrapped up in long, blue coarse cloth coats down to their heels, and the waist tied with a red scarf, leather thong, or rope. The hat is a queer-looking affair, very low-crowned and bell-shaped. I have never seen so many lifeless, inanimate faces as in Russia. The countenance is sallow, eyes sunken, and beards are mostly yellow. In these great streets, and over the vast admiralty-square, amid the palaces and vast buildings, I rambled by moonlight, and was never weary while watching the queen of heaven climbing over dome, minaret and façade. It was then that I realized the magnitude of this strange city, and felt that it had *now* an air of antiquity and grandeur that no other city I have seen can boast. By the light of the moon I could not distinguish the brick plaster and stucco from granite or marble; but by the light of day the illusion was dispelled.

Our visit to the Winter Palace had been arranged by the kindness of Mr. Muller, and we found free admission to every portion of this regal abode. This building presents a marble front upon the Neva of nearly eight hundred feet, and the rear, which lies upon the immense square, is of plaster, but richly adorned. Its form is a square. On entrance, we all had to deposit greatcoats, as only dress-coats are tolerated in the precincts of imperial majesty. The grand staircase is one of wonderful beauty, and we happened to see the great carpet put upon it, as the royal family were to visit the palace the next day. This wonderful mansion was destroyed by fire December 29, 1837, and was rebuilt in less than two years. I think no capital in Europe can boast of such a royal residence. It is vain to attempt a description of so much splendor as I saw; for one room after another, till we had gone through a hundred, seemed to surpass in magnificence all its predecessors. The St. George's Hall is the most beautiful apartment, I suppose, in the world; certainly it is superior to any saloon at Versailles. Imagine a room one hundred and forty feet by sixty; on either side are twenty columns of porphyry, the bases and capitals most richly gilt. These pillars are the support not only of the ceiling, but of a noble gallery, the balustrade of which is of the most highly elaborate workmanship. The Salle Blanche, where the great gala fêtes are held, is entirely decorated with white ornaments, profusely adorned with the richest gildings. In passing from the first room to this last, we went through a gallery of national portraits; and among the heroes of the empire we were much interested with the likenesses of Barclay de Tolly and England's Iron Duke, Suwarrow, and Kutuzoff. The empress' state drawing-room was thought by our ladies to be the gem of the palace; and certainly its pictures, vases, &c., are wondrous. It is gilt from floor to ceiling, except a space of two feet from the floor, which is a deep French blue. The hangings and furniture of all the royal apartments proper entirely surpass the splendor of Buckingham Palace, Windsor, and the Tuilleries.

The room containing the diamonds and regalia excited the interest of all in our party; and on no consideration would we have been deprived of the pleasure of seeing this unrivalled collection of treasures. Rubies, diamonds, emeralds, and pearls, — why, the room was full of them. The imperial crown pleased me better than any diadem I have seen in the regalia of other kingdoms. It is surmounted with a wreath of oak-leaves formed of diamonds, — and not small ones, — and in the sceptre is one supposed to be the largest in the world. Its history is remarkable. It was purchased by Catherine II., from a Greek slave, and for the small amount of four hundred and fifty thousand rubles, to which was added a pension for life. The time occupied by an examination of this palace was double what I have ever seen devoted to any other. The servants who escorted us all wore the imperial liveries, and were tall, fine-looking men. The great dining-room is a very noble saloon; and here and in the next room we saw the immense collection of gold plate, in which the Czar surpasses all his royal brethren in Europe.

The Hermitage was the favorite resort of the great Catherine, and it is united to the Winter Palace by a covered gallery, or, rather, I think, by several. This building received so much reconstruction when the Winter Palace was rebuilt, that it is essentially a new edifice. The portico of this building is really glorious. It is supported by ten colossal statues, of Finland granite, each eighteen feet high. The feet of these are twenty-five inches in length. Some of our party thought them the true lions of St. Petersburg. They are wonderful, no doubt. Opposite to this building is the palace where the Emperor Paul met with his tragical end.

I regard the Hermitage as the great affair of St. Petersburg, and certainly prefer it, as a museum of paintings and works of art, to the Louvre. I believe there are in this building nearly three thousand paintings; and the galleries embrace the works of all the great masters, and especially some of the works of Murillo, Snyders, Potter, and furnish the most interesting assemblage of Flemish pictures in the world; at least, it is a rival to the galleries of the Hague, Amsterdam, and Antwerp. I confess that the Dutch school is my passion; and here are Ostades, Boths, Neefs, Gerard Duows, Denners, Teniers, Wouvermans, and Mieris, to occupy a month in patient and delightful study. The pictures of game, and fruit and flowers, are very beautiful. All Europe has been ransacked, and no money has been spared, in obtaining these gems of art. It may be fancied that nothing can be much richer, when I state that the collections of Crozat, of Paris, Tranchini, of Geneva, Baudoin, of Paris, Sir Robert Walpole, the Prince of Condé, the galleries of Houghton, Prince Guistiniani's, Hope's, of Amsterdam, and the Malmaison and Coesvelts, are all concentred here. One excellence of this noble establishment consists in its order and arrangement. Every school and master is in its proper apartment; and no gallery in the world has been so admirably arranged, or placed in such superbly-finished apartments. In all the rooms of this building, as well as in the Winter Palace, the eye is charmed with vases and candelabra of jasper, porphyry and malachite, that can be seen nowhere else but in this wondrous capital.

The room devoted to Rembrandt has more than forty of his pictures, and some of them are his best. I would mention "The Prodigal's Return," "Old Woman and her Book," and "The Monk and his Pupil," and "Abraham Sacrificing Isaac," as peculiarly fine. Murillo's St. Mark is a fine production. We all stopped in admiration at two very small pictures, of aged women, by Denner. They are the most life-like pictures I ever gazed upon, not excepting the Raphael portraits in Florence.

PAINTINGS, OF DIFFERENT SCHOOLS. 133

The room which contains the Wouvermans pictures can never be forgotten by any one who has an eye for the beautiful. One, "The Interior of a Stable," is capital; but some of this painter's pieces here are poor enough; and I cannot feel that the Salvator Rosas and Leonardo da Vincis, are all of genuine parentage. One Holy Family, by this last artist, in which I observed St. Catherine is introduced in the place of Zecharias, is undeniably his, and is a great picture.

A portrait of Clement IX., by Carlo Maratti, is one of the most impressive portraits ever placed on canvas. Here are a large number of small cabinet pictures, which I could stand and gaze at and study for hours. I would rather look at one good picture for an hour, and correct my taste by its careful contemplation, than look at a hundred gairish daubs, which are called fine paintings by those who judge a picture by its dimensions and the quantity of bright coloring. I think I have seen finer pictures by Murillo, in some English galleries, and in Paris, than most of those here ascribed to the great Spaniard. An unfinished Holy Family, by Raphael, did not much please me; but I was greatly delighted with his St. George and the Dragon, and the Princess on her Knees. This great picture has been a traveller. It was painted in 1506, for the Duke of Urbino, and presented by him to Henry VII., at the death of Charles I. When all the choice works of art were scattered, this gem went with the rest, and has now a worthy home. A Madonna, once belonging to the Duke of Alba, and afterwards the great attraction of the Coesvelt gallery, is a world-renowned picture, and cost the emperor more than thirty thousand dollars. This has been engraved in London, and is, to my eye, one of the most pleasing Madonnas that I know. The Virgin Mother is seated in a landscape scene, the Saviour on her lap, while she is reading a book, and John, kneeling, offers the infant a cup. The mother's expression is exquisitely beautiful. I was greatly delighted with a Judith, ascribed to Raphael, but supposed to be a Moretto. The paintings by Domenichino are, I think, not at all equal to some I have seen in English galleries, and in the Louvre. And certainly this is true of the pictures by Rubens, if I except the Martyrdom of St. Sebastian, the Bacchus and Satyrs, Perseus and Andromeda. Vandyke has here Charles I. and his Queen, and noble pictures they are, too. A marriage of St. Catherine, by Corregio, is an interesting production of this great master.

Hercules strangling the Serpents, by Sir Joshua Reynolds, is a famous picture; but has recently been restored, and not very ably, I suspect. "The Repose in Egypt," by Murillo, is a great effort, and demands a careful study. Snyders' Bear Hunt is a wonderful piece of study, and pleased me as much as his great Boar Hunt, that I have seen, I think, in Holland. In one of the galleries we noticed a copy of Raphael's Loggie. This is by celebrated Italian painters.

The Loggie are galleries in a part of the Vatican palace, and are decorated by Raphael with paintings, and stuccoes, and arabesque ornaments. The subjects are chiefly mythological subjects. The ceilings describe a cycle of events from Scripture history, and these have been called "Raphael's Bible." I turned back to look again at Gerard Duow, and Mieris, and Ostade, and would gladly have tarried all day over these precious panels. But we were off to other portions of this vast curiosity-shop. Here is the Museum of Peter the Great. Here are his clothes, his work-tools, his lathes, his finished and unfinished carving and statuary; for he was no mean sculptor, as his Abraham and Isaac testify. In a glass case he is presented, life-like, in his wedding-suit of clothes. Never have I seen such a collection of jewelry and precious stones as are gathered together in these long, long galleries. Bouquets, that look as though they had perfume, are here by scores, all formed of rubies, emeralds, diamonds and amethysts, of inestimable value;

watches by hundreds, and snuff-boxes and works of art adorned by diamonds.

We came to the conclusion that the buried-up treasures of the Hermitage would meet all the expenses of a formidable campaign. No person, who has not visited this truly wonderful place, can imagine what knick-knackery and works of *vertu* are crowded into one room after another.

The snuff-boxes which have been presented from the Sultans of Turkey are almost too precious to be credited. Here is an escritoire that opens to the sound of music, and has hundreds of secret drawers, all starting out by hidden springs. One of the most gorgeous trifles is a vast clock, in a glass case, ten feet by six or eight. The clock is a large tree, of which the branches and leaves are gold. In the foliage is a peacock, who, when the chimes commence, expands his tail, and an owl turns up his solemn eyes, and a golden cock flaps his wings and crows lustily.

The Hermitage contains a fine library, containing the private collections of Voltaire, Diderot and Zimmerman, with those of other illustrious scholars. But the grand Imperial Library is one of the largest in Europe, and now contains nearly half a million of books. The MSS. here gathered are invaluable, especially those bearing upon French and English history. Here are volumes of original letters, unequalled in interest; and every facility is afforded to the students in obtaining access to these marvellous treasures.

One room was intensely interesting. It was devoted to antiquities brought from the Crimea; and, if I recollect rightly, from a town between the Sea of Azof and the Black Sea. These are of the purest gold, and of immense value. They were found in tumuli, and were of Grecian origin. The laurel wreaths are as perfect as if just from the goldsmith's hands. A helmet, or mask, with a shield, are of the highest order of artistic skill. No palace in Europe can match this unique collection. All the apartments in the Hermitage are adorned with the most costly furniture; chairs and sofas of exquisite design and material, and centre-tables of unknown value, of porphyry, jasper, lapis-lazuli, and malachite. One vase, of gigantic proportions, is made of Siberian marble: it is of an oblong form, and its circumference is fifty feet, and its weight forty-three thousand two hundred pounds.

It is tantalizing to look at this place, and to feel that, instead of spending a week or two in the treasury of art, science and beauty, you must "do it up" in three or four hours.

I forget whether here or elsewhere, but I think in the Hermitage, it was that I saw Bruloff's great picture of the Last Days of Pompeii. It is, I think, full twenty feet by fifteen or sixteen; its management of color is almost as wonderful as the work of Rembrandt, and there are figures in the grouping that will live in memory.

The marble palace contiguous to the Hermitage is one of the noblest mansions here, and is the residence of the Grand Duke Constantine, who, although it was closed for the summer, and all the rooms covered, had the politeness to have it thrown open to our party, and everything uncovered for inspection. Those who went through it were greatly delighted; but I was weary of splendid rooms, and preferred a quiet walk, and then a drive round and about the city.

Visits were made to the Admiralty, the Mint, the Arsenal, the Fort, the Custom-house and the Corps des Mines, where a large number of pupils are educated for governmental service in the vast mines of the empire. Here is the finest mineralogical museum in the world, and a description of it would make an interesting volume. Under ground is a fine model of a Siberian mine, representing all the various appearances of a natural formation.

Directly in front of the Winter Palace is the Hotel de l'Etat Major. On this very immense structure is a beautiful group of bronze,—a chariot of Victory, drawn by eight prancing steeds.

This is a noble work, and is universally admired. Between the palace and this edifice stands the famous Alexander's Pillar, a grand shaft of red marble, from the quarries of Finland. This is surmounted by an angel bearing a cross. The height of the monument is nearly one hundred and sixty feet.

In company with my old friend Mr. Evans, of New Bedford, who has the superintendance of the imperial cordage manufactory, I visited the Monastery of St. Alexander Neffsky; this is a very celebrated institution, and is the seat of a Metropolitan. Its situation is at the remote part of the Perspective, and encloses in its precincts churches, towns, gardens and cloisters; it was founded by Peter, on the spot where the saint won a great battle, and here he lies interred. The church is very large, and its pillars are of fine marble; and, although it has many adornments, it looked to me almost as dirty as the monks who were swarming round. The shrine of the saint is in a small chapel, and is of enormous value. The pyramid is said to weigh five thousand two hundred pounds of silver, and is fifteen feet high; a silver chandelier here is exceedingly fine, but the other silver work is in bad taste. The chanting by the monks was very solemn, and the conduct of the worshippers exceedingly devout. The Smolnoi Monastery I did not visit. The Sabbath day we passed in St. Petersburg, I attended morning service in the English church, — a very fine building, — the church will accommodate some four or five hundred persons. It is the best edifice I have seen as yet, on the continent, for Episcopal services. The clergyman in charge is the Rev. Dr. Law, who has been settled there about thirty years. The congregation was respectable, but not as large as in winter, owing to the absence of many of his parishioners in their suburban retreats. The sermon was truly excellent, but rather a controversial one. The text was "The brightness of the Father's glory." The discourse was very much after the style of Bishop Horsley, and had some ingenuity in its argument. The deportment of the audience was very devotional. There is also a Scotch church in the city; but I was not aware of it till Monday, or I should have been present part of the day. In the afternoon, at five o'clock, I went to the Kesan cathedral. This is a building in the form of a Greek cross, the arms of which are equal; in the centre is a large dome, and at the ends four small pointed cupolas. The position of this cathedral is imposing; it is on the Neffsky Perspective, and stands finely back from the street. The great external feature is the colonnade, of vast Corinthian columns, forming a semi-circle, and the end of which almost reaches to the houses on the street. Although the church, in its approach, disappointed me, yet I differ from those who censure this grand screen or colonnade. It strikes me as one of the sublimest pieces of architecture I am acquainted with. A walk under its lofty portico is no mean pleasure. In front of the cathedral are two fine statues of Kutuzoff and Barclay de Tolly. The interior is certainly grand, but heavy. The pillars are fifty-eight in number, if I reckoned correctly. The holy-place — the Ikonostast, where women never enter — has its beams, and what is usually wood-work, of solid silver. Every worshipper, I noticed, purchased a small taper of tallow or wax at the door; and then, going up to the Lady shrine, bowing his head to the pavement, and crossing his breast, he lights his candle from an ever-burning holy lamp before the Virgin, and kisses the pavement. His candle he places in a silver plate, where are many others burning, and he proceeds to say his prayers; and when he quits the sanctuary, it is with backward steps and repeated genuflections. In the Greek churches there are no images, but many pictures, and the Virgin is always adorned with gold and jewels. A diamond in the Virgin's crown, in this church, is the next in size to that on the emperor's regalia. I forgot to say that the pillars, and balustrades, and picture-frames of the Ikonostast, are all solid silver, — the donation of the Cossacks to the holy mother of Kesan.

At this shrine old Kutuzoff performed his solemn act of

worship, before he took command of the army in 1812. This church is adorned with military trophies in great plenty. I noticed some twenty French eagles, which were captured in Napoleon's great mistake — his Russian campaign. I was interested with the worship, which was even more gorgeous and formal than the rites of the Romish church. The chanting was very fine, and exceedingly solemn and impressive, without any musical accompaniment. All classes of society appeared among the worshippers, nor was there any lack of men. I saw nothing like want of thought or reverence, and I understand that all the duties of religion are urged upon the people by frequent visits at their own houses. The worship of the Virgin evidently prevails over that of her Son.

In leaving this temple, I felt that it was not equal in solemn grandeur to many churches in Belgium and France. The next day, when I visited the Isaac church, now in process of erection, I had far different emotions, and felt that here indeed was a fane worthy of its end and purpose. No man can fail to be impressed with this wonderful pile. The exquisite proportions of this church seem to diminish its apparent size. I have only to say that here are monoliths, of Finland marble, sixty feet high, forming perystiles of unsurpassed beauty; and in the interior are columns of malachite, fifty feet high, which adorn the altars. Malachite, lapis-lazuli, porphyry and gold, all seem to vie with each other for the preëminence in this glorious pile. Long years have been devoted to this sanctuary, and very many more must elapse before it will be completed. The dome is grand, and the granite pillars around have a noble effect. I think the Isaac church will take its rank with St. Peter's and Paul's cathedral; but my own preference is to the Gothic style of architecture for such vast buildings. The façade, windows and pediments, are in the hands of French artists. The angel at the Saviour's tomb, and the female figures and affrighted soldiers, are represented in gilt bronze figures, eight feet high, on one of the pediments, and are beautiful beyond description. The frescos on the dome are still in progress. The cupola is copper, richly gilt, and is surmounted by a small one, a miniature edition of the first; and above all is the golden symbol of the Christian faith. The malachite used for the holy of holies was given to the emperor by Count Demidoff, and its value is estimated at one million of rubles. St. Isaac happens to have his day in the calendar on the birth-day of Peter the Great, and so gets the patronage of this temple.

CHAPTER IX.

MAJOR THOMPSON BROWN — DROSKYS — WEDDING — GOSTINNOI DVOR. — STREETS — MILITARY — FAREWELL TO ST. PETERSBURG — RETURN TO THE YACHT — VISITORS — REGATTA — CRONSTADT — MR. WILKINS — DANGEROUS POSITION — VISIT FROM GRAND DUCHESS OF OLDENBURGH AND FAMILY — STEAMBOAT PARTY AND IMPERIAL BAND — THE EMPEROR — QUEEN DOWAGER OF HOLLAND — NARROW ESCAPE.

It gave me great pleasure to meet in St. Petersburg with Major Thompson Brown, Consulting Engineer to the emperor. This accomplished gentleman and his excellent lady were my old friends and fellow-townspeople in Newport, and here I found them most happily situated. The position which this gentleman occupies is one of great responsibility, and brings him into frequent contact with the emperor and the officers of state. Major Brown resides a few miles out of the city, in a delightful country villa. I was on my way to visit him, when horseflesh gave out, and I was reluctantly compelled to abandon the pleasure. I have been much amused with the drosky. This is the great carriage of the Russian everywhere. It has four wheels, and a long seat with a cushion; this seat is quite low. It is usually drawn by two horses; it has no top, and accommodates two persons, who have their feet on different sides of the seat. One horse is in the shafts, which are very strong, and made fast to the collar by leather thongs, and joined by a bow, four feet nigh, called a dooga, arching over the neck of the horse; at this point the traces start a foot back of the collar, rivetted to the shafts, and thence run to the axle outside the hubs of the front wheels. A stylish turn-out is a drosky, with one horse, a trotter, in the shafts, and a horse alongside in traces, made fast to a stationary bar, one end of which projects a couple of feet outside of the front end of the drosky. The rig of this horse is independent of the other, excepting his attachment, by an inside rein six feet long, to the saddle-girt of the shaft-horse. This rein enables him to travel at pleasure at an angle of about thirty degrees from the other, and he is kept at that angle by a rein from the outside of his bit running through a ring in his breeching to the hands of his driver, who holds the reins for the shaft-horse and one for this side animal; the particular department of which last one is to make a flourish, going on at a gallop, to which he has been trained, and swinging his head and neck, from the level of his body, towards the ground constantly. An extra flash establishment is with two outside prancers, one on either side the shaft-horse. This enables a fast trotter to travel with a galloping horse without discomfort to either, and produces no irregular motion in the vehicle.

The horses in the city are very fine, and some of the carriage-horses are quite large, and of excellent action. The harnesses are all light, if we except the collar, and many of them are richly adorned with polished plates of silver and brass.

On the Sabbath, which we spent in St. Petersburg, we found a wedding-feast celebrated at our hotel; and, in going to our dining-room at supper-time, the waiter took us through the room where the festivities were going on. Excellent music and spirited dancing seemed to have put the party into high spirits.

Our purchases took us into every part of the city, and, of course, we visited the far-famed Gostinnoi Dvor. This is an immense bazaar, where everything you can fancy or wish for is exposed for sale. It is a wonderful structure, extending through several streets, and reminded me of the great fairs which I remember in England in my early days, but which are now nearly abolished. The various trades are here found keepng company in their proper classes. The proprietors of these booths and stalls are perfectly importunate, and not a queerer set of men have I often seen. They stand waiting at their doors, and are as ready to solicit custom as a Chatham-street son of Abraham. On many of these stores I noticed a paltry picture of some saint, and in front of it a little lamp, burning. Here we bought boots, slippers, shoes, cushions, mats; and some of the ladies made expensive investments in sables, ermines, and other furs. On the Saturday we saw a great many of these shops closed, and the doors fastened with a string, and red seal upon it. Mr. Evans informed us that the Jews considered this a more secure fastening than the strongest lock, to protect their property. The engravings which we selected were very expensive, and were all of them executed in Paris, and when in that city I found it impossible to obtain them. In all parts of the city we found men vending tea and ice-water, quass, and other refreshments. We noticed, on three occasions, a large, shut-up, dark-looking carriage, with no windows, and door locked, escorted by twelve or sixteen soldiers. These were prisoners on their way to justice, or about to go off to Siberia, the great Botany Bay of the empire. I was much pleased with the fruit-stalls and shops, and have rarely seen finer fruit. The apples were the choicest specimens I could desire; but, having been brought from the southern provinces, and kept through the winter, were extravagantly high in price. The egg-plums, apricots, grapes and melons, were all fine; but very costly, as we found out at a dessert ordered at our hotel. The bird bazaar is an extraordinary spot, and will well repay a visit. Here are linnets, goldfinches, bulfinches and nightingales, and many other birds with which I was unacquainted.

The general appearance of what we have seen in St. Petersburg has pleased me exceedingly. Here is a capital that may vie with any in Europe for splendor and magnificence; and it evidently bears the impress of firmness, and promises to become second in grandeur to no other metropolis. The streets present a gay appearance, painted white, yellow, and light-green. The spires, domes, and façades of churches and palaces, are seen thickly grouped, and the canals are wide and river-like, and sweep round with much beauty; and then the glorious Neva adorns the city far more than the Thames or Seine does London or Paris. The streets, too, are well planted with trees. I do not well understand where the poor reside, as there seem to be no lanes, courts or alleys; all is wide, spacious street. I imagine that they live in cellars, and burrow under shops and the mansions of the wealthy. The roofs of churches and the rest of the building often have little agreement, and styles of architecture are strangely jumbled together,— Grecian façades, and Oriental, onion-shaped domes and cupolas. The police are dressed in the plainest garb, a drab long coat; one of this body is at every corner, armed with a desperate-looking axe. The military appear in the streets in considerable strength. The men seem to me rather like machines, — no force of expression. The most of them are *en route* for the south and the disputed provinces. The music of the bands was very good. The serfs, who are so numerous, come every spring from the country; each has to obtain a permit. In the autumn these men return with their small earnings. No small income accrues to the government from the payment on these permits to come and go. In all parts of the city I have seen vast flocks of pigeons. These birds are held in sacred estimation, because the dove is the scriptural emblem of the third person of the holy Trinity.

I imagine that the population of this city is not far from six hundred and fifty thousand. I was informed by a medical gentleman, long resident in Russia, that the mortality is great, and is unfavorable in comparison with other capitals of Europe.

We were all sorry when we had to bid adieu to this city of palaces, magnificent churches, and golden domes and spires. We cast one more look on that unrivalled square, a glance at the equestrian bronze, another at the ever-present admiralty spire, and we were on board the little steamer to take us to our noble ship. On getting on board the passage-boat, we met a goodly number of our friends to accompany us to Cronstadt; among them were Major Brown and his charming daughters, Mr. and Mrs. Evans, Mr. Bodisco, a Russian officer, and nephew of the minister from Russia to our country, and where our valued young friend has passed many years of his boyhood. We soon arrived at the yacht, and the day was spent most delightfully with our friends, to whom we had the happiness to receive an addition, in the company of Mr. and Mrs. Ropes, Mr. and Mrs. Prince, Mr. Endicot, of Boston, and several very agreeable and interesting English ladies, and also a number of French and Russian ladies and gentlemen, who came down in a charming little steamer, chartered for the occasion. Several of these little boats visited us during our anchorage, and hundreds of persons inspected the yacht with evident pleasure. More than once we had two steamers at once alongside. Mr. James Thall, a gentleman of great literary acquirements, and a remarkably good linguist, who had a country residence at Peterhoff, and paid members of our party polite attentions, came, with his family, in a fairy steamer. Amongst the numerous visitors at different times to the North Star, were Admiral Glassenapp, Prince Witgenstein, and Admiral Richord, the ex-Governor of Kamtschatka, an aged gentleman, of great good sense and tact. He examined everything carefully, and Mr. Vanderbilt was very much pleased with his visit. He is in command of the navy at Cronstadt.

Whilst we were lying at anchor, we had the pleasure to witness the annual yacht regatta. The prize, I believe, was a silver cup, given by the emperor. We saw the vessels return from the race of some seventy miles, and they all passed close to us. Some of them were very pretty schooners, and one noble one was evidently of English build, and had a happy-looking set of Englishmen on board. Mr. Baird's boat took the prize, if I remember rightly. We had, in our numerous parties who came on board, several treats in the efforts of ladies and gentlemen on the noble piano which adorned our saloon. One of these gentlemen had the reputation of being the best pianist of the city.

In our visits to Cronstadt, we had much polite and friendly kindness from Mr. Wilkins, the partner of the American vice-consul, Mr. Rowe. At Mr. Wilkins' hospitable abode Captain Eldridge, his lady, and a few of us, partook of an elegant lunch, which we shall often think of with pleasure. Here we partook of a variety of Russian luxuries, which we had not met with in the hotels. Such sweetmeats I never tasted. They were of various kinds; and one, made of berries, we thought superior to the strawberry. Caviare and mushrooms were on the table in perfection. At our request, we were treated to a taste of the national beverage, quass, and a very small taste sufficed; a more villanous compound I never tasted. The attentions of Mr. Wilkins and his family were constant. Our purchases in Cronstadt were chiefly Russian robes, Kezan soap, and shoes.

In going on shore on this occasion, with the captain, we nearly met with an accident. We proposed to go through the Merchant Dock, and it is so crowded as to make it a difficult navigation. Our boat got jammed between two vessels in motion, and such a cracking as the ribs of our gig made proved the sense she felt of injury. Luckily, one of the vessels yawed off, or we should have been crushed most certainly.

We noticed a steamer alongside, with an evidently distinguished party of visitors, — one of the gentlemen in full dress, and wearing the broad ribbon of a field-marshal. As soon as the visitors came on the quarter-deck, they announced themselves, and we had the honor to welcome the Grand Duchess of Oldenburgh, the niece of the Czar, and her family of seven children, attended by their tutors and governesses. The gentleman in charge of them was Field-marshal Toltog. As soon as the duchess came on board, she asked me if I knew her "very dear friend, good Dr. Baird, of New York," of whom she spoke in terms of the warmest friendship and respect; and also of other minister's, whom he had, she said, so kindly commended to her acquaintance. This lady speaks English fluently, and is, beyond all doubt, a decidedly Christian character. The party remained on board two or three hours, partook of refreshments, and were very much gratified. The daughter of the princess was a charming girl of about fifteen, very intelligent, and simple in her manners. The duchess, at leaving, begged me, if ever I revisited St. Petersburg, to report myself at once at her palace. All the members of her suite were English, and appeared to be pious people. On the evening before we sailed, we saw a steamer approaching from St. Petersburg, with streamers flying, and a band of music playing. As soon as she came up, we found that Major Brown, his lady and daughters, Mr. and Mrs. Ropes, and a numerous party of friends, had come down to take a farewell, and had brought with them the imperial band, the finest in Russia. This was an unexpected gratification, for which we were indebted to Major Brown. Mrs. Brown and I had a long talk over our old friends in Newport, and her deep interest in them led to a very protracted chat, during which the party, under the fine awning of our spacious quarter-deck, had been busily engaged in waltzing to music which is rarely equalled. Refreshments were brought to the company, and the band played Hail Columbia, God save the Queen, and The Emperor's March; and then, amid a display of rockets and blue lights from the North Star, and nine hearty cheers from both boats, our kind friends " all went home in the morning," — for it was one o'clock when they cast off. The player on the clarinet had recently received a diamond ring from the emperor, as an award of distinguished skill as a performer.

Our great regret at leaving Russia is not having seen the great, and, I believe, good man, the emperor, who has done so much to elevate the condition of the masses in his extensive dominions, and to improve the entire country. I leave Russia with exalted opinions of the wisdom and patriotism of the emperor, and doubt not that, if his life be spared, Russi will continue to advance in all that makes a country great and powerful and happy. I have heard anecdotes in plenty respecting the Czar, and all of them reflect great honor upon the qualities of his head and heart; but I do not feel that I am at liberty to state them in this public manner, as they were related to me in the social circle, by men who are favorably situated to know their truth. Some of our party saw the emperor at the church of the palace, at Peterhoff; but I spent that Sabbath in the city. Had we remained a day or two longer, we should have seen the emperor on board; but his time and thoughts had all been engrossed with the pressing affairs of the great vexed question between Russia and Turkey.

Our steam was now up, and just as we were weighing anchor a steamer hove in sight, adorned with flags and streamers; but she was too late; the North Star was under weigh, and close by us was an English steamer, bound to London, having on board the Dowager Queen of Holland, who has been making a short visit to her brother, the Czar.

Just as we were leaving the guard-ship, we were all much excited by a cry that a small boat was run over by our wheels. We flocked to the guards, and then found that a boat, with two boys and a man, from one of the neighboring ships, had got so close to our steamer that, in fright, one boy had jumped out of the boat, and was hanging on to the iron braces that support the guards. We stopped the yacht, and rescued the boy, who looked thoroughly scared; he was a fine-looking youth of sixteen, and hailed from Scotland. We were now off; and shall we ever again witness such sunsets, such evenings, such nights, as we have here enjoyed for the last few days?

CHAPTER X.

VOYAGE — COPENHAGEN — THORWALDSEN'S MUSEUM — FRUEKIRKE — THORWALDSEN'S CHRIST AND HIS APOSTLES — THE SCULPTOR — ROSENBERGH PALACE — ITS RICH COLLECTIONS OF ART — COINS AND MEDALS — PARK — STATUARY — COUNTRY — EXCHANGE — GALLERIES — AMALIENBORG PLADS — SONG OF THE WATCHMAN.

WE left Russia June 29, — weather fine. The 30th, the wind was strong and ahead, and more sea on than we had yet experienced. In the Baltic, the ship pitched considerably.

Friday, July 1st, — calm, — we again went along quietly, and with only two boilers. At ten o'clock P. M., we passed Bornholm, a Danish island, eighty miles from Copenhagen, and at half-past five in the morning were anchored off the city; and, after a hasty breakfast, went on shore in our own boats, determined to improve the day, as we were limited to five o'clock in the afternoon.

Copenhagen, the capital of the kingdom of Denmark, is situated on the eastern coast of the island of Zealand, at the southern extremity of a channel connecting the Cattegat with the Baltic, — this is called the Sound, — and partly on the north coast of the small island of Amager, or, as it is often called, Amak. The situation is favorable for commerce. The city is enclosed by ramparts, and is defended by several bastions and outworks, and, towards the sea, by a strong citadel; and powerful batteries command the entrance to the harbor. These forts are called the Three Crowns. The navy-yard is in front of the city, at the upper end of Amak, and appears to be in excellent condition, with immense store and ship houses. Here are several fine ships-of-the-line and frigates. The port is formed by an arm of the sea, and is capable of accommodating five hundred ships besides the navy; and, by canals, the shipping can pass into the town.

The aspect of Copenhagen from the sea is fine, and the palace spires and church steeples have a pretty effect. The climate is damp, and the bills of mortality are not favorable to its reputation for health. The cholera had just broken out here as we arrived, and its ravages were awful for the next six weeks, and gave a larger amount of deaths, in proportion to the population, than had before occurred in its history in Europe.

The population is one hundred and thirty-four thousand, of which about two thousand five hundred are Jews. The streets are in poor condition. The shops, with a few exceptions, are poor; the women were gayly dressed, and I noticed many in red apparel, with very handsomely-worked caps. The government is, since 1848, a constitutional monarchy, and the religion is Lutheran, and toleration given to other creeds; but, strange as it seems, certificates of baptism, confirmation and vaccination, are necessary to apprenticeship and marriage! I never found so many persons before in a foreign country who spoke English. We secured a good guide in a man who had formerly served my valued friend, Governor Arnold, of Rhode Island, in the same capacity, when he made an extended visit to the North Cape. I called on our United States Chargé d'Affaires, to whom I had letters of introduction; but he was absent from the city; and this, too, was unfortunately the case with Professor Rafn, the great northern antiquarian, to whom I had a letter from the Hon. J. R. Bartlett, the commissioner for the United States in the Mexican boundary affair. This was a severe disappointment, as I longed to see the great museum of northern antiquities, which was closed, but which I should have probably seen had this learned man been at home.

Our first visit was paid to the Thorwaldsen Museum, which is a very spacious and striking building, behind the royal chapel.

The style of architecture is Egyptian, and it is two hundred and thirty feet long, one hundred and twenty-five broad, forty-six high, and has two stoves. The exterior is decorated with Tuscan paintings in reference to the great artist. On the building stands a chariot of victory, drawn by four horses; this is executed in bronze. The interior apartments are painted in the Pompeiian style, in most glaring colors, and the work has been done by the ablest artists, as an affair of love. In the centre of the building is an open court, and here is the simple tomb of the immortal sculptor. The lower story of the museum is occupied with his works, and the upper one contains his collections of art, and his fine painting. Among so many glorious productions of art, it would be difficult to make a selection for special praise; but the *last* group of the Graces, the Shepherd Boy, Ganymede and the Eagle, Cupid and Psyche, are my favorites.

The bas-reliefs are very numerous, and attracted my eye as much as the statuary; and of these I prefer Alexander's Entry into Babylon, Night and Day, and some of which I shall speak hereafter. Well may the city be proud of this matchless collection of one life-long labor. I should much enjoy a week or two in this place, if it were only to afford a careful study of these noble productions.

From this museum we repaired to the Fruekirke, or Church of our Lady, which is the cathedral church of Copenhagen. It was completed in 1829, and is a tame building, with a Doric portico, and has no claim to notice beyond the fact that it is the depository of the master-works of Thorwaldsen. Here is his Christ and the Apostles. The very first object that arrests your eye on entrance is the vast statue of the Redeemer, just at the rear of the altar. Before the altar stands a fount of marble, which is a *Concha* in the hands of a kneeling angel. We were told that the first child that was christened here was one of Professor Bissen's; Thorwaldsen stood sponsor, and the king and queen were present. Around this beautiful angel is a needleworked carpet, presented by Madame Bissen. The apostles stand on the sides of the church, on pedestals four or five feet high. They are the most wondrous creations of art, and in pure marble of Carrara. They far transcend the idea which is obtained by one who looks merely at the casts. Judas was rejected by the sculptor, and Paul was substituted. The James is a charming figure, and so is Thomas; and, indeed, so I say of them all. These were all executed at Rome, where the artist spent a large portion of his life. We saw the favorite seat of the artist, when he attended this church; it was directly under the statue of James.

In front of this church, on the pediment, there is a group, in *terra cotta*, of sixteen figures, made by Thorwaldsen; it represents John preaching in the wilderness. This is a work alone sufficient to give fame to a man. In the portico, is a bas-relief of Christ's entrance into Jerusalem; and inside, one of Childhood's Guardian Angel on the right hand, and on the left, Christian Charity. A bas-relief behind the altar represents Christ on his way to Calvary; and in the confessionals are others of Baptism and the Last Supper.

Thorwaldsen was a native of Copenhagen. He went to study at Rome in 1796, and was first brought into reputation by Mr. Thomas Hope, who engaged him on the far-famed Jason. In 1819, when he visited Denmark, he was honored by all classes in the kingdom, and his fame was regarded as part of the national glory. He attained a good old age, and died lamented by his king and fellow-subjects. A bust of Byron, by this sculptor, is the property of Dr. Geo. Hayward, of Boston. This city is famous for its statuettes of Thorwaldsen's great works; but they are almost as expensive as they are beautiful. We obtained a few, as recollections of the place and artist. Thorwaldsen's portrait by Horace Vernet, his friend, bears a very strong resemblance to the late venerable Rev. Dr. Peirce, of Brookline, Mass.

We now proceeded to visit the Palace of Rosenbergh. This is a Gothic structure, of brick, with stone cappings, having a large tower to the west, two smaller ones to the east, each of which has a spire, and then a small tower between the two last, without a spire; and it is in this tower that the entrance to the palace is placed. Inigo Jones is said to have designed the building. This ancient residence of the Kings of Denmark has always been a popular show-spot with travellers, on account of its being a sort of gallery for the illustration of the national history. It dates its glories back to the days of its founder, Christian IV., who made it his constant abode, and filled it with works of art. The rooms in this palace are mostly small; some few are very spacious, and richly adorned. But it is all crowded with curiosities. Certain old ladies, who love old china, would go into ecstasies if they could see the *antiquities* of the celestial empire, Dresden and Sevre, in this particular department. Old cabinets, secretaries, tables, chairs, mirrors, are here in profusion; and they are of the costliest kind, and in grand preservation. I noticed silver andirons, that weighed at least a hundred-weight each; silver candelabra ten feet high, with twenty-four branches; four silver lions, large as life, and well executed; — these are guardians of the throne-room. The drinking-horns of the old northern magnates were very curious, and indicated that they drank deeply into some things. Here, too, is the far-famed saddle, and caparison for a horse, presented by Christian IV. to his son on his marriage, in 1664. This is literally *covered* with rubies, pearls, emeralds and diamonds, and the ground-work is heavy Genoa velvet, and was made in Paris, and must have been an expensive present. The throne-room is called the Riddersal, and the throne is massive silver. The tapestry of this room is very beautiful, and is descriptive of Christian's battles.

The collection of coins and medals is regarded as one of the finest in Europe, and would amply repay a careful study. I have never met with so intelligent and competent a guide as the gentleman who shows this palace. The gardens around the palace are remarkably fine and park-like, and situated in the centre of the city. They justify the pride and warm attachment of the good citizens. The noble old trees, flourishing shrubs and flowers, with very wide walks, make this a most agreeable promenade; and we saw a large number of children, under the eye of parents and nurses, enjoying the fine day, as we walked through the garden. In the centre, densely surrounded by venerable elms, oaks, &c., is a large circular basin, and in the middle of this is a bronze group, — a boy seated on a swan, — and from which issues a jet of water. In a pavilion, at the termination of a fine avenue, is a bronze group, of either Hercules or Samson, tearing open the jaws of a lion. This is a spirited work. There are also a few marble statues. I think these grounds must cover twenty or thirty acres. I very much regretted that we were unable to ride out to the far-famed beech woods; but we were forced to be contented with a charming ride through the Lánge Linie, which is a noble promenade. We went a mile or two into the country to see some pretty villas, and were much pleased with the most extensive tea-garden building that I recollect ever to have seen. The country houses were very neat, and the out-premises and gardens kept in good order.

The Exchange is a remarkable edifice, and was built by Christian IV. It is four hundred and six feet long, and sixty-six wide. It has a commanding entrance, with marble pillars, and two statues, representing Neptune and Mercury. The building is one hundred and seventy-six feet high, and is celebrated for its spire, formed of four dragons, whose heads point north, south, east and west, and their bodies are twisted together till their tails come to a point at the summit of the spire.

Few cities have finer museums, galleries of art, &c., than Copenhagen. We were sadly unfortunate in not being able to gain access to the royal gallery of paintings, and the northern antiquities. The paintings in this gallery number nearly two thousand, and the collection is rich in the Flemish and Dutch schools. But here is Salvator Rosa's noblest picture, — and this I did long to see, — "Jonah preaching to the Ninevites." The library, too, with its fine collection of prints, inferior only to the library of Paris, and, perhaps, Berlin, was also closed this day. In this library are very valuable MSS., both Icelandic and Oriental.

We were all much pleased with the Amalienborg Plads, — a fine octagon, formed by four palaces, of equal size and similar construction. In its centre is an equestrian statue of Frederic V.

It was my happiness to meet in Copenhagen with a lady from New York, a near relative of Mrs. Choules; and our thus meeting, so far away from home and family, was an agreeable incident. Our researches were now brought to a termination by a terrible storm of hail, thunder and lightning; and we afterwards found that, on the same day, the great hail-storm was experienced in New York.

Here we parted from our young friend Allen, who was to proceed from this city, by way of Kiel and Hamburg, to Leipsic, and resume his studies. We found a fine supply of strawberries in Copenhagen, and the people afraid to use them, owing to the existence of cholera.

I think it may be well to insert here a *literal translation* of the

SONG OF THE WATCHMAN.*

EIGHT O'CLOCK.

When day departs, and darkness reigns on earth,
The scene reminds us of the gloomy grave!
Then let Thy light, O Lord! before us shine,
While to the silent tomb our steps we bend;
And grant a blessed immortality!

---

* This habit of announcing the hours is still kept up in this city.

SONG OF THE WATCHMAN.

NINE O'CLOCK.

The day glides by, and sable Night appears.
For Jesus' sake, O God, our sins forgive!
    Preserve the royal family;
And guard the people which this land contains
    From danger of the Enemy!

TEN O'CLOCK.

Master, maid and boy, — would you the hour know?
It is the time that you to rest should go.
Trust in the Lord with faith, and careful be
Of fire and light, — for Ten o'clock has struck!

ELEVEN O'CLOCK.

Almighty God protects both great and small!
His holy angels guard us like a wall!
The Lord himself our city watches o'er,
And keeps our bodies and our souls from harm.

TWELVE O'CLOCK.

At the hour of midnight was our Saviour born;
Great blessing to a world which else were lost!
Then, with unfeigned lips, in prayer and praise,
Commend yourselves to God. — Past Twelve o'clock

ONE O'CLOCK.

O, Jesu Christ! we pray thee send us help
To bear our cross with patience in the world,
    For Thou art God alone!
And Thou, O Comforter! Thine hand stretch forth;
Then will the burden light and easy be!
    The clock has stricken One!

TWO O'CLOCK.

O, gracious Lord! whose love for us was such
That Thou shouldst deign in darkness* to be born;
    All glory's due to Thee!

* Obscurity.

SONG OF THE WATCHMAN.

Come, Holy Ghost ! and pour into our hearts
Thy heavenly light, that we may see Thee now,
    And in eternity !

THREE O'CLOCK.

Black Night departs, and Day begins to dawn.
Keep them far off, O God, who wish us harm !
    The clock has stricken Three !
Father, Thine aid we seek ! — and of Thy grace
    Give us abundantly !

FOUR O'CLOCK.

Eternal God ! who wouldst the keeper be
    Of us who dwell below, —
To Thee, surrounded by the heavenly host,
    Honor and praise are due !
For this good night give thanks unto the Lord !
Remember, "Four !" — we're summoned from our guard.

FIVE O'CLOCK.

Jesu ! Thou Morning Star ! we now resign
To Thy protection, cheerfully, our king.
    Be Thou his sun and shield !
And thou, bright orb of day ! begin thy course,
And, rising from the Mercy-seat of God,
    Thy radiant lustre yield !

CHAPTER XI.

OFF FOR HAVRE — SCENERY OF THE SOUND — ISLE OF HUEN — TYCHO BRAHÉ — NORWAY AND SWEDEN — GODWIN SANDS LIGHT-SHIP — DOVER AND WALMER CASTLES — HAVRE — STEAMER FRANKLIN — MR. VESEY, U. S. CONSUL — THE TOWN — HISTORICAL INCIDENTS — INGOUVILLE — LEAVE FOR PARIS — ROUEN, POISSY, ETC.

We now see the English steamer, with the Queen of Holland on board, — which left St. Petersburg in company with us, — just heaving in sight. Thus we beat her twelve hours!

At about six o'clock we got up steam, and were once more under way; and now we are heading for Havre. The heavy storm, which lasted for an hour or more, had cleared the atmosphere, and we saw two most beautiful and clearly-defined rainbows spanning the sound from Copenhagen to the Swedish coast opposite; and the width of the sound here is about twenty miles; but the distance grows less very fast as we proceed to Elsinore. We all kept our eyes upon the retiring city, in which we had passed a very pleasant, and, I am sure, a very profitable day. The coasts on either side are lovely, and the Swedish is in many places quite bold. The village of Landscrona shows up from the shore. On the Danish coast the scenery is very attractive, and presents a pleasing variety of lawns, orchards, farms, villas and forests. On our sail we came close by the small island of Huen, where the illustrious Tycho Brahé lived, and where he made his famous astronomical researches. It lies near to the coast of Sweden, and has a slight elevation, on which he built his observatory, in which he was nobly assisted by the King of Denmark.

Tycho Brahé was born in 1546, and was educated in Copenhagen, and, after spending some years in Germany, he returned, in 1571; but again visited Germany in 1575. He was induced to settle in Denmark by the extreme liberality of Frederick II., and received this island as a gift; and on it he spent vast sums of money, in the erection of costly buildings. He outlived his patron, and found less favor from his successor, Christian IV. He died, in 1601, in Prague, whither he had retired, by the invitation of the Emperor Rudolph. Never could the noble fortress of Kronburgh Castle be seen to finer advantage than as we swept by it. The evening was very clear, and its bold towers were defined most accurately against the azure sky. The standard of Denmark was floating from its flag-staff, and the lighthouse, in one of the turrets of the castle, looked cheerful, as it was kindled up soon after we passed it. We watched the grand old fortress as long as it remained in sight, and spent a pleasant evening on deck. The Sunday, however, proved squally, and we had rather an unpleasant day, but observed our regular service in the saloon. In the morning we had some good views of the coast of Norway and Sweden, as we passed the Cattegat, and rounded the Skaw, getting into the Skagerack. We saw several ships, apparently bound into Christiansand. The sea was, however, rougher than we had yet had it on our voyage. At two P. M. the breeze had freshened up, and the waves were high. We were now off the lee-shore of the mouth of the Sleive, about six miles distant. From two to six we only made twelve or fifteen miles. At ten P. M. the gale abated, and the ship made good way through the night; but the fog was as dense as I ever saw.

July 4. — The sea was yeasty, and the day very uncomfortable; the smoking-room deserted, but only two persons decidedly sick. The arrangements for celebrating the day fell through; and at dinner we talked patriotically, and did as a great many of our friends at home were doing.

July 5. — I have already spoken of the thick weather we met with; but it had little effect in delaying the voyage, or hindering our exact course, and the abilities of our accomplished commander were only made the more apparent. I shall not soon forget the satisfaction with which he made the light-ship on the Godwin Sands, after the thickest fog, coming down directly upon her, according to his prediction. I have never felt such abiding confidence in any man's judgment as in that of Captain Eldridge. All his movements are in exact unison with his statements made beforehand, and he exhibits that perfect acquaintedness with his profession which inspires confidence in the breast of every person around.

The sea had gone down, but the wind was ahead. At one o'clock P. M., we passed close by the cliffs of Dover, and had a fine view of Walmer Castle, where England's duke was conquered by the only enemy that ever vanquished him. The sight of Walmer brought to our remembrance those beautiful lines of Longfellow, called "The Warden of the Cinque Ports." I found in England the opinion was general, that Longfellow's was the noblest tribute which the death of Wellington had called out, and this piece is thought quite equal to Campbell's best pieces. We stood in, to have a near view of Dover and the fine coast adjacent. The town extends along under the stupendous cliffs. We had a fine afternoon to thread through the channel, and obtained pleasant glimpses of the English coast. We arrived off Havre at night, but lay to for morning light; and, besides, we could not enter the dock gates till nine o'clock. As we approached the gates in the morning, we found thousands of people gathered around to see the steamer Franklin depart on her homeward voyage. We instantly saluted her, which compliment she returned, and Captain Wotton very politely stopped his engine to receive our letters for home.* After giving her three hearty

---

* We all had our fears that we had missed the mail for New York, and were sad enough to see the steamer fairly under way; but Captain Eldridge told us that he knew her captain was by all odds too noble a man to disap-

cheers, which were reciprocated by her passengers, she went on her voyage, and we entered the great port of the Seine; and a more beautiful sight is not often witnessed than the docks and banks thronged with citizens, who were having a double gratification; they came out to see an American steamer go away, and, unexpectedly, they found a still nobler one coming in to occupy her place. Out of the vast concourse I soon singled out my friend Mr. Vesey, the recently-appointed consul at Havre, and he was the first on board to greet our arrival. It would be a happy thing for the American tourist, if at every foreign port he could meet with such a representative of his country; but this is too much to expect. It is enough to say that a more thorough gentleman and warmer-hearted man than Mr. Vesey cannot be found; and his appointment to this valuable and important post reflects honor on President Pierce's administration; while the retention of Mr. Vesey as consul at Antwerp, despite his politics, was one of the many acts which adorned the official career of that pure patriot and enlightened statesman, MILLARD FILLMORE.

Mr. Vesey and our American fellow-citizens resident in Havre were much gratified at our arrival, and felt proud of their country when they saw this noble specimen of naval architecture, and the property of a private American citizen, and could point to her owner as a merchant prince, who, by the force of character and enterprise, had made his way from obscurity to a place beside the noblest and wealthiest of the old countries of Europe. We were gratified to notice a large number of noble ships bearing the starry banner of freedom. Several of their commanders soon came on board, and with them my good friend Captain Wood, of the packet-ship Germania, and his excellent wife, and their little girl. The entrance to the docks is fine, and the

---

point his countrymen, and assured us that we were all right. "I know him," said Eldridge, "and, my word for it, Wotton will come to." The prediction was verified, and our friends at home owed their letters to the kind-heartedness of the captain of the Franklin.

appearance of the old portion of the town, its vast amount of shipping, its venerable fort, and high hills off to the right, and covered with villas overhanging the town, is one not soon to be forgotten by a stranger who gazes at it. On our left was the charming Marine Hotel of Frescati, with its garden and bathing-ground directly in front. Havre is comparatively a modern city; it was established as a town by Francis I., in 1516, who built the ancient tower at the left bank of the port. The present population is about eighty thousand, and it is now in a career of rapid progress and improvement. The docks are large, finely built, and numerous. Hundreds of men are now at work on a dry dock of large dimensions. The importance of this place is at once seen by reference to the map of France, when its relations to Paris and Rouen, as a port of entry, will appear. The large number of Americans, resident and seafaring, to be met in the streets, renders it a pleasant spot to the wanderer from his own happy home in the far west. Havre is rich, too, in its historical associations. It was from this place that the Earl of Richmond sailed when he went to England to contest its crown with the hunchbacked Richard, in 1485. It was here, too, that the gallant Sir Sidney Smith, the hero of Acre, was captured by the gun-boats in 1796, when he had grounded upon a sand-bank in an effort to cut out a French frigate. In Havre was born the famous St. Pierre, who wrote the charming tale of Paul and Virginia. Havre has nine quays, and a vast number of public fountains. The church of Notre Dame is not at all remarkable, but has a fine organ, which was the gift of Cardinal Richelieu. The Palais de Justice is a plain edifice. The Ursuline Convent is a large building, and the nuns are engaged in the education of young ladies; and very often English girls are placed here, under the preposterous idea that these ignorant women can enlighten them. What Protestant, with his eyes open, would trust his daughter to the care of women who believe that there is no salvation out of the Church of Rome, and, if honest, must therefore take every opportunity to make proselytes of the children under their influence? We took carriages to explore the town, and, after riding through its principal streets, many of which are very good, we ascended one, which, after an ascent of half a mile, through a road which presented the noblest stone walls we ever saw of similar extent, we arrived at the Cote, where, on a vast elevation, are the exquisite residences of the wealthy. I think this part of the town is called Ingouville. Here are terraces, gardens and pleasure-grounds, laid out in the most tasteful manner. Homes of greater beauty are nowhere to be seen. I think it would be hard to meet with sweeter models for country residences; and as for the gardens, trees, shrubs and flowers, now all in gayest garniture and brightest bloom, they are types of Eden. I visited an American lady, whose house is on this paradisiacal spot, and, as I gazed on her beauteous Yankee children and saw the elegant associations of her foreign home, I rejoiced at the comforts which alleviate her absence from early friends and the haunts of childhood. Her husband met us at his gate, and we thought that, with such a home, such a family, and a prosperous business, Mr. C——e must be a happy man. I longed to visit Harfleur, once a Roman station, and long in the possession of the English; but time forbade me. All around I could see that beauty invited me to become a wayside wanderer. I yearned to ramble over to Tancarville, on the Seine, about twenty miles off, and where I know, from the accounts of early friends, there are charming ruins and the most enchanting views. It was at Tancarville that the Meluns, the Harcourts, and the Dunois, became the worthy successors of the Chamberlaines, the fellow-warriors of William the Conqueror.

It was a boyish notion of mine to walk through Normandy; and there are few things I would like better than to spend three or four months in such a pilgrimage, even now. These walking tours are, after all, the thing to make a man know a country, and remember it forever. Give me the treasures which it affords to memory, the play it gives to imagination, the illustrations it contributes to historical association, and I will let who may choose it travel by railroad speed through a land, and know nothing that is valuable, and see little that he can remember in future life.

From Havre we started for Paris, and the route is upon the banks of the Seine. Of all railroad routes that I am acquainted with, I regard this as the most pleasant one I ever travelled. I cannot conceive of more rural happiness and comfort than appears to be spread over the glorious fields of Normandy, and between Havre and Rouen. The country is far more wooded than I had supposed, or had seen in other parts of France, in former travels. From Rouen to Paris we passed through many spots of interest. I must not omit to mention Poissy, where the infamous Charles IX., and his more infamous mother, Catherine de Medici, met in conference, in 1561, with the great divines of the Catholic and Protestant churches. This town is thirty miles from Paris. Certainly the country appears to be prosperous, — the farms are well cultivated, and the residences gave an idea of far more enjoyment and comfort than many of our party expected to see.

Our entire party went to Paris, excepting Mr. Vanderbilt, who was indisposed, and preferred to remain for a quiet day on board the yacht.

CHAPTER XII.

HOTELS — HON. S. G. GOODRICH — AMERICAN CLERGY IN EUROPE — REVIEW — REV. ROBERT LOVETT AND HIS CHAPEL — CONFERENCE OF AMERICANS — METHODIST CHAPEL — LOUVRE — JARDIN DES PLANTES — PALAIS DE JUSTICE — FLOWER-MARKET — HOTEL DE CLUNY — ENGLISH FRIENDS — VERSAILLES — GARDEN OF THE TUILLERIES AND CHAMPS ELYSÉES — PONT NEUF AND OLD PARTS OF PARIS — HOTEL DE VILLE — CHURCHES — ROYAL LIBRARY — GOBELINS — ST. DENIS — NEUILLY — CHAPELLE ST. FERDINAND — CHAPELLE EXPIATOIRE — FONTAINEBLEAU.

On reaching Paris, we found the weather as hot as it generally is in any of our Atlantic cities in August. We were soon stationed in comfortable hotels — as the Hotel du Rhin, in the Place Vendome, and the Hotel d'Albion. I took up quarters at the Hotel Windsor, on the Rue Rivoli, where I put up in 1835, and afterwards in 1851. And, strange as it may appear, I have on every occasion had the same suite of rooms, so that I had here quite the home feeling. This is a capital house, and its landlord all a traveller can wish. My first business was to call on our distinguished fellow-citizen, the Hon. S. G. Goodrich, late United States Consul in Paris, and still discharging the duties of consulate till the arrival of his successor. Peter Parley is a man of whom his country ought to be proud; he has done more for the instruction of his young countrymen than any other living man. He has been the author to whose pen every section of our land has been indebted for the reading of its children and youth. A few years ago, the State of Louisiana and the city of New Orleans paid him public honors rarely ever equalled upon our continent; and when Mr. Goodrich was sent abroad as Consul at Paris every one acknowledged the fitness of the homage done to talent, and genius, and high patriotic spirit. On his arrival in the French metropolis, Mr. Goodrich found his countrymen next door to being without any representation. Instead of shutting himself up, and keeping his fellow-citizens at an unapproachable distance, and aping an etiquette which a British plenipotentiary would hardly establish, he at once made his residence a pleasant resort for all his countrymen, and every Friday evening he had a soirée for his friends, where the New Englander, Pennsylvanian, South Carolinian or Louisianian, was sure to meet with a hearty welcome, and where, for the evening, an American felt sure that he had one representing his country in Paris to whom he could look with pride and pleasure, and on whom he could rely for advice and assistance in any emergency. There, too, American ladies, when in Paris, met with friendly and serviceable attentions from Mrs. Goodrich and her accomplished daughters. Americans abroad felt the importance of having such a man retained at this post. Numerous signatures were attached to a representation of the earnest desire of men of all parties that Mr. Goodrich might be retained. His services in having greatly extended the business of the office, and his merits, were urged upon the attention of the powers that be; but in vain. The operation of such a measure abroad is injurious. No other country displays such antics, and plays shuffle-board in this style. I have no doubt that Mr. Goodrich's successor is a most worthy man, and he will be a fortunate and enviable one if, at the termination of his consular life in Paris, he shall possess one-half the reputation which Mr. Goodrich has acquired with all who have witnessed his labors and the spirit in which they have been discharged.

At the time of our arrival in Paris there was a large delegation of American ladies and gentlemen in the city, and it was very pleasant to meet some intimate friends. The Rev. Drs. Crocker, of Providence; Lamson, of Dedham; Krebbs, of New

York; Vinton, of Boston; Bishop McIlvaine, of Ohio, and Rev. Messrs. Kirk, Jameson, Cook and Bidwell, were all here.

A party was made up to visit Versailles, in the vicinity of which a great review was to take place. The excursion was exceedingly agreeable, and the pleasure of the day was enhanced by the company of my valued friend and former pupil, Robert Schell, Esq., his lady and her sister. The emperor was not present, as expected, but a large body of soldiers was under arms, and the Minister of War, with other generals, conducted the operations of the day. A sham fight followed. The ladies were very much interested in the various manœuvres of the skirmishing parties. A very large company of spectators was on the ground. Departing from this gay and one-sided view of war, we betook ourselves to an excellent café, and enjoyed our dinner; after which, the party had a delightful stroll through the palace grounds and gardens, and then, resuming the carriages, returned to Paris, having passed an exceedingly pleasant day. The examination of the palace was deferred for another day. It was with great pleasure that I met my friend, Mr. Henry T. Parker, of Boston, with whom I had been in Europe in 1851. A pleasant day spent with him in the Palais Royal, I shall not soon forget. On the Sabbath day I attended divine service at the Episcopal church, in the Marbœuf chapel, the minister of which is the Rev. Robert Lovett, chaplain to the Right Honorable the Earl of Rosse. This gentleman has occupied this important post about twenty-five years. The congregation was large and very respectable; every seat was occupied, and I think the audience was between five and six hundred. The service was read in a very impressive manner. I do not recollect that I ever heard it better read, — the prayers were *prayed*, not *said*. The text was Psalm 93: 5, — "Thy testimonies are very sure; holiness becometh thy house, O Lord, forever." The sermon was delivered without notes, — it was simple, earnest, evangelical, and adapted to usefulness. We were very much gratified, and, if we were to remain in Paris, I think I should seek no further for a Sabbath sitting. After service, I had a pleasant interview with Mr. Lovett in the vestry; he told me that on the last Lord's day Bishop McIlvaine had preached a most excellent sermon in his pulpit. I would strongly recommend travellers, when in Paris, to attend the ministry of this "good minister of Jesus Christ."

In the afternoon I met a number of American ministers and friends at the residence of Mrs. Deming, to consult upon the advisableness of the establishment of an American chapel in Paris. I have no doubt that this is a desirable measure; and, if a place of worship could be procured, and a suitable minister placed in it, I think the advantages which would result from the institution would be numerous and certain. A large number of young business men are always in Paris, and a minister, with a home, would be of incalculable service to the hundreds of Americans who sojourn in this great city. In the evening I officiated at the English Methodist chapel, in the Rue Royale, very near the Church of the Madeleine. The congregation was as large as the chapel would hold, but it is quite a small one.

We devoted a day to the Louvre, which is now in fine condition, having undergone entire reparation; the gildings are fresh, and the frescoed ceilings are looking as if they were just executed.

The great picture of Murillo's, which was purchased from Marshal Soult's estate, and cost more than one hundred and twenty thousand dollars, is now in this gallery; it is a wondrous production, and it is difficult to believe that it is not a new picture, the colors are so very brilliant. The subject is the Assumption of the Virgin. Here are some glorious pictures, but I miss many that charmed me long years ago. I am always pleased with the pictures of Philippe de Champaigne; his portraits have an individuality about them, and I feel that they must have been likenesses. Two of his portraits of old French royalty were once in New York, and I remember them offered somewhere for sale, and wondered that they were not taken up. If I am not mistaken, they were at the Clinton House when it was kept by its fine old host, Mr. Hodges. The *chefs-d'œuvre* of this great collection have been so often engraved, that the enumeration of the sources of pleasure connected with the originals seems unnecessary. The apartments devoted to sculpture are immense, and the arrangement was made chiefly by Denon. In them are about fifteen hundred statues, busts, bas-reliefs, altars, brackets, candelabras, sarcophagi, &c. I was pleased with some exquisite gates of steel, finely carved, belonging to the days of Henry II. In the Musée Grecque et Egyptien are vast treasures of mosaic, chalices, porcelain; and here, or in some other part of the building, I was charmed with a bas-relief, the production of Benvenuto Cellini, executed for Francis I. In this part of the Louvre are about thirty saloons, into many of which strangers rarely enter.

Our friend Dr. Linsly was exceedingly laborious during our stay in Paris. Every morning he was up at five and off to the hospitals, where, through the courtesy of the professors and surgeons, he was taken through the daily walks, and had a fine opportunity to see the treatment of hundreds of patients by the renowned physicians and great surgeons of this celebrated medical school. We had a very delightful occasion on one day here, when Dr. Linsly and I had the pleasure to have Mr. Goodrich and his family as our guests, and we sat down quite a large party. Our visit to the Jardin des Plantes was on a fine day, and this noble institution appeared, I thought, more attractive than I had ever beheld it. We went to it by crossing the fine iron Bridge of Austerlitz, — it has five arches. The garden was established in 1635 by Louis XIII., and the talents of the greatest naturalists of Europe have been placed under contribution to make it what it is, — the most famous garden on the continent. It has been the scene of labor for Herouard, De la Brosse, Tournefort, Vaillant, Jussieu and his son, Buffon, and more recently the illustrious Cuvier has devoted to it his great talents. When revolutionary barbarism devastated the city, this spot fortunately escaped destruction, and Bonaparte took it into his special favor. The care of this garden and its valuable adjuncts is in the charge of the Minister of the Interior.

The Botanical Garden, its noble conservatories, museum of natural history, anatomical gallery, laboratories, lecture-rooms and menagerie of animals, birds, &c., constitute a combination of advantages for study that no other capital in the world presents to the enthusiast in natural science. The menagerie was brought here from Versailles, by Louis XVI. The palm-trees are in fine condition, and date back to the days of Louis XIV.; and the tropical plants are in conservatories, kept warm by steam-pipes. I was glad to see again the glorious cedar of Lebanon planted in 1734. One gallery, that of natural history, is more than four hundred feet long; and in the cabinet of comparative anatomy are more than fifteen thousand specimens, all arranged by Baron Cuvier. Haydon was quite right when he said that the Jardin des Plantes was "a place of Roman magnificence." On our return we saw the Halle aux Vins, or great wine-dépôt; here are about five hundred and fifty thousand casks of wine, and two thousand casks frequently come in during a single day. This is the custom-house for wine, and the excise duties on wine are here paid on the sale of the article.

Our visit to the Palais de Justice was very interesting. This building is as old as Notre Dame, and was formerly the royal residence; indeed, as late as the days of Francis I. The present front was built in 1760. Here is a vast gallery of more than two hundred feet by about eighty, in which the clients may perambulate whilst their cases are going on in court; and here is a monument to the courageous Malesherbes, the advocate of Louis XVI. The courts of law are venerable halls, but too small for the demands of the city. The Conciergerie was the prison used for state purposes when the Palais was a royal mansion. It was from this place that Lavalette escaped, aided by his heroic wife and Sir Robert Wilson. Here Marie Antoinette was confined; but the cell, which was made by Louis XVIII. into an expiatory chapel, was destroyed in the revolution of 1830. Sad scenes of blood and murder were witnessed here in 1792. We were greatly interested here with the Sainte Chapelle, altogether the finest Gothic relic in Paris. It was built 1245, as a sanctum to receive the true cross and crown of thorns, purchased from the Greek emperor by St. Louis. The condition of this chapel is wonderful, considering its great antiquity. The glass windows are perfect treasures of art, and look as if just executed. The chapel is unique, and is, I think, one of the greatest curiosities in Paris. It is at present receiving a perfect renovation, and will be the noblest architectural bijou in Europe. Boileau, the great satirist, was buried here. Close by is the Quai Dessaix, where the great flower-market is held, and to which we paid frequent and charming visits. It is a pleasant thing to see the almost universal passion which exists for flowers. Go through the narrowest streets of Paris, and at the windows of the poorest houses, and up four and five stories, you shall see pots of green things, and gay, blooming flowers. I like to watch the faces of the country people who bring in the flowers, — and they are here by hundreds; they seem to be alive to the beauties of nature; they look as though they had gained some refinement from their gazing on these faint reflections of uncreated excellence and beauty. And then I was delighted to see the feeling of content and pride with which a man in blouse, or a hard-working woman, or a poor little child, would carry off a pot of some verdant thing, to make home look a little more bright and cheerful. These flower-markets are pretty things, and they are good things, too. Bad people do not love God's handiworks, and seldom do they care for plants and flowers. I wish that parents would cultivate the taste for beauty and the love of nature in their children. A good flower and a fine plant are far better presents for a child than a noisy drum, a cruel sword, and a miniature gun. Passive impressions lead to active habits, and many a fond but foolish mother has contributed her aid to make her darling boy food for bullets.

I managed to have a long day and a pleasant party at my old favorite haunt, the Hotel de Cluny, in the Rue des Mathurins. This is a rare spot, and one that I never feel wearied in visiting. It was the town residence of the influential Abbots of Cluny, a Benedictine monastery at Cluny, and, before the revolution, it had six hundred houses in connection with it, and an income of three hundred thousand francs. It was built in 1480, on the ruins of the Roman Palais de Thermes, where Julian made it his palace in 360. Here many a Pope has had a home when visiting France, and here did the Abbess of Port Royal and her nuns find a resting-place from 1579 to 1584. In this glorious old spot lived Mary, daughter of Henry VII. of England, and widow of Louis XII. of France; and, while living here, she was privately married to the Duke of Suffolk, and it was from this event that the claim of poor Lady Jane Gray was laid to the crown of England. Between forty and fifty years ago, M. Du Sommerard, a gentleman of great antiquarian taste, purchased the place, and expended a vast property in collecting works of art of the mediæval age, the whole being classified according to chronological order. At his death, which occurred a few years ago, the French government wisely determined to purchase the hotel and its unique collection, and large additions have been made to it of every curiosity that can serve to illustrate the early history of the country. The first appearance of this edifice, on entering the court-yard, is very striking. It has several Gothic turrets and rich windows. No one can walk through this building without being satisfied that the Abbots of Cluny and their brethren must have had good times when they came up to court. Room after room is filled with bas-reliefs, sculpture, carvings and casts. The furniture of the 14th, 15th and 16th centuries, is in great profusion, and the tapestry is very beautiful and perfect. Perhaps there are no cabinets and presses to be seen in Europe that are more exquisite than those in this museum. We went from one saloon to another in the upper story, and revelled in the examination of the richest old curiosity-shop in the world. The catalogue contains nearly two thousand items, and weeks of study might be spent to great profit in this wonderful place. I would not forget to say that the handiwork of Bernard de Palissy is here in great plenty, and some of the superb designs of Benevenuto Cellini. Cups, goblets and drinking-horns, of all the great men of French history, gems, enamels and armor, abound, and porcelain of every variety and age. A small chapel, whose ceiling is sustained by a single shaft, is very interesting, and the carving in this sanctuary describes several sacred subjects. Just as we were going into this charming place, I met with a venerable English lady and her female companion, and, on offering her my arm to aid her ascent of some steep steps, we entered into conversation. I found her an exceedingly interesting woman, of fine taste, and possessing much valuable information. We went through the entire collection in company, and, at parting, she gave us a kind and pressing invitation to visit her at her mansion near Plymouth, in Devonshire. We were fortunate in meeting with very pleasant people at our hotel, and we shall always look back with interest on an acquaintance which we formed here with Captain Masters, of the royal navy, and his son and daughter. This gentleman resides at East Ryde, on the Isle of Wight. His son was a Cambridge man, and was spending the vacation in travel. In their company was an excellent clergyman of the English church, the Rev. Mr. Swainson. With these friends we arranged for a visit to Versailles. On this occasion, we took the railroad, and in the cars found a large school of noble-looking boys in uniform, attended by a bevy of tutors — priests, in clerical costume. They were bound to the grand reviews.

Versailles has been so often described that I need only say

that, though I have been through its splendor again and again, I found it full of interest. The palace is now used as a grand receptacle of the objects which minister to national pride. Louis Philippe turned his attention to this palace, and gathered together in these gorgeous saloons all the pictorial history of France. Verily, this is the place to study the history of this great country; and, when I look at the magnificent portraiture of the personal career of the great emperor, I cannot, for a moment, doubt that Louis Philippe did more than any other person to create that wave of popular feeling which carried the present Napoleon into his imperial throne. I do not think that any other nation has such an illustration of its ancient and modern history as this.

The works of sculpture which pleased us best were a Joan of Arc, sculptured by a deceased daughter of Louis-Philippe, and bearing her cypher; Cardinal de Retz; Chancellor L'Hospital; Sully; the late Duke of Orleans, by Pradier, of Geneva; Cardinal Mazarin and Colbert, by Coyzevox; Molière, by Houdon, the sculptor who made the noble statue of Washington at Richmond; Fenelon and General Washington, by Houdon; Napoleon and Ney, by the same; Marshal Davoust, by Bosio; Bossuet, Coligny.

In the saloons of paintings, we were much gratified with those descriptive of the Crusades, the Battle of St. Jacques, by Johannot, — this is a noble piece; the Interview of the Camp of the Drap d'Or, by the younger Debay; the Battle of Ivry, by Steuben; the Instituting of the French Academy, in 1634, — a most spirited picture, with capital drawing, by H. Lecompte. The Passage of the Rhine, 1672, has employed several artists; I prefer the one painted by P. Franque. Napoleon receiving the Senatus Consulte, at St. Cloud, on his proclamation as Emperor, 1804, by Rouget, is good. A picture that I cannot forget was Napoleon receiving at the Louvre, after his coronation, the deputation from the army. The Proclamation of the Lieutenant General, read at the Hotel de Ville, 1830, and a Celebration of Mass by the Pope and Cardinals, are full of interest.

But why should I particularize? for here are more than two thousand, and of these probably five hundred have great merit. The recent paintings, by Horace Vernet, illustrative of the battles in Algiers, are vast as to size, and deeply interesting in their details of African scenery, and exhibit wonderful brilliancy of coloring. Our visit, also, to the great and little Trianon, was very agreeable; and we were delighted with these charming little palaces, where, I have no doubt, more comfort has been experienced by their royal owners than in the gorgeous chateaux close by. Monarchs are but men, and, like other people, they feel more real pleasure in homes of comfort than in magnificent and spacious solitudes. Bonaparte loved a small house, and once wrote to his brother at Paris to get him one ready on his arrival from Egypt; George IV. had his snuggery close by the glorious old castle at Windsor, and Queen Victoria spends her happiest hours at Osborne House, which is a modest mansion, not equal to many gentlemen's family houses.

The garden at the great Trianon pleased me, perhaps, as much as anything of its size that I ever saw, and, in my opinion, is far more beautiful than the gardens of the great palace close by. The little Trianon we all felt interested in, because it was the favorite retreat of Marie Antoinette.

After dining at a café, we took the rail on the other side of the Seine, and, riding up the river, had a good view of St. Cloud, and passed through Sevres.

The walks which I had in the gardens of the Tuilleries and in the Champs Elysées are all, I think, become parts of myself, and will be forever with me. The exquisite order in which everything is kept delighted me; and then the perfect behavior of the thousands who resort to these promenades! It was just the right season to enjoy these spots; the noble orange-trees were still many of them in fragrant blossom, and the marble statues beside them afforded a fine contrast. It is the fashion to criticize the Tuilleries; but I must always admire the fine long line of elegant old buildings.

As to the Champs Elysées, it is a place to think in and to think of, but cannot be described. I can forgive a Parisian for his pride; he has whereof to glory, indeed, as he carries his children into the woody walks of this pleasure-ground of the people. I can turn from the thronged street and be instantly among the finest flowers, the noblest walks, the gayest company and the prettiest children; for, although I do not think the women generally handsome, yet the children are very beautiful. O, these fountains! how refreshing is the spray they cast off so freely! I cannot express myself in reference to this locality more happily than by quoting a description given of it by Mr. James A. Robinson, who was one of my young travelling companions in 1851. He said, writing to a friend: "Turn round, and look at the gardens we have left. There, see the long, low Tuilleries, the palace of the Bourbons, the home of Napoleon, the residence of the Citizen King, and now the Palace National. Off to the right is the Seine, and its long line of quays; here is the bridge, and just across it is the chamber of the Assembly, with twelve Corinthian columns. To our left, is a long, stately range of buildings, known as the Rue Rivoli, in which we reside; it has an arched arcade in front for foot-passengers, and some hundreds of columns to support and adorn it. At this end are public offices. Now turn, and look at our right; and see, a street cuts through this noble row, and, at its end, you behold the pride of the city, — the Madeleine. There it is, all white, and its stately columns tell of Greece. Now gaze upon the open space of the Champs Elysées, and look down through that splendid avenue, and there see the finest thing in France, — Bonaparte's triumphal arch."

I have never visited Paris without having my admiration of the Pont Neuf increased. It is my favorite stand-point. The bridge is of stone, and not marked by any architectural beauty; but from it you obtain the best view of the olden portion of the city, and here is the finest one of its venerable streets, quays and ancient houses, that I know of. The buildings are very old, — six, seven, and some eight stories high. The Ile de la Cité makes two streams of the river, and off behind all stands Notre Dame. I have spent hours here, looking at the prospect in early morning light, and in the glowing colors of the setting sun; and I have wandered off to this bridge many a night to watch the effect of the moon upon these relics of other ages. A favorite walk with me is to the Hotel de Ville, a grand old edifice of the sixteenth century. It was on the 1 lace de Grève, in front of it, that the bloody scenes of the revolution were enacted, and here stood the guillotine. Perhaps the best view of this municipal palace is had from the quay on the other side the Seine. It was here that many of the most exciting scenes of the first revolution transpired, and the very room in which Robespierre held his council is shown, and the table on which he was placed when his jaw was fractured by the pistol-ball. Very near to this is the old church of St. Germain l'Auxerrois, said to have been founded by Robert, in 998. The part which remains dates from the 13th century, and the front is the great western doorway. From this church the bell sounded out which summoned the Catholics to the infernal butchery of the Protestants, on Bartholomew's day, 1572, — a work of piety which the Pope, Gregory XIII., approved, and in honor of which he commanded a medal to be struck. This medal is scarce; but I have seen it, and the following is the inscription, which 1 copied:

Around the head: GREGORIVS XIII. PONT. MAX. AN. II.
On the reverse: VGONOTTORVM. STRAGES 1572.

This medal is in the British Museum, among the Papal medals. The silver medal was cast in the first year of his Papacy, and the copper one in the second.

We visited a number of churches, and were much gratified with St. Germain des Pres, St. Sulpice and the Pantheon, — which last the piety of Napoleon III. has again put into the hands of the priests. It is now dedicated to St. Genevieve. Certainly, this is a most charming specimen of the Grecian style. This church is three hundred and two feet long, by two hundred and fifty-five in width. In the crypt are the tombs of renowned men. The dome is lofty, and is finely painted, by Gros. The work is principally illustrative of French history, and it is supposed that some sacred subject will soon take the place now devoted to kings and queens. The portico of this church is exceedingly impressive, the Corinthian pillars of which are sixty feet high and five feet in diameter.

The portico of St. Sulpice is truly majestic; it has a double row of columns. I am always gratified in looking at the west front of this fine sanctuary. No traveller should fail to go into this church to see, in a deep recess beyond the altar, an extraordinary sculpture of the Virgin and her Son, in marble. They appear with the globe at their feet, and immediately under their feet is a bruised serpent. Very wonderful is the effect of a concealed light, falling upon this beautiful work of art.

A wet day was selected for a visit to the Royal Library. It is in a central situation, and the entrance is from the Rue Richelieu; the building occupies a square, and extends to other streets. Very dark and unpromising are its walls; and, when I first visited Paris, I passed it in full faith that it was a prison. I was desirous to see the bust of its late librarian, the renowned bibliopolist, Van Praet. There it stands, in a spot where he passed his useful and agreeable life. A greater enthusiast never lived. The cabinet of medals is, in many respects, unique, and has been the care of the monarchs of France since the days of Francis I. Very few persons obtain access to the ground-floor of this collection, in which are the vases, gems, cameos, and precious works of art. The vase of Ptolemy cannot be forgotten by any one who has seen it. I can only say that the wondrous library is all open to the students' use. I shall not attempt a description of its tomes; but here are first editions, vellum copies.

rare Boccacios, unaccountable Dantes, impossible to be found; Virgils, and not-to-be-understood first editions of Homer, as poor Haydon, in his charming autobiography, said of Lord Spencer's library. On this visit, I was most attracted by the large collection of prints, which comprises all the successive periods of art. The accommodations for these matchless engravings are far too contracted. I found that there were more than eleven thousand bound volumes of prints. The library of MSS. is very rich, and I should enjoy a week spent in rummaging these old cabinets and presses, where are missals bound and illustrated as the piety of other ages deemed fitting for books of devotion. On a former visit I saw many of the rare and early editions. Only a book-worm can understand the gratifications of hours and days passed in this quiet retreat. There are some twenty or thirty other libraries of great interest in Paris; and in no city in the world can a literary man obtain all the information that he needs with so much ease as in this capital.

Our visit to the Gobelins was a source of much pleasure. I am happy to say that this interesting manufactory is now receiving the patronage of the government, as it did under Napoleon and Louis Philippe. We found a large number of workmen employed upon tapestry and carpets. There are about one hundred magnificent specimens of these curiously-fabricated pictures hanging on the walls of spacious apartments, and we were courteously shown the tapestries in course of execution. I am not mechanic enough to attempt a description of the process which is employed. A son of the Emerald Isle, who was watching the operation of making a grand picture from a Raphael, brought here from the Louvre to be copied, was standing near us, and broke out, "Holy Father, Jimmini! what a thing man is!"

A very beautiful day invited us to go out of the city, and we took carriages for the abbey church of St. Denis, which is about four or five miles from Paris This church has been the great burial-place of the monarchs of France, from the days of Dago bert, in 580. Louis Philippe laid out vast sums of money in restoring this church, which suffered sadly in the first revolution. It is a truly noble structure; and we entered the porch with a feeling of interest, from the recollection that in this porch Henry IV. made his abjuration of the Protestant cause. The west front is very fine; it has two towers, and over the great gateway is a bas-relief of the Judgment. This temple is one of the most impressive that I have seen. On every hand are monuments of great merit, and some exceedingly curious. Directly behind the altar, floats the oriflamme, or national standard. The restoration appears to be in excellent taste, and the windows are among the best we have seen. We descended into the crypt, and here we found, in exact chronological order, the remains of the kings from Clovis down, or, rather, their monuments; for the bodies of many were taken up by the madmen of the revolution, in 1793. Some of the sculpture is very fine. I greatly admired the kneeling effigies of Francis I. and Claude, his queen. Here is also the tomb of Charles, Comte d'Alençon, who fell in the battle of Cressy, in 1346. The marbles of this royal charnel-house are many of them exceedingly fine, and in far better preservation than I had expected. The many chapels on the aisles are exquisitely beautiful.

On leaving the abbey, we drove to Neuilly, the favorite residence of Louis Philippe. This delightful spot is in ruins, it having been sacked and burned by the Parisian mob, in 1848. We walked through the charming grounds, which were now all staked off, ready for a great sale of the property, which was to take place soon. The severity of the new government, in confiscating the family property of the Orleans dynasty, is a lasting blot upon the new régime.

The chapel dedicated to the memory of the Duke of Orleans, eldest son of Louis Philippe, stands not far from the Arc de l'Étoile. He was unfortunately killed by being thrown from his carriage, July 13, 1842. The duke was carried to a small shop

CHAPEL OF ST. FERDINAND.

opposite the scene of the disaster, and there laid on a pallet in a back room. He lay insensible till his death, which took place at ten minutes past four P. M. This chapel is dedicated to St. Ferdinand, the duke's patron saint, and was built by his afflicted father. The chapel is a pretty stone edifice, about fifty feet long, by twenty in height. In the transept, on the left, is an altar to St. Ferdinand, and off to the right a group representing the duke upon his death-bed, while at his head is an angel in prayer. This exquisite statue of the angel was the work of his sister, the Princess Marie, and bears the initials M. O. The rest of the group is by Triquetti. In front, as we enter, is the altar to the Virgin, and surmounting it is a statue of the Virgin and Child, by Triquetti. Directly behind this altar, we went down three or four steps, and entered the room in which the duke died. This is very plainly furnished, and is used as the sacristy. Opposite the door is a picture the size of life, by Jacquand, describing the tragic scene. The duke is lying on a pallet, physicians supporting his head, the queen and one of his sisters kneeling at his side; the king is gazing in the agony of hopeless grief, and the royal Dukes D'Aumale and Montpensier, and Marshals Soult and Gerard, Guizot and a priest, fill up the group. In this room I noticed a small, gilt-framed painting, which the guide informed me was the only article saved in the sacking of Neuilly, and was deposited here.

A neat building faces the door of the chapel, which was intended to receive the royal family in their frequent visits. I observed a richly-embroidered cushion, which was the work of the queen. One clock here has the hands pointing to ten minutes to twelve, when the accident happened; and another clock opposite, whose hands stand at ten minutes past four, when the heir apparent of this beautiful land expired. In the court is a cedar of Lebanon, brought home from the Mount by the Duke of Orleans, and here it was planted by his son, the Count de

Paris. I do not envy the man who can visit this spot unmoved. And this is all the real estate that the Orleans family is permitted to hold in France!

We next drove to another place of deep historical interest; it was the Chapelle Expiatoire, in the Rue d'Anjou St. Honoré. This is to the memory of Louis XVI. and his ill-fated queen, and stands on the spot where, for twenty-one years, their remains were interred, till they were exhumed, and carried to St. Denis. As you enter the chapel, on the right, you see a fine statue of Louis, executed by Bossio. Never did chisel define ermine so delicately as on this marble; and the lace scarf and frill-work is like lace itself. On the left is a statue of Marie Antoinette, in a kneeling posture, as if supplicating Madame Elizabeth for aid and support, who, in the person of Religion, stands beside her. The queen's face is almost one of imploring agony, and more of earthly emotion than heavenly grace is depicted. Descending to the crypt, our guide pointed out the four columns on which the chapel rests, and which serve to support the pillars of the roof, and told us that within those vast square columns were enclosed the remains of those who perished in the revolution, thrown in a promiscuous heap, and mixed with quick-lime, and among them was the saint-like Princess Elizabeth.

Leaving the chapel, we begged a flower from the garden. The faithful Swiss guards lie on either side of the garden, and their resting-place is marked by stone columns. These two chapels are among the most interesting objects we have visited in Paris.

In former visits, I had not been to the Chateau of Fontainebleau, but had only passed through by rail. On this occasion, we made a pleasant party with some valued friends from New York, and went out for a long summer day. The railroad goes through a fine country, rich in corn and pasturage; the views are bold, some of the hills are bordering on the romantic, and the private residences are many of them very beautiful.

The town is finely situated in the midst of the extensive forest. Fontainebleau is about fifty miles from Paris, on the railroad to Lyons. On our arrival, we ordered our dinner at the Hotel de Lyons for four o'clock, and then started for the palace. This is esteemed the most beautiful one belonging to the crown. It has been built at different periods, but has been put together in the finest taste, and the parts are in good keeping. This was the resort of several of the early kings, but the present chateau was erected by Francis I.; here Charles V. was received by him, and here poor Biron was arrested by Henry IV. Like other palaces, it has been a scene of horrors; in its walls Monaldeschi was murdered. Here, too, Louis XIV. signed the revocation of the edict of Nantes. Napoleon loved Fontainebleau, and here he passed much of his time. He made it the prison-house of Charles IV. of Spain, and here kept the Pope Pius VII. in custody. The great event which has given this palace a lasting interest was the abdication of Napoleon, in 1814. Louis Philippe spent vast sums in the restoration of this palace; and everything done to it, as it regards the building or the furniture, was in perfect accordance with the style of the edifice.

This palace is very extensive, and you are conducted through vast ranges of apartments. I was most pleased with the rooms occupied by the Pope, and with the private apartments of the great emperor. The table on which he signed his abdication is a plain little affair, not worth two dollars or three at the outside. It is covered with a glass case, to preserve it from the hands of the curiosity-hunters. The works of art and paintings are very numerous, and some of the last are of a high order. The great ball-room is a very noble affair; it is of oak, and richly gilt, and equal to anything I have seen since I left the Winter Palace, in St. Petersburg. Some portions of this building date back to the eleventh century, and the chapel on the lower floor is said to have been consecrated by Thomas à Becket, in 1169. Here are fine gardens, in capital order, and a large fish-pond, well stocked with carp. We looked with intense emotion at the stairway of the chateau where Napoleon took his farewell of the army. That must have been the hour of his soul's darkness. In this palace Louis Philippe had collected the entire history of France from its earliest records, upon Sevres china plates, which are here framed, and suspended on the walls of a gallery. The bedrooms of Henry IV. and Mary de Medicis, Louis IX., and Marie Antoinette, are fine apartments. In this queen's boudoir is a vase of gold and ivory, given to her at her ill-starred marriage. Here is a vast quantity of Gobelin tapestry; the history of Esther is one of the subjects.

A very severe thunder-storm kept us prisoners for some time. On its passing off, we repaired to the hotel, and had a comfortable dinner. We met with an agreeable travelled gentleman at the table, and, after finding that the cosmopolite was a New Yorker, we invited him to join our party for a visit to the forest. We had a large carryall, with side curtains. The driver was communicative, and called attention to the most famous trees of this beautiful spot. I think some of the oaks transcend in beauty any that I have seen before. The three brothers are wondrous productions, and cannot be less than six or seven hundred years old. Just as we were midway in the forest, it began to rain furiously. The curtains were no defence, as they had no fastenings; and we proposed that the ladies should sit down on the floor of the carriage, and we would protect them with the cushions as far as possible, and then over all we threw the ladies' woollen shawls. Such times of fun and laughter I have rarely seen, as we had amid the storm, thunder and lightning.

Soon after our return, the sun shone forth brilliantly. Our good friend Mr. Leggett will not soon forget his ride with the young ladies in the forest of Fontainebleau. This forest is about thirty miles in circumference, and contains more than thirty-two thousand acres. The scenery is very diversified, and in some parts the rocks and waterfalls are highly romantic. Wolves are still troublesome to the farmers, and a price is yet set upon their heads. The town is quite pretty, has fine clean streets, large shops; and, if I wanted to sit down quietly in France for the autumn months, I think it would be in this grand old town. The grapes of this vicinity are exceedingly fine, and the vineyards have been famous since the days of the jovial Francis, who introduced the best varieties of the grape.

CHAPTER XIII.

REV. J. R. PEAKE — NAPOLEON'S TOMB IN THE HOTEL DES INVALIDES — LOUIS PHILIPPE — DESCRIPTION OF THE CRYPT — GALLERY, ETC. — MOSAICS — CARYATIDES — SARCOPHAGUS — RELIQUARY — ALTAR AND BALDAQUIN — GUIDE — CLIMATE OF PARIS — OVERTURES MADE TO MR. VANDERBILT — WOODMAN AND FORR — RAILROAD TO ROUEN — HISTORIC NOTICE — POPULATION OF ROUEN — CATHEDRAL — INTERIOR — MONUMENTS — RICHARD CŒUR DE LION, ETC. — ABBEY OF ST. OUEN — PALACE OF JUSTICE — JOAN OF ARC — CORNEILLE — ENGLISH CHURCH — VISITORS.

DURING my stay at the Hotel de Windsor, I enjoyed much pleasure in the society of an English clergyman also resident in the hotel, the Rev. J. R. Peake, of Whitchurch, in Shropshire. This gentleman was a most pleasant companion in my city rambles, and we both had many views and opinions in common, though belonging to different pales of the Christian church. Mr. Peake, like myself, is engaged in the education of lads, and was now passing his vacation on the continent. I really hope that we may meet again, and am disposed to believe that the desire is entertained by my friend and brother. Mr. Peake joined our entire party in visiting the Hotel des Invalides, for the purpose of seeing Napoleon's tomb. This required some management, as the great work was not quite finished, and the public were not admitted. All difficulties being removed, we made our visit.

The remains of the emperor were brought to France in triumph, in 1840, in a frigate commanded by the Prince de Joinville. A noble procession of steamboats conveyed the body to Neuilly. On a car thirty feet high, and drawn by sixteen black horses, it was carried to the Invalides. Galleries were erected to accom-

GRAND ENTRANCE TO THE CRYPT, AND VIEW OF BONAPARTE'S TOMB.

modate nearly thirty thousand persons. Candelebra of vast size adorned and illuminated the church, and in front of the altar was a magnificent catafalque, covered with violet-colored velvet, and this adorned with imperial emblems to receive the sarcophagus. The pall-bearers were Bertrand, Gourgaud, and the surviving marshals of the empire. The king and his family were present. How much Louis Philippe was accessory to his own dethronement, is a question that may well be pondered.

The body was then placed in a chapel of this church, which was itself elaborately fitted up. But the government immediately addressed itself to the preparation of a tomb befitting the greatest man who ever ruled in France. It would take a volume to describe the gorgeous arrangements for this unrivalled sepulchre. I have, therefore, preferred to give a good engraving of the entrance to the crypt; and through the door-way is seen the tomb itself, and the monuments of Duroc and Bertrand are seen on either side.

The tomb is surmounted by a marble balustrade breast-high, and the entrance-door is guarded by two colossal funeral genii. This engraving shows the high altar of the church, as you enter the edifice. The other side, towards the tomb, is still more elaborate. The altar, the balustrade around it, the hand-rail and the pedestals which support the candelabra, are formed of black marble from the Pyrenees and green marble from the Alps. Over the door-way leading to the tomb is Bonaparte's dying request:

"I DESIRE THAT MY ASHES MAY REPOSE ON THE BANKS OF THE SEINE, IN THE MIDST OF THE FRENCH PEOPLE, WHOM I LOVED SO WELL."

The crypt is a circular gallery, of about seven or eight feet wide, with a central space, formed by twelve marble arches, and the before-named balustrade connecting them with each other; and between these arches are twelve caryatides, fifteen feet high. The sarcophagus stands in the centre, with the ends towards the doors.

190 MOSAICS — BAS-RELIEFS — SARCOPHAGUS.

This gallery around is paved with mosaics, and its wall is thrown into divisions, which correspond with the arches of the centre work. The doors of the crypt and reliquary occupy two of these divisions, and the other ten are devoted to marble bas-reliefs. Twelve bronze lamps are suspended from the roof of this circular gallery. The bas-reliefs are the exquisite production of Simard, and are allegorical representations of the great acts and institutions of the emperor's reign. The subjects are the Institution of the Legion of Honor, Encouragement of Commerce and Industry, Public Works, Establishment of the Audit Office, Establishment of the University of France, the Concordat, the Civil Code, the Foundation of the Council of State, Organization of Public Administration, Pacification of Civil Troubles.

The mosaics in the passage leading to the tomb are very rich, and here are two of them. A larger one is an eagle surmounted

by the imperial diadem. Each of the caryatides, with the pillar against which it stands, is formed of a single block of marble. The sarcophagus is very imposing from its simplicity. It is composed of quartz gritstone, and was procured from a quarry in Russia. The cover is of one slab. The coffin, of tin, is enclosed in mahogany; this has two cases of lead, and over all is an ebony coffin. The sarcophagus itself is lined with gray Corsican granite. Here, then, will lie the remains of Napoleon Bonaparte till the last trumpet shall sound, and all ranks shall be abolished, and he will stand with the humblest of his subjects before the King eternal — *unless* the good pleasure of Parisians shall by and by decide upon pulling down what they formerly built up with so much enthusiasm.

The Reliquary, or sword-room, is a very elegant apartment, lined with white marble. Directly facing the door stands a marble statue of Napoleon in imperial costume, the sceptre in one hand and a globe in the other. In front of this statue is a pedestal of dark porphyry, from Finland, on which is a rich bronze cushion, where repose the hat which Napoleon wore at Austerlitz, his sword used at that battle, his epaulettes, orders, and a gold crown. On either side is a tripod supporting the flags which are identified with his military exploits. On the walls are recorded the names of battles in which he commanded in person. The pavement of this apartment is inlaid with mosaic medallions, descriptive of imperial power.

I think the Altar and Baldaquin exceed in magnificence any work of man that I have ever seen; and, standing before it and looking around upon the entire scene, I feel that all of earthly splendor that this world has witnessed in the monumental art must pale before this sepulchral *chef-d'œuvre*. Twelve years have been devoted to this national labor, and it is now nearly finished. Our guide was one of the Old Guard who accompanied Napoleon to Elba and St. Helena, and is now the custodian of his tomb. We saw the coffin in a chapel, where it lies in great magnificence, awaiting its final removal.

During all my visits to Paris, which have been in June, July, December, January and February, I have been observant of the weather and climate. I have noticed no fogs nor mists. The air is dry, and those who have had a tendency to cough, bronchial irritation, or asthmatical symptoms, are always relieved. In no place have I felt the state of the skin so healthy as in this city. In all cases where invalids visit Paris and find that they improve, I think they would do well to abide quietly. I have seen bad consequences ensue from not letting well-enough satisfy. We all, as a party, had our health perfectly in Paris; enjoyed every hour of our visit, and left this beautiful city with regret.

I ought to mention that our stay in Paris was one of nineteen days. During our abode here several gentlemen and noblemen called on Mr. Vanderbilt, expressing an earnest wish to have him identify himself with a new steam-ship line which the government proposed to open with North, South and Central America. To these overtures, which were urged in the most flattering terms, Mr. Vanderbilt gave no encouragement; but freely communicated his views, and offered the results of his experience. The subject was afterwards revived, and the most pressing invitations to revisit Paris were forwarded to Mr. Vanderbilt at Constantinople, and the first names in France, both civilians and capitalists, were involved in the proposal. And had Mr. Vanderbilt gone abroad with any desire to advance his interests by commercial operations, the opportunities afforded him were as brilliant as a business man could desire. But his aims and objects were strictly private, and personal enjoyment and the happiness of his circle was all he attempted.

Having finished our business with Mr. Woodman, the prince of tailors, and Forr, the best shoemaker in Paris, we took the train of cars for Rouen, which is eighty-four miles from Paris. Our route lay on the banks of the Seine, and we passed through Clichy, Colombes, where the queen of Charles I. died in poverty; Poissy, Meulan, Mantes, where William the Conqueror met his death-wound; Rosny, the favorite residence of the great Sully. On our way we noticed some exceedingly fine churches, of apparently an early date. The town of Vernon is a fine-looking old place. Every time I pass this road I long to make a sauntering tour along the banks of the Seine. How much I wanted to make a tarry in Andelys, Gaillard, and other sweet

spots on the river-side. Elbœuf is a large, flourishing town, with many manufactories of cloth, and around are villas indicative of taste and wealth. The Seine, in all its course, winds through a cultivated valley, and presents at every bend the most picturesque views. Next to Paris, I regard Rouen as the most interesting city in France, and, in some respects, one of the most extraordinary cities of Europe. This place lies on the north bank of the river, across which there is a fine stone bridge, and I believe also a suspension bridge; but I was engaged in noticing the glorious approach to this city, and the show which it presents of its venerable cathedral, and the abbey church of St. Ouen. Ptolemy speaks of this city by the name of Rothomagus. The Romans occupied and fortified it, and remains of their walls are yet to be traced. The Church of Rome claims that Christianity was introduced here by the apostles. Saint Ouen built churches here during his episcopate, in the seventh century. Rollo, the Norwegian, who became Duke of Normandy, was a great benefactor to Rouen. Under his care it grew and flourished.

This city was strongly fortified at an early period, and has often been the scene of siege and carnage. Its sieges date in 949, by the Emperor Otho, and Louis IV. of France; in 1204, by Philip Augustus; in 1418, by Henry V., King of England; in 1449, when Charles VII. took it from England; in 1591, by Henry IV. This is quite a place of business, and it has numerous manufactures, which are prosperous. The city is engaged in foreign commerce, and I saw vessels at the quays of three hundred tons. The custom-house is a good building. The population is about one hundred and twenty thousand inhabitants. The narrow streets are thronged with people, and everywhere the hum of cheerful industry was heard. The streets are precisely as they were when Francis I. was in power; and I am carried back to the days of the sixteenth century more really than I ever was before. I feel that I am gazing at the very houses on which

Joan of Arc has looked, and am amid the same scenes that pleased and occupied her cruel tormentors.

Every one said, " Let us go to the cathedral; " and on the way we picked up a boy, who was a willing, cheerful, chatty guide. On our way, I was tempted to explore sundry portfolios of engravings, and made a quick but very satisfactory investment. After rummaging the quays of Paris in vain, I here stumbled upon the objects of my earnest desire. I think everything in Rouen looked better after my purchase of sundry Woolletts and Sharpes, &c. O, what steep streets, what narrow streets, what beetling house-tops, what moss-covered fountains, what dusty, cobwebbed curiosity-shops, I passed, that hot morning! "There! there!" says good Dr. Linsly, as he caught the west front of the cathedral, " what a church!" And it is indeed a sight to wonder at, admire, and then think about. I wanted to stand and spend an hour at this spot. No engraving can describe the glories of this front. It reminds me of Wells Cathedral, which was the first large ecclesiastical pile of great merit which I saw; and I well remember that it affected me to illness; it overpowered my mind, at my childish age. This front is one hundred and eighty feet wide, and one hundred and fifty feet at its loftiest pitch. It has three porches between the two towers, and the bas-reliefs are illustrative of Herodias' dancing, and the decapitation of John the Baptist. We entered by the middle door, and at once saw the length and altitude of the nave. Our attention was directed to the lantern of the tower, which is upheld by four immense pillars, which cluster thirty-one columns into a circumference of forty feet each. The windows of this edifice are one hundred and thirty, and these are the best specimens of painted glass in France, especially those of the time of the *Renaissance.* The rose windows of the transept and over the organ are deemed matchless. One of these represents the Father, surrounded by angels, with music; and again these are surrounded by ten angels, each holding emblems of the Passion.

The dimensions of the cathedral are about four hundred and forty feet in length, the transept one hundred and seventy-five feet, and the nave is ninety feet high. The chapels are twenty-five in number, and I noticed several females at the confessional. Old Rollo lies in the chapel of St. Romain; he was removed here from the nave in 1063. Here is the grave and monument of John, Duke of Bedford, the Regent of France, 1435. King Louis XI. was great enough to refuse to destroy this tomb. His language was, "I say, God save his soul; and let his body now lie in rest, which, when he was alive, would have disquieted the proudest of us all!" The most splendid monument here was that of the two Cardinals Amboise — uncle and nephew. The uncle was the liberal restorer of this church. The monument is of black and white marble, — the figures, of white marble, kneeling beneath an elaborate Gothic canopy. Below is St. George, in gilt; and the frieze is surrounded by six small female sculptures, which are emblems of the virtues displayed by the cardinals. In this church is the grave of Richard Cœur de Lion. I was interested in looking at the freestone statue which decorated his tomb. He is in a recumbent posture, his head on a cushion, and his feet against a crouching lion. A search was made in 1838, and the heart of Richard was found in a double box of lead, and on it this inscription, in letters of that age:

HIC : JACET : COR : RICHARDI : REGIS : ANGLORUM.

This heart our party afterwards saw in the museum, in the glass case in which it was originally placed. It had much the appearance of a piece of leather, but was evidently a heart. We were all pleased with the tomb of Louis de Brézé, 1531. This monument was erected by his widow, Diana of Poictiers. This is a monument having four pillars of black marble, between which is a coffin, on which is laid a white marble statue of the deceased.

The body is quite naked — the left hand on the breast. This is a wondrous resemblance of death. Diana is kneeling at the head. She afterwards forgot her sorrows in the arms of the Second Henry. Over the monument, the warrior is on horseback in full armor. I should much like to have an engraving of this tomb. A fine staircase leads to the ancient library. In the altar of the Lady Chapel is a grand picture, " The Adoration of the Shepherds," by Philip de Champagne. The exterior of this edifice is grandeur itself. The west façade was built by Cardinal Amboise. The spire was burned in 1822; but a cast-iron open-work pyramid now takes its place, composed of two thousand five hundred and forty pieces, and put together by twelve thousand eight hundred and seventy-nine iron pins; its elevation four hundred and thirty-six feet, and its weight one million two hundred thousand pounds.

We now went to the Abbey of Saint Ouen, the oldest church in Normandy. It was founded in 533, in the days of Clothaire I. The Normans landed in 841, and burned it; but Rollo, on becoming a Christian, rebuilt it. It was built and rebuilt; but, in 1236, ten years after its completion, the work of eighty years was destroyed by fire. Again was it burned in 1248. Early in the fourteenth century *this* edifice was commenced, and was finished early in the sixteenth. I was again awe-struck with this western rose-window, of which Dibdin said such beautiful things, declaring this church "could hardly have a rival, and certainly not a superior." Here are one hundred and twenty-five windows, and the dimensions about the same as the cathedral. I really felt grateful to the workmen who are so carefully repairing this exquisite piece of architecture. I must say no more of this precious pile, but away to other objects; only observing that I saw the ruins of noble churches now used as warehouses and factories.

Rouen reminds me of Chester; but it looks more ancient, far, than that city. We hurried to the markets, and found everything exposed for sale that can be imagined. As we walked along, we could not help paying attention to the strongly-built Norman Horse, which looks like the embodiment of endurance. We now went to the Palace of Justice, built 1499. A more beautiful bit of architecture cannot be found in France. The roof has no pillar of support. This edifice is one side of a square, and is adorned with all that the architecture of the age understood of delicacy and splendor. The angular pillars of the piers are covered with canopied statues and miniature steeples; numerous ornaments surround the windows, a leaden balustrade surmounts the roof, and an elegant octangular turret occupies the middle of the façade. Hence a massive flight of stone steps leads to the Salle des Procureurs. The Palace of Justice is almost as beautiful as the Hotel de Ville, at Brussels.

We were all anxious to find our way to the Place de la Pucelle, where Joan of Arc was burned, in 1431, in accordance with the superstition of that age. How little is popular opinion worth! One generation says, Crucify! — the next says, Hosanna! This girl was burned for a heretic, and is now well-nigh worshipped for a saint. Here, turning from the spot, we found a house regarded as one of the oldest in Rouen. At the left-hand entrance the wall is covered with bas-relief figures, representing Henry VIII. and Francis I. going to the Champ de Drap d'Or. Here, in this very hall and entry, walked the gay and jovial monarch Francis I., and in this gateway sounded his bugles. The work on these walls is very elaborate, and every portion of the relievo ought to be engraved. Prevort, who has published a memoir on this building, called " The Hotel du Bourgtheroulde," fixes its date at 1486.

The roofs of the houses are covered with wood, in various tile-shapes. I stopped at several shops, to admire the cabinet furniture. The wood is chiefly black walnut, and several articles were of great beauty of finish.

The ladies were mostly bent on seeing sights, at a rate which some of us thought beyond the bounds of moderation; and Mrs. T—— and I quietly retraced our steps, and found the comfort of a good dinner no mean restorative of wearied nature. I got, in Rouen, some glimpses of the neighboring heights, which satisfied me that from their summits a prospect of the valley of the Seine, with the antique towers of this incomparable old city, would amply repay the wayfarer who should ascend them. On the stone bridge is a statue of Corneille, who was born here.

Our route to Havre, by rail, was in the dark, and we saw little, of course. On reaching Havre, we found the operation of coaling going on; and a sad, dirty affair it is, especially in wet weather. We passed the Sabbath day here, and attended service at the English church, where we heard a rather dull sermon. The American Sailors' Chapel was not open that Sunday, owing to the absence of the chaplain. At this port we met with the Humboldt steam-ship, and had much pleasure in welcoming her commander, Captain Lyndes, on board the yacht. He is a fine specimen of the American seaman. Captain Eldridge and his friend Lyndes had a good time; they are men made for each other.

While the North Star lay at Havre, she was visited by thousands of persons, many of whom came from Paris and other cities. Among other distinguished visitors was the Minister at War. We were under many obligations to Mr. Vesey and Mr. Smith, for kind attentions; and, on Monday, July 25, we steamed off for the Mediterranean, amid the cheering of a large crowd gathered upon the docks.

CHAPTER XIV.

VOYAGE RESUMED — BAY OF BISCAY — VIGO BAY — LOSS OF ROBERT OGDEN FLINT — ROCK OF LISBON — CAPE .ST. VINCENT — TRAFALGAR — TARIFA — COAST OF AFRICA — ROCK OF GIBRALTAR — MALAGA — QUARANTINE — WATERING — VISITORS FROM SHORE — FUNERAL SERMON — CATHEDRAL — BEGGARS IN THE STREETS — A PRETTY BOY AND A STRONG RESEMBLANCE — JOSE CUBERO — PRIEST WITH BELL AND BOX — BULL RING — REV. CHARLES BRERETON — BISHOP OF BARCELONA — CALECHES AND DRIVERS — RIDE TO MR. DELIUS' VILLA AND VINEYARDS — ALAMEDA — MULETEERS — MR. CONSUL SMITH — HARBOR OF MALAGA.

MONDAY *July* 25. — On a bright cheerful day we left the dock gates, at noon, sailing to make Cape Barfleur, La Hogue, Casket lights, Isle of Ushant light, — having passed the channel islands to our left. The swell from the westward was heavy, and the ship's motion grew uneasy, and we soon realized the truth of the character usually ascribed to the Bay of Biscay; it was a disagreeable pitch —

> "All the day,
> As we lay
> In the Bay of Biscay, O!"

but we were spared from appropriating to our own experience the entire song of old Andrew Cherry. We now made Cape Finisterre, on the morning of the 28th, with a clear balmy sky, and moderate breeze from the north-west. We ran down the bold coast of Spain, and skirted it closely, so as to obtain fine views of its prominent points. Cigars were again in brisk demand, and the temperature was as fine as we could desire. Our distance from shore was from five to eight miles; we looked into Vigo Bay, and, with our glasses, had a distinct view of

Camina, the boundary town between Spain and Portugal, and here we saw an English homeward-bound steamship.

On the morning of the 29th, at about half-past five o'clock, I heard an unusual noise on deck, and the cry of "man overboard." I hurried up, and found Mr. Cope and three of the sailors getting down the boat, and just got a glimpse of a poor fellow, with his hands up, astern. I was, with others, busy in throwing over the life-preserving stools, before I asked who the man was. I was grieved to learn that it was Mr. Flint, one of our quartermasters. The boat was off, our steamer stopped, and a search of an hour made, but in vain; the ocean was calm, but our poor shipmate was unable to swim, and he probably went down almost without a struggle. As we had been going fast, we were far from him instantly, and the chances were small to recover one who had no power to sustain himself. He was on the quarter deck when the men were shifting the main-sheet, and a flap from it struck him off as he stood at the extreme edge of the stern, outside the netting. With heavy hearts we watched the boat slowly return from the unsuccessful search, and we left Robert Ogden Flint to rest in his ocean grave till the sea shall give up its treasures. All was done by Captain Eldridge and Mr. Cope that was possible. The sad event took place in N. lat. 39, 55, and 9, 43 W. long. This was our only gloomy day since leaving New York. Mr. Flint was a young man of respectable connections; his father was an eminent physician in Massachusetts, and his brother, Dr. Flint, of Buffalo, one of the most scientific practitioners in our country. Our young friend was fond of his profession, and we had often spoken of him as affording high promise; he was only twenty years of age, had just been promoted at Havre to the rank of quarter-master; highly intelligent and affable, he had made himself a favorite with all our party. Our hearts ached for his widowed mother, and we offered sincere prayers that God, the widow's God and husband, would comfort her in her sore bereavement. At a subsequent period, a gentleman started a subscription paper, which was filled up by the officers, crew, and the members of the party, to place a suitable monument to the memory of Mr. Flint, in the Greenwood cemetery; and, as I am writing, I learn that a granite one is in course of erection.

Coasting south, we came to the Farilhoens, and steered close to the Burlings isles and light, which lie a little off the shore. These islands are high, rugged-looking rocks, and they made quite an appearance from our deck. The Farilhoens have near them a cluster of islets, called the Estellas. Our course was then direct for Cape Roca, or the Rock of Lisbon; to this we came very close at twelve o'clock. Behind the rock I observed that the land rose to a great elevation, with many ridges. On the northern slope of this range stands the town of Cintra. We longed to visit this fine city, — visit the beautiful Cintra; and still more I desired to meet with a friend whose society on a former voyage had made much of the pleasure I experienced in crossing the ocean. This was the Honorable Mr. Haddock, who represented the United States at the court of Portugal. To be so near him and his charming family, and yet not see him, was a mortification. We made direct for Cape St. Vincent, — remembering Jarvis and Nelson in 1797, — and passed so close as to have a capital view of this remarkable headland, on the summit of which stands a venerable-looking convent, with several towers. What a look-out the old monks must have had over the Atlantic waves! And though to-day it was bliss to breathe the clear, warm element of life, and all around was calm as a summer evening, yet I fancy that Cape St. Vincent is familiar with other phases of ocean wave. The cape is very precipitous, and off to the north it presents some broken rocks, which stand up like the Needles. Off this cape we passed five steamers. We pursued our course to the straits, passing by Cadiz, into which we had a pleasant peep, and then on over Trafalgar Bay, where the subject of conversation was chiefly upon Nelson and his victory. I could not forget that in these same waters another of Britain's great and gifted sons had found his last resting-place. It was off Trafalgar that Sir David Wilkie was buried, from the Oriental steamship, in 1842. We were off the cape July 30th, at twelve o'clock. The elevation of this famous spot is not considerable, and on one of its corners stands a round tower. This is the north-western point of the entrance to the straits, and we now shaped a line to Tarifa, a very old and fine-looking place, settled by the Moors, and called after a Berber chief. It has long since lost the importance which it once possessed. The town looked venerable and picturesque, but small for a population of more than ten thousand. In 1812 it was possessed by the English, and was besieged by Marshal Victor, who was compelled to retreat. The light-house stands on an island rock, and on this is the chief fortress of the town. This is the most southerly point of Europe. All around us were ships of various descriptions, making for the Mediterranean, with a fine westerly breeze. Our awning was now desirable, as the sun was very powerful; and under its shade we greatly enjoyed the prospect, as we gazed upon the African coast from Cape Spartel down to Ceuta. The shore is grand and rugged, and is very high, elevated in some places to about three thousand feet. But every eye is turned to the north-east, and many voices exclaimed, "There's the Rock!"

Never was I more enchanted with the sight of any spot than that of Gibraltar. This was the accomplishment of a day-dream of early life; and now here I was, under a class of advantageous circumstances such as I could never have anticipated, and few men can possibly enjoy. The straits are nearly twelve miles wide, and the prospect on either coast is clearly defined. There we were now off Gibraltar; we slowly passed, and every opera-glass was in requisition. We did not propose to stop till our return; and now only looked at the crouching lion, of which it has been said that the rock is a striking resemblance. "His fore head, high and massive, rests upon the fore-paws, doggedly overlooking the low beach, which, *Nahant-like*, connects it with Spain; and the bristling mane and back are the rock outline against the sky. The formidable monster is three miles long from the forehead and nose to the tip of the tail, and of the exact proportions in height and breadth of a well-shaped lion. Against his left ribs are a brood of houses, which nestle under his protection, and are washed by the waves of the bay." This very graphic description is taken from "The Shores of the Mediterranean," a work written by the Hon. Francis Schroeder, our present Chargé d'Affaires at Sweden, and published by the Harpers in 1846. Of these volumes I would say that I read them with pleasure, on their issue from the press, and very carefully consulted them whilst coasting through the sea; and I am so satisfied of their accuracy, and impressed with the great beauty of their free sketches of scenery, that I would earnestly advise no traveller to go through the Mediterranean without them; and all persons who desire to have an acquaintance with these enchanting shores, and cannot go abroad, to study them carefully. I regard Mr. Schroeder's work as the best guide-book extant; and I am sure that the wayfarer who may use these volumes will often thank their author for much enjoyment.

The African coast attracted me, with its lofty Abyla, on whose summit was a fleecy cloud; far away was the range of the Atlas Mountains. Abyla was the African pillar of Hercules, and Calpè the European one. At eight o'clock we were beyond the rock, and in this latitude there is no northern twilight, but

"As sets the sun on Afric's shore,
One instant — all is night."

We lay our course off for Malaga, and the night was thick and murky, but at day-light, on Sunday, July 31st, we were in its charming bay.

As soon as we had anchored, our party were on deck, and I never saw persons more charmed than we all were with the splendid panorama which lay before us. The town is built on a circular bay; — it is on a gentle hill, and all around is a background of lofty and romantic mountains. Directly in front of us was the cathedral, a very large and imposing edifice; off to its left a ravine, between the mountains, and a plain, on which a large part of the city is built, and through which runs a small river. Off further left, are vast manufactories and lofty chimneys, which make a fine show against a blue and cloudless sky; and away to the right of the cathedral is a picturesque Moorish castle, and immense fortifications, with zig-zag roads up to them, that, as we look up at them from the deck of our yacht, seem impracticable for anything but goats or mules. The city is very fine looking, a great deal of white and green. We are pretty close in, — and what a noise and clatter! A Spanish lad, who belongs to our ship, is a native of Malaga, and he tells me that it comes from the market, which is now just opened, and hundreds are praising their fish, flesh and flowl; and he says the noise will increase till nine or ten o'clock, — and we found it so. Now the health-officer came off, and found that we came from France, which receives ships from parts of Europe where cholera exists; so we are to perform two days' quarantine. Well, be it so, — with such a sky, such a temperature, such a prospect, I never could be better off. And there came a boat full of good things, vegetables of all sorts, but, best of all, grapes; the grapes of Muscat, the Frontinac and Sweet Water. We all felt acquiescent, and unanimously voted that quarantine was not so bad a thing as we had heard it alleged to be.

But I suspect that, after all, quarantine is not always seen from the deck of a steam yacht, by men sitting under a spacious canopy, and surrounded by every luxury. Our consul, Mr. Smith, came off, and from his boat held a friendly chat, and we made arrangements for our supply of water.

This had to be brought us in hogsheads by boats, and then they were hoisted into the yacht; and on their return to the boat, it was amusing to see the farcical purification to which they were subjected before they were again deposited. Each hogshead was abundantly aspersed and besprinkled with salt-water. Nothing but money escaped, and that seemed to be regarded as the root or cause of no evil. We received an assurance from the town authorities that at twelve o'clock on Tuesday our imprisonment should terminate. And, as soon as the hour arrived, the bay was crowded with boats and feluccas, and we had visitors in shoals; and some of them were really not likely soon to be forgotten. We had on board our ship that day some of the prettiest girls I ever saw; and the older ladies, too, had eyes of wondrous power. The Spaniards were in ecstasies with the ship, and I think hundreds that day enjoyed the visit. The governor and his staff honored us with their company. Our great object in submitting to quarantine was to obtain a clean bill-of-health for the Mediterranean ports. The thermometer was at eighty-five, as we sat looking from our awning over the bay of about fifteen miles' extent.

On the Sabbath-day we observed our service at eleven o'clock, and I preached a funeral-sermon for our lost friend, Mr. Flint, from Jeremiah 12 : 5 — " What wilt thou do, in the swellings of Jordan ? "

In the absence of our visitors, we took our boats and landed in Malaga — most of us for the first time touching Spanish ground. Our first attention was directed to the cathedral, which we had looked at for two days. This stupendous temple was begun by Philip II. in 1538, and only finished in 1719. The style is not good; it wants unity. It is intended for Grecian, and has a bold façade between two dwarf towers. The interior is very rich, and yet not in keeping. The choir has good carved work, and the roof is richly adorned with oak and chestnut carvings. The pulpit is very fine, of reddish marble. I noticed several pictures, but the light was bad. A Madonna struck me as good. The choristers were preparing for vespers, and a dirty-looking set of children they were. I observed one boy who had six fingers and a thumb on his left hand. Leaving the church, we were surrounded by a crowd of children, half-grown men and women, and several old crones. I think our body-guard numbered from twenty to thirty, and they stuck close to us; and, as we were some sixteen or eighteen, we made quite an array passing through the narrow streets of Malaga, many of which were not more than ten feet wide. If we entered a shop, they guarded the doors, and as we came out they smiled and took up their march. Some of the boys were, though poorly clad, of exquisite beauty. One, about thirteen, was as fine a faced boy as is often seen. Murillo would have made a picture of the chap. I see him now, all radiant with smiles. He attached himself to our party closely, and greatly pleased Mrs. ———, who imagined that his glorious black eyes strongly resembled those of her dear absent boy of the same age, whom she had left at home. Again and again did she speak of the strong resemblance, and called my attention to the fact. Presently her kind feelings, which were strongly enlisted towards the lad, led her to ask her husband to give him a quarter-dollar, which he received with sunny smiles, and then deposited in his mouth for safe-keeping. Again the lady exclaimed, " O, how much he resembles my dear ———!" There he was at her side trotting along and looking up in her face, when suddenly he unbuttoned his ragged pants, pulled out the tail of his shirt, whipped the coin from his mouth, tied it up in the corner of the nether garment, and went on readjusting his dilapidated trousers. I could not help asking Mrs. ———, "Now is he not the very picture of your boy?" We visited the celebrated Jose Cubero, who is the maker of the Malaga terra-cotta images of the Spanish characters in national costume. These images are admirably painted. We purchased several, but they are expensive here, and in England and America are very costly. We were accosted by a priest, who rang a bell and held a small box in his hand for alms. On asking what the objects of his solicitation were, we were informed that a murderer was to be garrotted the next day, and the good padre was taking up alms to pay for his funeral masses. Such is Popery in Spain. They can "pray a soul out of purgatory;" but even this poor murderer must bring fish to the priest's net.

We now went to the bull-ring, an immense amphitheatre, capable of holding ten thousand persons. We were taken into the apartments where the animals are kept. Saw one in his prison-house, — the implements of torture, the saddles, &c. A great bull-fight came off a week before our arrival. We visited the Church of the Martyrs, a fine building, but had no time to examine its interior as I could have wished. We were sadly fatigued with a heat perfectly tropical.

Among our visitors from this town was the Rev. Charles Brereton, the English chaplain, and his family; with him I had a pleasant interview; and, on landing, I found he had kindly sent his secretary to render me any aid in making my way. Mr. Brereton preaches regularly at the house of the English consul, Mr. Marks, who was now absent. But his excellent mother, a fine old lady, whose husband established divine service in his consulship, came on board. From the chaplain I learn that about one hundred English Protestants reside here, and eight hundred and fifty British sailors come into port during the three months of vintage; and then there are many American seamen and visitors. About three hundred British travellers visit Malaga every year. Mr. Brereton and Mr. Marks have succeeded in getting a beautiful cemetery for the use of Protestants, and the way in which it is planted and adorned is an honor to them and all who have aided them. A more befitting spot for the worn-out pilgrim at the end of life's journey I have seldom seen. This was the first burial-place granted to Protestants in Spain. Now an effort has been made to secure one in Madrid; but the Bishop of Barcelona has fiercely denounced the measure, and he is unwilling to allow religious rites at the grave.

Amongst other pleasant things, this Catholic bishop says, "The desired of the nations, God, and true man, conversed with men, and formed his church. He placed in it as his vicar the most high Pontiff, centre of unity, rector, doctor and universal master. Whoever is not with him is not in the church; and whoever has not the church for mother has not God for Father. Without necessity of prolix explanations, what is a Protestant? An unfortunate, a bastard, without father or mother, and consequently without God.

I hope, if any Americans visit Malaga, they will call on Mr. Brereton, who seems imbued with the spirit of his office, and is a liberal, Christian man. He resides here on account of his health, and speaks loudly in praise of the climate. I think a winter here must be pleasant for the invalid. Having received in the morning an invitation to visit the vineyard of a wealthy Spanish gentleman, we took carriages and drove some three miles into the country. The vehicles hired were caleches, and held four persons. Besides several of these, we had a gig that held two, and the driver sat on the side. O, how much of amusement would that procession have created in Broadway! I did not imagine that such carriages and such drivers could be obtained in such a city as Malaga. The man who drove one caleche positively resembled a baboon. He might have been an importation from Abyla, the ape's mountain. His face was the most shrivelled-up affair I ever saw,— of a tawny-red color, with an awful grin,— whilst his arms and legs were in perpetual spasmodic motion. The harnesses were exceedingly rude. The head-stalls run down to an iron nose-piece, of semi-circular form, a half-inch wide, strapped over the nose, and having in it two rings; from the outside one of which a rein passes to the driver, and from the inside one of which a rein is attached to the corresponding ring of the mate in a double team. This nose-piece answers the purpose of a bit. The team is guided by single reins. Through the pole, about a foot from its outer end, is an iron pin projecting its extremities some four or five inches; outside this pin is a layer of three or four strands of half-inch rope, folded around and then twisted together so as to bring it snugly against the backing-pin, and thence separated to run through supports on the collar, and thence to large rings in the breeching, which is of leather, and three inches wide.

Our ride out of the city was very pleasant, but we were jolted over the worst road I ever travelled; leaving Welsh ones with a character of comparative goodness. We passed an acqueduct, and here for the first time saw the prickly-pear in its gigantic form, making an impenetrable boundary-hedge. It was now covered with its yellow fruit, which we did not think as palatable as did the urchins of Malaga, who were munching it at every corner. We now realized that we were in a tropical climate, for on every side we saw the agave, or American aloe, and in several instances had the gratification of looking at its towering, spear-like blossom. A ride of about three or four miles brought us to the charming habitation of Edward Delius, Esq., a merchant of Malaga. The name of this estate is, I think, Teutinos. The house is an elegant summer residence, and the grounds were laid out in much taste immediately around it. I perfectly revelled in the show of geraniums, myrtles, ranunculuses and oleanders. At every turn we took in these grounds we met with orange and lemon trees in full blossom, and the fig in several varieties. The vineyard occupies about fifty acres; and here we found the delicious muscatel just ripening, and picked its noble clusters from the scrubby vines. The prospect from these gardens of the city is very fine; and, as the cathedral loomed up in the evening sky, and beyond it were the blue waters of the Mediterranean, and the dark Moorish castle and its battlements frowning over all around, we thought that we could spend more time with our kind host very agreeably; but we were obliged to take leave. In walking to our carriage, I observed that Mr. Delius had some Durham cattle on his place, and they looked in good condition.

On our return, we rode through the Alameda, which is well shaded by fine trees, and under which the pretty women were using their fans most bewitchingly. This spot is adorned with statuary and fountains. We walked through the Zacatin, a sort of bazaar. It has some good shops, and the buildings are supported by columns. We resumed our carriages and drove round the mole, and had a fine view of the vast Moorish castles, Gibralfaro, and the ruins of Alcazaba, which crown the overhanging mountain. The soldiers were just marching up the zig-zag road to relieve guard for the night. The costume of the muleteers, who come into town with mules and asses, and are numerous, is very picturesque. The gay handkerchiefs, and richly-buttoned jackets, and heavy leather leggings, make quite a figure; and Jose Cubero has immortalized them in his capital statuettes. I am sure we all felt indebted to the friendly attentions of Mr. Consul Smith; and it was with reluctance that we were obliged to decline the friendly proposals for our more public entertainment the next day. At about eight o'clock we mustered our party, and, shaking hands with our kind Malaga friends, rowed off to the North Star.

No place have I ever seen to which the approach is more impressive. The back-ground of mountains is superb, and the outline of the city at the water-edge is very pleasant. No winter is experienced at this place, and the air is balmy. We all thought that we had never breathed so freely as whilst anchored in this charming harbor; and I really think our sympathies with those who suffer from quarantine will always be abated, in consequence of our delightful recollections of the days of our embargo off Malaga. This harbor can receive four hundred merchantmen and twenty ships-of-the-line, and is accessible in all winds, and affords complete shelter to shipping.

CHAPTER XV.

OFF FOR LEGHORN — CARTHAGENA — IVICA — MAJORCA — MINORCA — CORSICA — SCENERY — GORGONA — LEGHORN — HOTEL ST. MARCO — FREE PORT — OPERA — SCOTCH FREE CHURCH — SERVICE ON SABBATH — STREETS ADMIRABLY PAVED — EVENING SERVICE — THE PARSONAGE-HOUSE — GOSPEL IN ITALY.

AUGUST 2. — At half-past nine P. M., we steamed off for Leghorn; standing out from the light about five miles, and making a direct course for Cape de Gat, and running in very close to the Spanish coast. Wednesday, the 3d, we had fine views of the grand and mountainous shores; which, however, under a scorching August sun, looked brown and barren enough. Rounding Cape de Gat, we made for Carthagena, the new Carthage of the Romans. We were off this place in the afternoon. It lies in a deep basin, and is well sheltered, having one of the best harbors of the Mediterranean Sea. We longed to enter, but were obliged to content ourselves with a sight. The population is about thirty thousand. This evening, we saw fifty-three sail at once from our deck, and met two British steamers. Our lightest clothing now came into requisition. We next passed Cape Palos in full sight, with its square tower, and then bore away for the north coast of Ivica, distant about seven miles. All along its shores we observed watch-towers on the chief headlands, and passed a rock which resembled a venerable cathedral. We now bore away for Majorca, and coasted it at a distance of about five miles, having a fine view of its grand shores. The scenery is very romantic; and, from the Drogonera Island light to Cape Formenton, the voyage was one of exquisite enjoyment. The sea was of glassy smoothness, and off to our right one long succession of ever-changing beauty for about fifty miles. The hills are some of them most tastefully formed, their peaks lancet-shaped, and the summits of many are tipped with snow. The slopes of these mountain ranges, which appear to be volcanic, are luxuriant vineyards, and inland the island is very productive; its exports are grapes and oranges. In the evening, late, we passed off Minorca, and saw its lighthouse, on the north-eastern coast. The wind rose during the night, and the 5th was a rough day, the sea quartering upon us, and raking from the Gulf of Lyons. During the night, the ship rolled. In the early morning, we were off the coast of Corsica, made Cape Ridellata, and crossed the Gulf of Fiozenzo. The sun rose gloriously behind the mountains. We then passed Giraglia revolving light, and on close to the small island of Gorgona, so famous for its anchovies. We now made direct line for Leghorn, and anchored in its harbor August 6th, at two P. M.

The appearance of this city is fine from the water, and its fortifications and grand Lazaretto give it a very imposing aspect. We were boarded by a health officer, and ordered on shore, where we soon had our passports put in order, and were allowed to land, Mr. Binda, our consul, becoming our security.

Here are two large basins, which are shut up at night by a chain and boom, and the entrance is strongly guarded by important fortresses. The mole extends almost a mile seaward, is a favorite promenade, and, running out parallel with the sea, forms the harbor. The lighthouse stands upon a rock, and is a pretty feature in the view of the town. We went immediately to the St. Marco Hotel, kept by Mr. Smith, an Englishman. We found this a very well-conducted establishment, with spacious rooms, and an excellent table. The walls are covered with pictures, and some are quite good ones. After dinner, we walked out, made a few purchases, and found all articles of clothing as cheap as we could desire. This is a free port, and the stores

VIEW OF LEGHORN.

are admirably supplied with English and French goods. We went to a café, and, after having partaken of some capital cream and water ices, were surprised at finding how trifling the charge was made for them. Some members of the party attended the opera, and the performance was Semiramis. They returned much pleased, and reported the soprano, contralto, barytone and bass voices, as very superior, and the choral and orchestral performers more efficient than they had found in London or Paris. The house, they said, was elegantly fitted up, and they judged the audience was about two thousand. There are five rows of boxes — in all, one hundred and thirty-six; the Grand Ducal one elegantly furnished. The box-fronts are painted in illustration of Greek and Roman history. The drop-curtain bears a fine representation of Cæsar's triumphant entry into Rome.

The Sabbath day, Aug. 7, was a delightful day. At our breakfast we had a fine supply of figs and peaches. After breakfast several of our party took the railroad for Florence. I remained to pass the day in Leghorn, and inquired my way to the Scotch Free Church. I was delighted to find so good a building. It is one of the neatest chapels that I ever worshipped in. It is a model church, for its size, and will accommodate, I should think, about three hundred persons. Elegance and taste are apparent in every arrangement; and, though destitute of any gaudy ornaments; it is rich and noble in appearance, and would do no discredit to a palace, for a monarch's private chapel. I heard a capital sermon, — really an eloquent one, — from a gentleman who is supplying Dr. Stuart's pulpit during his visit to Scotland for the benefit of his health. After service, I went into the vestry and library, and spoke to the clergyman. He warmly pressed me to take the evening service, and this, too, was urged by Mr. Henderson, a leading member of the church; and, on my consenting, we were invited to take tea in the evening after sermon. I found a noble library belonging to Dr. Stuart and a capital library for parish use.

Leghorn is a well-built city, and the best paved one that I ever saw. The streets are wide, paved with granite blocks about three feet long, fifteen inches wide and six inches in depth; they are very solid and even, and are laid in cement, the surface being chiselled to accommodate horses. The streets were really crowded all day; the people well dressed, and having a happy, contented air. In the evening, I noticed that the opera was open. After preaching at the Scotch kirk, we followed the Rev. Mr. Cicely and Mr. Henderson, the banker, into the parsonage, which is under the same roof as the chapel. At the tea-table we met a very learned Swiss clergyman, the Rev. Dr. Schaffter, who has travelled much in the East, declined several professors' chairs in Prussia, and is now expecting to labor as a missionary in Canada. Mrs. Choules presided at the tea-table, and we had a long session, dawdling, as Dr. Johnson called it, over our cups of tea. Mr. Cicely showed us over the spacious manse, which is by far the handsomest parsonage I have seen. The rooms are large, the ceilings lofty, and every part of the house commodious. The drawing-room is very elegant, with inlaid floor; and all the stairways are wide, and of the finest workmanship.

I would not omit to say that a small but interesting Sabbath-school is in connection with this place of worship. It is pleasant to know that pure evangelical truth is here proclaimed, even amid the black darkness of Popery; and I was glad of an opportunity to preach the gospel in Italy, and there to join in prayer with God's people, that He would soon overturn the Man of Sin, who, impiously placing himself in the seat of the Almighty, lays claim to infallibility. But God declares that he will not give his glory to another; and Popery, by this fatal assumption of a divine attribute, has tied around her neck the apocalyptic millstone, which is at last to sink her to the bottomless abyss. Mr. Henderson is a Scotch gentleman, who has long resided here; he is an eminent merchant and banker, and has a mercantile house in Liverpool and Canada. He sent the first export of marble to New York, and a small quantity overstocked the market. Now every ship from Leghorn carries out vast quantities of marble from the quarries of Carrara. I was delighted with the general character of this excellent man, and much regretted my inability to visit him at his villa in the country. Mr. Henderson was as kind as possible, and, on our return from Florence, proffered me very friendly letters of credit to his correspondents at Rome and Naples. In the English burying-ground at Leghorn is the grave of Tobias Smollett, the novelist.

CHAPTER XVI.

ARRIVE AT FLORENCE — HOTEL D'ITALIE — RIDE — CITY AND STREETS, ETC. — PITTI PALACE — PICTURES — CANOVA'S VENUS — DUKE'S APARTMENTS — MUSEUM — POWERS AND HART — POWERS' STUDIO AND HIS WORK — HART'S STUDIO — BUSTS OF AMERICANS — STATUE OF HENRY CLAY — UFFIZII GALLERY — STATUARY — TRIBUNE — VENUS DE MEDICI — KNIFE-GRINDER, ETC. — TITIAN'S VENUSES — RAPHAEL'S PICTURES, ETC. — NIOBE — RUBENS — POWELL'S DE SOTO, ETC. — CATHEDRAL — CAMPANILE — BAPTISTERY — SANTO CROCE — CHAPEL OF THE MEDICI — ST. LORENZO — SACRISTY — MICHAEL ANGELO'S DAY AND NIGHT — PALAZZO VECCHIO — DUCAL PIAZZA — STATUARY.

On Monday, we took the rail for Florence, and greatly enjoyed the journey, which lies through a beautiful region, giving proof of careful cultivation. The fields are small, and almost everywhere divided off by elms, mulberry and plum trees; and these trees are gracefully festooned with vines laden with grapes. We found the dépôt at Florence situated in the Cascine, which is the Hyde Park of this city. On our way hither we had frequent and beautiful sights of the Arno, and saw some charming villas perched on the eminences above its waters.

On arrival, we found that Mr. Vanderbilt had politely sent a messenger to conduct us to our quarters, which were provided at the Hotel d'Italie, kept by Signor Baldi; and here Mr. V. and his own family were also established. Our elegant apartments looked out upon the Arno, and upon the iron balcony into which our windows led we passed many pleasant hours watching the fishermen, who stood up in the water breast-high, casting a net, which looked like a balloon, and which they elevated every few minutes. The fish appeared very small, and not as large as smelts. The prospect beyond the river was exceedingly fine; height upon height, and church and convent crowning each eminence, and then giving us glances of the bridges. That balcony will long live in our memories, and I commend the apartments in the rear of the Hotel d'Italie, to all wayfarers.

I always commence a new city by a ride through its streets, that I may have a general comprehension of the "lay of the land." I was at once satisfied, with a rapid survey, that Rogers had not overcharged its character.

This city, which deserves its appellation, *the fair*, is situated in a beautiful valley at the base of the Apennines. It is nearly six miles in circumference, almost oval in its plan, and its population is about one hundred thousand. Many of the streets are narrow, but there are several very fine ones. The squares do not please me as much as those in other cities. The great feature of the city is the picturesque Arno, which, shallow in the summer, becomes a swollen stream in winter, from the rain and snows of the mountains. The palaces are numerous, and very imposing in their appearance. Some are built of massive stones, in a rustic style of architecture. The walls of the city are in good preservation, and two or three of the eight gates are very handsome. The pavement is composed of broad flag-stones, and these, as in Leghorn, are chiselled to save the horses from slipping. All around the city are delightful gardens and fertile meadows. The four bridges which span the Arno are all fine ones; but the bridge of the Trinity is regarded as the most beautiful one in Europe. The old bridge has a covered way, and on each side are jewellers' shops, or stalls. All around the city are hills covered with villas, churches, convents, olive-trees, and vineyards.

Our first visit was made to the Pitti palace, which is the present ducal residence. It was built by Luke Pitti, who intended to rival the Strozzi palace. A reverse of fortunes caused it to pass from him while yet unfinished; and, in 1559, it came into possession of the Medici family.

PITTI PALACE — PICTURES.

Although this palace is heavy in its appearance, owing to the massive rustic style, yet it is a most admirable royal habitation. Every part of the palace is spacious, and adapted to its purpose. I found everything in that order which indicated care and preservation. The entrance is by a corridor and stairway of noble dimensions. The great attraction is the treasure of art which is here to be found, both in sculpture and painting. The arrangement of the apartments deserves praise; and, as in the gallery at the Hermitage, the spectator is provided with sofa, chair and lounge, for his comfort while enjoying this wondrous collection. The pictures at present number nearly five hundred and fifty; and this gallery embraces the treasures of the Medici family, and the two last dukes have lavished vast sums in additions from the churches and monasteries of Tuscany. The apartments take their names usually from the subjects of the gorgeous frescos which adorn the ceilings. Thus the halls of Venus, of Mars, of Saturn, &c., are all adorned with allegorical descriptions of the virtues of the Cosmo family. The pictures which are world-renowned must not be criticized by the ignorant. But I may mention those which pleased me best, and have made a lasting impression upon my mind.

Let me name the portraits first. I regard the Pope Julius II., by Raphael, as the grandest portrait I ever looked upon. The duplicate in the Uffizii is, fine as it is, another thing. I have seen nothing to compare with it but a portrait in St. Petersburg, to which, I think, I have alluded. Next, I liked Vandyke's Cardinal Bentivoglio, which no living painter can equal. Two portraits by Raphael, of a female and her husband, are wonderfully effective. The Leo X., by Raphael, does not strike me so pleasantly. The picture lacks ease, and the grouping of the three figures is constrained. The head of Grotius, by Rubens, is full of energy. A portrait of Philip II., by Titian, is a life-like picture; it is all but living. An old man, by Titian, is a wonderful execution. Some writers call it a Rembrandt.

The Madonna della Seggiola brought us all to stand and admire. I have seen good copies all over the world, but they lose their charm after seeing so much of heavenly beauty and earthly sweetness as this glorious work of Raphael exhibits. After leaving this, I lingered longest over a small picture — Ezekiel's Vision — by Raphael. This is strangely beautiful. God, the Father, appears in celestial glory, surrounded by cherubs, his arms supported by genii, and resting on the ox, lion and eagle. And here, too, is an angel rapt in adoration. Everything is easy, free, and the eye is fastened on the canvas of this remarkable picture. The Fates, by Michael Angelo, is a very striking picture, and pleased me more than it does the critics usually. It is also ascribed to Rosso Fiorentino. Titian's Magdalen is hardly a penitent, but is perfect beauty. Two Marine Views, by Salvator Rosa, are exceedingly fine. A St. Mark, by Fra. Bartolemeo, is a grand effort. The Murder of Abel, by Andrea Schiavone, has a sweet bit of landscape, and is a picture richly deserving of careful study; this is in coloring very like Titian. I dare not omit Guido's Cleopatra, of which I obtained a copy; and also one of the Madonna in the chair on ivory. In a saloon of this palace stands the famous Venus of Canova. I have rarely ever had my expectations so raised as in reference to this sculpture. I was entirely disappointed, although Canova was the artist, and his statue is renowned. The attitude is forced, unnatural, and next to impossible. The head cannot be turned off at such an angle without doing a violence to the mastoid muscle, which precludes the idea of ease and comfort. No being can direct the head as the Venus does, without producing a distortion of the muscle. That which is not natural cannot be beautiful. The finish is fine, but everything is over-done, too labored, and that evidently. The private rooms of the palace were shown us, and they are very magnificent. The floors are richly inlaid, and the ceilings exquisitely frescoed. The apartments are filled with tables of the costliest character, and the doors are many of them of exquisite workmanship and design.

From this place we repaired to the museum. This is eminently adapted to the use of medical students, as some fifteen or twenty rooms are filled with wax preparations, illustrative of anatomy and morbid appearances of the human system, and several rooms are devoted to natural history. The representations of the human body are entirely life-like, and the descriptions of the progress of the plague upon the patient are terrifically minute. The plague desolated Florence in 1348, and more than forty-five thousand fell as victims.

Mr. Vanderbilt's family having pressed him to favor them by sitting to our honored countryman, Mr. Powers, he called at his studio, and made arrangements for a bust; and at the same time Mrs. Vanderbilt was requested by her sons-in-law to sit to Mr. Hart.

Our visits were frequent to the studios, and we had much pleasure in examining the charming productions of the chisels of our distinguished countrymen. I couple these gentlemen together, because, though Powers is the sculptor of the world, and is the foremost artist of the age, still Mr. Hart has distinguished genius, and, with the opportunities now afforded him to make his countrymen know him, will soon obtain their highest plaudits. Powers is a glorious, noble creature; he is a man to look upon, and his eye is the finest that I know of, since death closed those orbs of light around whose flashes was sometimes thrown a terrible darkness, — eyes which this great artist will soon attempt to place forever in his country's gaze. On every side Powers has forms of beauty; but I am jealous of the labors of such a man, when appropriated by individuals; he should work only for cities, states and the Union. Talents like those granted to Powers should be devoted to the adornment of our national buildings, our halls of science, our great squares. I regard Powers as a true object of American pride. If he died to-morrow, his fellow-citizens all over the Union would lament his loss; every newspaper would exult in recapitulating the wonderful works of his genius; but how few of these would be found on the high places of his country, to incite and stimulate the talent of the American youth! Some female heads in his studio are very beautiful, and I was much struck with an exquisite bust just completed of Mrs. Penniman, of New York. His heads of the great men were very noble representations; but I was far less pleased with that of Webster than with many of the others. Those of Calhoun, Cass, Everett, Winthrop, are all that can be asked; but Webster is not sufficiently massive. I doubt not that the great work just placed in Mr. Powers' hands will be his *chef-d'œuvre*, for he will make it, I know, a work of love. It is certain, when he has seen the latest representations of the great statesman, that he will send to Massachusetts a statue worthy to be placed near to Chantrey's favorite one of Washington.

In Mr. Hart's studio, which is elegant and spacious, I was delighted with his heads of Wickliffe, Cass and Crittenden. Governor Crittenden's bust is, I think, as perfect a realization of the man and his character as was ever chiselled out of marble. I could almost say to it, "Now utter words of wisdom, — or a joke." It does all but speak. The great work on which Mr. Hart is employed is a statue of Mr. Clay, for the ladies of Virginia. The cast is completed, and is the only likeness of the great man that ever quite satisfied my eye. Nearly every bust and picture is a likeness, ay, and unmistakable; but generally there is a coarseness which did not belong to the orator. Here the likeness is perfect, and yet the air and spirit is gentlemanly; the attitude cannot be improved. We all felt that we were only admiring the first appearance of a work of genius which will be sure to become the praise of the whole country. We saw the immense block from which the statue is to be created. How long will it be ere nature's quarry shall again furnish us with other Clays, Calhouns and Websters? At present, in lack of them, we are called to bow down to small lights, and moderate talents, and magnificent pretensions. I saw Hart at work; he, too, is a genius. He works easily; has a large heart, good head, is no pretender, but can, with confidence, point to his labor, and say, "Look at it." I am sure his head of Mrs. Vanderbilt, in four sittings, was as complete a likeness as was ever moulded. Hart is about forty years of age, and his name will soon be one of the honored ones in the heraldry of American art.

Mr. Powers' efforts on Mr. V. we all watched with great interest. The artist was delighted with the head and figure, and he was engaged evidently *con amore;* his subject sat charmed with the originality of his eloquent conversation. If the result was not a perfect representation of a head of rare power and command, I am no judge, and we were all of us mistaken. Long as the marble lasts will that face evince its striking force and power.

I shall never forget the day I entered the Uffizii gallery. It is to every man who makes his first visit a memorable day. The palace was commenced in 1560. It was built by Cosmo I., and is the noblest collection of statuary in Europe, if, perhaps, we except the Vatican. The gallery was organized in 1765. Its two longest sides are five hundred and twenty-five feet long, and thirty-five in breadth. On one side there is a vast number of windows, to afford proper light in the galleries; all these apartments are lofty, and adorned with rich frescos. The statues and busts of the Roman emperors are exceedingly rare and valuable; and here are those of Agrippa, Otho, Caligula and Nerva. A vast many of these busts are indicative of brutal character.

I hurried through this gallery of marble, that at last I might enjoy the desire of my life, and stand in the Tribune. Was I disappointed at my entrance? No; the apartment itself is a fitting home for the rich treasures which it contains. The dome is radiant with mother-of-pearl, which is copiously inlaid, and the pavement is a mosaic of the costliest marbles, in the most tasteful forms. This is the *holy place* of art, and here sculpture and painting nobly contend for the preëminence. And there is Venus: — men may talk and censure long and severely; but, so long as the eye can find charms in beauty, so long will this marble find admirers. It is another thing than Canova's, over in the other palace. The Scythian ordered to flay Marsyus, or, as some call him, the knife-grinder, is a long study. What wondrous knowledge of the frame the sculptor possessed! It is lifelike, and its details are as minute and truthful as are the pictures of Teniers or Ostade. The Appolino is the perfection of grace. The Wrestlers belong to the same class of art as the Knife-grinder or Scythian. The two Venuses, by Titian, are paintings which do more to educate our taste for coloring in an hour, than a month's survey of painted canvas, spread over acres of common galleries. The portrait of Julius II., grand as it is, does not strike me as at all equal to the one in the Pitti palace; both are by Raphael. The Fornarina did not come up to my anticipations, after seeing it engraved. The two Holy Families, and John in the Desert, are holy, heavenly things. What are paintings worth but for *the effects which they produce* on those who see them? What every one feels is nature, is truth. The man who addresses human sympathies, and speaks a language that his fellows comprehend, is beyond the paltry criticisms of the artists of this age.

The Holy Family, of Andrea del Sarto, is as lovely a representation of maternal love as the gallery contains. I differ from many in relation to the Holy Family by Michael Angelo, called harsh, severe, rigid; the wretchedly bad taste in throwing in the back figures has done much to destroy its effect; but the drawing is masterly. A Madonna, by Corregio, adoring the child, is very lovely. A Charles V. on horseback, by Vandyke, is a noble picture. I was greatly pleased with the pictures of the Florentine school. A gallery of portraits of painters is interesting, and here are fine autograph portraits of Raphael, Perugino, Velasquez, Rubens, &c. In this room, I was struck with the Medicean Vase, which represents the sacrifice of Iphigenia; it is very ancient, and came from Greece, but was found at Adrian's villa. The Hall of Niobe presents these wondrous remains of antiquity, — statues supposed to be the work of Praxiteles. The Dying Son is a death-like figure. In this saloon is a picture which I would walk far to see again, — Rubens' Henry IV. at the Battle of Ivry. This is very fine, and the horse is one of almost unsurpassable beauty.

This horse reminds me that I omitted to speak, in my record of Paris, that we were very kindly called upon by Mr. Powell, the distinguished artist, to invite the party to see his great picture ordered by Congress for the last vacant niche in the rotunda of the Capitol. The subject, as is well known, is the scene of De Soto taking possession of the Mississippi country. We were very much delighted with this grand picture; and Mr. Vanderbilt, an admirable judge of a horse, regards the horse on which De Soto sits as the best he ever saw. In the same studio we saw some capital portraits of Lamartine, Hugo, Dumas, and other famous men of the day.

I repaired again and again to these charming rooms, and spent hours of happiness, which will, I hope, prove fruitful of much future pleasure.

My visit to the Cathedral was on a fine morning, when a high mass was in celebration, and about four hundred priests were in full canonicals and parade. Its foundations were laid, 1298, by Arnolfo, and the building was designed to be between the pointed and ancient style. The walls on the outside are covered with colored marbles. Its length is four hundred and fifty-four feet; its elevation from the pavement to the summit of the cross three hundred and eighty-seven feet; the transept three hundred and thirty-four feet long, the nave one hundred and fifty-three feet high, and the aisles ninety-six and a half feet high. When Arnolfo died, in 1300, Giotto became the builder, in 1331. He erected the façade and the campanile, which was his pet work. Up to the sixteenth century it was adorned with the best works of the great masters, especially of Donatello. In 1558, it was almost destroyed, to be rebuilt in modern style. In 1636, another façade was begun, but was abandoned; and now a more miserable-looking, unfinished stone front can hardly be seen; it looks all the worse by a comparison with the splendor of the rest of the edifice. A popular notion exists that churches in Italy are kept in an unfinished state to avoid a tax to the Pope, which never commences until the completion of the edifice. In 1420, Brunelleschi was employed to construct the cupola. This architect studied at Rome, and there projected what before was deemed impossible, namely, to unite the four naves of this great cathedral by throwing over them a spacious cupola. Although opposed by ignorance in high places and the selfishness of his rivals, yet he lived to complete his design, with the exception of some outside work, for which he left plans. This cupola is octagonal, one hundred and thirty-eight feet six inches in diameter, and one hundred and thirty-three feet three inches in height from the cornice of the Duomo. Its greatest praise is that Michael Angelo made it his model when he erected the dome of St. Peter's. This is the largest dome in the world. The exterior view from the south-east is most imposing, and here is seen the dome rising from the surrounding smaller cupolas. The dome is painted by Vassari and Zuccheri; the subjects are prophets, angels, saints, Paradise, and the figures are colossal.

I felt gratified to see the graves of Giotto and Brunelleschi, who sleep in close neighborhood. A David, by Donatello, is very fine; and an unfinished group in the rear of the high altar, of the Entombment of the Saviour's body, by Michael Angelo, is so beautiful as to create regret that it was not completed by the great artist. It was in this duomo that Julian was murdered by the side of his brother, Lorenzo the Magnificent, in 1478. The general aspect of the church is fine and devotional. The Campanile, or tower for the bells, is the work of Giotto, and is a remarkable edifice; with all its altitude, it has but four stories. The architect intended to surmount the tower with a spire, and the piers are visible which were to support the erection. As a matter of course, we looked after Dante's stone, where he was wont to gaze upon the growing wonder of the rising cathedral. Close by are the modern statues of Arnolfo and Brunelleschi.

In front of the Duomo and Campanile stands the Baptistery of St. John. The bronze gates of this building are the chief supports of its fame. They must be wondrously beautiful to have caused Michael Angelo to say that they were fit to be the gates of Paradise! The south gate, designed by Giotto, was completed by Andrea Pisano in 1330, and its erection was celebrated as a festival all through Tuscany. The northern and eastern gates were added in 1400–1422, by Ghiberti. The north gate illustrates the life of Christ, the south the life of John, and the east the events of the Old Testament. The Baptistery is an octagon, supporting a cupola and lantern. The wall was erected by Arnolfo, 1293. Vast figures in mosaic adorn the dome, and the Lucifer of Dante appears in the frescos. All the baptisms of Florence occur here; and several of our party, at various visits, saw the ceremony of christening.

From this place we turned our attention to the Westminster Abbey of this city, — Santa Croce. This was established by monks sent by St. Francis, 1212, and Arnolfo commenced this church 1294. The exterior is as rude as anything can be in architecture, but the interior is grave and majestic. Here are the monuments of Michael Angelo, Dante, Alfieri, by Canova; Machiavelli, Fossombroni, Alberti, Galileo. A series of chapels are well worthy of careful notice, and in one is Bartolini's exquisite monument to a Russian princess.

W had read and heard so much of the gorgeous Chapel of the

Medici, that we fully expected a treat, nor were we at all disappointed, although I do not think it has been marked by good taste. It was intended for the resting-place of the holy sepulchre. This chapel is far from completed. The walls are literally covered up with the richest specimens of marble, lapis-lazuli, jasper, chalcedony and Florentine mosaic, in which all the colors and shadings are natural to the stones employed. All the coats of arms of the Tuscan states and cities are ranged around, in mosaic work. Nothing can be more elegant than the cenotaphs of the Medici family. The bodies are in a crypt beneath this chapel. Seventeen millions of dollars have been expended upon this sepulchral palace!

The church of St. Lorenzo, which dates from 1425, has much that is beautiful; and this cannot fail to be the case where Brunelleschi designed and Donatello adorned a building. The sacristy, or a small chapel, is the great attraction of this church. This small erection was designed by Michael Angelo to receive monuments for Lorenzo de Medici, the grandson of Lorenzo the Magnificent, and Giuliano de Medici, a son of the Magnificent. The monuments to these individuals are in white marble, by Michael Angelo, and are regarded as his undoubted masterpieces. They have a strong characteristic resemblance, and are somewhat enigmatical, as it is hard to tell what Day and Night, Morning and Evening, have to do with these worthies. No satisfactory solution has been afforded; but there is the marble, and there, as long as that marble lasts, will men congregate to admire, and wonder at the near approach of sculpture to language.

The figure of Lorenzo creates awe. He sits in armor, and he chains the eye. Poor, indeed, are most other statues after this has been seen. I do not like the chapel in which they stand; each should have a Gothic sanctuary for its own sole occupation, of which it should be the shrine.

I scarcely ever walked out but I found myself attracted to

the Palazzo Vecchio. This building was erected 1298, and was the dwelling-place of the Gonfaloniere. In 1540, when the republic died, it became the palace of Cosmo I. I know few buildings that can compare with it in dark, awful grandeur. The battlements are massive, and the overhanging machiolations, and the tower springing up from their support, give it an imposing air, such as I have seen nowhere else. All around are wonderful things. There, is an equestrian statue of Cosmo I.; there, a fountain of Neptune. Near this fountain, in the days of the republic, stood the Tribune. Here is the glorious David of Michael Angelo; and there, as a match, is Hercules destroying Cacus, by Bandinelli. The David is far the finest, and belongs to the same class of statuary with the Medicean statues just alluded to in the sacristy. Here are large porticos, which you ascend by steps, and in front a spacious square. On these porticos are some wonderful pieces of artistic excellence. There, at the corner, stands the Perseus of Benevenuto Cellini, the casting of which is so graphically recorded in his life. At the other end, as a match-piece, is the Rape of the Sabines, by John of Bologna. Judith slaying Holofernes, by Donatello, is a pretty bronze, but small. Here are several colossal females, lions, &c.

PALAZZO VECCHIO, FLORENCE

CHAPTER XVII.

SANTA MARIA NOVELLA — PAINTINGS — SPEZIERIA — RESIDENCE OF MICHAEL ANGELO — CHURCH OF THE ANNUNCIATION — THE CASCINE — SCENERY — MOUNTAINS — THE BRIDGES — FRIENDS IN FLORENCE — OLIVER CROMWELL'S PORTRAIT — IMPRESSIONS OF FLORENCE — LEAVE FOR PISA — THE CITY — LEANING TOWER — CATHEDRAL — CAMPO SANTO — THE BAPTISTERY — SANTA MARIA DELLA SPINA — THE CAMELS — LEGHORN — GOVERNMENT ALARMED AT OUR YACHT — VISITORS, ETC.

I MUST not omit a visit which we paid to the church of Santa Maria Novella, belonging to the preaching friars. They made a missionary effort here 1216, and in 1222 had a small church, the ground of which is included within the confines of their noble convent. This is a large establishment, and comprises a church, two cloisters, several quadrangles, refectory, sacristy, chapterhouse, &c. This edifice is a finished one. The grand façade was completed 1470, in the Pisan style. The church was begun 1279. The Campanile is a tower with a spire, which is Romanesque; but the church itself is Gothic, and is adorned with fine stained glass. The fresco of the choir is by Ghirlandio. In the arches of the roof are the four Evangelists, by Strozzi, which were finished 1583. Here, at the altar, is the famous Crucifix, by Brunelleschi. In the Strozzi Chapel are frescos of Orgagna. A very famous picture is in this church by Cimabue. It is a Virgin and Child, on a gold ground. Vasari says it was executed in a garden, and carried to the church in solemn procession, with the sound of trumpets. Several good monuments are to be seen; one of a Saint Villana, canonized in 1824, but whose sanctity is called in question; she is sleeping in death, and two most beautiful angels are looking over her, bearing a scroll on which her epitaph is written. The sacristy is an exquisite room, and has fine windows of painted glass. The cloisters are filled with many works of art. The chapter-house contains a representation of the church militant and triumphant, and is curious enough; and also the triumph of the schoolman, Thomas Aquinas. The monks of this convent, like the shaking quakers, have an eye to profit, and they have long been famous for the preparation of medicines and essences; and a most beautiful establishment they have, called the Spezieria, which is fitted up in more style and elegance than any druggist's store in London or Paris. We were interested in the place and the attendants, who are very polite; they seem to drive a thriving business. We brought away quite a quantity of their precious perfumes.

I felt unwilling to leave Florence without visiting the house in which Michael Angelo lived, and which, I understood, was full of his relics. We made the necessary arrangements for admission, and repaired to the Via Ghibellina in which it stands. It is yet in possession of a descendant of this great man. The entire interior is preserved as in the time of the artist, and no one can doubt it on a survey. Much of the furniture remains as in his day. The apartments open from one to the other, and you meet with a step, down or up, in going from room to room. Here is a small saloon or gallery, the ten large panels of which illustrate the artist's history. They were done by the best painters of the age, and some of them as a work of love. One, Michael Angelo showing his plan of the Library to Leo X., is very striking. Another, in reference to Solyman proposing a bridge at the Dardanelles, is impressive. In one room is his statue, by Novelli, and near it a Holy Family, in oil. It will be remembered that he only painted three easel-pictures. His actual studio we entered with reverence, and all around were the works of his hands, — sketches, bas-reliefs, &c. Here are his brushes, color-jars, and other articles of professional use. In one room we saw his walking-stick, his cup, his slippers, and some finely-preserved letters, — his rosary, his writing-desk, &c. We were shown a crucifix given him by the Pope, containing a vast number of relics, set in small circles covered with glass. I remember here was a bit of the stone which was thrown at Stephen, a bit of the true cross, a stone from the grave of Lazarus, a morsel of the pillar of flagellation, and some twenty other equally precious pieces of papistical gammon. I was much pleased to see here the first marble sculptured by the artist, — a group in quarrel. To walk through the house of a man who was the favorite of seven Popes, who painted the Last Judgment, executed the Moses, and erected the dome of St. Peter's, is an affair that furnishes food for thought, and demands the exercise of one's best affections.

A hasty visit to the Church of the Annunciation showed me that it contained many beauties. The arches spring from columns. Here are many very good paintings; one by Andrea del Sarto, the Wise Men and the Star in the East, is full of beauty. The small chapels are exceedingly costly, and abound in silver. A festival service was going on, and I did not like to injure the feelings of those who were devoutly engaged by any mere curiosity on our part.

The Cascine, at Florence, was too renowned for the beauty of its drives and scenery not to have our attention; and we frequently rode to the Royal Farms, which the name signifies. All that art and wealth can effect by combination has been here effected; and the good Florentines have a place of enjoyment close at hand, on the banks of the Arno, which I think is unsurpassed in Europe, unless the Summer Islands of St. Petersburg furnish the exception. The drives are crowded by the rank and fashion of the city, and the roads are about one mile and a half long, and are double; and between them are plantations, grass-plots, preserves of game. In front of one of the duke's buildings, — I think the dairy, — is the circus, where you find scores of carriages drawn up for rest, and where the afternoon high exchange of fashion is held. I have seldom seen more beautiful equipages than we passed on the Cascine. The views of the villas lying off on the base of the mountains are enchanting. How any one can depreciate this ride and its scenery, I am at a loss to understand. Certainly, till we have any city that can approximate to the convenience and charm of this suburban region, we ought not to undervalue it, though it is not American. I shall ever remember the Cascine, its long range of hills, its sunset hours, and its charming cottages, looking like diamonds set in emeralds. I have been struck with the fertility of all the sides of the hills around. The uprising terraces seem to embody a vast mass of vines. The leaves of the olive-trees, with their delicate light-green, serve to variegate the scenery, and the tree itself is quite ornamental. The summits of the mountains are nearly all crowned with chestnut woods, and everywhere are villages perched upon what appears at a distance an inaccessible spot. The chestnut is a source of great income to the inhabitants of these mountain ranges; the fruit, made into meal, forms the principal food of the peasantry, — and they seem to thrive on it; for a nobler-looking race cannot easily be found. Sismondi speaks of the beauty of the women, and the clearness of their complexion, which probably arises from the simplicity of their fare.

Our last ride in Florence was to the very top of the hill which formed the back-ground of our prospect in the rear of our hotel. We passed through the gates of the city, and drove some three miles up a road which, at every winding, gave us glorious glimpses of the beautiful city. At the summit we came to a convent, and from this point enjoyed the last rays of daylight on the Apennines. These hills reflect the sun's rays most brilliantly, and give a coloring to evening light which I have seen in no other place. From these eminences we had all Florence at our feet. It was one wide scene of grove, garden, pinnacle and tower; and the river winding along through the Val d'Arno, the fertile granary of corn, oil and wine. Go into the city, and there are all the treasures of art, both ancient and modern, —

"The past
Contending with the present."

The bridges are all picturesque, but that of the Trinity, completed in 1569, is exquisitely beautiful. It has three arches, of which the central span is ninety-five feet three inches, and that of the side ones eighty-five feet six inches. The rise of the arch is one-seventh of the span, and the arches are slightly pointed. On this bridge are the statues of the Seasons. The length of the bridge is three hundred and twenty-three feet.

In many little affairs of business I found great service from the politeness of Mr. Goodban, the English bookseller, who has a capital collection of the best engravings. We enjoyed much pleasure in meeting with Mr. and Mrs. White, of New York. Mr. White is pursuing his profession as a painter with enthusiasm, and has many fine works in his studio. In Florence we were happy to meet with Mr. Taylor Root, of New Haven, to whose kindness we were indebted for many attentions.

My last hasty visit was to the Pitti palace, to get another sight of its pictures, and especially to see the famous portrait of Oliver Cromwell, by Sir Peter Lely. The noble old Protector has his likeness in the Tuscan palace; tho. he is not *yet* to be seen in the royal galleries of the land he governed. But England will hereafter give him room, and perhaps place him, as Walter Savage Landor recently suggests, "on a charger" now occupied by "a royal swindler."

I am pleased with this city; it is as orderly as any American town, and the people are well-dressed and happy. I have seen no case of intoxication; and, wherever I have been in a wine country, I have seen the people a sober one. There is nothing wanting to make this country a happy one, and its people a prosperous and contented population, but the existence of civil and religious liberty; and this blessedness will yet be the lot of its inhabitants. The tradesmen of Florence are very civil, and I saw far fewer beggars than in Malaga. The clergy of all sorts, dressed in black, brown, gray and white, are numerous in the streets; and they are decidedly a better-looking class of men than the Irish and French priesthood.

We took the cars for Pisa, leaving our guide Sebastian, whom Mr. Vanderbilt engaged at Leghorn, to take charge of the luggage, and come on in a subsequent train, which we were to join at Pisa, and all go back to Leghorn in company.

The railroad passes through a level country, but in full sight of a lofty range of hills. This plain is ten or twelve miles wide, and covers the interval between the sea and the Monte Nero range, on which the wealthy men of Leghorn reside in summer. Every part of the road indicates good farming and a contented population. On every hand are ruined towers, which tell of other days, and remind us of the civil discords which have marked Italian history.

Pisa is a fine large-looking city, with wide streets, and the houses many of them noble in appearance; but there are very few persons to be seen; and, instead of a population of nearly one hundred and twenty thousand, as it is said once to have had, there are hardly twenty thousand residents at the present time. The Arno runs through the city, and it is crossed by three fine bridges; the central one is of marble. This is the seat of a university with a large faculty, and some of the chairs are filled by men of eminence. The former splendor of the city is still visible in its desolate mansions. The great attraction to travellers is a few famous buildings, which all lie close together, — the cathedral, the Campanile, or, as it is designated more commonly, the Leaning Tower, the Baptistery, and the Campo Santo. In the winter there are many English who reside here on account of the mildness of the climate, which is deemed much more genial than that of Florence.

We first repaired to the Leaning Tower, which contains the seven bells of the Duomo. It is about thirteen feet out of the perpendicular, and, beyond a reasonable doubt, I think, this is owing to the nature of the soil in which the foundation was placed. The tower is round, and built of white marble; and its bright appearance is remarkable when its age is remembered, as it is nearly seven hundred years old. It is one hundred and seventy-eight feet high, and the ascent is by easy steps. It has eight stories, each resting on arches. The prospect from the top is quite enough to repay the labor of the ascent, and the view extends to the Mediterranean, and commands a vast mountain range. The Duomo was commenced 1063. Its architect was Buschetto, a Greek; and Rainaldo, who succeeded him, executed the stately façade, with its five stories; the sides of the church have but three. This building is covered with marbles of various colors; the roof flat, and the interior richly gilt. It is supported by seventy-two columns, most of which are of granite. The cupola is frescoed by Riminaldi; the subject is the Creation. The church is lighted by one hundred painted windows, and here are several gems of beauty in bronze statuary, by John of Bologna. The paintings are very good, and among them some capital works of Andrea del Sarto, whose pictures do not strike me as being so "feeble" as they have been styled. St. Margaret, St. Catherine and St. Agnes, are pretty enough for belles, to say nothing about saints. A Sacrifice of Isaac is a picture of great power, and has much true conception of the father's heart. God Speaking from the Burning Bush is a picture not often equalled. The church is in the form of a Latin cross. It suffered from fire in 1596. The beautiful bronze doors were modelled in 1602, but are inferior to those at Florence, by Ghiberti. One door in the transept escaped the fire, and contains a number of rude reliefs from the history of Christ.

A silver altar in the Chapel of the Annunciation is of great beauty, and is said to have cost thirty-six thousand crowns. In the nave is a bronze lamp of fine workmanship, which suggested to Galileo the idea of the pendulum. A nobler church is seldom entered, and it is kept in admirable order. The pavement is very rich, and composed of marble laid down with great beauty. This church is called Gothic; but is destitute of the leading characteristics of Gothic architecture, as clustered pillars and pointed arches, &c.

I hardly know what to say of the Campo Santo, which is an ancient cemetery, around which are spacious cloisters, but is as much a museum as a Golgotha. It is more than four hundred feet long, and nearly one hundred and fifty feet wide. The cloisters are forty-six feet high, and thirty-four and a half wide. The interior is filled up with earth, brought by a crusading bishop from Mount Calvary, in fifty-three vessels. This structure was commenced in 1278 over this sacred deposit. Sarcophagi have been gathered here from various quarters, and many stones commemorate the death of early Roman Christians. The principal attraction, however, is the extraordinary frescos which adorn the cloister walls, and afford the earliest specimens of the art. The great work of Orgagna, "The Triumph of Death," and the Life of Job, by Giotto, and the Drunkenness of Noah, by Gozzoli, are the principal subjects of interest, although there are a variety of other illustrations of sacred subjects. The costumes of these paintings are those of the age in which they were executed, and many an actual portrait is here on the walls. In a small chapel into which we entered, our guide called our attention to a remarkable echo, to produce which he chanted grandly. His fine voice was very rich and musical.

We now went into the Baptistery, which was built in 1152. The pulpit is wonderfully beautiful; it was made by Nicolo Pisano. It stands on nine pillars, and has two marble desks for the gospel and epistle. The bas-reliefs of this exquisite piece of statuary are as perfect as when they were completed. The cupola is lofty, — one hundred and two feet from the pavement. The fount is fourteen feet in diameter, and Murray says " was *formerly* used for baptism by immersion." Popery is fond of antiquity, but has gotten rid of some *old* things, and tried her hand upon many inventions. The Baptistery of Pisa is a noble edifice, and full of curious and beautiful things.

We next rode over the river to see a little church called Santa Maria della Spina. It is a miniature Gothic structure in marble. Giovanni and Andrea Pisano were the artists to whom are ascribed several of the small statues which adorn this church. The church takes its name from a thorn of the Saviour's crown, brought from the Holy Land by a Pisan merchant, and given to this chapel in 1333.

At the Dairy farm (belonging to the Grand Duke, who resides at Pisa in winter), about three miles out of the town, there are more than two hundred camels. They are the descendants of those brought home by the Crusaders. We wanted to go to see them, but had not sufficient time; but, just as we were regretting it, I saw three of them bringing in immense loads of hay from the farm. They were fine-looking animals, and in better condition than those we see in menageries.

Having taken dinner, we hastened to the cars, where we were to meet Mr. Vanderbilt and our friends Messrs. Powers and Hart, who were to visit the yacht, and see us sail from Leghorn. Our guide got off the train to speak to Mr. Vanderbilt, and was in the act of jumping on as the train was in motion. This was contrary to law, and he was snatched from the platform, and we went on without him; but he telegraphed us, so that we heard of him on reaching the station at Leghorn, and he made his appearance soon after, having taken a gig and driven rapidly to the city.

Our ladies immediately went about shopping in Leghorn, and I looked round upon the city. The Via la Grande is a fine busy street, and on its pavements I felt that I was again in a place of trade and commerce; for here were Turks, Moors, Armenians and Chinese, and the Dutch sailors were smoking as if as much at home as in Amsterdam. The population is rather more than sixty thousand, of which one-sixth are Jews.

La Grande Piazza is a noble square, and here is the great church, into which I did not enter. The Jews' synagogue is supposed to be one of the finest in Europe.

A Turkish bazaar which we went to was filled with Eastern articles of great beauty, and with plenty of French trifles; but, as we were bound to Constantinople, we refused to be tempted.

On our arrival at Leghorn, we were surprised and amused to learn that the fact of the yacht's anchorage in the roadstead had excited an alarm. Orders had been received to place guard-boats off the North Star, and we were suspected of having arms on board, and it was thought that we had come to take or bring some "Liberals." It was not quite certain that Kossuth himself was not on board. Great excitement existed, and orders had been received, from further off than Florence, to keep a vigilant eye on our movements. Our consul protested against these jealous fears of a gentleman's yacht, but in vain. Austrian imagination could not conceive of such a ship being the ocean home of a private American merchant. The yacht was thrown open to visitors, as in other ports; and many hundreds came from Pisa, Florence and Lucca, as well as the good people of Leghorn.

Our friends, Powers, Hart and Root, all seemed glad to walk our decks, and felt proud that the flag of their country waved over them on such a vessel. Our guide, Sebastian, who lived here, determined to go with us to Rome, and so he left his family for another week.

We were most kindly waited on by Mr. Henderson and his nephew, Mr. Miller, to the last moment, and letters to Rome and Naples politely presented us for our service.

VISITORS.

We had difficulty in getting rid of our visitors; and, when the steam was up, and the wheels revolving, a gentleman on deck would run into " that great cabin " with his wife and daughters, " for one little minute." We hurried him up, and when he took his boat, and we steamed off, there were at least one hundred boats around us, all filled with visitors.

We left the port amid the hearty cheers of the vast fleet of boats, many of which were gayly decorated with colors.

20*

CHAPTER XVIII.

LEAVE LEGHORN FOR CIVITA VECCHIA — HARBOR — DIFFICULTIES ON OUR WAY — DISAPPOINTMENT — VOYAGE RESUMED — SEE ST. PETER'S AFAR OFF — ISCHIA — PROCEDA — BAIA, ETC. — BRIDGE OF CALIGULA — NAPLES — THE BAY — RENEWED DISAPPOINTMENT — SWIMMERS — LADY MORGAN — VESUVIUS, ETC. — CAPRI AND SUNSET — STROMBOLI AND ÆTNA — CAPE FARO, OR PELORUS — SCYLLA — EARTHQUAKE OF 1783 — MESSINA — SCENERY OF THE STRAITS — RHEGIUM — MOUNT ÆTNA — SYRACUSE — CAPE PASSARO — MALTA.

From Leghorn, August 12, seven P. M., our course was directed for Palamjolu light, on the east coast of Elba, lying between that island and Piambino, thence south and east for the inside of the islands of Giglio and Gianuto; then running still south-easterly for Civita Vecchia, where we anchored at seven A. M. the next day.

The town is small and clean-looking, has strong forts built out on a little rocky islet, and an old monastery off at the left serves as a Lazaretto. The small harbor is well protected from the sea by a mole which has two entrances, — one at each end. Inside the town is a basin to receive vessels, which was built by Trajan. This is guarded by a strong chain every evening. We took a health-officer on board, and our captain and one of the party landed with the ship-papers. They soon returned, and stated that, owing to a defect in them, we could not be allowed to land until we had performed quarantine, or till the governor had communicated with Rome. The difficulty was that some names had been omitted on the bill of health at Leghorn, so that more persons appeared to be on board than the papers had specified. Mr. Vanderbilt was unwilling to suffer a detention, and it was supposed that, as we had a Chargé d'Affaires at Naples, our best course was to go direct thither, and trust to his influence to get us admitted to pratique, and then go from Naples to Rome. This prospect kept up our spirits under the cruel disappointment of being so near to the Eternal City, and yet debarred the privilege of visiting the old Mistress of the World. I really did pity the poor ladies' maids, who were Catholics, and our purser, Mr. Keefe, who also was a son of the church, and had letters from his clergy in New York, commending him to sundry of the faithful at Rome. One of the girls burst into a passionate flood of tears, and declared that all which had induced her to come on board was to go to Rome; and now the vexation was too hard for flesh and blood to bear up under with any patience. After laying close into the town for two or three hours, we weighed anchor, and, standing out about three miles, took a line from Cape Linaro to Mount Circello. About three o'clock P. M., we were off the mouths of the Ostia, and, the day being beautifully clear, we had a capital view of St. Peter's dome and the small cupolas. All our party came on deck, and every glass was in demand. The distance from Rome was, I imagine, about twenty-five miles. So we saw Rome. I have learned to bear with disappointments, and have often seen the happy results which frequently appear from having our anxiously-desired paths hedged up. We had a fine night upon the sea, and a delicious air.

From Mount Circello we ran across the Gulf of Gaieta, and made for Ischia. This island, with the small one of Procida, forms the north-western shore of the Bay of Naples. Passing Point Antonio, our course lay direct in for Naples. The night was very splendid, and I spent most of its hours on deck, to watch a coast of so much interest and scenery so romantic as now surrounded us.

Ischia is a spot full of wonders, and was once as famous for its volcanic eruptions as Vesuvius is at present. The last great outbreak was in 1302, when the island was almost desolated. Here are lofty hills, rugged rocks, and barren mountains; but there are many spots of beauty and fertility, where the vine and myrtle flourish, and all the tropical fruits abound. In the centre of Ischia rises Monte San Niccolo, a volcano which once ravaged the island; and from the summit of it the view must be most lovely. A few hermits dwell on this elevated rock, and their cells are cut out of the stone and lava.

The town of Ischia lies about two miles off from Proceda, and a strong castellated fortress, on a precipitous rock, is united to the island by a stone bridge of great length. The ancient name of Ischia was "Inărĭme," and its circumference is about sixteen miles. Proceda is about two and a half miles long; the town occupies the shore, and there appeared to be a large number of fine buildings. Sailing on about two and a half miles from the eastern point of Proceda, we came to Point Misenum, the northern boundary of the bay. Here, on a high point, are two watchtowers and a large house. The scenery was very picturesque, and off to the northward there were several large steamers at anchor. We now passed Baia, and saw the ruins of ancient temples, and several apertures from the sea leading through the solid rocks. Near to the shore are the baths of the Cumæan Sibyl. All along the shore from Baia to Pozzuoli, which lies in a bay, the navigation near the shore is rendered dangerous from the ruins of houses and towers which are submerged, and which extend so far from the coast as to reach where seven and eight fathoms water are close to them. Near to the town are the pillared ruins of the mole and the splendid bridge of Caligula, which once reached over to Baia, two and a half miles in length. East, lies the small island of Nisita, which is the quarantine station. To the north of this is a mole, and midway from the island to the land is a steep rock From a point of land on which is a large white building, much like an American hotel, you get the first view of Naples. Off this spot are vast ruins which lie in the sea, and the towers of other ages now require that the navigator should give them a wide berth. Having turned this point, we came to the Castle del Ovo, upon a rock. Mergillena Point is lined with charming residences, and the shore on to Naples is one unbroken line of villas, palaces and imposing structures. And now before us was the Castle of St. Elmo, and, hard by, the Convent of St. Martino; there was the royal palace and the arsenal, all lying on the noble slope of the hill on which the city stands. As for church domes, I can't pretend to number them, — they were everywhere. A mole is built out before the town, on which is erected a high brick tower, which serves as a light-house.

This city stands where Palœpolis and Neapolis formerly stood. Neapolis was desolated by the great eruption of Vesuvius in 79, when the elder Pliny was destroyed. This glorious bay is, I should think, nearly twenty-five miles across from Ischia or Misenum to the opposite shore — perhaps more. As we anchored in the harbor on a lovely Sabbath morning, everything seemed beautiful. Before us lay the city, like a crescent; and off to the right the Villa Reale, well thronged with the Neapolitans; and, turning round, we saw Vesuvius and the road leading off to Pompeii, and off to the left lay the grotto of Posilipo and the tomb of Virgil, while stretching far northward are hills of quiet beauty, with the lofty Apennines forming a back-ground.

The health-officer who boarded us took our papers, and then went on shore to report; and when he returned brought us word that we could not land, owing to the condition of our bill of health. We found that our Chargé d'Affaires had left for America; and, unwilling to stay for a long quarantine, we were once more doomed to be satisfied with the sight of our eyes. From the entire tone and bearing of the official, it was clear that the authorities did not much care to have Americans land there; and we did not seem to have favor in their sight. While at anchor, boats came off in great numbers, with fruit and vegetables, and a vast number of men came swimming around us. One very good-looking man, with gold spectacles on, and carrying a silk umbrella and smoking a cigar, swam from the shore to our yacht, — full one-third of a mile. He trod the water as though on a pavement, and was breast-high out of the waves. Mr. Vanderbilt now determined to try his hand with the English, and ordered our course to be directed for Malta.

We have seen Naples, — ay, and seen it in great beauty, — and we have gazed for four or five hours upon the unrivalled shores of her glorious bay. To say that we longed to tread the classic haunts with which our early studies had made us familiar is but what we shall gain credit for. O, it was hard to see and turn away; but then how much had we enjoyed since the dawn of this lovely day!

Well did Lady Morgan remark, in her work on Italy, which I confess I always read with interest: "In the environs of Naples there lies subject-matter for the antiquary, the painter, the naturalist and the philosopher. Its coasts are bathed by the sea of Homer; its lakes and hills afford the topography of Virgil; its vineyards bloom over caves where the Cumæan Sibyl composed her oracles; and every cliff and headland is a history, the register of a crime, or the landmark of an adventure which has made the immortality of him who recorded or him who performed them. The whole of these shores look as if they were etched and painted, the drawing and coloring equally exquisite. The sea-pieces of Salvator Rosa are recalled at every step." — Vol. III. pp. 155–6.

The ladies had for several days determined upon the ascent of Vesuvius, and had most industriously prepared a general equipment of Bloomer apparel for the occasion. The clothing market fell, upon the news of the Neapolitan embargo, and great bargains might have been made at this moment of depression.

We were fairly moving out past the mole, and every eye was

on the city, then off to the sweet village of Portici, built almost upon the ruins of Herculaneum, and then upon Vesuvius, mounting to the clouds and throwing off a slight vapor, and, beyond, the Apennines. Then there is Posilipo point, with its white mansions, and off before us Capri, of olden fame; and our course lay between this island and the cape on the main. This island takes its name from the goats that used to browse upon its cliffs; it became part of the empire under Augustus Cæsar, who made it a place of occasional retirement. It has always been regarded as a most healthy spot; and here Tiberius spent the last days of his shameful career, amid the most cruel and abominable debaucheries. Every part of the island was studded with palaces, groves, gardens and grottos. On a lofty hill stands a ruined fortress; and on the eastern point of the island is a vast ruin, which indicates the splendor which once reigned here. Medals, statues and other ancient relics, are often found here. The panoramic view from Capri, embracing the bay, its beautiful islands, the promontories north and south with their bold cliffs, and a bright blue sea, is altogether the most beautiful one that I have seen. As we came to the southern point, we were delighted to see the Scopuli spoken of by Virgil. An arch, as perfect as could be made by art, opens through these rugged rocks, and is said to be of enormous height, — I believe four hundred feet.

The sun was shedding his evening rays upon Vesuvius, and throwing violet hues all over the mountain sides, as we took our latest look at the enchanting scenery. This was perhaps the most brilliant sunset that we ever witnessed. As the sun neared the horizon, it appeared like a ball of fire. The back-ground was of shaded crimson, deepening towards the sun; above it there was a deep-blue cloud fringed with gold, and above this streaks of the most delicately-formed clouds, all crowned by a canopy of exquisite shading; then, diverging from the sun, came pillars of parti-colored light, gradually losing themselves in the clear sky, at about twenty-five degrees from the horizon. To-day we observed divine service at eight o'clock P. M.

We now made a straight course for Stromboli, and discovered this light-house of the sea. At about two in the morning Captain Eldridge kindly came below, and called us up to see the ever-burning faro of the seas. There it was, long miles off, flaming away just as brightly as it did when Carthaginian navies and Roman consuls ploughed the waves in their war-galleys. Here am I, looking upon an object which has fastened the gaze of millions; and they wondered as I do, and then they perished in successive periods; and here we are from the New World, gazing on the same wondrous exhibition of terrific power, and are reminded that "one generation passeth away and another cometh, but the earth remaineth." How unchanged are its grand features, while the long generations of men who have lived have returned to the dust from whence they sprang! Nature is as young and lovely as at her birth; the stars shed as bright a radiance as when Job wrote about the Pleiades and Arcturus; the meadows are as green as when Isaac walked out to meditate at the evening-tide, and the waves are as restless and rolling as when the Saviour calmed them down by the power of their Creator; but the nations that lived on these shores, the navies that sailed these seas — where are they? They have grown old, — and they are not.

Stromboli lies about thirty-three miles north of Sicily, and is nearly ten miles in circumference. It is a cone rising up to the height of twenty-five hundred feet above the sea. All round its base and sides are scattered hamlets, with a population of nearly fifteen hundred, who are on the edge of destruction, and live and act, ay, and sleep, on the surface of an eternal volcano. I do not quite understand how men can become reconciled to such appalling danger. This is the only volcano that is known to maintain constant eruption. Its earliest mention is two hundred and ninety-two years before Christ, and it was burning in the days of

LIPARI ISLANDS — ÆTNA.   251

Augustus and Tiberius. Part of the island is very fertile; the soil is black mould, and abounds in corn, cotton, grapes, figs and currants. In the island are many curious caves, and the Grotto del Bovi Marini is eighty-one feet long and thirty-five wide, and is full of crystallizations. This volcano is probably supported by oxygen, pyrites and sulphur, — there are no signs of bitumen.

The Lipari Islands were known to the ancients as the Æolian Islands, and the poets feigned that Æolus here shut up the winds. These islands were vastly useful to Homer and Virgil, in furnishing them with poetical materials. In Hiera Vulcan's forge was placed. Twenty-seven years ago a damsel on the Hudson river asked me if I knew her brother-in-law. I replied Yes. "Well," said she, "don't you think he is an interesting man?" To this I agreed. She then said that she thought him very interesting, adding, "O, he has seen so much of the world! He has been all through the Mediterranean river; he's seen the burning mountains, and seen them make nuns, and seen them after they were made." I could not help remembering her ideas of the *interesting*, whilst I was enjoying the same privileges. Poor girl! her romantic notions have long since given place to the every-day duties of a good Dutchman's wife.

At the earliest dawn of day, we saw the peaks of the gigantic Ætna far away, and soon discovered the smoky cloud which ever covers his hoary head. Every eye was fastened upon the increasing view which our rapid headway now afforded. But we were to see Ætna to greater advantage as the day advanced. What a remarkable thing it was to see these three great volcanoes of the world — Vesuvius, Stromboli and Ætna — in the short space of less than nine hours. This could only happen to a voyager by steam.

We now steered direct for the Faro Point, the famous promontory of Pelorus, which took its name from the pilot of Hannibal, who was put to death on suspicion of bad faith to the Carthaginians. Here we obtained fine views of the Calabrian coast, which is grand in its rugged mountainous aspect. Just as we passed Faro we saw the famous Scylla of classic story, which occasioned so much dread to the early navigators of this channel. It is a bold rock, and is perhaps one hundred and fifty feet high, and is the jutting-out cape of the western part of Calabria. Underneath it are caverns and pieces of rock around, and a strong western current from the Tyrrhene Sea sets in with violence, which formerly produced frequent disasters to the Greek sailors who drifted on the dangerous cape. Much of its horror, however, may be ascribed to the poetic imagination of Homer and Ovid.

Now the name of the cape is Sciglio, and a castle strongly fortified forms a striking object upon the rock, as it is approached from the Pelorus. This town of Sciglio was the scene of an awful visitation in February 1783, when an earthquake nearly destroyed the place. The castle, churches, houses, &c., were extensively injured; and the prince, with more than two thousand of his people, fled to the beach for safety, when the promontory of Campala, falling into the sea, caused the waters of the straits to rush over to the Pelorus, and as they receded it was with a tide of violence that carried off the unfortunate prince and every one of his people. The exact location of Charybdis is a matter of doubt. Some place it at the light opposite the harbor of Messina, others at the Faro Point. Captain Smyth says, "Outside the tongue of land that forms the harbor of Messina lies the Galofaro, or celebrated vortex of Charybdis, which has with more reason than Scylla been clothed with terrors by the writers of antiquity." Our passage from Faro to Messina which is a distance of ten or twelve miles, was one of great interest, for the landscape on the coast of Sicily was adorned with every beauty. On the shore were charming villages, noble convents and venerable churches, and the back-ground composed of lofty hills finely cut into ravines. The straits here are narrow, and resemble a noble river; and the Calabrian shores present a glorious line of mountains.

The approach to Messina is very fine. It stands at the base of a picturesque mountain-range, belonging to the Neptunian chain. The city is large, and the cathedral and the noble towers of churches and convents rise from among the mass of buildings. Behind the city, and far up the mountain, are two very ancient-looking forts; and midway between them is an old monastery, in which Richard Cœur de Lion resided in 1190, when on his crusade to the Holy City. The buildings, mostly white, are in beautiful contrast with the rich green foliage behind. The population is about eighty thousand. We saw a large number of vessels lying at the Marina, which is a fine wharf in front of the city. The scenery reminded several of our party of the banks of the Rhine; and the passage of this piece of water is, I think, a sufficient reward for all the trouble of a voyage from America.

Let me speak of the great pleasure with which I here read a little volume called "Sicily, a Pilgrimage," by Henry T. Tuckerman, and published by G. P. Putnam & Co. It is a book of beauties; and then its delineations are so graphic, and its descriptions of nature so truthful! I think it is written in its author's happiest moments, and it has made many of my hours at sea pass away delightfully. Our course lay straight for Syracuse, and, passing by Messina, we soon came to Rhegium, a neat little place on the Calabrian coast. This is the town to which Paul came after his shipwreck, when on his way to Rome. Now we have a noble sight of Ætna. It is capped with snow, and we can well see the beauty of Pindar's description, when he calls it "the snow-clad pillar of the heavens, this nurse of endless frosts." It lies before us, and will be in sight all day, and late into the evening. It is divided into three ranges, known as the cultivated, the forest, and the desert regions. The crater is said to be two miles in circumference. From Mount Ætna are derived those supplies of snow and ice which the towns of Italy and Sicily require. What a map must be laid out to the view of the man who stands upon Mount Ætna, and what a survey of cities, mountains, coasts, bays and capes! It was a fine evening, on the 15th of August, when we made Syracuse, which stands upon a neck of land divided by a very small arm of the sea from the main island. The name of the island is Ortygia. It has two harbors, and one affords the best anchorage in the world, and is large enough to accommodate the navy of any country in Europe. This city once had a circumference of twenty miles, and a population of five hundred thousand; now it has only about fifteen thousand. Here are the two columns of the temple of Jupiter Olympus, and they are now good landmarks for entering the harbor. In this port Lord Nelson supplied his fleet when he was in his celebrated pursuit of the French fleet, in 1798. It is something to have seen this remarkable city, which was founded seven hundred and thirty-two years before Christ, by Archias of Corinth; and we cannot look at it without remembering Dionysius, Thrasybulus, Agathocles and Archimedes.

It was owing to the Mammertines, who lived in the southern part of Campania, and who served as mercenary troops under Agathocles, having rebelled afterwards against the Syracusans and appealed to Rome for protection, that an army of Romans, under Appius Claudius, came against the Carthaginians, and commenced the celebrated Punic wars, which at last destroyed Carthage, and annexed Sicily to the empire. This city has been battle-ground for Greeks, Romans, Saracens, Normans and Spaniards. It was off Syracuse that the great battle was fought between the Dutch and French fleets, in 1676, when Admiral De Ruyter was killed.

Our course was now directed for Malta, and we made Cape Passaro at night, and thence arrived off Malta on the morning of the sixteenth of August, before day-light. As we lay off, a copious shower of rain fell; but we found that it did not extend to Malta, where no rain had been known for many months. At six o'clock we entered the port of Valetta, with our anticipations highly raised as to the gratification which awaited us in this celebrated island.

21*

CHAPTER XIX.

HARBOR — ARABS — ALLOWED TO LAND — VISIT FROM MR. CONSUL WINTHROP — DIVERS — HISTORICAL NOTICE — VALETTA — THE RACES — MALTESE BOATS — INVITATION FROM THE GOVERNOR TO TAKE DINNER — INVITATIONS FROM THE OFFICERS OF THE GARRISON — VISIT TO SIR WILLIAM REID — GOVERNOR'S PALACE — MR. WINTHROP'S RESIDENCE — MSS. OF ITALIAN OPERAS — CAPTAIN THOMAS GRAVES, R.N. — CITTA VECCHIA — SHOPS — THE GOVERNOR AND SUITE VISIT THE YACHT — ST. JOHN'S CHURCH — WALLS OF THE CITADEL — COUNTRY PEOPLE — COSTUME — FORTS ANGELO, RICASOLI, MANOEL, TIGNÉ AND ST. ELMO — TURKISH SIEGE IN 1565 — DEPART FOR CONSTANTINOPLE.

WE found a large quantity of small shipping in the harbor, and one vessel thronged with Arabs, bound for a pilgrimage to Mecca. Some of them were the ugliest-looking customers I ever saw. We were soon at anchor, and a health-officer came on board, and we were at once allowed to land, — but were full of fear when he took our papers up with tongs. As soon as we had taken breakfast, our consul, Mr. William Winthrop, came off to us and gave us a cordial greeting, and offered us his best services to render our visit agreeable. When we came on deck from breakfast, we found a number of boats around us, with bands of music of a rather primitive character, as regards the instruments; but our attention was riveted to two or three boats in which were divers. They were fine-looking young men, and were ready, for a small silver coin, to go to the bottom, and they invariably brought it up in their mouths. These fellows were admirable specimens of muscle. I never saw such perfect development. One of them had a lad of fifteen who sat on his shoulders, and they dove down together. Often did they pass under our yacht, and came up at a distance on the other side.

This same island is a most remarkable one, and, excepting the rock of Gibraltar, no other rock has greater claims to notice. I say rock, for it is nothing else. We have read of Malta in the entrancing pages of Virtot, and have fancied that we knew something about the forts and bastions; but the thing itself is wondrously beyond description. I will not say more of its history than that it has been in the possession of Phœnicians, Greeks, Carthaginians, Romans, Vandals, Goths, Normans, Germans, the Knights of St. John and the French, and it has been held by the British since 1800. All of the appearances of nature are African; nothing is European but the modes of life and the habits of civilization. The celebrity of Malta arises from its having been so long the great bulwark of Christendom against the blood-stained crescent banner of the Turk; and from this island a signal check has been given to the corsairs of the African shores. Now it is the great stopping-station of travellers to the East.

Malta, in 1516, fell into the hands of Charles V.; and when the Knights of St. John, who had been expelled from Rhodes, were in search of a new home, the emperor determined to cede the islands of Malta, Gozo, Comino, and Tripoli in Africa, to the order. The grand master at this time was Philip Villiers de L'Isle Adam, a Frenchman. The Knights took possession of their acquisitions October 1530. The castle of Angelo was the only fortified place, and efforts were at once made to strengthen it; and from that period down to the capture of Malta by the French, in 1798, the Knights devoted their attention to strengthening the defences and increasing their number, till they made it one of the most renowned military stations in the world. Every one has read of the bloody sieges which were carried on by the Turks and corsairs, and so gallantly withstood by the Knights of the Cross.

> "There, like an eagle in her rocky bower,
> The gallant order braved the Moslem power,
> While Europe echoed with their martial fame,
> And rung with La Valette's undying fame."

The town of Valetta was founded by this illustrious Grand Master. It stands on a peninsula, crowned by Fort St. Elmo. The foundation was laid in March 1566, and in 1571 it became the seat of government. The city of Valetta is fully equal to any town in the Mediterranean, as respects the beauty and elegance of its streets and buildings. Its position between two arms of the sea, running very nearly parallel into the land, is commanding; and on each side of it is a spacious and commodious natural harbor. The streets are wide, and intersect each other at right angles, and the dwellings are thrown into blocks. The material of building is a fine cream-colored stone, and the flat roofs furnish a good promenade. I greatly admired the architecture; nearly all the houses have projecting balconies, and the windows are adorned with deep cappings, affording a very picturesque appearance to the streets. We landed at the wharf near our ship, and soon found that everything was novel. We passed a magnificent gate, and discovered that to get into the city we had to ascend the streets of steps immortalized by Byron, who said, "Adieu, ye cursed streets of stairs," — queer enough they are; but, on gaining the level ground, we were all charmed with a city which strongly reminded us, in some of its streets, of the grand city of Bath. We had the good fortune to reach Malta on St. Roch's day, the 16th of August, on which day the annual races occur, and were advised by Mr. Winthrop to be present. They take place on the shore road, at the head of the quarantine harbor. Mr. Vanderbilt engaged two Maltese boats, and our party, in company with Mr. and Mrs. Winthrop, were to go by water. Our route lay through our harbor, round Fort St. Elmo, and up the quarantine harbor. Of all the boat excursions that I ever made, this was by very far

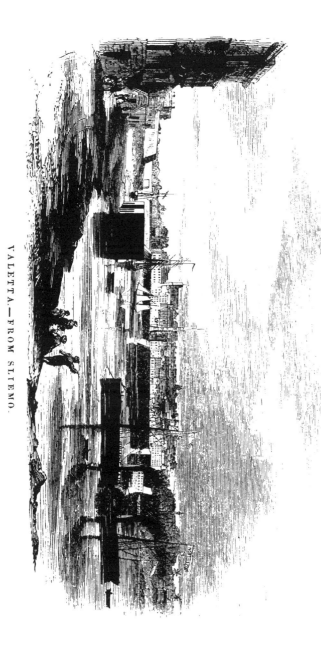

VALETTA—FROM SLIEMO.

the most enchanting. We had as fine an evening as sunset ever lighted up with its parting beams. We sailed close under the rocky ramparts of Fort St. Elmo, and then entered the quarantine harbor, passing Fort Tignè and Fort Emanuel, and having the town of Valetta now upon our left. At the head of this harbor we found the race-road on its shore, and a vast multitude assembled. There were three prizes, — one for donkeys, one for fillies and one for horses. The animals were ridden by boys, and they used no saddles or bridles, but displayed great dexterity in riding. The race seemed to call out the mass of the population, and the shops were closed. The donkeys ran well under severe whipping, and the horses made fair speed. There was a strong police upon the ground, and many priests present. We remained in our boats. In consequence of the nature of the harbors, and the position of Valetta and the other towns and collections of buildings, a vast fleet of boats is necessary, and hundreds of men are employed in the transport of passengers from one side to the other. The Maltese boat is about twenty-five feet long; the two ends are higher than the midships, the stern-piece running up about two feet above the gunwale at that point, and both ends are alike. They are something in general shape like our whale-boats, but broader and heavier. The after end is fitted up with seats, under an awning rigged on a stationary frame, with side-curtains, and a very comfortable accommodation is afforded. The boats are fancifully painted, and are kept in admirable order. We found the Maltese boatmen active and obliging, and quite intelligent. For fifty cents we could command a boat and two men from sunrise until midnight.

Our return home was diversified by a visit which we made to the new English steamship Valette, which had that day arrived from Marseilles, in forty-six hours. She is deemed the fastest steamer in the Oriental line, and this is the best time ever made from Marseilles. The officer in charge was very polite, and conducted us over every part of the ship, which is fitted up in excellent taste; but the accommodations of the passengers seemed very limited, when compared with our own in the North Star. The sunset of this evening will long be remembered by us. The sky was cloudless, — not as deep a blue as we have at home; but off to the west there was a broad magnificent expanse of golden effulgence, and we can fully appreciate an Italian sunset.

On our arrival at the yacht, we found an invitation from the Hon. Sir William Reid, the Governor of Malta, inviting Mr. Vanderbilt and the party to dinner at the palace; but Mr. V. was obliged to decline this polite attention, in consequence of his arrangements only allowing us two days in Malta. Invitations also were kindly sent us from the officers of the 3rd regiment, — "the Buffs," — the Royal Engineers and Artillery, and the 68th Light Infantry, requesting us to dine with them on successive evenings. All these kind overtures we were reluctantly compelled to waive. The 3d regiment, known as "the Buffs," is the only regiment which has the privilege of passing through the city of London with their flags flying and drums beating.

The next day Mr. Vanderbilt invited me to accompany him in a call upon the governor. The day was as hot as I ever experienced, and even in a carriage it was fearful. The palace is situated in a spacious square. It is a vast edifice, of plain architecture externally, and is three hundred feet square. It is surrounded on each side by the four principal streets, and on three sides has a row of open or covered balconies. The palace has two grand entrances in front, opening into a court, and one entrance on the other sides of the building. The interior of the mansion has been the care of the different Grand Masters of the order. It consists of two stories, each containing a series of apartments which traverse the entire quadrangle. In the court is a portico, covering a fountain with a statue of Neptune. The upper story consists of numerous and elegant apartments, and very spacious saloons, richly adorned with paintings in commemoration of the battles of the Knights. Some of these are excellent productions. Here are many of the works of the first masters. In the waiting-room at the end of the hall, as we ascended the grand staircase, we noticed St. George and the Dragon, St. Peter, Æneas, &c. In the corridor leading to the armory, we entered a room hung with tapestry representing scenes in India and Africa. These tapestries were brought from the Gobelins one hundred and fifty years ago, but still look fresh and beautiful. The armory is very splendid; and here you see the warlike equipments belonging to the brave old Knights of Malta. Here was a suit of black armor seven feet three and a half inches high. Among other Turkish trophies, is the sword of the renowned pirate and Algerine, Admiral Dragut. The best painting that I ever saw of Louis XVI. is in this palace. It was sent to the Grand Master by the unfortunate monarch. We found his Excellency in a large room, surrounded by his papers, and evidently in his usually occupied room. Sir William Reid is a fine-looking, elderly gentleman, of very quiet manners. He received Mr. Vanderbilt with great cordiality, and expressed his happiness that the yacht had visited the port. The governor made particular inquiries after his friend Mr. W. C. Redfield. Sir William is an officer in her majesty's army, and was once Governor of Bermuda; but he is well known as the author of various publications on the theory of storms. He told us that his attention was first directed to this subject by Mr. Redfield, of New York. Governor Reid took an active part in the management of the London Exhibition, in 1851, and probably owes his present exalted position to the eminent services which he rendered upon that occasion. Captain Hoare, the son-in-law of the governor, was present at our interview. He is a gentleman of much intelligence, has been in the United States, and had crossed from San Juan in one of Mr. Vanderbilt's steamships, in company with Mr. Jacob Vanderbilt, after whom he inquired with friendly interest. The governor made many inquiries in relation to American steamships, and their power of speed. As we were taking our leave, Sir William informed Mr. Vanderbilt that he should pay a visit to the yacht the next day at twelve o'clock. Master George Vanderbilt was with us at this call, and it happened that when he and I were at the Crystal Palace, in London, we both met Sir William Reid, who kindly introduced us to Mr. Nesmith, who had charge of the machinery, and from him we had much information as to the steam-power of the exhibition. The lad was remembered by the governor in connection with some inquiries that he made of me, and which were heard by him, and led him to place us under Mr. Nesmith's care.

I went from the palace to take a family dinner with the consul. Mr. Winthrop has a fine residence in a house once occupied by the Prior of the Knights of St. John; it is close by St. John's Church. I can hardly imagine a more pleasant home than he possesses. His rooms are very spacious, and extend through a long suite of apartments, on one side of which is a gallery, lined with exquisite shrubs and flowers; and on the other sides the rooms open upon a balcony, which overhangs a fine street. The ceilings are many of them beautifully frescoed, and the staircase is of massive and elegant stone-work, richly carved. Mr. Winthrop has been consul here for nineteen years, and finds the climate adapted to his health, which has been feeble; but he now appears likely to live a long life, which all who know him will, I am sure, desire most earnestly. Our consul is a hard student; he has devoted himself to historical pursuits with great ardor. He has contributed a series of admirable papers to the Southern Messenger upon the history of the Knights of Malta, and is one of the principal contributors to the admirable "Notes and Queries," published in London. In his library I was much interested with an extraordinary collection of two hundred and twenty-four MS. volumes of Italian operas, from 1596 to 1824, with the names of the persons to whom they were dedicated, and the places in which they were performed. They contain upwards of seventy thousand pages, and are most admirably written. Mr. W. has received applications to part with them to go to England, but he would prefer selling them to an American library; and he would readily find a purchaser, I think, if they were seen by some of our collectors

At Mr. Winthrop's I had the pleasure to meet with Captain Graves, of the royal navy. This gentleman has obtained much celebrity by the admirable charts which he has constructed for the coasts of the Levant. These he presented to Captain Eldridge; they were of great service to us. Since we left Malta, I am happy to notice that Captain Graves has been appointed Superintendent of the Ports in Malta; he is also President of the Literary Society of Malta. I visited Captain Graves, and saw his noble library; and he most kindly favored me with the loan of several exceedingly rare and valuable books, which I was to leave at Gibraltar on my return to that port.

After dinner, our party took carriages, and we rode out to Citta Vecchia, sometimes called La Notabile. The hack-coach here in use is new to us. It is a close coach-body, of antique style, capable of holding four persons, but with no box for the driver; and rests on two leather stretchers, which run from the axle to the cross-bar behind the horse. It has but two wheels, the ends of the long shafts being mortised into the axle, and thence running straight to tugs formed in a strap traversing a huge saddle, at which point they are made fast. The entire weight of the carriage is thus thrown on the shafts. The collar and breeching are very rude affairs, and the driver runs barefooted at the head of the horse, governing him by a long rope, the spare length of which he carries in a coil in his hand.

This old city is on the highest ground of the island, and nearly at its centre. This is the head-quarters of the Catholic Church, and the bishop is also titular Archbishop of Rhodes. He has a palace here, and one in Valetta. This city, though small, is surrounded with walls and bastions, and is regarded as a strongly-fortified place. Its ancient name was that of the island, Melita, and is so spoken of by Ptolemy in his geography. It was once a stately city. The inauguration of the Grand Masters took place here.

Our ride was through a country of entire rock. The soil has been brought here from Sicily, and is mixed up with the friable portions of the rocky native soil. We found some few good houses on the road, but the poor Maltese live in worse huts than the Irish cabins; and they who labor in the city walk in and out, eight, ten and fourteen miles a day, in this burning sun. Assiduous labor has rendered even this rocky island very fertile, and the products are strawberries, figs, pomegranates, grapes, peaches, nectarines, apricots, oranges, lemons, melons, medlars, plums, pears, apples and prickly pears. The great object of curiosity at the old city is the cathedral, the site of which is said to be the spot where Publius resided, who was governor when Paul was shipwrecked here.

The church is a fine edifice, in the rich Corinthian order, and it has a very splendid altar of marble. Some of the party visited the catacombs of St. Paul, and explored these ancient sepulchres. I went with a procession into a church, to witness a mass on behalf of some person who had just departed this life. The priests were returning with the host, and a number of boys carrying lamps and tapers, headed the array. Here we found more beggars than at any other place, and they were wretched-looking ones, too. Children without eyes, or perhaps some with only one, were held up by parents for alms. Eye-diseases are awfully prevalent, owing to the white dusty clouds constantly flying from the rocky ground.

On our return, we passed the governor's country-house, which has a very fine garden. It is at St. Antonio. Here are ponds and fountains.

We found the shops well supplied, and the goods quite reasonable. In a bookseller's shop I was pleased to see a fair representation of American books. Harpers' publications were here in considerable numbers. Several of us took a dinner on shore at Baker's Hotel, and found it an excellent one; and Mr. Baker was exceedingly kind, and rendered me very valuable services by procuring for me some things which I had in vain attempted to obtain. The hotel is thoroughly English, and the attention all that can be wished.

On the morning of the 18th, we had a large number of visitors from the city; and at twelve o'clock precisely we observed the governor's boats on their way. His excellency came on board under a royal salute from the North Star of twenty-one guns. He was accompanied by his sister-in-law, Lady Bolland, the widow of the distinguished English Judge Bolland, Rear Admiral Houston Stuart, General Ferguson, and some thirty British officers of the garrison, and a number of ladies. General Ferguson is a noble-looking man; he is one of the most distinguished officers in the English army, and holds his present honorable position in acknowledgment of his long services and great bravery in many hard-fought battles. He is regarded as one of the noblest ornaments of the profession. Our visitors appeared to be very much pleased and surprised with the yacht, which they examined very thoroughly. Admiral Stuart and several of the officers complimented Captain Eldridge upon the admirable manner in which the salute was fired, and said it would have been creditable to a man-of-war.

As soon as our friends left us, I went on shore to visit St. John's Church, which is the great church of Malta. It was built in 1576, and has been adorned at large expense by all the Grand Masters of the order. The façade of the church is anything but attractive. The interior is fine, and the choir has an admirable sculpture in marble, representing the Baptism of Christ by John, by Bernini. The roof is adorned with paintings, in illustration of the life of John. The pavement is richly adorned with sepulchral slabs in mosaic, with colored marbles, jasper, agate and precious stones. These cover the graves of the knights who died here, and there are many declarations on these slabs of the virtues of the departed heroes. The grand altar is very superb, and chairs of velvet are placed for the bishop and governor. The chapels which used to belong to the chapters or languages of the order run parallel with the nave, and constitute the aisles. They are very richly embellished, and the roofs are all dome-shaped. From one of these chapels is a staircase leading to the crypt, in which are the tombs of the Grand Masters. Here is interred L'Isle Adam, the first Grand Master in Malta. Of this great man I was so fortunate as to procure a grand portrait, which is as old as his time, but in perfect condition, and a painting of much merit. The Decollation of St. John, by Michael Angelo Caravaggio, is a noble picture; and so is the Flagellation, by Sebastiano del Piombo.

The Catholic clergy of this island are thought to be more than one thousand. An English church, known as St. Paul's, was built here in 1839, by the Dowager Queen Adelaide. It is a plain and neat edifice, and well adapted for divine service.

In this place we found some excellent statuary cut out of the soft yellow stone used in the buildings here. The workmanship was very good, and the men have taste enough to make use of the classical models of antiquity. We obtained some fine vases and figures, which are lifelike.

More than once did I wander over the walls of Valetta which overlook the ditch, and where are monuments to the memory of former governors of this fortress and other persons of note. The tomb of the Marquis of Hastings is under the Cavalier St. John, and in another place the sepulchre of Governor Sir Thomas Maitland. The view is as fine as seems possible; the walls overlook the great harbor and its lateral creeks or openings, which accommodate so many vessels, the three towns opposite,

COSTUMES. 269

and the castles which defend them; and there, too, you have a distinct view of the Floriana suburbs. This is a place of great resort, and the prospect of the sea in the evening is very charming. The native dress is much worn by the lower classes; a long cap, hanging down behind, of various colors, I saw on many men; and this is used as a pouch for small articles. Many of the Maltese wear a silk or cotton sash to hold up the pantaloons. The white clothes of the poorest were beautifully clean. Many of the country people looked quite jauntily; the costume is seen in the illustration.

I greatly admired the dress of the Maltese ladies. It consists of a black silk petticoat, which is worn over a body of some other silk or print, and this is called a *half-onnella*. The upper part is called the *onnella*, and is also of black silk, drawn up into gathers at the centre of one of the outer seams. In the seam of one of the remaining divisions is enclosed a thin piece of whalebone, which is drawn over the head, and forms an elegant arch, leaving the face and neck perfectly open. The left arm is covered with part of this habit, and the right is used for keeping down the angle of the other. The whole is very neat, and the Maltese ladies are not deficient in grace to show their dress off to advantage. I hope this account may be intelligible; if it be not, I may be pardoned when I say that it is the description given in one of their publications at Valetta. The countrywomen usually wear striped native cotton; the head-dress is a *tsholkana*, instead of an *onnella*. The *doublett* is in shape the same as the *half-onnella;* but on gala occasions they put on the *gezuira*, which is a kind of petticoat of blue cotton striped with white, drawn up in thick creases round the waist, and open on the right side, where it is tied with bows of ribbon. The poor women of the island rarely wear shoes, but have one pair which they keep for special occasions. The *onnella*, no doubt, took its origin from the oriental veil. I have noticed vast numbers of the laboring men lying down in the streets and on the docks, and I am told that they often sleep all night exposed to the air.

I will not close this notice of our visit without a slight account of the forts, which are so marked a feature of the place.

CASTLE OF ST. ANGELO.

In 870 the Arabs erected here a small fort to guard their piratical craft which anchored in the great harbor. The Knights of St. John, on their settlement, made it their chief bulwark, and added greatly to its strength. In 1686 it was very much enlarged, under the Grand Master Gregorio Carafa, and it took its present appearance in 1690. It presents a most formidable appearance, and consists of four batteries, one above another, in the style of an amphitheatre, and mounts fifty-one guns, and others upon the cavalier and adjacent walls. This fortress is garrisoned by British artillery.

FORT RICASOLI.

This was founded in 1670, by the Cavalier Ricasoli, at his personal expense; and the Grand Master Cottoner ordered it to be called by his name, as a mark of his gratitude for such generosity. This fort is built on a point of an angular projection, and corresponds with St. Elmo, on the opposite shore, in front of Valetta; and thus the two forts command the entrance to the great harbor. From the sea, if well garrisoned, the fort is quite impregnable; and from the land it could only be reached by surmounting a long succession of very strongly-defended forts, which would threaten destruction to any assailants.

FORT MANOEL.

This was erected in 1726, and is now used as a Lazaretto.

FORT TIGNÈ.

This fortress was built in 1796, and named in honor of the Cavalier Tignè, who planned the barracks of St. Elmo. This fortress, in connection with St. Elmo, defends the entrance to the quarantine harbor; it is regarded as a very strong work, and has extensive mines cut in the solid rock. It is garrisoned by the artillery and a company of the line. It answers to Fort Ricasoli, and St. Elmo is the great central point between the two harbors; the wings of defence are Ricasoli and Tignè.

THE CASTLE OF ST. ELMO.

This, I have already mentioned, stands upon the extremity of the peninsula which separates the two chief harbors; and the great harbor on the left has three lateral inlets, which are defended by Fort St. Angelo, and on the shores of which stand the towns of Burmola, Senglea and Vittoriosa, — all nearly opposite to Valetta. The Fort St. Elmo was built by the Viceroy of Sicily, against the Turks, in 1488. On obtaining possession of the island, the knights saw the vast importance of this point; and when they commenced the city of Valetta, they made St. Elmo the citadel. In 1565, the Sultan Solyman, angry at the seizure of a Turkish galleon belonging to one of his favorites, threatened the destruction of the order; and, for this end, sent a powerful fleet under Dragut, the admiral of the Algerine navy. This armament appeared off the island in May. The attack was made on St. Elmo, usually defended by sixty men under the command of a knight; but on this occasion sixty knights and a company of Spanish infantry were sent in as a reinforcement. The Turkish artillery battered the fort from sea and land. A breach was effected, and a bloody contest followed; and the result would have been the destruction of the garrison, had not supplies arrived in the night from the other side of the great harbor, and the wounded were carried back in the boats. The ravelin was stormed by the Turks, and fell into their hands after a loss on their part of three thousand men. But the courage of the knights was unabated. At last, in their exigency, they sent a knight to the Grand Master, to request permission to evacuate the fort. La Valette, knowing the vast importance of the place, would not permit it to be abandoned, but managed to excite the emulation of the garrison, who were now determined to die rather than surrender their charge. On the 16th June, a general assault was made by the Turks, and the walls were laid level with the rock on which they were built. The enemy entered the ditch, and a heavy fire was kept up on both sides. The assault lasted for six hours, when the Turks retreated with a loss of three thousand men. Seventeen knights perished in the breach, and three hundred soldiers were killed and wounded. A volunteer reinforcement from the other side, of one hundred and fifty men, came over; but it was stated that this was the last aid that could be afforded. The 22d of June the assault was renewed at break of day; and, after defending the place for four hours only sixty men remained to man the breach. At eleven o'clock the janissaries took possession of the Cavalier, and Dragut entered the fort. Not one knight survived, and every soldier perished in the breach. The Turks lost eight thousand men, and the order had to mourn the deaths of three hundred knights and about one thousand three hundred soldiers. The bloody conqueror, anxious to revenge the death of his men, ordered a search for the dead knights, ripped out their hearts, cut their breasts in the shape of a cross, and set them afloat on boards, for the tide to waft them to St. Angelo, and the head-quarters of the Grand Master, at Borgo. La Valette, by way of reprisal, put his prisoners to death, and, loading his cannon with their heads, fired them into the enemy's ranks. The next year after the defeat of the Turkish invasion, the first stone of Valetta was laid, and the Castle of St. Elmo built in great strength. In 1687 it was almost entirely rebuilt, and early in the seventeenth century the bastions of hard limestone were added, and supplied with artillery.

On the angles of the ramparts which command the entrance into both harbors are seen two turrets, originally intended for the purpose of watching all vessels entering and departing the harbor. A treble row of magazines, nineteen on each story, now forms a barrack for two regiments of the line, and a safe asylum for females in case of a siege. These magazines are bomb-proof, and are within the walls under the western wing of the fort.

I must not forget to name the vast chambers which are dug in the rocks to preserve grain in case of siege. These caves are hermetically sealed, and will preserve grain for one hundred years. A vast quantity of wheat is brought here from the Black Sea, and consequently there are in this port many Turkish and Greek vessels, the sailors in which do not appear very ship-shape, or, as Captain Eldridge says, "don't look cut the right way of the leather." Valetta is a free port, but wheat and oil pay a small duty. Rents are quite reasonable in Valetta, and good houses can be had from one hundred dollars per annum upwards.

Having purchased laces, mittens, corals, vases, statues, pictures, &c., we prepared to depart. We did not leave Malta without regret; for we had formed very pleasant acquaintances. Mr. and Mrs. Winthrop and Captain Graves were very kind and friendly, and placed us all under lasting obligations. They dined with us while the anchor was being weighed, and at seven P. M. on 18th August we left Malta for Constantinople.

CHAPTER XX.

MOREA — CERIGO — CAPE COLONNA — TENEDOS — PLAINS OF TROY — ENGLISH AND FRENCH FLEETS — SIGÆUM — HELLESPONT — DARDANELLES — CASTLES OF EUROPE AND ASIA — PROPONTIS, OR SEA OF MARMORA — FIRST VIEW OF STAMBOUL — SCENERY — ANCHORAGE OFF PERA — MR. BROWN AND OTHER VISITORS — VISIT TO PERA, GALATA AND TOPHANA — SULTAN'S NEW PALACE — GULLS — SULTAN'S FIRMAN — SERAGLIO — ATMEIDAN, OR HIPPODROME — SUBLIME PORTE — LIBRARY — ANCIENT ARMOR — MOSQUE OF ST. SOPHIA — HISTORICAL NOTICE, ETC.

On a fine evening we steamed out of the famous port of Malta, and lay a direct course for Cape Matapan, the southern point of the Morea. During the night the wind freshened, and at about twelve o'clock we passed a man-of-war, which we supposed to be a United States ship, as one was expected to arrive in Malta.

The nineteenth was not quite so pleasant a day; it was close and muggy, and no bad imitation of an American dog-day. It was in charming weather that we made our first view of the Morea, and went close by Matapan, which runs out to a lofty, precipitous jut, and at its base is a cavern, which looks as if it bore marks of volcanic action. My copy of Lord Byron was now in demand. We next crossed the mouth of the Gulf of Kolokythia, and obtained a good sight of Mount Taygetus, which takes its name from Taygete, the daughter of Atlas. Its highest point is about three miles south of Sparta. We were now making the north point of Cerigo, the chief of the Ionian Islands. The coast was precipitous and barren, but its valleys are exceedingly fertile, and produce wine, oil, flax, cotton and silk, and corn enough is raised to support the inhabitants. The population is about nine thousand. We saw a vast number of fishing-boats engaged in their business, which seemed very profitable, as they caught a great many. These islands are now under British protection, and enjoy a greater degree of prosperity and more commerce than formerly.

We passed Cape Spati and its chapel, and made Cape St. Angelo and its rocky shore, and then bore away north-easterly for the Straits of Doro, passing between Zea and Macronisi Islands, and leaving St. George to our left. Off Cape Colonna we caught a glimpse of the ruins of the Temple of Minerva, of which several columns remain; and they stand on an elevation of two hundred feet above the sea, and are visible midway in the straits. The passage between Macronisi and Zea is about eight miles, giving us a fair prospect of both shores. The port of Zea is an excellent one, and we passed by it, as it stands on the northwest part of the island; on some charts it is put down as the Port, in others as St. Nicholas. The wind was ahead, and the sea rough for many hours.

Passing the Straits of Doro, we bore away for Tenedos, and on the morning of the twenty-second we came up with the Island of Mytelene, at early light. This was the Lesbos of classic story, and here Sappho and Alcæus were born. We were off Tenedos at seven o'clock. This island is six miles in length, but only about two and a half in width, and is a rocky spot. The town is small and mean looking. I noticed the first mosque that I have seen. A fortress with a large number of guns mounted, and a number of soldiers on the shore, looked as if it were regarded of some importance. The Turkish flag was waving from the walls. It was to this island that the treacherous Greeks withdrew their fleet, to induce the Trojans to imagine that they had abandoned the siege, and then sent the wooden horse to Troy. Almost directly opposite to Tenedos are the Plains of Troy. The exact position of the renowned city is a matter of dispute. On the coast are many hillocks, which tradition declares to be the tombs of Achilles, Hector, Ajax, Peneleus and other magnates of the Homeric song. Here, too, are ruins of vast magnitude. Off at a little distance west lie Lemnos and Imbros, the hiding spots of the Greeks, and the former famous for the ancient assertion of the rights of the ladies, who took a short cut to their object by murdering all the men. But now, at a little past seven o'clock, we were interested by observing, just ahead, a vast fleet of ships of the line; this was the combined fleet of England and France lying at anchor in Beshika Bay. Captain Eldridge, to give us a fair view, shaped his course directly through the fleets, and we had a capital opportunity to see these noble ships. The French ships were very fine, and looked in good order. The combined force consisted of about twenty-five ships of the line, and perhaps twelve or fifteen steamers. As we passed we dipped our colors, and the English returned the compliment; but the Frenchmen were not so polite. Besides these large ships, there were probably twenty-five or thirty small vessels and tenders engaged in purveying for the armament.

Cape Janissary is the site of the ancient Sigæum, and is the south headland of the entrance to the Hellespont. Here the Scamander pours its waters into the sea. The scenery on the Asiatic side immediately improved on doubling this point, and the shore looked more fertile than on the European. The Hellespont here is about three miles wide, and gradually diminishes its breadth. We passed about midway, and saw both the castles distinctly. On the European shore there is an old battery outside the Hellespont, and a new castle on the promontory, at the entrance, of seventy cannon and four mortars. On the Asiatic side stands an old castle, with a battery of eighty guns and four mortars. All our party spent the forenoon on deck, and we made advantageous use of the volumes of Schrœder, Stephens, and the ancient but invaluable folio volume by Sandys, who, though he travelled and wrote two hundred years ago, is still unsurpassed as a local guide in the East. I left my own copy at home by a mistake; in London I could not get the old book for less than four guineas; and when at Malta, my friend Captain Graves, hearing me lament the loss of it on this voyage, kindly allowed me to take his copy. Several fine locations now appeared on the European side, the country-houses looked quite cosey, and the cypress was abundant. Some of the hill-tops were very lofty, and we observed tents on their summits. A large number of vessels lay at anchor waiting for a fair wind, and, by comparing their height with the elevation of the land, we concluded that it must be at least two thousand feet. Six or seven miles brought us to the famous Dardanelles. Here, on the Asiatic side, is the fortress or castle called Sultani Kalessi, with one hundred and twenty guns, many of which discharge immense stone balls. Kilid Bahr is the name of the castle on the European side, and it mounts sixty-four guns. We now approach to Sestos and Abydos, and the spot which has been immortalized by Leander, Lord Byron and Dr. Holmes' oyster-man. The town of Galipoli, at the promontory which makes the entrance to the Sea of Marmora (the ancient Propontis), has an old castle, with a mole and lighthouse. The country directly round it is very pretty and English-looking. We directed our course for the northern point of the Isle of Marmora, and during the night had more motion than we had expected in this inland sea; and here we shipped our first sea on the voyage. At break of day we were getting near to Constantinople, — and I am sure that the impressions of this day will never be erased from my memory. Like Mr. Schrœder, we made this port at early day, and I shall appropriate his description of the scenery, which is, in my opinion, a most felicitous attempt at the creation of a verbal panorama.

"The sun was peeping, with half-closed eyelids, through the woods on the heights beyond Scutari; the sea lay in breathless quiet, and the brilliant city glittered with its minarets, its mighty domes, its towers and the white sheen of palaces. The Seraglio Point jutted out, a mass of cupola and a forest of rich foliage; and its walls skirted round the margin of the point, a compact and massive front of elegance. The city rose loftily behind this garden fore-ground. Scutari sat like a rival, opposite; Pera on a cape just beyond the Seraglio; and the Bosphorus opened in a vast perspective of palaces, on either shore, far into the distance, the banks rising with rich foliage, and every height crowned with some noble kiosk. The gilded tops of a hundred minarets caught the sun-rays in fire, and the domes seemed to hover over all lesser things. We neared rapidly, in the still morning, passing on our left the famous 'Seven Towers,' — a fortress famed in the annals of tyranny and cruelty, — and wound along the whole elegant curve of the Seraglio Point, which is inconceivably beautiful from the water; a grand composition of foliage, and every Turkish architectural fancy. We entered the Bosphorus, and looked still further into its beautiful distance. On the right, in Asia, was Scutari, only a lesser Constantinople; and the distance across to the Seraglio Point, in Europe, cannot, I think, exceed a mile and a half. Pera was on the other side of the Golden Horn, which opened from the Seraglio Point on the left; and before I could well recover from my bewildered feelings we had advanced into the Golden Horn."

It was a matter of some difficulty to find suitable anchorage for our yacht, as all around us were large vessels and steamers at anchor, and the currents set in at this point with tremendous force. We at last selected a spot in front of Pera and Galata, and perhaps three hundred yards from the shore. Near us lay a ship which hoisted the English yacht flag. She was about four hundred tons, and belonged to Mr. Leyland, of London. Close by, also, was the British war-steamship, the Firebrand, which had just arrived with despatches to the minister. A lovelier position than we lay in could not be found. The hills of Constantinople were off to our left, Pera and its heights before us, and the Golden Horn dividing these cities, and over the Horn a bridge which unites the two places. Scutari, with its crowded houses and charming back-ground, lay off to the south; and on all sides were ships of various sizes, and hundreds of the graceful caiques shooting in every direction, and impelled by noble-looking Turks.

I think we hardly felt like leaving the deck to take our breakfast, and every moment was a loss that deprived us of the opportunity to gaze upon the wondrous shores on either hand.

An elegant caique soon came alongside, and we had the happiness to meet with Mr. Brown, the dragoman, or secretary of our embassy, who very politely offered us his own and Mrs. Brown's friendly services while we remained in port; and he chalked out a plan of operations by which we might make the most of our time. Visitors in vast numbers now dropped in, and among the many, I remember with pleasure the call which we received from a young officer of the Firebrand steam-frigate, Mr. J. B. Butler. Mr. and Mrs. Leyland, and their son and daughter, tutor and governesses, came from the yacht Sylphide, and we were much gratified with the party.

After dinner we landed in Pera, which, with Galata and Tophana, are the suburbs, in which all foreigners reside; and they answer to Constantinople as Brooklyn does to New York, but are united to Constantinople by a bridge resting upon boats, which spans the Golden Horn. Tophana and Galata are on the water's edge, and Pera covers the hill-top. In Galata is the naval arsenal, and the military affairs are chiefly carried on in Tophana. The impressions produced upon a foreigner at landing are very strange. He has been gazing upon a capital of wonderful splendor and magnificence, and he finds himself at once in scenes of dirt and filth which cannot be surpassed in the narrowest lanes of New York, or in the worst streets leading to the piers of the North river. Streets we did not find on landing, but old wooden shanties seemed to have been rained down, and our

VIEW OF CONSTANTINOPLE.

course was between them, and round them, and all the time up, up. We had a kind guide in Mr. G. De Giacombo, a Greek, who carries on the ship-chandlery business, and had the supply of our yacht. He piloted us round, and took us to several stores; and at one house, up stairs, we saw some exquisitely-embroidered muslin dresses, wrought by Armenian women. The ladies thought them more beautiful than any similar work in Paris. The heat was intense, and the labor of ascending the wretched streets, and getting out of the way of asses laden with stones, who went straight on, was considerable. The loads on these donkeys were immense; bricks, stones, timber, were tied up with cords, and thrown over their backs, and a Turk walked behind smoking. We entered a café for the purpose of obtaining ice-cream, but found the preparation not at all palatable. We then made our first acquaintance with sherbet. It was rather poor stuff, made of fruit and water, and is better in poetry and on the page of oriental romance than in the streets of Pera. We could not avoid noticing that which all travellers allude to, — the multitude of dogs in the street. They are only the frames of dogs; for such skeletons I never before looked at. They are mostly of a dirty-red color, and are the ugliest-looking specimens of the canine tribe that can be imagined. At one spot I reckoned thirty-seven. They were all lying down, and, to pass along, you have to accommodate their slumbers, and give them a wide berth. We reached Pera, the residence of the ambassadors during the winter months. It is rather better laid out than Galata, but struck us as a miserable place. At length we came to a burying-ground, densely shaded with cypresses. Here was a café with grounds laid out in front, and tables under the shade of cypress and other trees. We took our places, and called for coffee, which was handed to us in small cups of china, which held no more than egg-cups. The prospect extending before us was glorious, and a great many persons were there, apparently enjoying it as much as we did.

On our return, we descended the hill, and came back by Tophana, so as to see the gateway of the new palace which is building for the Sultan. It is a very noble building of white marble, with extensive wings, faces the Bosphorus, and is on its banks. The style is Grecian, and its architect, I was told, is a Greek. The grand gate of entrance at the west is the most elaborate piece of marble-work that we have ever met with. On our way, we met an Araba, with one of the sultanas and three other ladies. The carriage was an old-fashioned affair, — green, yellow and gilt. There were two black eunuchs on horseback, with pistol-holsters at the saddle. The lady had been down to the shore to look off at the yacht.

All around our anchorage we were amused with thousands of immense gulls, which were as tame as barn-yard poultry. They skimmed close to our decks, and swam up to the very sides of the yacht and other vessels; and on the wharves I observed hundreds of them perched upon the sheds. They are never molested; no gun is ever allowed to be fired at them, and their lives are as sacred as are those of the horrid whelps on shore. The porpoises, too, in the harbor, are evidently quite at home. They rise up close to the caiques, and fear no evil. This sacred regard to life is a striking feature in Mahometanism; and if it only had reference to the preservation of humanity, it would be a happy circumstance. The following day, our friend Mr. Brown having procured a firman from the Sultan, we landed in Constantinople, to visit the places of prime interest to foreigners. This firman, and the guard who goes with it, and has us in safe-keeping at the peril of his life, is a mightily expensive affair, and cost us rather more than sixty dollars. We landed in caiques, and went off under the charge of Mr. Brown's special guard, who was one of the janissaries.

Our first visit was paid to the seraglio, on the grand point. We entered through a desolate-looking court, on one side of which stood a clump of fig-trees, the only sign of life or vegetation to be seen. At the entrance into the seraglio we exchanged our boots and shoes for slippers, with which we all came provided. Proceeding up a long flight of marble steps, we followed the Turkish conductor through long galleries and apartments, which were profusely adorned with engravings, and among them I noticed a series of French ones, illustrating the campaigns of Napoleon. The ceilings of most of the rooms were painted with flowers, and so were many of the walls. The apartments were generally matted with straw, and many of them opened upon the Bosphorus, others into charming flower-gardens. We were shown the most lovely bath-room that I have yet seen; it is composed entirely of white marble, and is as luxurious a spot as can be contrived. It was quite a large room. From the principal room of the harem there were a number of smaller apartments leading off by separate doors. The furniture was generally quite plain and old-fashioned; not a footfall can be heard upon the thick mattings.

Descending a few steps on our way to the flower-garden, we entered a secluded retreat overhanging the Bosphorus. It had a bow-window, marble floor, and a fountain in the centre, that discharged and sent up a stream which spread into grateful showers of spray. The light was softly mellowed by the curtains, and from the ceiling a lamp was suspended, which the crystal drops just failed to reach. All around were small jets and fountains flowing into the basin of the larger one, amid which were large golden fish disporting themselves. One room, which was that devoted to the Sultan, was very large and lofty. All around are immense sofas, and on one side an imperial couch of vast size, covered with a canopy. Around the opened door we were allowed to stand, but not to enter.

The garden is very tastily laid out, and filled with trees, shrubs and flowers. I noticed verbenas, gilly-flowers, geraniums, marygolds, roses, and wall-flowers, and orange and lemon trees were very abundant. The seraglio has not been occupied for several years, except by the officials who keep it in order. The reason of its desertion, although so supremely beautiful, arises from the unpleasant associations which are connected with the murder of Sultan Selim; and the late Sultan and his son, now on the throne, have neither been willing to reside here. The dragoman informed us that in case of an insurrection escape from this point would be impossible. A walk of some little distance led us by the spot where Sultan Selim was murdered by the janissaries.

We then entered the Hippodrome, which was built by the Roman Emperor Alexander Severus. It is now probably two hundred and fifty yards long, and one hundred and fifty wide. Many of the monuments which used to adorn this place were demolished or stolen by the Crusaders, when they took Constantinople, in 1204. Among its present striking features I may name the obelisk, of red granite, which was cut in Egypt more than three thousand three hundred years ago. Its height is sixty feet; it is supported by four bronze blocks, which rest on a foundation of marble, on which are bas-reliefs representing the races which used to occur in the Hippodrome.

Here, too, is a brazen pillar of three serpents. entwined; it was brought to Constantinople by Constantine from Delphi. The heads of the serpents are wanting, and it is said that one was struck off by Mahomet II., on his conquest of the city. A square marble pillar, erected in the eighth century, and covered with brazen plates, was known as the Colossus. It stands at one end of the Hippodrome, and served as a meta in the races.

Not far from the Hippodrome, or, as it is now called, the Atmeidan, is the burnt column, which is ninety feet high, and composed of porphyry; but it has so frequently suffered from fires, that it is hard to tell of what it is made. It came from Athens to Rome, where it adorned the great Temple of Apollo, and afterwards was brought here by Constantine; and it is said that he placed in the foundation one of the nails used in the crucifixion, and several other sacred relics. The inscription placed the new capital under the protection of the Saviour of the world. The famous bronze horses which now adorn the portico of St. Mark's, at Venice, formerly stood at the corners of this place. The Atmeidan was the scene of the massacre of the janissaries, and here they met with their fate by order of Sultan Mahmoud, who saved his own life by this sad sacrifice of thousands of men.

We now approached a marble gateway, which presents nothing very striking in its appearance, but which has afforded its name to the city and government, — "the Sublime Porte." We were here shown the ancient throne-room where the Sultan gave audience. The throne is not very unlike an old-fashioned four-post bedstead, and stands in one corner of the room. It is gilded, and profusely ornamented with precious stones. The pillars at its corners are thickly studded with rubies, emeralds and turquoises.

Leaving this, we entered the library, which has a flight of steps leading to it. The room was dark and cheerless. Our dragoman opened a huge genealogical parchment, which contains the pedigree of the Sultans and their portraits, to the time when Selim ascended the throne. The MSS. were closely arranged on shelves, guarded by an open net-work of iron wire. We were shown some beautifully illuminated copies of the Koran. When we were at the Sublime Porte, we saw a lad of about fourteen, reciting his lessons to a priest. The boy went on with a gentle recitative chant, book in hand, as he squatted down before a stool, accompanying his voice with a gentle uniform swaying of the body to and fro. He looked on us, and smiled, but by no means intermitted his employment.

Our next visit was to the armory in the ancient Church of St. Irene. Here we found all descriptions of weapons, some of which were of great antiquity. We were much gratified at seeing in this place some links of the chain used by Xerxes at the Hellespont.

And now we turned towards the renowned Mosque of Saint Sophia. The history of this wonderful structure of Greek architecture for more than one thousand five hundred years is very interesting, and I have condensed the leading features of its vicissitudes from Von Hammer.

In the year 325, when the council of Nice was held, Constantine erected the Temple of Divine Wisdom. In 404 it was burned down. It was rebuilt by Theodosius, 415. In the fifth year of Justinian it was again burnt, and was reconstructed with greater splendor by that emperor. The building occupied seven years, and was completed in 538. Twenty years after, half the dome fell in; but Justinian restored it with an additional magnificence, and at Christmas, 568, it was solemnly reöpened. The walls and arches were of brick, and the marble columns were of the most admirable character; every variety of marble, porphyry, granite, white marble with rose-colored veins, green marble from Laconia, blue from Lybia, black Celtic with white veins, Egyptian granite and porphyry, was employed. Here were eight columns which Aurelius took from the Temple of the Sun, at Balbec; eight green columns from the Temple of Diana, at Ephesus; and several others carried off from Troas, Cyzicus, Athens and the Cyclades. Thus had the spoils of idolatrous worship been devoted to a Christian church; and the dome of St. Sophia proudly rested upon the pillars of the ancient temples of paganism. The cross was planted upon the column which supported the statue of Justinian. This cross fell in the great earthquake of 1371. In 987 a portion of the dome was again thrown down and restored; so that this magnificent work is partly composed of the first edifice of Justinian, partly of the second, and then was renovated by Basilius and Constantine. Mahomed the Conqueror erected the two pillars toward the sea, and one minaret. Selim II. built the next one, and Murad III. erected

MOSQUE OF ST. SOPHIA.

the other two minarets, at the north-east. All history testifies that this was the most splendid temple of the Byzantine empire. The tradition is that an angel delivered the plan of this church to Justinian, and also furnished large treasures for its completion. At the dedication, Christmas eve, 548, the emperor slaughtered one thousand oxen, one thousand sheep, six hundred deer, one thousand swine, ten thousand fowls; and, in addition to this, distributed thirty thousand measures of corn to the poor. Entering the church, he said, "God be praised who has thought me worthy to complete such a work. Solomon, I have surpassed thee!"

This mosque is in the form of a Greek cross; three of its sides are surrounded by vaulted colonnades with cupolas, and the other side is the entrance.

At entering, we had to put on slippers, or walk in our stockings. The walls are of stone, and highly polished; while the floor is of stone and marble, and covered almost entirely with matting. The dome is very grand, and its centre is one hundred and eighty feet from the floor, its diameter one hundred and fifteen feet, and its height one-sixth of the diameter. The extreme interior length of the mosque is one hundred and forty-three feet, and its breadth two hundred and sixty-nine feet. The eight porphyry columns from the Temple of the Sun, at Rome, support the dome; and, with smaller ones of white marble, the cupolas, also, on either side of the dome. Twenty-four Egyptian granite pillars sustain the galleries. The columns in all amount to one hundred and seven. On the vault of the dome are four immense seraphim in mosaic work, and beside them are, in giant characters, the names of Ebubekr, Omar, Osman and Ali, the companions of the Arabian impostor. In the dome itself is inscribed a verse of the Koran, — " God is the light of the heavens and the earth." These words are illuminated on the nights of the Ramazan by a large number of lamps. The cupola is lighted by twenty-four windows. The *Minber*, or pulpit, where prayer for the Sultan is read on Friday, has two flags, one on each side, to denote the triumph of Islamism over Judaism and Christianity. The pulpit for instruction, but which is seldom employed, was given by Sultan Murad IV.; and it rests on, I think, four marble columns.

On one column of this church is a large impression of a hand, made, it is said, by one of the early Sultans; and there is a popular notion that when that impression disappears the Turkish power will pass away.

Two large vases, or fountains of water, are placed here, the gift of Murad III., for the refreshment of worshippers. The Sultan's seat is elevated, and enclosed in a gilded lattice-work. Many of the priests seem to live here day and night, and we saw many of the Turks reclining at full length on the floor, some evidently asleep. Several of the faithful were reciting their prayers in a loud and monotonous tone; and their eyes followed us in all our movements, with no very benignant expression. Certainly, if I had not placed implicit faith in the virtue of the firman, I should have had serious apprehensions of our personal safety. Never did I see men scowl at their fellow-men as did some of these worthies upon our ladies, as they walked through the mosque. We left it with emotions of thankfulness that men are not always to believe a lie, and glad to know that the crescent must surely give way to the cross, and the Crucified One yet prove the resistless attractions of his deathless love by drawing all men unto him.

CHAPTER XX.

MOSQUE OF ACHMET — MUZZEIN'S CALL — COSTUMES OF THE JANISSARIES — REV. MR. BENJAMIN — TOMB OF SULTAN MAHMOUD — BAZAARS — SHOPPING — VISIT TO THE ENGLISH YACHT SYLPHIDE — TURKISH VISITORS — AMERICAN MISSIONARIES — EXCURSION TO SCUTARI — HOWLING DERVISHES — CEMETERY — WEDDING — BULGURLU — SCENERY — CHALCEDON — A KIOSK — HOUSE IN WHICH THE LATE SULTAN DIED — SOLDIERS COMING IN FROM ASIA — DARK RIDE — SAIL TO BEBEK — AFFECTING INCIDENT — VILLAGE OF BEBEK — MISSION PREMISES — EDUCATION OF BOYS IN MECHANICAL ARTS — PERSECUTION — MR. HAMLIN — ARMENIAN PRIEST — THE FAMILY CIRCLE — "LIGHT ON THE DARK RIVER" — MISS LOVELL — MR. MINASIAN.

We continued our exploration by a visit to the Mosque of Achmet. This building has one peculiarity : it is the only mosque in the empire with six minarets, and has two more than the famous one at Mecca. The location of this beautiful edifice is on a part of the ancient Hippodrome. The most impressive feature, on entering the mosque, is the group of massive columns which support the dome. The circumference of each of these four columns is not less than thirty-six yards. The cupola of the great dome is surrounded by four half-cupolas, each of which is joined by two entirely round cupolas, which form behind the four enormous pillars the four corners of the mosque, which therefore appears on the outside to be composed of nine cupolas. The Minber is a copy of the pulpit at Mecca, and is surmounted with a gilt crown, and over this a crescent. This mosque is the richest in Constantinople, and its treasures are said to be immense. As we entered it the Muzzeins were calling aloud the hour of prayer from the minaret.

In our morning perambulation we met with every variety of costume. The full-bearded Turk, with the old turban, which is much less common than it was a few years ago, — the Fez cap is everywhere seen; the smart-looking Armenian, with his well-to-do air; the ill-clad Jew; Albanians in gay apparel; beggars of all ages; women, with their white yashmak and fancy-colored robe, shuffling along in their yellow boots; even the colored women wear the yashmak.

We now took carriages and proceeded to the gallery containing the costumes of the janissaries; and here we passed a delightful hour. The massacre of this formidable body was ordered by the late Sultan Mahmoud II., and it took place on the 15th of June, 1823. They would not brook the idea of reform, and had so long been accustomed to guide the councils of the Sultan, and even change the person of the sovereign, that Mahmoud, who had seen the murder of his cousin and predecessor, well understood how precarious was his hold on the throne, and determined to extirpate this proud body, or perish in the undertaking. The Atmeidan was the scene of their slaughter, and the survivors were sent to distant parts of the empire.

We received much information, all the morning, from our kind friend the Rev. Mr. Benjamin, a missionary at this city from the American board. Mr. B. married the sister of Mr. Daniel B. Allen, one of our party. He has long resided here, and is well acquainted with the objects of interest.

In this gallery the figures are lifelike, made of wax, and dressed in the identical clothing of the different orders and offices of the body. The dresses were very richly adorned with embroidery and costly trimmings. Here, too, were the wax effigies of some Circassians, who were very beautiful. On our way here we passed the marble mausoleum of Sultan Mahmoud. It is in a neat flower-garden, and is surrounded by a richly-gilt iron fence. In the interior is a room with large glass chandeliers. The coffin is covered with a pall of red velvet, embroidered with gold, surmounted by the Fez cap of the Sultan, with an aigrette of heron's feathers, looped by a diamond clasp.

Our steps were now turned to the bazaars; and these must be seen to be at all understood. They are very narrow alleys; the buildings having iron roofs in some cases, for safety. These alleys are a perfect labyrinth, and each trade has its own precincts; thus shawls, glass, slippers, rugs, furs, gilt goods, perfumeries, embroideries, silks, are all to be found in different localities. Up and down the narrow hill-side alley you must travel many a weary step in search of articles; and horses belonging to pachas, and attended by servants on foot, are liable to be met at every other step. I went into several carpet and rug stalls, and found their owners cross-legged and sipping coffee, which they offered me in the early period of our negotiations. These rugs and carpets are of exquisite fabric, the Persian being much finer and more compact in texture than the Turkey article. The goods are all placed in open sight, and the salesman usually sits on his stand, and manifests no anxiety to dispose of his goods. We went to a diamond merchant's, and certainly, when entering the narrow and dirty-looking quarters, should never have supposed that such immense wealth was there concentrated. Vast quantities of precious stones were exposed to our examination, and, a young man coming in with a bit of paper, one of the concern opened an iron safe, and I saw a box full of gold coin, in which, I suppose, there was at least half a bushel. One thousand sovereigns were taken out, but still it was a box full of gold. Shopping is a queer business in this city. Rarely do you give more than half the price demanded for anything offered you in the bazaar. No sooner did we stop at a stall than we were beset with a motley crowd of lookers-on, — Jews, Turks, and boys of all ages, — crying, Bucksheesh. Then there were always people waiting to carry your parcels, and Jews drumming up for the benefit of other merchants, who they know will suit you better. One old Jew, named Moses, really pleased me; he seemed to be an honest fellow, and certainly knew more about goods than the rest of the hangers-on; he really gave us assistance in the purchase of several articles. Glass, boots, shoes, silk goods and jewelry, are all to be bought at low prices. The silversmiths are chiefly Armenians. Almost every burden is transported in the streets of Constantinople upon men's backs, and often did I pity the poor creature who was borne down nearly to the earth under a weight which would have better suited a horse.

Satisfied with our purchases, tired with that most laborious work, sight-seeing, we were glad to resume our carriages at the entrance of the bazaar; and thankful we were to reach the shore, and place ourselves, Turk-fashion, on the cushions of the charming caique, which soon propelled us to the yacht.

Thursday morning, we made an early return-call upon Mr. and Mrs. Leyland, on board their yacht, the Sylphide. We were received with much courtesy, and spent a very agreeable half-hour in the cabin. We were then politely shown over every part of this charming craft. I think the internal arrangements of this ship hardly allow of improvement. The saloon occupied by the ladies had far less the appearance of a ship's cabin than of a parlor in a well-arranged gentleman's mansion. Books, engravings, maps and works of art, adorned the apartment; and the dining-room was as completely adapted for comfort as it could have been on shore. The access to the state-rooms was very well contrived, and they were spacious and elegant. The arrangement, I remember, admitted the entire suite of rooms being opened to a current of air from forward to aft. In the saloon was a fireplace; the panels of the room were mahogany and rosewood. Elegant book-shelves encircled the base of the mast, and on the mantel were Maltese stone vases, filled with flowers of delicious perfume. Sofas of crimson plush and comfortable arm-chairs gave a home-like air to the apartment. In the state-rooms the beds were swung between the ports, and more luxurious chambers no lady could desire. The same comfort extended to the rooms of the doctor, and all others that we saw. The family, during the summer, Mrs. Leyland told me, usually dined upon deck.

The yacht was weighing anchor and getting ready for sea, and when we went on deck we found a pen of sheep, just got ready for the voyage; among them I noticed a fine specimen of the Cameronian breed, remarkable for its enormous tail. There was in a separate pen a beautiful deer. He had become such a pet with all on board, that his life was to be spared. Playing by his side was a noble Newfoundland dog, the favorite of his young master. On the upper deck cane-bottomed swinging settees gave us pleasant seats for a few minutes before we took our leave of this pleasant family circle. More perfect taste and elegance I have never seen in a sailing ship.

On our return to our steamer we found the saloon filled with visitors. Pachas of all ranks, and officers of the Turkish army and navy, Armenian merchants, English and French residents, were all in strong force; and, in addition to these, several of the American missionaries who dwell here and at Bebek, a town on the Bosphorus, about five miles east. We were delighted to meet with the Rev. Messrs. Schauffler, Hamlin, Dwight, and their amiable families. Mr. Dwight left his card for me, but I was not able to meet him. Mr. Hamlin was very anxious that Mrs. Choules and I should take breakfast with him the next day, and kindly offered to come down and fetch us in a caique. To do this, he would have to leave his home at half-past four, so that we might have an early repast, and be back to the yacht in time to see the Sultan attend mosque.

The Turks appeared to enjoy their visit on board. Some of them conversed fluently in English and French. One pacha, who had been educated in England, had charge of the manufacture of fire-arms for the Sultan. He was a noble-looking man.

After our visitors left, I, in company with Dr. Linsly and his lady Mrs. Cross, Miss Thorne, Mrs. Choules, and Mr. George

Vanderbilt, joined our good friend Mr. Brown, in an excursion to Scutari. On landing upon the Asiatic side, we noticed a tower, known as the Maiden's Tower, and to which tradition attaches a story. We were shown the kiosk where the Sultan fainted when he learned the death of a favorite slave, who had been poisoned. The Asiatic side is a mile and a quarter from the city, and has a back-ground of richly-cultivated hills, which are well planted with trees of various kinds. We left our boat at the quay, and ascended the long and narrow streets of Scutari. Our intention was to be present at the service of the howling dervishes. Our janissary went with us, and, after threading several wretched lanes, we came to the monastery of these strange religionists. Everything looked wretched and forlorn. As we entered, the dance was closing by the kissing of hands, and the exhausted dervishes were leaving the hall. We went in; the company was small, the room filthy, and a mean-looking divan ran round it. On the walls were hanging various implements, cords and irons, and nothing looked like adaptation to comfort, but rather a manufactory of misery. The retiring brotherhood had a dried-up, shrivelled expression; they were lank, and seemed worn out. We regretted the loss of the only opportunity to witness the extraordinary spectacle. We repaired to a coffee-shop near by, and seating ourselves on stools under a fine spreading tree, were refreshed with excellent coffee and fine grapes. Mr. Brown's janissary now procured us carriages; they were as gay as red paint and gilding could make them. The drivers ran by the sides of the carriages. We ascended the hill, and came upon the famous cemetery of Scutari. The Turks are fearful of being ultimately expelled from Europe, and are very anxious to be buried in Asia; so that the cemeteries in Scutari are much employed by the inhabitants of Constantinople. The position is certainly most charming, and all around are noble groves of cypresses. We met with strange-looking vehicles on the road, and one araba was filled with a party evidently dressed for a festive occasion. It was drawn by four white oxen fantastically dressed, and having red tassels hanging from a frame over their heads and shoulders. One of our carriages broke down, but the ladies were not injured; and, leaving the driver to repair his damage and follow on, we walked up the hill.

We soon came to a kiosk where a wedding-feast was in course of celebration, and a large company seemed gathered. Here we saw a number of dancing boys, who had been entertaining the guests. The assemblage was breaking up as we approached. In about fifteen minutes more we ascended the hill which is called Bulgurlu, and I am sure that we shall none of us forget the scene that opened upon our gaze. Two quarters of the world were before us. The evening was balmy, and the atmosphere perfectly clear. The panorama is unrivalled upon earth. There was Constantinople, the Golden Horn lying between her and her sister cities. Off at our left are the gardens of the old Byzantium, and the white buildings of the seraglio in their front. Off to the right there are Pera, Galata and Tophana. There, are a hundred mosques and minarets; between all this and Scutari there is the Bosphorus, its innumerable vessels, and its arrowy caiques; all along its banks are ranges of terraces and rows of houses of different colors, each residence surrounded by groves and gardens.

As we stood on this eminence, off to our left lay Chalcedony, so famous for a council held here against Eutyches; and again to the right, far away in the Bosphorus, I could descry the masts of the combined Turkish and Egyptian fleets; and beyond were the dark waves of the Euxine. The sun, breaking from his curtains of gold and purple, cast a mellowed glory over this wondrous prospect. For more than half an hour we sat under the shade of a venerable oak, sipping coffee, and gazing upon scenes we were unwilling to leave. Close by was a kiosk and a charming garden; it belongs to the physician of the late Sultan. He is not in favor, and is regarded as one of a party opposed to the present Sultan's measures. A party was dining with him, and we saw the servants carrying in the covers. Mr. Brown, who knew the proprietor, obtained permission for us to walk in the garden, and a servant gathering grapes presented a noble cluster to one of the ladies. The grapes were the largest we had yet met with, and exquisitely flavored. Close by our shady seat was a spring of water, known as the Sultan's Fountain, from which we drank cooling draughts as it flowed up from the rock. Here we listened to Mr. Brown's localizations of the different spots. Directly below us, and a little to our left, he pointed out an insignificant painted wooden house, of small dimensions, in which the late Sultan died. He was brought here for change of air, and to be under the eye of his physician. The air of the mountains could not give health to the monarch of this beautiful land, and he now lies in his sumptuous mausoleum. We reluctantly bade adieu to this mountain, and, resuming our carriages, had a long down-hill ride in the shades of the evening. The roads are beyond description wretched and full of rocks, and it required very little aid of the fancy to believe that they had never been repaired since Xerxes travelled over them. Dr. Linsly preferred the use of his legs. As we went out in the afternoon, I ought to say that we met with a number of soldiers coming in from remote places as volunteers for the army. They were warlike-looking fellows, well mounted. They came by twos and threes, and I suppose we passed fifty or sixty. It was pitch dark when we reached the water-side, and as we were entering our caiques I lighted my cigar from the chibouque of a solemn-looking Turk. A pleasant sail to the yacht closed one of the most agreeable excursions that I ever remember to have made.

Friday morning, in accordance with our previous engagement, Dr. and Mrs. Linsly and Mrs. Choules were all up at four o'clock, in order to be ready when Mr. Hamlin should fetch us to Bebek. At five o'clock he was alongside, and we at once took our seats in a noble caique; and how did we enjoy that quiet morning on the beautiful waters of the Bosphorus! The exquisite scenery and the swift sailing were all new to us. Rapidly did we glide by the palace of Sultan and Pacha, until, nearing another, we were told of a heart-rending affair which was identified with its magnificence. By Ottoman law, the male children of the reigning Sultan's daughters are destroyed at birth. The late Sultan Mahmoud had one daughter, to whom he was ardently attached. When she arrived at a marriageable age, every overture of marriage was declined on her part, on this account. At length her father, prompted by paternal affection, gave her a sacred writing, under his own hand and seal, that if she had any sons they should be exempt from the universal law. She married, and three daughters in succession cheered her heart. At length her royal father died, and, soon after, a son was born. Never was the precious treasure suffered for a moment to be absent from her sight; fully aware of the frail tenure of her darling boy on life, she vainly hoped by anxious watchfulness on her part to preserve the child. Alas! in absence of all other means, the infant's garments were poisoned, and, seized with convulsions, it expired in her presence. Too well she understood the cause; delirium followed the terrible consciousness, and in ten days her life was a sacrifice to the barbarity of this murderous custom, and she died a maniac. "I was passing the Sultana's palace," said Mr. Hamlin, "when the prolonged and awful death-wail announced that the tragic scene was over." It is quite possible that the Sultan knew nothing of this sad story until all was over. The Turks do not like innovations upon their national habitudes.

The entire sail this morning was past a long line of palatial kiosks, and in the Bosphorus were innumerable vessels of almost every flag. We soon reached Bebek, which has a lovely position in a small bay; this is a populous village. On the landing are some magnificent oaks, and trees which look as if they had the growth of two or three hundred years. Dr. and Mrs. Linsly went to the Rev. Mr. Schauffler's to breakfast, and we accompanied Mr. Hamlin to his abode, which is romantically situated midway on the hill. The house is of wood, painted black, and is of large dimensions. It was purchased of a Greek; was built about fifty years ago, as an inscription of date records; and, when I asked why it was painted black, I was informed that it was intended by its original proprietor to denote his humble, submissive spirit in relation to the government and people. This is the location of the educational affairs of the mission, at the head of which our friend Mr. Hamlin presides. I went into the school-room, which was spacious and well-arranged, having the necessary apparatus for imparting knowledge. The present number of pupils, who are boys of different ages, up to twenty, is fifty-four. On the premises are shops and out-houses for mechanical purposes. The pupils are taught to make stoves, pipes, watering-pots, &c., for all which a ready sale is secured. A steam-engine of considerable power is on the premises, and a building is now going up for a bakery, which is an operation that can only be carried on in Turkey under a special firman from the Sultan. This privilege is allowed to every embassy, and has been recently claimed by Mr. Marsh, our minister at Constantinople, and made over to the institution at Bebek. This will be a very profitable employment, and of great benefit to the school. Several of the pupils have been sent to America to improve themselves in the mechanical arts, and on their return have proved eminently useful.

Much persecution is endured by the Christians, not so much from the Turks as from the Catholic part of the Armenians. They are, in almost all instances, thrown out of the way of obtaining business. Mr. Hamlin stated that the night before a man called on him to procure employment; he was a tailor. A few months before, he had united with the church; he had now no means of supporting his family, because, since his conversion, all his trade had been withdrawn, orders previously given for clothes were countermanded, and he could not support his family unless he could obtain employment from the work-shops of the mission.

I was exceedingly pleased with the aspect of the premises. Everything looked like good management and thrift. Mr. Hamlin is an extraordinary man; he has great mechanical talents, and appears perfectly at home among brick, mortar, lathes and steam-engines. The engine is of his own construction. The interior of the house showed that strict frugality was the rule of the domestic economy. The furniture was plain, — exceedingly so; and I did wish that those who complain about the luxury of missionary life could have seen this establishment. The breakfast-table was a cheerful spectacle. Everything was neat, but far from luxurious, and certainly was only what every New England country pastor, who has four or five hundred dollars a year, would have daily on his morning table. We had the pleasure to meet at breakfast with an aged Armenian priest, who, on account of his embracing evangelical truth, had been subjected to deprivation of office and the grossest personal indignities. He is now the faithful and efficient deacon of a church in the country, and has a high character for piety and usefulness. He is a most venerable-looking man, and would make a good study for a painter. Mr. Hamlin's daughters are fine girls; they have never seen America, and they will excite the interest of hundreds and thousands in Christian America who may peruse the most fascinating piece of female biography of our day, in a volume just published by Messrs. Ticknor & Co., of Boston, called "*Light on the Dark River.*" The volume is the life of the late Mrs. Hamlin, the mother of these dear girls. This work is written by Mrs. Lawrence, a daughter of the Rev. Dr. Woods, of Andover, and is, beyond all question, one of the most charming and pathetic productions recently issued from the press. I wish I could think that my notice of this little volume might induce some who have never seen it to at once do themselves the pleasure and benefit. Mr. Hamlin has married again, and his lady was well known as Miss Lovell to American Christians, from her devoted labors as a teacher in Turkey. When Mr. Goodell visited the American churches a few months ago, and made his touching appeals to us on behalf of Turkey, he often stated the successful labors of this gifted and energetic lady. I have no doubt that he was correct when he said that probably she had done more good by her efforts than most ministers who had remained at home in her native state of New York. Seated at the table, I told Mr. Hamlin how deeply I was interested in listening to Mr. Goodell's warm-hearted and simple statements about Miss Lovell, and expressed my wish to see her. He smiled, a lady blushed, and I was again presented to Mrs. Hamlin as the late Miss Lovell. Long may these excellent friends live to toil and labor for the good of Turk, Greek and Armenian! The Great Day will pronounce their blessedness!

On our return, we were accompanied by Mr. S. M. Minasian, a former pupil of this school, and who, having passed some years in America, now carries on business in Constantinople. He was our kind guide for the day, and greatly aided Mrs. C. in obtaining articles which she wished to purchase. I would earnestly commend this gentleman to all Americans who may visit Constantinople as one who will gladly render them the most valuable services, and on whose knowledge, judgment and integrity, they may most implicitly depend. On our way back to the yacht we saw many of those small brown birds which are so common in the Bosphorus, and are supposed by the Turks to be "lost spirits." They are continually on the wing, wending their way from the Black Sea to that of Marmora.

Our reason for returning so early to the yacht was to see the Grand Sultan go to mosque; and then, after that pageant was enjoyed, we were to go through the Bosphorus up to the Black

Sea, and have a sight of the combined fleets of Turkey and Egypt.

The Protestant community in Turkey, as far as it consists of native subjects of the Porte, is principally Armenian, and contains about three thousand five hundred. There are seventeen churches, and a large number of common schools. The seminary at Bebek is designed to furnish teachers, pastors and translators, for this community, and for the extension of missionary labor. The course of instruction at Bebek embraces a period of five years, except for those who have thoroughly studied their own language previous to entering the institution; in such cases the term is lessened one year.

LANGUAGES.

Ancient and modern Armenian, Turkish, Greek and English. The Armenian, Turkish and Greek, are spoken languages of the country, and demand far less time than the English.

MATHEMATICS.

Arithmetic, algebra, geometry, trigonometry, measuring heights and distances, surveying.

PHYSICAL SCIENCES.

The following text-books are used in courses of experimental lectures:

Olmsted's School Philosophy, Smillie's Philosophy of Natural History, Silliman's Chemistry, Herschel's Astronomy. The lessons are prepared in English text-books, but are recited in Armenian, in which language the lectures are delivered.

INTELLECTUAL AND MORAL SCIENCE, AND RELIGIOUS INSTRUCTION.

Upham's Intellectual Philosophy; Upham on the Will; Wayand's Moral Science; Paley's Evidences; Philosophy of the plan of Salvation; Butler's Analogy; a Theological lecture Wednesday evening; Sermon on Sabbath morning; Exposition Sabbath afternoon; Bible-class and Prayer-meeting in the evening.

Geography, Rhetoric and History, are studied in connection with the Armenian course, in that language.

After going through this preparatory course, such as are fitted by talent and influenced by grace to undertake the work of the ministry commence theological study in a separate and additional course.

I have already alluded to a manual-labor department in the school, and which has grown to great importance. In a stone magazine, used by the Greek proprietor as a wine-cellar, are fitted up a japanning oven and camphene factory. The machine-shop is in excellent order; and there are assaying furnaces and a blacksmith's forge. In addition there is now a bakery, granary, flour-mill and a last-factory. Thus labor is furnished for ten or twelve persons, and a large amount of profitable employment for the students, most materially lessening the expense.

This course of operation, it is probable, will introduce the useful arts, with their modern improvements and machinery, into the country, so as to raise the Protestants in public esteem. Many of the students are now engaged in the useful arts in Constantinople; and, if they succeed, those who have formerly been excluded from labor by the combined influence of the Armenians — both Greeks and Catholics — will attain respectability and comfort.

Six pupils have been ordained as pastors or evangelists; two licensed to preach. Six are now studying theology, and several are engaged as proof-readers, translators and teachers.

The manual-labor department has been carried on without any support from the missionary society. Many travellers, and, I am happy to say, some of our North Star party, have cheerfully placed a few stones in the structure. English merchants and residents have been generous, I learn, in aiding the good work, and the American legation has always been kind and liberal. I found the missionaries all unite in expressions of kind respect for the important services of Mr. Brown whilst acting as Chargé d'Affaires in Mr. Marsh's absence in Greece. The bakery will be fully equal to *ten scholarships*.

The editing and printing of missionary matter is done at Constantinople. At present there is in press, I learn from my valued friend Rev. Mr. Benjamin, an edition of the New Testament in ancient Armenian; Flavel on Keeping the Heart; Lucilla; Lives of the Patriarchs and Prophets, in Armenian and Turkish; a Bible Dictionary; Commentaries on separate books of Scripture; and a newspaper, in Armenian, will soon appear. A boarding-school for girls is established at Hasskerry, and contains about thirty pupils.

It gives me great happiness to bear my testimony to the sense which I cherish of the vast importance of these labors, and the fidelity and zeal in which they are evidently discharged.

Mr. Hamlin has just put up an electric telegraph in the Sultan's palace, and during his engagement had much opportunity to see and converse with the Sultan, of whom he speaks as being mild and gentlemanly, conversing fluently in French, and tolerably well in English.

Mr. and Mrs. Benjamin have been seventeen years at Athens and Smyrna, and now reside in Constantinople. They have a chapel in their own house, and service three times on the Lord's day, in Armenian. Mr. Benjamin preaches, and is occupied in translating books.

CHAPTER XXI.

SULTAN GOING TO MOSQUE — CAIQUES — A STEAMBOAT CHARTERED — EXCURSION UP THE BOSPHORUS — EUROPEAN BANK — TURKISH AND EGYPTIAN FLEET — SYMPLEGADES — BLACK SEA — ASIATIC COAST — LAND AT KANDALI — RETURN TO YACHT — DEPARTURE FROM CONSTANTINOPLE — VOYAGE TO GIBRALTAR — ARRIVAL AT THE ROCK — APPEARANCE OF ROCK AND TOWN — THE METHODIST CHAPEL — REV. W. H. BIDWELL — STREETS AND MARKETS — SHOPS AND GOODS — EXCURSION TO THE ROCK — ENGLISH OFFICERS — ST. GEORGE'S HALL — ST. MICHAEL'S CAVE — MONKEYS — DINNER AT MR. SPRAGUE'S — HISTORICAL NOTICES — SMUGGLERS SHOT — PROFFERED HOSPITALITIES — EXCURSION TO THE CORK WOODS — "CHARLEY," THE MOORISH MERCHANT — DINNER WITH THE FORTY-FOURTH REGIMENT — VISITORS TO THE YACHT.

FRIDAY is the Turkish Sabbath; and every Friday the Sultan goes in state to some one of the numerous mosques of the city or neighborhood. On this occasion he had selected the mosque in Galata, close by our yacht. At about ten we saw the imperial caiques going up to the marble palace to fetch the Sultan and his suite. All the ships of war and vessels of commerce were richly decked with flags. An Austrian steamer was one mass of colored bunting. The North Star was gayly caparisoned for the day, and looked finely. I have never seen so much river show and display, since the 4th November, 1825, when the Erie Canal celebration came off at New York.

Presently there is the loud booming of cannon from the Seraglio Point, and it is echoed and reëchoed from Scutari and the hills back of the cities. Finer echoes I never listened to. Hark! there are ten thousand reverberations, for every ship in the Bosphorus, and every fort in Stamboul is discharging guns in rapid succession.

There come the caiques, — four of the most graceful creations of art that I ever saw. They are very long — at least eighty feet, — and are in color of white and gold, each with beautiful canopies in the stern. They move with vast rapidity, impelled by twenty-eight oarsmen. In the third caique sat the Sultan on his throne, under a velvet canopy; and with our glasses we saw him distinctly. Our yacht gave a salute of twenty-one guns as the procession passed. On arrival at the wharf the oars were uplifted, and the shore lined with troops. The Sultan lands, and several of our party in a caique are close by, and see him distinctly. He is in European dress, — black frock-coat and pantaloons, — and wears the Fez cap. As he steps on shore, every one bends lowly and gracefully in salutation. He walks through the ranks; the noise of cannon ceases, and the crowd quickly disperses as he enters the house of prayer. A richly-dressed and very able band received the Sultan as he landed. Several boats kept around the aquatic procession, and I noticed men holding up papers in their hands; and to these boats two or three smaller ones of the royal cortege immediately pulled up, and took the papers. These were petitions to the Sultan, and which are never rejected. Every one has the right to appeal to the Sultan in this way.

Mr. Vanderbilt did not like to risk taking the North Star up the Bosphorus, as it is so thronged with all descriptions of vessels; and he deemed it best to charter a small steamboat for our party. This was done at an expense of about sixty dollars.

As the Sultan was again entering his caique, after short services at the mosque, we moved slowly and bore off, that we might again see the ruler of this great people. He returned with less splendor, — only with two caiques. He sat under a red umbrella, and we could see him to advantage. He landed at the new palace, which is nearly finished, and we went on.

Far up on the high hill on our left, commanding a glorious prospect, stands the military school. The Seraglio Point and the

Golden Horn are now left behind. Our boat hugs the European side, so that with our opera-glasses we can note every object of interest; but it is impossible to do justice to the surpassing beauty of this ever-changing panorama. Long rows of marble palaces, with gardens of great beauty, kiosks, mosques, high hills, clothed with the richest shades of foliage, and thickly sprinkled with princely residences, meet the eye at every glance on either side. There is a noble palace, built by the late Sultan for his son, now on the throne. When Mahmoud died, it was not quite finished, — lacked the upper story; in accordance with the custom, it has never been resumed, is fast going to decay, and one of these days it will be hinted that it looks badly, and a lighted coal will be quietly dropped into its apartments, and it will disappear. It is of wood, as a prejudice exists against stone; and the new palace, now in course of erection, is the only marble one in the empire. We now approached the palace of Mahmoud, which had been unoccupied since his death. Just beyond is a long range of columns shooting up from low buildings, which resemble cupolas. These are chimneys of the imperial kitchens, and next is a fine edifice, which is the Sultan's present home, and into which he removed just before his father's death. And now come the abodes of vizier, pacha and state officers; the palace of the late Sultana Validè, the mother of the present Sultan; those of his sisters; and here are the brazen gates of that unfortunate one whose sad end I have alluded to before. Now we are on a point of the Bosphorus of great historical interest. These towers of Europe and Asia mark the spot where Darius, and afterwards the Crusaders, crossed the Bosphorus. Here are the fortifications built by the latter. On the bold European cliff stands the tower built by Mahomed II., when, as conqueror, he entered Europe. The strait is very narrow, and the view both up and down the water gloriously beautiful. High projecting cliffs, not rough and cragged, but clothed with soft verdure; hills and slopes dotted with imposing habitations;

smiling villages adorned with cypress, plane and olive trees, make up the prospect.

About two miles from the Black Sea we came to a fine bay, in which lay at anchor the noble fleet of Turkey and Egypt. They are exceedingly fine-looking ships; some of them are of immense size. One — the Mahmoud — is a four-decker, and looks as large as any ship I ever saw. They all have the old square-built sterns, with side galleries. I reckoned about thirty ships, and there were probably not fewer than ten or twelve steamers, and a vast number of tenders and other craft engaged in supplies for the fleet.

Not far from this spot is Therapia, a most charming retreat, where the foreign ministers reside in the summer. Here, I suppose, was Mr. Marsh, of whom we saw nothing during our stay.

The light-house on the mouth of the Bosphorus, at the entrance to the Black Sea, was the limit of our excursion east. Just opposite to it are the Symplegades of mythology. We now came down the Asiatic side, passing the fortress of Riva; the cape of Jum Burun; Poiras, — which fortress stands opposite to the European castle; Anatoli; the Giant's Mountain, which is the loftiest elevation on the Bosphorus; Unkiar Skelessi, or the landing place of the Sultan, and once a favorite resort of royalty, but now the site of a paper-mill; Begkos, a pretty village; Sultania, a pleasant bend of the Bosphorus; Kandali, the most beautiful place on the Asiatic side, and renowned for the purity of the air. Here we all landed, so that the entire party might claim to have been in Asia. We were politely invited to visit a mansion on the hill, owned by a French gentleman, but our time would not permit. We took coffee at the little café on the dock. I never saw a place where I so longed to tarry, and enjoy the unnumbered beauties of the scene. Every word that Murray says is true. " Vain is the attempt to describe the separate or collective beauties of hills and dales; of bights and bays; of meadows and springs; of dark cypress groves and light rose-beds; of roaring currents and flowing streams; of golden kiosks and marble fountains; this confusion of flag-bearing masts and towering minarets; of cupolas floating in air, and caiques cleaving the waves." From the eminence you can see the Euxine and the Sea of Marmora by only turning your head. Again in our little steamer, we pass by several charming places, as Begler-beg, Istawros and Kusghundschik, which is hard by Scutari; and at five o'clock we were on board the North Star, having spent a day which is ever to be remembered by us with pleasure in future life.

We now prepared for our departure, and Mr. Giacombo, our kind and indefatigable agent, was busy with us putting our supplies on board. At six o'clock we took leave of Mr. and Mrs. Brown, to whose friendly attentions we were much indebted during our short stay.

We left Constantinople August 26, at eight o'clock P. M., with the finest weather.

In the Sea of Marmora we passed Mr. Leyland's yacht, which sailed forty hours before us. Our back course lay to the north of Tenedos, and we steered between that island and Lemnos, and made for the Doro Straits, leaving St. Estraite and Skiros to the northward. Passing the Sea of Candi, we steered between Zea and Macronisi, and directed our course for St. Angelo and Matapan. Never, perhaps, was weather more propitious than we now had it, and our progress was rapid. On the 28th, we observed divine service. On the 29th, at two P. M., we passed Cape Passaro and the rocky shore of Sicily near Cape Scalambra, a few villages dotting the coast. The 30th, we made the island of Pantellaria, known to the ancients as Cossyra; it is about thirty miles in circumference, and is of volcanic origin. Passing to the north of this island, we steered up to Cape Bon, on the coast of Africa; and here the weather became too intensely hot for comfort, and coats and neckcloths were oppressive.

Heading north and by west for Cape Bianco, we thence

GIBRALTAR,—FROM THE SPANISH SIDE.

steamed westerly, and at noon on 31st we were off Cape Mavera light, having passed the island of Galita, and made a west course along the coast of Algiers, which we passed September 1st, at noon, the weather hazy, so that we only saw the outline of the shore. At twelve o'clock, on the 2d, we were just north of the small island or rock of Alboran, and in the evening there came up a terrible thunder-storm, accompanied by a gale from the westward. Our ship behaved well; but it was decidedly a rough night, and the breeze came on us charged with the cold air of the Atlantic, and felt very different from the atmosphere we had enjoyed for the past month. We lay off the harbor of Gibraltar at half-past twelve, thus performing our voyage from Constantinople to the Rock in seven days; a thing which has never before occurred, — yet we only used two boilers, and had the power to have made the passage in five and a half. The distance was one thousand eight hundred and forty miles.

All ships coming from the Levant are compelled to undergo a quarantine. We were kindly limited to one day, and during that time suffered to commence coaling. We had abundant opportunity, during this quiet time, to notice the position of the celebrated town and its circumjacent country.

At first sight, we can hardly believe that the rock is connected with the main land; but, on inspection, there is seen a long, low, sandy bar, which unites it to Spain, and is well known as the neutral ground. The rock is two and three-quarter miles in length, and about three-quarters of a mile wide. The side towards the Mediterranean is almost perpendicular, and so is the north side. The side towards the harbor has a very gentle ascent from the water, and then at once becomes precipitous. At the south end of the rock are two different planes of the formation; the upper one is called Windmill Hill; the most elevated spot above these planes is called O'Hara, after the general of that name. It is above the lower plane that the 44th regiment is in barracks. The telegraph station is, I think, very nearly at the middle of the rock. It is remarkable that though the side is so inclined, and almost precipitous, yet the water rarely reaches the town, even after violent rains. The mountain is full of caverns, and from these the water is discharged by unknown caverns into the sea. From the rock there is a prospect which includes four kingdoms; — in Europe, Spain; in Africa, Morocco, Fez and Barbary.

The scenery of the bay is delightful, and St. Roque stands on a hill at the foot of a mountain range which stretches away north and west. Further east are the lofty mountains of the Sierra de Ronda. West of the rock, and at the head of the bay, is the charming white-looking town of Algeciras. This was for a long time the Moorish key to the possession of Spain, but it was captured by Alonzo XI., in 1344, after a protracted siege of nearly two years. It is a neat town, with about fifteen thousand inhabitants, and there is frequent intercourse between it and Gibraltar, and boats are continually crossing the bay,— a distance of less than ten miles.

Looking off from the bay, there are the lofty mountains of Barbary, which bear such a marked resemblance to Gibraltar that it has been supposed that a separation has been produced by some great convulsion of nature in former ages. This theory has been supported by the circumstance that monkeys are found in great numbers upon the rock, and in no other part of Europe. There, too, as we look away at Africa, is the island fortress of Ceuta, which belongs to Spain, and where some of the Cuban prisoners are still confined. On entering the harbor, we found that our expected supply of coals from Wales had arrived in three Bristol schooners. Mr. Sprague, the United States consul, came to us, and, in the kindest possible manner, proffered his services, and placed his mansion at our disposal. During the dirty operation of coaling, most of our party took up quarters at the Club-house.

September 4 was a charming day, and, it being the Sabbath, I felt desirous to visit the Methodist chapel, of which a beloved friend, fellow-townsman, and fellow-collegian, had once been pastor, and fell at his post, a victim to the yellow fever, in the year 1828. We made a little party, and found the chapel. It is a very neat edifice, and the officiating clergyman delivered an excellent sermon. The principal part of the audience was composed of soldiers, who were accompanied by their officers, and appeared very devout and attentive, — as they might be, while listening to such admirable instruction. I had the melancholy pleasure of standing by the marble mural tablet which records the faithful services and the early death of the Rev. William Barber. On returning to the hotel, I enjoyed the unexpected pleasure of again meeting with my valued friend the Rev. Mr. Bidwell, who had parted from us in Paris on his tour through France and Spain, which he spoke of as fatiguing; and very evidently he had toiled hard and suffered much in crossing the Pyrenees. He was to depart that evening for Cadiz, by the steamer; and since my return I have read with great interest the capital letters which he has furnished to the *New York Evangelist*, — a paper owned by him, and conducted in a manner which renders it a welcome visitor in every house it enters.

Monday was a busy day, and I made a general survey of the place. The population of Gibraltar, inclusive of the garrison, is more than twenty thousand. The landing is on a good dock, outside the gates; and here is a capital fish and fruit market, in which we made daily observations. Every description of fruit was in profusion and perfection. Peaches, plums, grapes, lemons and pomegranates, were all fine, but no such nectarines as we found at Malta, and which were very superior to any I have ever seen in England, France, or in the United States.

On passing the gates, where the custom-house officers were very polite, we came into a square, where the soldiers were quartered in considerable numbers; and their fine, athletic figures, healthy appearance and neat uniform, presented quite a contrast to the Turkish soldiery. We now came into the main street, which is long and rather narrow, and full of shops. Many of these are well supplied. This is a free port, and goods are consequently quite reasonable. To the left of the rock, and above the town, stand the remains of an old Moorish castle, built in the eighth century, and which is supposed to be the earliest trace of occupancy now left in Gibraltar. Far to the right, and higher, stands the signal-post, from which vessels on approach are reported to the town. Above the densely-built town are stationed the barracks; and there is the governor's house, with its fine garden, and just below lies the Alameda. What a strange medley of characters the streets present! Here are white-turbaned, white-trousered and petticoated Moors; keen-bargaining, black-eyed Jews; swarthy Spaniards; bright-tartaned Highlanders; gayly-dressed English officers, beautiful women in mantillas, and red-coated soldiers, at every step. The streets are all alive with a busy, bustling population.

Our party are watched closely by the shop-keepers, and a good-looking Jew has caught the ladies; we fill his shop, and even crowd his back-room. The shelves and counters are loaded with Spanish and Moorish curiosities. Andalusian scarfs, embroidered table-covers, Malaga figures, costumes, cushions, slippers, vases, coral, silks, old laces, china, and I know not what else, were the sore temptations. One thing I do know, that before the ladies left they had well-nigh emptied the store.

But we had an engagement at the consul's, and the party gathered there by appointment. The plan was to see the rock, and a number of English officers were at Mr. Sprague's to escort the ladies. Mules, donkeys and horses, were in front of the mansion in great force, and on a burning day some thirty persons made the ascent.

Indisposition hindered me from going, but I give the narrative as it was given me, on the return of the pilgrim band. The officers were Messrs. Brown, Higgins, Turner, Thornhill, and others

EXCURSION TO THE TOP OF THE ROCK.

whose names I cannot now recall. The cavalcade I watched as it slowly wound up the hill, and I last saw the party on the winding ascent leading to the excavations, and then retraced my steps.

The party was greatly delighted with the galleries cut in the rock, which are wide enough for mounted cannon to be dragged through with ease, and receive light from port-holes cut in the sides, through which the murderous cannon are pointed. Leaving the mules and horses to join them at the summit, the ladies and gentlemen ascended a spiral staircase, which led them to St. George's Hall, which is a large, circular apartment, with a vaulted stone roof; the sides and flooring are of the solid rock, and from this apartment several large cannon shoot out of the embrasures. Stepping upon one of them, our friends looked down from this dizzy elevation upon the beach and harbor, and obtained a noble view of the adjacent country. The town lay beneath them as an extended map, and every house and garden was clearly defined. The African coast appeared in all its beauty, and the vast Abyla lifted its dark form against the bright back-ground of a tropical sky.

After a protracted enjoyment of this exquisite prospect, the march was resumed, until the signal station was reached; and here, through the thoughtful attention of the officers, a pleasant lunch had been provided. Here the horses and other animals were waiting, and again put into requisition; and a circuitous path led to St. Michael's Cave, the entrance to which is through a fissure in the side of the rock, barricaded with boards. This is a large and lofty circular room; from the roof immense stalactites are hanging, which reflected the light shining from the pine-knot torches. The ground was very damp, and even wet. On the mountain sides are vast numbers of goats, which browse the scanty herbage. The eastern side, which is inaccessible from its perpendicularity, is the safe home of the monkey population, who are in quiet possession of their fastnesses, and are never permitted to receive molestation. During the prevalence of a Levanter, or north-east wind, they occasionally appear upon the rock. The party was gratified by observing one whose large size and grizzled head denoted him as a patriarch of his tribe.

The path down the mountain was delightful. The most charming scenery discovered itself at every turning of the serpentine pathway, in which were some places so narrow as to afford no more than necessary foothold for a single horse, and a false step of the animal would have involved the certain death of its rider. The return was through the charming Alameda, after passing the pleasant residence and gardens of the governor, and the Jews' burying-ground.

On reaching the town, we all met, at four o'clock, at Mr. Sprague's, where he had prepared an elegant dinner. The table was covered with every luxury that the climate furnishes. The game and fruits were in rich profusion, and the dessert was principally furnished from his country house and gardens. The hospitalities of this day are inscribed upon our memories. Mr. Sprague is a gentleman of the most polished address, resides in a noble mansion, and is the worthy successor of his honored father in an office which he long held to the credit of his country. The mother of Mr. Sprague did the honors of the table with great dignity, and our ladies probably enjoyed the day as much as any they had passed upon the excursion. Mrs. Sprague's daughters were in Boston, on a visit to a sister who resides there. Mr. and Mrs. Vanderbilt earnestly pressed Mrs. Sprague to join the party in our yacht, and allow her children the surprise of a visit; but she had never crossed the ocean, and feared to make the voyage.

The annals of the Rock afford interesting passages in relation to this place, so long in possession of the Moors. Wrested from them by conquest, it remained in the hands of Spain, in spite of various attempts on the part of the Moors to regain this stronghold. The following dates may be useful as affording a key to the history of the renowned fortress.

Gebal Tarik, the Berber chief, landed here 711. It was taken from the Moors 1309. Recaptured by the Moors 1333. Taken by Guzman, a Spaniard, 1462, and became part of the Spanish crown 1502. Fortified by Charles V. 1552. Captured by the English, under Admiral Rooke, 1704. Stood a siege against France 1783, and was defended by Eliott. The force of this garrison is about one thousand pieces of cannon, and the fortress in siege would require ten or twelve thousand men. At present the garrison is about four thousand five hundred men.

A great deal of smuggling goes on here, by men who carry articles into Spain. This morning, September 6, a sad occurrence took place; at early daylight one man was found dead and two others mortally wounded, on the sandy bar known as the neutral ground. They had been pursued by the Spanish revenue force, and shot whilst attempting to escape. They were brought into the town, but the wounded men were regarded as beyond cure. These smugglers are known as "rock scorpions,"— persons who live by a contraband trade, and by their wits.

The kindness and attention of the British officers was constant during our entire stay in Gibraltar, and Mr. Vanderbilt and his friends received invitations from the gentlemen of the various regiments in the garrison to dinners. The regiments stationed here, and whose officers all visited the yacht and urged our partaking of their hospitalities, were the 92nd, 44th, 13th, 30th and 35th.

On Wednesday, 7th, several of the officers of the 44th regiment of infantry, and of the Royal Artillery, proposed to the ladies and gentlemen an excursion on horseback to the Cork woods, a place famous for picnics, and situated a few miles within the Spanish dominions. From a lady who made one of the party I received the following account of the jaunt, and thankfully make use of her kind communication. The events

A PICNIC IN THE CORK WOODS.

of the jaunt I heard most graphically described the next evening by several of the English gentlemen, and one bore the marks of his accident.

"*Gibraltar, Sept.* 8, 1853.

"My dear Doctor Choules: According to promise, I proceed to give you a brief account of a most delightful picnic to the Cork wood groves, in the vicinity of Gibraltar, given us by several of the officers of H. B. M.'s 44th regiment, and of the Royal Artillery. The invitation was kindly extended to all our party (as you are aware), but from indisposition, and dread of the long ride on horseback, several declined. At ten o'clock of a rather cloudy morning, we were equipped in our travelling-dresses, and mounted on very tolerable horses. I was more fortunate than the rest; Mr. H., of the artillery, having insisted upon my riding one of his horses, a very beautiful animal, which had won the races at Seville not long previous. I gladly availed myself of his kind offer, I can assure you, and off we started, in great spirits. We soon reached the neutral ground, dividing Spain from Gibraltar, and it certainly looks as if it had no owner. It is quite barren, with scarcely a habitation upon it, about a mile in length, and half a mile in width. The outposts, only a few rods apart, soon told us we were in her Spanish majesty's dominions. We passed a few miserable-looking houses, the inhabitants eying us rather suspiciously, as they do not like the English officers to enter their territory.

"In a short time we arrived at San Roque, a quiet little town, about two leagues distant from Gibraltar. It is to this town that the newly-married couples of Gibraltar generally repair to spend their honeymoon. Here we stopped a few minutes for refreshment, and to readjust our dresses. San Roque, like other Spanish towns, has an amphitheatre for bull-fights, and an Alameda, or public shady walk. Our way now lay through a wild country, the only road a foot-path, over which we had to pass in Indian file. I was told by Capt B. that a British officer had been attacked and robbed, recently, in passing over this very ground. This in no way excited our fears, our escort being gallant and powerful. We were obliged to ford several small streams, and in crossing one Mr. L.'s horse very coolly laid down and took a refreshing roll in the water, greatly to his discomfiture.

"We soon came in view of the cork-trees. They are a widespread, shady tree; the foliage is very thick, and of a dark green. There is nothing particularly remarkable about the tree, except the bark, or cork, which covers the trunk to the depth of six inches. We rode through the wood for about two miles, until we reached a very humble country inn, where the only accommodation found was an empty barn, from which was separated, at one end, an old wine-shop. We tasted some of the wine, but found it disagreeable. We expected that the officers' 'tiger,' whom they had sent with lunch, would be here awaiting our arrival. In about half an hour he made his appearance, having had great difficulty in crossing the Spanish line. We dismounted, and, after selecting a large tree, the ladies reclined under its shade, while the gentlemen provided our repast. A large pine table was brought, also a few rustic chairs, and we were soon engaged doing ample justice to the liberal entertainment set out for us. The chicken salad was made by an artist; and, as we had been well appetized by our long ride, the viands and wines were very grateful to our hungry palates.

"We were disappointed with the appearance of the cork groves; they were not so picturesque as we had expected. The tree is large and beautiful, but the forest, covering a vast plain, is monotonous. After passing a couple of hours agreeably enlivened by social chat, and having cut off some pieces of cork as reminiscences, we set out on our return, which proved to be full of adventures. As we were going along at a smart canter, a herd of cattle rushed across our path. Mr. T., a young artillery officer, was so intent following one of the ladies, that he did not perceive the interruption until he came in full contact with a large bull, causing him to be thrown with great violence. Although a good deal stunned, he was happily not much hurt. His horse, finding himself at liberty, started off, and joined a drove of young horses, which were running about wild. Then began an earnest chase after the runaway. It was only after a hard pursuit of two hours that he was captured. All the gentlemen joined the chase, save one or two who remained with the ladies. In leaping a ditch, one of the hunters was thrown, escaping with a bruise on his lip. Another of the party, Mr. S., in crossing a farm, was denied passage by the peasants, who seized hold of his bridle, and threatened violence; but Mr. S. nothing daunted, laid about right and left with a heavy riding-whip, and forced his way through. We then made a fresh start, and, as it was getting late, took a short cut across the sandy beach at the head of the Bay of Algeciras. We were galloping away finely, when suddenly K——'s horse, completely blown, stopped short, and we had to wait a while until it recovered itself.

"We now came in sight of the mountain called the 'Queen of Spain's Chair,' facing Gibraltar and the bay. It is said that during the celebrated siege of Gibraltar, by the Spaniards, towards the end of the last century, the Queen of Spain, exasperated at its prolonged and successful resistance, seated herself on this mountain, and vowed she would not leave her chair until she saw the Spanish flag waving over the Rock of Gibraltar. This coming to the ears of Governor Eliott, the gallant veteran in command, he determined to relieve her from the personal inconvenience to which her rash vow had subjected her, and hoisted the Spanish flag on the battlements, and the English beneath. We reëntered the world-famed fortress of Gibraltar just before gun-fire, having ridden twenty-five miles. Independently of the novel incidents of our excursion, we were charmed with the gentlemanly demeanor and courtesy of our entertainers, and we shall long look back with pleasure to their picnic to the Cork woods of Spain. S—— T——."

In our shopping expeditions we found ourselves in a curiosity store, kept by a Moor, who is known as "Charley." He is the handsomest black man I ever saw. His eyes are wondrously fine, but his face has been tattooed in his early youth, when he was a slave in Barbary. Charley has been to Timbuctoo, has been a great traveller, speaks several languages, and has managed to accumulate some considerable cash. This man is, in my estimation, "the character" of the town. His costume is thoroughly Turkish, or, more correctly, Moorish; parts of his dress very costly. In his shop we made many a pleasant lounge, and ate his dates, which he always brought out. I think that our acquaintance was mutually agreeable; for certainly Charley, having found favor with our ladies, made extensive sales to all our party, and I fancy at leaving he must have had possession of several hundreds of dollars. His card of business is as follows:

HAGGE SAID GUESUS,

DEALER IN

MOORISH CURIOSITIES, ETC. ETC. ETC.,

No. 7 Main-street,

GIBRALTAR.

A shrewder salesman than "Charley" is not often found. I am writing from an inkstand which I purchased from him, and he said, "O, you will wish you had bought a dozen when you get home!" Well, Charley, you were right there; for my Moorish inkstand, with its castellated sides, is a general favorite, and nearly every one covets it; but I shall keep it in remembrance of as clever a darkey as I know. But he was far too clever to let me off with an inkstand, and sundry other memorials have I to show of our transactions in trade. I wanted some large vases. "Well," said Charley, "what you want such big things; you can't car them a-ship and not break." And he strongly urged smaller matters; but I was set on my idols, — a pair of large vases, made in Barbary. Charley was wrong; the big things reached home in safety, and Charley, like his prophet, was a false one. I commend all travellers to the Rock to put themselves at once into commercial intercourse with Hagge Said Guesus; and I do not think that there is one of the North Star party who would not like to shake hands again with "Charley." I had nearly forgot to say that Charley always addresses the ladies as "my dear;" and the good-humored expression which is enthroned on his handsome round visage is only clouded when a customer objects to his prices, which he prides himself upon never abating.

Mr. and Mrs. Vanderbilt and Mrs. Cross paid a visit to his excellency the Governor, and were very courteously received, and returned pleased with their call.

On Thursday evening, Mr. Clark, Major Labau and I, accepted an invitation to dine with the officers of the 44th at their quarters upon the Rock. At six o'clock we repaired to the Clubhouse, where we were to meet our kind friends, who would take charge of us. At sundown we had the pleasure to listen to the noble band which plays every evening in the square, and never did music sound more sweetly than that calm night. Having ordered our boatmen to meet us at the Ragged Staff, as the town gates would be closed on our return, we at a little past seven got into the carriage and ascended the rock, which is a slow process, but every winding turn showing us new beauties, and at eight we reached the comfortable quarters of the regimental mess. A more superb look-out was never seen than this building affords.

The accommodations are very fine, and all that gentlemen can desire. At a little past eight we were summoned to the dining-room, and a more magnificent one is not easily found. It was a company night, of which there are two every week. There were twenty-two or twenty-four officers at table, all in uniform. The table was loaded with massive plate, belonging to the regiment, which is distinguished for the elegance of its equipage.

Our dinner was one of the best I ever met out of Paris; indeed, it was thoroughly Parisian, as the arrangements of the mess are under the supervision of an artist from the French capital. The Epergnes were very large, and bear the name of the regiment; and the immense candelabra and other adornments rendered it a brilliant scene. The band played during the evening, and I deeply regret that I cannot lay my hand upon the musical programme with which we were provided. The evening was passed in pleasant interchange of views and opinions upon national and local matters, and the Russian and Turkish difficulties came in for a share of our conversation. The gentlemen here, as in Malta, strongly sympathize with the Sultan. A more agreeable party I never met than surrounded that table; every one seemed happy to meet us as Americans, and there was a general sentiment expressed of strong aversion to the tone of the articles which appear in one of the leading London papers, and which most surely are not the just exponents of English opinion and feeling towards the United States.

As the gates are closed at ten for the night, we could only leave the rock at the Ragged Staff gate, and that by the favor of the powers that command. Having the staff in their own hands, and the charge of the carriages which were to convey us to the shore, our hospitable friends kept us late. I am quite sure that the kind speeches of the generous, high-minded officers of the 44th, and their friends of other regiments, will long be remembered by each of their American guests. I shall never hear the Rock of Gibraltar spoken of without thinking of the 44th regiment, and our friends Brown, Higgins, Deering, Thornhill, and others whose faces I can recall much easier than their names. These gentlemen insisted upon escorting us down to the shore, and some fifteen of them got in and on our two carriages, and the descent of the Rock of Gibraltar by a bright moonlight, and the hearty English huzzas with which they took leave of us, are never to be forgotten by either of their guests.

A charming row of two miles brought us to the yacht, and some amusing events which there transpired deeply convinced us that it is never a wise thing to be in "a hurry."

Among those whose politeness I feel bound to record I will mention Mr. Roberts, who keeps a fine chemist's store, where every drug and chemical may be procured in as much perfection as in London or Paris. Mr. Roberts, with hundreds of the inhabitants of the Rock, visited the yacht; and when he came off to us the day we sailed, he politely brought a box of ice, which for a day or two proved exceedingly comfortable and refreshing. Our own stock had been exhausted, and the good people at the only port in the Mediterranean where it could be obtained asked the moderate price of one hundred and twenty dollars per ton. Our ice procured at St. Petersburg lasted us into the Mediterranean, but soon wasted in that region.

Here we had to take leave of our friends and fellow-voyagers Mr. and Mrs. Daniel B. Allen. Mrs. Allen came on board the yacht from a sick bed, and in a condition of extreme debility. The voyage proved eminently serviceable, and now, in much improved health, she leaves us. Our friends took a steamer to Cadiz, and proposed to pass a year in Europe. They carried with them the best wishes of all our company, and sorry were we to lose the companionship of those who ever looked upon the bright side of each passing event.

On leaving the harbor we fired a salute, which was replied to by the guns of the fortress.

CHAPTER XXIII.

LEAVE GIBRALTAR — TANGIER — SAIL FOR MADEIRA — PORTO SANTO — MADEIRA — FUNCHAL, AND ITS ASPECT — LANDING IN THE SURF — HISTORIC NOTICE — LEGEND OF MACHIM — OBSERVATIONS ON FUNCHAL — CATHOLIC INTOLERANCE — MANNERS OF PEOPLE — EXCURSION TO THE CHURCH OF OUR LADY OF THE MOUNT — SCENERY — A MIRACLE — MR. GEORGE BROWN — BEGGARS — ARTICLES FOR SALE — YATES' HOTEL — HIS STUDY — CLIMATE — SIR JAMES CLARK AND LEIGH HUNT — POPULATION — BOARDING-HOUSES — MODES OF TRAVEL — SHOPS — THE BOY-BEGGARS — BLAST OF THE VINEYARDS — THE VINE — WINES OF THE ISLAND — FRUITS AND VEGETABLES — TREES AND FLOWERS — BIRDS — FISH — DEPARTURE.

SEPTEMBER 9th, we left Gibraltar on a fine morning, at about eleven o'clock, and, with a brisk breeze, stood over for Tangier, We soon made the headland of Cape Spartel, and had a glorious view of the straits. This is the north-west point of Africa and of Morocco, and forms the south-western boundary of the Straits of Gibraltar. On its summit we observed an old tower, which appeared in ruins. The sea was rolling into the Bay of Tangier, with a strong northerly wind, and it was soon very clear that we were to be deprived of the pleasure which we had anticipated in landing on the continent of Africa. The surf was rolling in white sheets of foam, and, as a landing could only be effected by the use of the surf-boats from the shore, we at once felt that it was unwise to hazard the inconvenience for the gratification of an hour. We were about one mile from the shore, and our consul's flag was at once exhibited from his house-top. This gentleman had expressed to us at Gibraltar his earnest hope that we would show our yacht to the Moors.

The town makes a fine appearance, as the buildings are all white. It stands in a small space, and within a line of old

Moorish fortified walls; the buildings come down very close to the shore. Not a vessel was in the little bay, which is exceedingly exposed to the north-west winds. Tangier is an old place, and when won by the Romans, under Sertorius, was known as Tingris. Saracens, Moors, Portuguese and English, have all by turn claimed possession of this spot. Charles II. of England received it as part of the portion of his wife, Catherine of Portugal. It was abandoned in 1684 by the British. The present population is about seven thousand five hundred, of whom one-third are Jews. It carries on extensive trade with Gibraltar in cattle, poultry, &c. Not often have I seen a finer outline of coast than that which encircles this little town. A noble range of hills extends off to the east and south, and, as far as we could see, the most luxuriant growth of trees. Palms and aloes were abundant, and the cultivation looked as though it were of a high order. Certainly a sail along this part of Africa is most delightful, and it is hard to believe that such scenes of beauty are inhabited by barbarous Arabs, who are ever prowling for their prey.

We now, at half-past two P. M., made our course direct for the island of Madeira. In the evening the breeze freshened, and all night and throughout Saturday we had good headway. On the evening of the 11th, at six, we made the island of Porto Santo, and lay to under its lee, waiting for daylight to enter the roadstead of Funchal. This island presents a remarkable appearance, and is seen at a great distance. Three large hummocks enable the mariner to distinguish it from Madeira. The mountainous heights appear barren, and everything, as far as we could see, looked unpromising. The population is about one thousand two hundred.

In the early dawn of day we were passing north of the Desertas, a group of rocky islands which are not inhabited, and only visited by a few fishermen, who have huts here for occasional use. One rock, called the Pyramid, bears a very strong

MADEIRA—FUNCHAL FROM THE SEA.

resemblance to a ship with her sails spread. The Table Rock is a flat island, and takes its name from its formation. The passage between the Desertas and Madeira is about eight miles wide, and we lay pretty close to the island, which rose up with its lofty mountain range before us, in the bright morning light. Madeira opened to our view as a long range of rocky hills, dotted with white houses, church-towers, villas, trees planted in rows, and looking like orchards. As we passed along, the scenery became exquisitely beautiful. Precipitous cliffs, deep ravines and beds of mountain torrents, are clearly discernible; and gorges cut out as by the convulsions of nature, between vast mountains, extending from the sea up to the summits of the cliffs, till hidden from sight by the clouds resting on the peaks of the range, present a most majestic landscape.

Funchal now opened upon our gaze in all its beauty. This famous bay, which hardly, however, comes up to this geographical appellation, begins to recede from the Cape Garajáo at the east, a distance of nearly three miles, and then runs out more boldly towards Ponta da Cruz, a little west of Funchal. The entire indentation is, I think, less than a mile. From Garajáo to Fort St. Jago, which stands as an eastern boundary to the town, the coast is very bold, and has but one mountain gorge, at the foot of which stand the quarantine buildings.

At Fort St. Jago a rough shingle beach begins, which fronts the entire town, and extends to the western extremity of Funchal, known as the Ribeira de Saŏ Paulo, and then on to the narrow point called the Pontinha and the Loo-Rock; these are both surmounted with forts, and are striking features from the vessels in the bay. Loo-Rock stands out more than one hundred yards from the line of the coast. Not far from this, and bordering on the town, are the Portuguese cemetery and a fine plantation of cypress trees. The town lies directly on the water line, and ascends the eminence, which extends to a high mountainous range behind it, and is at least three thousand five hundred feet high. I am sure that no artist has ever done justice to the scenery of this island. It reminds me of Gay Head, on Martha's Vineyard; and has as rich variety of soil as that remarkable headland, mingling black, yellow, red and white, with the living green of the luxuriant foliage, under the perpetually shifting shadows of the clouds.

Our vessel was soon surrounded by a fleet of boats from the shore. The health-officer came off to us, and, taking our papers, soon returned, giving us permission to land. We then landed, and on gaining the shore had to have our boats drawn up through the surf, which breaks strongly on the strand. This is sometimes quite an undertaking. As soon as the boat nears the shore it is turned stern end to the beach, and the oarsmen, with their pantaloons tucked up, seize the opportunity when a large wave rolls up to back the boat upon its force, till it touches the beach; they then jump out, and pull the boat and passengers up high and dry. We at once repaired to the hotel kept by Mr. Yates. Among our visitors from the town, before we landed, were Mr. Borden and Mr. George Brown, both of whom rendered us kind and friendly attentions upon shore during our entire stay upon the island.

Before I record our movements, I would here say a little about the history of this interesting place. It seems probable that in the days of Augustus Cæsar something was known of the existence of these islands. Pliny unquestionably speaks of these groups, and adds that they were "discovered by Juba." After the decline and fall of Carthage, it is certain that all intercourse with the Atlantic islands was cut off. In 1419 the Prince Henry, son of John, King of Portugal, sent out ships to double Cape Bojador, and the captains were driven so far from shore, that they fell in with an island, which they called Porto Santo. Henry sent out a colony to this island, and the inhabitants soon noticed a dark spot still westward, and Zarco, the commander of one of Henry's ships, sailing west, discovered an island, 1420, to which he gave the name of Madeira, because it was covered with trees.

The Portuguese determined to colonize the island, and made Zarco, and his fellow-navigator Teixeira, captains of the place. Zarco ruled forty-seven years, and is buried in St. Clara convent. In 1508 Funchal was made a city. In 1580 Madeira passed into the hands of Spain, and continued in her possession until 1640. From 1801 until 1807 it was under English protection. In 1847 a popular effort was made, but the place was restored to Portugal, and is still in her power.

The Spaniards say that Columbus was once a resident on this island. It is certain that his wife was the daughter of Pestrello, one of the discoverers of Porto Santo. A romantic story is also told of the re-discovery of Madeira. This narrative, by Alcaforado, was translated into French in 1671, and was printed in Paris.

HISTORY OF MACHIM.

An Englishman of obscure birth, named Robert Machim, who lived in the reign of Edward III., fell in love with Anna d'Arfet, a beautiful damsel of noble family. Her father, incensed at his presumption, obtained the imprisonment of the lover, and married his daughter to a more illustrious suitor. The bridegroom, however, having left his castle, near Bristol, to attend the king in his wars, Machim, when released, procured access to Anna, and persuaded her to escape with him to France. They sailed, without a pilot, for the coast of Bretagne; but, a storm arising, lost their reckoning, and, after running ten days before the gale, at length discovered the coast of Madeira, and landed, in 1346, in a bay, afterwards named Machico, from him. A storm drove Machim's vessel from its anchorage, leaving those who had landed from it in such distress, that the lady died of grief. Machim, refusing all food, did not long survive her, and was buried in the same grave. The rest, having ornamented the tomb with a large wooden cross, and placed near it an inscription which Machim had prepared, requesting the first Christians who might read it to raise a chapel on the spot, took to their boat, and, being carried to the coast of Barbary, were made captives by the Moors. While in captivity they related their adventures and described the position of Madeira to a fellow-captive, who communicated the facts to a Spanish pilot, called Morales, in the employment of Gonçalves Zarco. Antonio Galvano, in his account of Portuguese discoveries, relates that this Machim, after Anna's death, left the island in a boat, and it was picked up on the coast of Africa, by the Moors, and sent as a curiosity to Henry III., King of Castile.

Funchal is built in an irregular manner, and its streets are laid with a pavement of small stones, of the size of an egg. The stones are basalt, and are furnished by the beach. The streets are narrow, and the rich and poor seem to live in harmonious contiguity. Most of the dwellings have balconies. In a large number of instances I found the ground floor of the houses used as wine-cellars. The people deserve much credit for the great cleanliness of their streets. Rivers, or, more properly speaking, mountain-torrents, at least three pass through Funchal, and have in their autumnal swell frequently devastated the place; but their beds and channels are now dammed up by stupendous walls These channels were perfectly dry when we were here. I have never met with such hosts of beggars as at this place. Men, women and children, assail you. The principal street is called the Carreira, at the end of which is the English chapel. It is a plain building, having no very striking exterior appearance of a church; but this arises from Portuguese intolerance. Catholics prate about their rights and liberties in England and America, where they have perfect liberty to observe *their* religious services, but not an atom of this will they afford to Protestants in any land on which they have power and entire foothold.

It is about time for England and the United States to demand from Catholic countries the liberty of worship for their citizens abroad. Will Americans ever learn that Popery is an unchangeable system, and that *wherever it has power there it persecutes?* Our Catholic bishops must laugh at the facility with which they delude our statesmen and our citizens by talking about liberty, republicanism, and other matters which they abhor, and would exterminate from the face of the earth.

The most agreeable walks in the town are the Praça Academica, and Praça da Rainha, on the border of the sea, and the Praça da Constituiçaõ, which is in front of the cathedral. On these promenades there are fine shade-trees, and conveniences for the invalid to take repose. These are great places of rendezvous in the cool of the evenings, and on gala occasions the band plays for the entertainment of the company. I have seldom seen finer-looking men and women than the peasantry who come into town from the mountains, bearing supplies of produce and fuel in burdens on their heads. These people struck me as possessing much politeness, for men and women in their station of life. I never passed them but they made a respectful recognition, and at the same time touched or removed the jaunty, funnel-shaped cap, with a long peak slightly topping off to the right. The costume of the country people is very picturesque. The women commonly wear printed calico, and a petticoat of striped linsey-woolsey, bound with a gay color. The men wear white linen trousers, the shirt adorned at the neck with a gold button, a showy waistcoat, generally worn open, or with bright buttons, and a short jacket thrown across the left shoulder. The carapuça is worn by men and women. My impressions of the common people at Madeira are very favorable; they are always clean-looking, but their reputation is not good for honesty. The state of religion is very low, and I am told by residents on the island that the priesthood are very indolent and inattentive. Dr. Kalley was spoken of with respect, and it was conceded that when residing here he effected much good. The rugged roads occasion most of the burthens to be conveyed on the shoulders of the peasantry, and long journeys of seven and ten miles are made with two hundred and even three hundred pounds, up and down ascents which really appear well-nigh impassable for an ordinary foot-passenger.

On a beautiful afternoon, several ladies and gentlemen formed a party at the hotel, and, under the guidance of Mr. Borden, set out to visit the Chapel of Our Lady on the Mount, which is a most prominent object from the deck of our yacht, standing high up in the back-ground of Funchal. The party were supplied with horses, and Burroqueros, who are the attendants of the horses and mules, and, hanging on at the animal's tail, manage to regulate his movements; they keep up with the horse, in spite of the toilsome ascent. The ladies on their return reported to me, for I did not go, that their road lay through narrow streets, enclosed on either side by high stone walls, rising like parapets, every now and then low enough to give peeps of the enclosed gardens and scenery beyond. But, to atone for this concealment, on all sides of the broken heights, or clinging to and overhanging the walls themselves, were large shrubs of heliotrope in full flower, perfuming the air with their fragrant petals; geraniums of immense growth and charming variety; luxuriant fuchsias, obtaining a size and vigor denied them in our less genial clime; multiflora roses, sweet myrtles, huge oleanders, filled with rose-like blossoms; these and many other floral beauties feasted their senses during that pleasant ride. About twenty minutes before arriving at the church, they rested at a platform which overhangs a vast gorge, and commands the most splendid scenery imaginable. Sea and sky lay before and beneath, blended in one heavenly azure, clear and blue in the softest summer radiance. Two cone-like mountains in the distance at the right uplifted their bluish-gray outline against a most exquisite back-ground; and all around were wooded heights, deep ravines, and beautiful beds of wintry torrents; pretty little thatched garden-cottages, surrounded by plantain, banana and fig trees; mountains, around whose summits clouds ever lingered, — all were thrown together in one picturesque combination. As they ascended, the high walls had disappeared, giving again occasional glimpses of the surrounding country. Large growths of aloes were seen at every turn. The Church of Our Lady presents nothing particularly striking, on a near survey. It is approached by long flights of stone steps from the platform in its front. Like all Popish churches, it has several small side chapels. From the platform there is a charming view of the bay and its boundaries.

The descent from the mountain was by another path, equally precipitous, but even more beautiful than the one by which the ascent had been made, because it commanded a more unobstructed view of the beautiful country. Many a lovely little nook and precipitous ravine, clothed from the top to the bottom of its steep sides with shrubs and verdure, lives a green picture in memory; and that ride to Our Lady's Church of the Mount is daguerreotyped upon the tablets of recollection.

The next day, Mr. Cope, our first officer, joined Mrs. Choules and myself in this same excursion. We went up in a carriage drawn by a pair of oxen. Mrs. C. was as much delighted as on the previous ascent. I think the church stands at eighteen hundred feet above the town, immediately in its rear. Mr. J. A. Dix, in his charming volume of "Winter in Madeira," says that "the ascent is at an angle of not less than fifteen degrees with the horizon." Much of the ascent is far more precipitous. I do not remember any day in my life in which I have enjoyed the beauties of nature so keenly. We stopped on our way at a lovely villa, and walked through the sweetest garden I ever entered. I know not the names of half the trees that were there; but I shall not forget the glorious camellia japonicas, some of which were at least eighteen or twenty feet high, and in luxuriant bloom. The geraniums were of extraordinary growth and beauty. Here I first saw the coffee-tree. An intelligent gardener led us from one spot of beauty to another, and furnished me with some seeds of various kinds. The prospect of the mountain beyond the church is sublime, rising up thousands of feet. This sanctuary is very dear to the population; it not only serves as a landmark, but the devout Catholic sailor, as he comes into port, recognizes it as the church of the saint whose protection has saved him from the dangers of the sea, and here he makes his vow to the object of his trust.

It is said that Our Lady of the Mount once vouchsafed a miracle when the people were threatened with a famine. A pilgrimage to the mount was undertaken by the principal inhabitants to invoke the aid of Nossa Senhora, and, lo! the next morning a vessel came into Funchal from Lisbon, laden with corn! On examination, the clothes of the saint were saturated with seawater, and the sailors declared that during a long calm a white figure arose from the ocean and drew them into the harbor!

I spent a very pleasant hour with Mr. George Brown, at his residence. This gentleman has had a checkered life, and few men have passed through more vicissitudes. The history of his adventures would be an interesting one, and afford a striking illustration of the benefits to be derived from a cheerful, hopeful temper. Mr. Brown occupies a large house, and employs himself in the education of some twenty or thirty lads. I found him surrounded with the unmistakable proofs of his admiration of our country, in which he had passed several years. The walls of his parlor have on them the Declaration of Independence, Jackson's Proclamation, the likenesses of the Presidents, and maps of the United States, and some of the single states. The books, too, indicate the bent of his predilections.

I made minute inquiries as to the studies of his pupils, and was gratified to find that he makes American history a very large part of the course of instruction. Mr. B. showed me the copybooks, compositions, etc., of his lads; and it was a curious thing to find that he makes them translate the Declaration of American Independence into Portuguese. He allowed me to carry away a fine copy of it, the production of a youth of fifteen years of age. The governor often visits Mr. B., and he regards the arrival of United States ships with much interest, as he then makes his solitary abode head-quarters for our officers. His card-basket showed quite an extensive circle of acquaintance with our naval gentlemen.

With my friend I rambled through the town, and had my attention directed to many curious matters. The Reading-room is quite a snug little place, delightfully embowered by vines and creepers, close to the water.

Whenever we landed we were surrounded by beggars, and many of them were very interesting children. We often think of one fine-looking boy, about eight years old, who pressed forward with two smaller ones, imploring alms on their behalf. He told me, in pretty good English, that they had "No father, no father, poor forlorn ones." This was his moving exclamation. I told him I would give them something next day, at which the poor children's faces brightened up, and were radiant. They had not yet learned to distrust man's word.

During our visit at Funchal, we were constantly beset with men and women offering articles for sale. Baskets in vast variety of form and fashion, straw-hats, lace, mats, mittens, walking-sticks, tables, writing-desks, chess-boards of the most exquisite construction in mosaic work, were pressed upon us at every step, and at prices astonishingly low. I do not believe that such a market is often thrown open to the good people of Funchal as they found on the arrival of the North Star. We all dined on shore, at Mr. Yates' hotel, and found an admirable table, with the best of attention.

Mr. Yates was formerly a sergeant in the British army, and resides here on account of his health, which is much improved by the climate. On conversing with our host, I was surprised to find him possessed of so much intelligence; and, in reply to my inquiries on many subjects, I at once discovered that he was a man of considerable reading. Mr. Yates invited me into his study, and I was conducted into a very charming retreat, where I met with a far finer library of the best books than can usually be met with in a clergyman's study in New England. The cast of the proprietor's mind was evidently in favor of theology and metaphysics, and not often do I fall in with a better collection of the best authors. Mr. Yates is a hard student, a close thinker; and, although at least fifty, he is diligently employed in the acquisition of the Latin language. I was delighted with my visit to this charming study, which commands a view of the ocean and the unrivalled beauty of the island mountain range.

Madeira is known to all the world by its production of wine, and as a favorite resort for consumptive persons. The climate appears to me to be all that can be desired for the invalid. The mean temperature at Funchal is reported at 66° of Fahrenheit for the whole year. February and March are the extreme of winter, and August and September furnish the greatest heat. Between March and September the mean difference is not greater than about twelve degrees. A variety of causes operate to produce this charming climate. The towering mountains which extend to the entire north shelter it from the weather at every point of the compass except from the south-east and south-west. Then the general absence of forest and wood meliorates the climate, and the perfect steadiness of the land and sea breezes keeps up a state of exquisite temperature. The rainy season takes place in autumn and the early part of spring, and seldom lasts more than three weeks.

Occasionally, at distances of a number of years, this island has been visited with deluges or freshets of an alarming character. The water comes down in torrents through the ravines, bearing before it vast masses of rock, and the noise is tremendous. In 1803, no less than five hundred persons perished, and it was supposed that a water-spout had broken upon the mountains.

I was very particular in my inquiries as to the dampness of this place, and am satisfied that at Funchal there is no undue excess of moisture; fog is unknown, and the dews are very moderate. I do not believe that climate can save a man whose lungs are nearly consumed by disease; but I have no doubt, where individuals have a tendency to disease, and many sure, unerring symptoms of its approach, that if they repaired to Madeira and lived prudently, perfect health would generally be the happy consequence.

Sir James Clark, writing upon the climate of Madeira, says: "It (Madeira) is warmer during the winter and cooler during the summer; there is less difference between the temperature of the day and that of the night; between one season and another; and between successive days. It is almost exempt from keen, cold winds, and enjoys a general steadiness of weather to which the continental climates are strangers." Acute rheumatic affections are very rare in the island, and the dangerous concomitant disease of the heart. Persons laboring under chronic rheumatism almost invariably receive benefit from a visit or residence here. In the island are excellent English physicians, — men of high professional eminence.

The general opinion here is that a residence through the summer is quite as useful to the patient as in the winter. If the population were not so ill-fed and hard-worked, the longevity would be much greater than the bills of mortality indicate. The physicians say that all diseases brought to the island, as small-pox, scarlet fever, &c., appear here in their mildest forms, and very soon disappear. On no occasion has Madeira been visited by the Asiatic cholera.

I am quite satisfied, if a person has to leave the northern part of the United States or England for a milder climate, that the best places I have ever seen for his purposes are Madeira and Malaga. At either of these spots he will find a charming climate, magnificent scenery, interesting associations, good society, the best of medical advice, and the religious privileges which a sick man ought to appreciate.

I am quite of Leigh Hunt's opinion about the state of those who are *threatened* with consumption. He says: "I suspect that people of this tendency, with a proper mode of living, may reach to as good a period of existence as any others. The great secret in this, as in almost all physical cases of ill, seems to be in diet and regimen. If some demi-god could regulate for mankind what they should eat and drink, by what bodily treatment circulate their blood, he would put an end to half the trouble which the world undergoes."

The population of the island is not more than one hundred and fifteen thousand. A large emigration has taken place to Demarara, where laborers were in great demand. This commenced in 1835, and about one thousand two hundred young men left Madeira; others went in 1840. A heavy fee is paid by each emigrant. It is supposed that since 1835 nearly thirty thousand persons have gone to the West India Islands.

All who resort to this island speak favorably of the local authorities; the officers of the custom-house are very polite, and the most liberal course is adopted in reference to the admission of personal goods.

The boarding-houses are numerous, and very comfortable. Mr. John Yates' family hotel is all that a gentleman would desire, and the charges for board vary from forty to fifty dollars per month, inclusive of the wine of the island. There are several villas to let, furnished, and on reasonable terms. These houses can be had for three, six or twelve months. Good servants can be procured at the following rates, as I was informed: Good men-cooks, seven to eight dollars; plain do., five to six dollars; house-maid, three to four dollars; boy, two dollars; groom, five dollars,—without food. Good horses are easily procured, but good saddles are scarce, and a visitor should bring his own. The roads are entirely unfit for carriages, and those who do not ride on horseback generally make use of the palanquin, a sort of cradle suspended from a pole, and hanging about twelve inches from the ground. It has curtains and awning, and a low seat. This is carried by two men, and the charge is about twelve and a half cents an hour. The ox carriage of which I made mention will hold four persons, and is like a large sleigh, moving on wooden or iron runners.

I found the shops, both English and Portuguese, well supplied with everything that visitors would need; but their exterior appearance is by no means inviting. Reading-rooms, clubs, &c., are all open to the stranger. The Commercial Reading-room, near the pier, with its charming veranda and beautiful view of the sea, would be a favorite lounge of mine, if I were to pass any time at Funchal.

Divine service is performed here every Sabbath, both in the English Church and in the Free Church of Scotland.

It is hardly necessary to say that every part of the island abounds in the most picturesque and romantic scenery. I procured some excellent engravings of cataracts and ravines in distant parts of the island, which are awfully grand and sublime. Our limited stay did not allow me to visit them.

On one of my visits on shore, I again met with " the forlorn ones," and their eloquent little advocate. I took him on board the yacht, and made up a large bundle of clothes, including a bonnet for his mother, and never did I see more perfect joy in a human countenance. He went back in the boat, and divided up his spoils; and that day several little hearts were made glad.

Mr. and Mrs. Vanderbilt and others of the party visited the elegant abode of Mr. Gordon, on the mountain, and were greatly delighted with his charming residence. This gentleman, and our worthy consul, Mr. March, were absent on a visit to

England, having left Madeira by the steamer a few days previous to our arrival.

We were all very sorry to find the island laboring under a sad calamity in the total destruction of the vineyards. Instead of producing twenty-five thousand pipes of wine, as used to be done, this year the amount will fall below two hundred! No one can form an adequate idea of the blasted appearance of the vines who has not seen them. They look as if they had been scorched by fire. We could not obtain grapes to eat. The fear is entertained that the vines are so injured that several years must elapse ere another crop can be realized. The vine was brought here in 1425, but the best varieties were introduced by the Jesuits in the close of the 16th century. I observed many of the vines trained on chestnut-trees; but the impression is entertained that the grape is better when grown near to the earth. The vintage occurs early in September. The usual rate of production is calculated in good seasons at a pipe of wine to the acre. The inferior wines are sent in large amounts to Hamburg and Cologne, where, under the hands of doctors, it is made into hock, and sent over Europe and to America.

Very many of the wines here raised are rarely seen off the island. The principal wines of Madeira are as follows:

Malmsey, a light-colored wine, made from a large oval grape, which, when ripe, is of golden hue; its bunches are thin and long. The best wine of this grade is made on estates belonging formerly to the Jesuits. It is difficult to raise the vine, as a little fog or dampness destroys the flower. This is the costliest wine of the island, and is worth about four hundred dollars a pipe on the spot.

Bûal. — This is a delicate wine, produced from a round, straw-colored grape, the size of a small marble. This grape is now scarce, and the wine is very high.

Sercial is a dry, light-colored wine, produced from the round hock grape, which hangs in thick clusters. This wine must obtain considerable age to become acceptable to the palate. The grape is never eaten; its price is high.

Tinta or *Madeira Burgundy.* — This is made from the small black Burgundy grape. It receives its rich claret color from the husks of the grape, which are left in the casks during fermentation. This wine is best when newly made, and after two years loses its aroma. Its value has been from three hundred to three hundred and fifty dollars a pipe.

Tinto is a dark wine from the Negra Molle grape, which is larger than the Burgundy. It is used with others in the composition of Madeira wine.

Madeira. — This is the great wine of the island. It is made from a combination of grapes. When new, it is of a light claret, violet hue; but this subsides as it advances to maturity. This wine is usually sent on a voyage to the East or West Indies, and takes its name accordingly in the markets. It has generally commanded on the island from one hundred to two hundred and sixty dollars a pipe.

Besides these, there are Verdêlho, Palhête, Surdo and Negrino wines.

All the wines of Madeira require an equable temperature.

The fruits and vegetables of Madeira are fine and abundant. Oranges, lemons, citron, coffee, arrow-root, the guava, banana, custard-apple, mango, peaches, pomegranates, apricots, figs, and most of the fruits of temperate climates. The sweet potato is largely produced, and its leaves are given to cattle. The tea-plant has been raised by Mr. Veitch at his quinta, near the magnificent and sublime Curral, at an elevation of two thousand seven hundred feet above the sea.

I was much gratified by seeing several new descriptions of trees. The Til; — this is the *laurus fœtens*, and when cut, it smells like sulphureted hydrogen. Age and exposure turns it of a beautiful black color. The Vinhalico, or island mahogany, is highly valued for cabinet work. The dragon-tree is nearly extinct. The palm is not very common, but here and there I saw some aged ones. It needs, according to Humboldt, a mean temperature of 80° or 81°. The aloe and prickly pear I found everywhere in luxuriant vegetation.

I ought not to omit naming a vegetable which Mr. Yates placed on our table, and to which he directed our attention. It was the Tchu-tchu (Sechium edule), called also by the people *pepinella*. It is a small gourd, very much like vegetable marrow; one seed covers a wall with its ramifications.

This is the very home of Flora. I have already named camellias of twenty feet in height, and I afterwards saw them still higher. The fuchsias grow into perpetual hedges. In every garden we were charmed with the fragrance arising from old favorites and newly-discovered friends. Magnolias were very fine, and in bloom. We noticed the Solandra datura, Judas-tree, spike coral, the turpentine-tree, oleanders, euphorbia, the hibiscus, &c.

It was pleasant to observe the English black-bird here, and to listen to its cheerful note. Here, too, is the green canary, — the primal ancestor of the yellow variety. It is found here in flocks with other birds. The English goldfinch is very common. Partridges and quails are scarce; the woodcock is more common. Humming-birds were in every garden, and on every trellis.

In the fish-market I saw the tunny, of large size; the red and gray mullet, and many kinds which were new to me. The turtle taken here is not the green turtle; and one we purchased did not seem at all equal to the West India ones at home.

I was exceedingly pleased with the appearance and deportment of the common people at Funchal and the vicinity. Men, women and children, however poorly clad, were all clean. Sometimes the clothes were so patched that it was difficult to say what had been the original texture of the garment. Owing to the warmth of the climate, a shirt and pantaloons, without shoes, is all that a boy requires.

At four o'clock in the afternoon we left this most enchanting island, amid the farewells of a vast multitude, who crowded the beach and wished us "a pleasant voyage," and told us truthfully that they hoped to see us again. I do not think that we touched at any place where we were the means of doing the people so much real good as at Funchal. We all made large purchases, and the poor folks who live by manufacturing baskets, mats, feather-work and cabinet-ware, seldom, I fancy, find such a set of customers. Mr. Borden and others said that it was a providential affair to many of the poor people, and would help to make them comfortable through the winter. Most certainly, if I had no duty to keep me at home, I know of no place where I should so like to pass a winter as at Funchal. I could not leave it without a hope that I might see it again, and yet this is vastly improbable; but its mountain range is impressed forever in my recollection.

CHAPTER XXIV.

LEAVE FUNCHAL — APPEARANCE OF THE ISLAND — SKIRT THE SHORE — ROUGH WEATHER — LIVE STOCK — A WRECK DISCOVERED — FLYING-FISH — SANDY HOOK — SALUTATIONS ON ARRIVAL — SUMMARY OF THE VOYAGE — OUR OBLIGATIONS TO MR. AND MRS. VANDERBILT — CAPTAIN ELDRIDGE AND HIS OFFICERS — THE VOYAGE A SOURCE OF PRIDE TO THE COUNTRY.

SEPTEMBER 12, at half-past four P. M., we steamed off from the roadstead of Funchal. The sun was shining beautifully through dark clouds of singular shape resting upon the island. A shower came on, and almost immediately we were delighted with a most brilliant double rainbow. One foot of the exterior arch rested upon the very edge of the water, and the bow bathed the back-ground of ravine and mountain in rich and varied dyes. This is the second instance we have observed of double bows appearing as we have left port. The other one occurred at our departure from Copenhagen. Our course was shaped by Captain Eldridge close along shore, so that we might have good views of the grand coast scenery of this beautiful island.

The back-ground of the town, running up to about five thousand five hundred feet, now showed finely, and presented a map-like delineation of its terraced villas and gardens. On the shore of Funchal stands a lofty pillar, which was erected in 1796–8, by an English merchant, for the purpose of landing goods from ships. This, however, has proved a failure. It stood originally in the very margin of the sea, and now it is considerably inland, indicating the receding of the ocean during the last half-century. The Loo Rock, which in the engraving looks merely like a projecting fort, is really an island, and has a channel between it and the point of land. Now we had a good view again of the governor's palace, which is seen over the Loo Rock, rising behind the gardens of the Praca da Rainha. It is called the Fortaleza, and looks very much like an extensive barrack.

And now from Ponta da Cruz we obtained fresh glimpses of the island, as we passed slowly along. The chief point of interest was Camera de Lobos, and then a little west of this the back-ground was very lofty, and broken in the finest manner. The tops of these mountain peaks seemed vanishing in hazy distance, and against the dark masses of cliff and wood I could see the wing of the sea-gull flashing in the sunshine. Next, we came upon the opening made on the shore by the mountain streams, and around these the coast broke into jagged masses like clouds, and afforded picturesque and startling scenery, in which the precipitous crag and roaring surge awakened sublime emotions.

The little town of Magdalena, on the very edge of the ocean, with its neat little church and its forest-crowned hills, richly gilded by the western sun, delighted us all as we gazed upon it in our too hasty passage. Calheta was the last hamlet we could recognize clearly, and now we lay off our course for New York by the southern passage, making west-half-north till we made latitude 35 N., longitude 52 W.; then west by north-half-north to latitude 37, longitude 64; thence west-north-west.

As soon as we passed beyond the west end of the island, we found a head sea and heavy swell. The night was a very unpleasant one, and probably the ladies suffered more than on any other occasion during the whole voyage. This weather lasted for two days, and the wind kept steady from the north-east. The first three days, we made our way running only two boilers, but then put on all four.

The 14th was a charming evening, and we had a good quiet night, which brought all hands to the breakfast-table. We had several additions about this time made to our live stock from the sheep taken on board at Gibraltar, which gave us four or five lambs. Of these every possible care was taken, but in vain; the bad weather was more than they could manage to bear up against; and now a worse misfortune befell us, in having all our beef taken on board at Madeira prove unfit for use. However, we had other stores to make good this loss; but it was provoking to see so much good provision become worthless.

The 15th was a fine day, and our four boilers now carried us along at a rapid rate. Sunday, 18th, was a rough day; every one seemed to feel under the influence of the storm, though very few were sick. The motion of the ship was unpleasant, and we generally voted it to be a mean kind of time. This was the only Sabbath at sea on which divine service was not held, and its non-observance to-day was owing to my indisposition from severe headache. The deepest interest was awakened in all on board by a report made whilst we were at dinner that a wreck was in sight. Captain Eldridge immediately altered our course, and bore down for it. On coming up to the hulk, it appeared to be the wreck of a ship which must have long been buffeting the ocean wave; her decks were broken up, but her chains still lay on board. Her stanchions really looked like men standing up, and at a distance we all supposed that they were two or three men on deck.

Monday, 19th, was stormy. One of our gentlemen this day lost his hat overboard. The water of the ocean was now tested by the thermometer, and gave 81° 2'. We were greatly amused with immense quantities of flying-fish, several of which were caught forwards. For several days we were surrounded by these pretty fish, and some of them made quite long flights. Almost all our course was through masses of sea-weed, which abounds in the Gulf Stream.

The 20th was a fine day, and our firemen, who were much exhausted with the weather, made noble efforts. Our progress this day was three hundred and six miles. I was greatly amused with an animated discussion between two of our party on the character of the weather which we had experienced on our entire voyage. One, who had never been at sea before, reckoned up sixteen days of bad weather; the other, who had often crossed the ocean, thought there had not been one bad day. I confess that, though I think we had a few unpleasant days, I did not remember one that I should call a regular storm. On our passage through the Gulf Stream we had three or four squalls of considerable force; but I have seen far worse weather in the same region; so that I was quite content to allow this passage to pass as a pretty fair one.

Some of the party had at Gibraltar thought of dear friends at home, and purchased the best grapes the market would afford, and these were carefully packed up in casks. One was now opened, to see how the experiment had succeeded, when the proprietors were vexed to find that they were packed up in pine sawdust, and were thoroughly impregnated with turpentine! In other respects they had kept tolerably well.

Until Thursday, 22d, we saw very few vessels. For days we had seen but two or three, and they were standing east; but now we felt that we were homeward bound, and all around us were ships, brigs and schooners, standing in for a port which, like ourselves, they longed to make, but not with our speed. Passing them all by, we felt our advantage in the possession of that mighty power which has revolutionized the state of the world.

Friday, 23d, at early daylight, we made the light at Sandy Hook, and, without waiting for a pilot, we gradually approached the shores of our beloved land. Staten Island looked as lovely as ever, and she is one of the sweetest spots upon our globe. Travel where he may, the voyager fails to find a place where all the comforts and elegance of life are more profusely concentrated than on this island-suburb of the great metropolis of America.

Just as we passed the residence of Mr. Vanderbilt's mother, a salute was fired, and a boat boarded us from the quarantine, reporting good news for all on board. At the wharf lay the

Hunchback steamboat, and as we passed her the cheering of welcome home fell on Mr. Vanderbilt's ears from those on board who had known him in all his career of life, — from a lad laboring for daily bread, up to the moment when, as a merchant prince, he was returning from a voyage in his own steam yacht to almost every great port of Europe, having received the respect and admiration of the Old World as the successful architect of his own fortunes. We went off from the island side by side with the Hunchback, and in going up the bay received the hearty salutations of every ship and steamer that we met. We steamed up the North river, and were saluted by the Cunard boat at Jersey city, the Collins steamer at Canal-street, and then rounding, we went past the Battery, where hundreds were gathered and on the neighboring wharves, and then went up the East river, and, at about two o'clock, brought up at the spot whence we originally departed, in front of the Allaire works. On the dock were kind friends and beloved relatives, and soon they stood upon our deck, and I almost felt that the entire four months of absence was a dream! But I soon learned a painful fact, that convinced me that all was a reality; that the sweetest joys of life are dashed with bitter waters, and that however bright may be the morning, the clouds may and will often gather ere the day comes to a close.

There are many items, which may, perhaps, prove of interest to others, which are not alluded to in my record. It has occurred to me that some would like to see a summing up of the work done by the North Star, and I therefore add an account of the miles steamed on our voyage.

	MILES.
New York to Southampton	3140
Trip round Isle of Wight	73
Southampton to Copenhagen	807
Copenhagen to Cronstadt	655
Cronstadt to Havre	1461

Havre to Gibraltar	1200
Gibraltar to Malaga	60
Malaga to Leghorn	807
Leghorn to Civita Vecchia	120
Civita Vecchia to Naples	155
Naples to Malta	340
Malta to Constantinople	838
Constantinople to Gibraltar	1838
Gibraltar to Madeira	600
Madeira to New York	2930
Total	15024

We were actually engaged in sailing fifty-eight days, making our average of speed to rate at two hundred and fifty-nine miles per diem, or within a fraction. On the entire voyage, our consumption of coal amounted to two thousand two hundred tons, averaging twenty-eight tons daily. It has rarely happened to any but those of our own party that it could be said, "We have been in the four quarters of the world in twenty-eight days;" yet this was the case with our yacht.

I cannot close this narrative of days precious to memory without expressing my gratitude to Mr. Vanderbilt for his uniform kindness and delicate attentions to me as an individual during the whole excursion; nor would I forget to mention how, every day, every one on board was made to see and feel the excellent qualities of his lady, whose uniform amiable spirit was the regulator of the circle. I do not believe that it is possible for a party of twenty-five persons to spend four months in such close and daily intercourse with less of collision or loss of feeling and temper than was seen in our whole excursion. I am sure that when we landed at New York one of our pleasantest hopes was that we might often meet in future life, to revive the memory of events which have marked our lives in 1853.

CAPTAIN ELDRIDGE AND OFFICERS.

Every one on board the yacht felt the amount of indebtedness under which he labored to Captain Eldridge, whose nautical skill is only equalled by his cheerful-hearted every-day kindness. I do not exaggerate his merits when I say that those who have seen him navigate the Mediterranean, where he had never been, and enter ports without a pilot, are quite satisfied that an abler seaman never trod a quarter-deck. Long may he live, an honor to his profession, and the object of regard to his friends! Mrs. Eldridge, I will simply remark, will have through our lives our highest respect, to which her admirable good sense and virtues entitle her. Our friends Messrs. Cope, Peterson and Germaine, will always be remembered by us with respect.

The gentlemen of the party, under a sense of obligation to the officers of the North Star, decided to present a silver tea service to Captain Eldridge, and a gold watch to each of the previously-named gentlemen, and also to Mr. Larner, the excellent steward.

The presentation of the silver service to the captain took place at Mr. Vanderbilt's house in December, on a very pleasant reünion of the North Star party, when it was handed to him, and an address made by N. B. Labau, Esq., on behalf of the gentlemen.

Mr. John Keefe, our purser, was, perhaps, more constantly with our party than any one of the other members of the ship's company. He was always attentive and obliging, was a most observant traveller, picked up a vast amount of new ideas, and very often made remarks which I shall remember as long as I live. If his numerous friends who visit him at his establishment in Broadway do not get amused by his stories of foreign travel, while regaled with his delicacies, I am much mistaken.

Much of the comfort of the ladies depended upon the good temper and willingness of the stewardess; and I am very sure that none of the ladies would forgive me if I did not say that

Harriet Johnson was always kind and cheerful. Her ready wit and pleasant jokes I do not forget.

The press of the country, with one or two exceptions, spoke favorably of the project; and in several of the papers of the day letters were published from various members of the party. Mr. W. H. Vanderbilt wrote a very interesting series, which appeared in the *Staten Islander*.

I do not believe that such a cruise as we made in the steam yacht North Star, was ever attempted before; and I much doubt if, under all the same circumstances of splendor and enjoyment, it will ever be again undertaken.

It is, I know, to American citizens generally, a matter of proud satisfaction, that a private individual has thus shown the mechanical skill and ability of our country to almost every nation in Europe; and it must be a subject of pleasure to Mr. Vanderbilt to reflect that his enterprise, so nobly conceived, was satisfactorily carried out and happily consummated.

IMPORTANT
LITERARY AND SCIENTIFIC WORKS

PUBLISHED BY

GOULD AND LINCOLN,

59 WASHINGTON STREET, BOSTON,

ANNUAL OF SCIENTIFIC DISCOVERY; or, Year Book of Facts in Science and Art, exhibiting the most important Discoveries and Improvements in Mechanics, Useful Arts, Natural Philosophy, Chemistry, Astronomy, Meteorology, Zoölogy, Botany, Mineralogy, Geology, Geography, Antiquities, etc. ; together with a list of recent Scientific Publications, a classified list of Patents, Obituaries of eminent Scientific Men, an Index of important Papers in Scientific Journals, Reports, &c. Edited by DAVID A. WELLS, A. M. 12mo, cloth, 1,25.

This work, commenced in the year 1850, and issued on the first of March annually, contains all important facts discovered or announced during the year. Each volume is distinct in itself, and contains *entirely new matter*, with a fine portrait of some distinguished scientific man. As it is not intended exclusively for scientific men, but to meet the wants of the general reader, it has been the aim of the editor that the articles should be brief, and intelligible to all. The editor has received the approbation, counsel, and personal contributions of the prominent scientific men throughout the country.

THE FOOTPRINTS OF THE CREATOR; or, The Asterolepis of Stromness. With numerous Illustrations. By HUGH MILLER, author of "The Old Red Sandstone," &c. From the third London Edition. With a Memoir of the Author, by LOUIS AGASSIZ. 12mo, cloth, 1,00.

Dr. BUCKLAND, at a meeting of the British Association, said he had never been so much astonished in his life, by the powers of any man, as he had been by the geological descriptions of Mr. Miller. That wonderful man described these objects with a facility which made him ashamed of the comparative meagreness and poverty of his own descriptions in the "Bridgewater Treatise," which had cost him hours and days of labor. *He would give his left hand to possess such powers of description as this man;* and if it pleased Providence to spare his useful life, he, if any one, would certainly render science attractive and popular, and do equal service to theology and geology.

Mr. Miller's style is remarkably pleasing; his mode of popularizing geological knowledge unsurpassed, perhaps unequalled; and the deep reverence for divine revelation pervading all adds interest and value to the volume. — *N. Y. Com. Advertiser.*

The publishers have again covered themselves with honor, by giving to the American public, with the author's permission, an elegant reprint of a foreign work of science. We earnestly bespeak for this work a wide and free circulation among all who love science much and religion more. — *Puritan Recorder.*

THE OLD RED SANDSTONE; or, New Walks in an Old Field. By HUGH MILLER. Illustrated with Plates and Geological Sections. 12mo, cloth, 1,00.

Mr. Miller's exceedingly interesting book on this formation is just the sort of work to render any subject popular. It is written in a remarkably pleasing style, and contains a wonderful amount of information. — *Westminster Review.*

It is, withal, one of the most beautiful specimens of English composition to be found, conveying information on a most difficult and profound science, in a style at once novel, pleasing, and elegant. It contains the results of twenty years' close observation and experiment, resulting in an accumulation of facts which not only dissipate some dark and knotty old theories with regard to ancient formations, but establish the great truths of geology in more perfect and harmonious consistency with the great truths of revelation. — *Albany Spectator.*   A

VALUABLE SCIENTIFIC WORKS.

A TREATISE ON THE COMPARATIVE ANATOMY OF THE
Animal Kingdom. By Profs. C. TH. VON SIEBOLD and H. STANNIUS. Translated from the German, with Notes, Additions, &c., By WALDO J. BURNETT, M. D., Boston. Two volumes, octavo, cloth.

This is unquestionably the best and most complete work of its class yet published; and its appearance in an English dress, with the corrections, improvements, additions, etc., of the American Editor, will no doubt be welcomed by the men of science in this country and in Europe, from whence orders for supplies of the work have been received.

THE POETRY OF SCIENCE; or, the Physical Phenomena of Nature.
By ROBERT HUNT, Author of " Panthea," " Researches of Light," &c. 12mo, cloth, 1,25.

We are heartily glad to see this interesting work republished in America. It is a book that *is* a book. — *Scientific American.*

It is one of the most readable, interesting, and instructive works of the kind that we have ever seen. — *Phil. Christian Observer.*

THE NATURAL HISTORY OF THE SPECIES: its Typical Forms
and Primeval Distribution. By CHARLES HAMILTON SMITH. With an Introduction, containing an Abstract of the Views of Blumenbach, Prichard, Bachman, Agassiz, and other writers of repute. By SAMUEL KNEELAND, JR., M. D. With elegant Illustrations. 12mo, cloth, 1,25.

The history of the species is thoroughly considered by Colonel Smith, with regard to its origin, typical forms, distribution, filiations, &c. The marks of practical good sense, careful observation, and deep research are displayed in every page. An introductory essay of some seventy or eighty pages forms a valuable addition to the work. It comprises an abstract of the opinions advocated by the most eminent writers on the subject. The statements are made with strict impartiality, and, without a comment, left to the judgment of the reader. — *Sartain's Magazine.*

This work exhibits great research, as well as an evident taste and talent, on the part of the author, for the study of the history of man, upon zoological principles. It is a book of learning, and full of interest, and may be regarded as among the comparatively few real contributions to science, that serve to redeem, in some measure, the mass of useless stuff under which the press groans. — *Chris. Witness.*

This book is characterized by more curious and interesting research than any one that has recently come under our examination. — *Albany Journal and Register.*

It contains a learned and thorough treatment of an important subject, always interesting, and of late attracting more than usual attention. — *Ch. Register.*

The volume before us is one of the best of the publishers' series of publications, replete with rare and valuable information, presented in a style at once clear and entertaining, illustrated in the most copious manner with plates of all the various forms of the human race, tracing with the most minute precision analogies and resemblances, and hence origin. The more it is read, the more widely opens this field of research before the mind, again and again to be returned to, with fresh zest and satisfaction. It is the result of the researches, collections, and labors of a long and valuable lifetime, presented in the most popular form imaginable. — *Albany Spectator.*

LAKE SUPERIOR: its Physical Character, Vegetation, and Animals,
compared with those of other and similar regions. By L. AGASSIZ, and Contributions from other eminent Scientific Gentlemen. With a Narrative of the Expedition, and Illustrations. By J. E. CABOT. One volume, octavo, elegantly illustrated. Cloth, 3,50.

The illustrations, seventeen in number, are in the finest style of the art, by Sonrel; embracing lake and landscape scenery, fishes, and other objects of natural history, with an outline map of Lake Superior.

This work is one of the most valuable scientific works that has appeared in this country. Embodying the researches of our best scientific men relating to a hitherto comparatively unknown region, it will be found to contain a great amount of scientific information.   **B**

GUYOT'S WORKS.

THE EARTH AND MAN. Lectures on COMPARATIVE PHYSICAL GEOGRAPHY, in its relation to the History of Mankind. By Prof. ARNOLD GUYOT. Translated from the French, by Prof. C. C. FELTON, with numerous Illustrations. Eighth thousand. 12mo, cloth, 1,25.

From Prof. Louis Agassiz, of Harvard University.

It will not only render the study of Geography more attractive, but actually show it in its true light, namely, as the science of the relations which exist between nature and man throughout history; of the contrasts observed between the different parts of the globe; of the laws of horizontal and vertical forms of the dry land, in its contact with the sea; of climate, &c. It would be highly serviceable, it seems to me, for the benefit of schools and teachers, that you should induce Mr. Guyot to write a series of graduated text books of geography, from the first elements up to a scientific treatise. It would give new life to these studies in this country, and be the best preparation for sound statistical investigations.

From George S. Hillard, Esq., of Boston.

Professor Guyot's Lectures are marked by learning, ability, and taste. His bold and comprehensive generalizations rest upon a careful foundation of facts. The essential value of his statements is enhanced by his luminous arrangement, and by a vein of philosophical reflection which gives life and dignity to dry details. To teachers of youth it will be especially important. They may learn from it how to make Geography, which I recall as the least interesting of studies, one of the most attractive; and I earnestly commend it to their careful consideration.

Those who have been accustomed to regard Geography as a merely descriptive branch of learning, drier than the remainder biscuit after a voyage, will be delighted to find this hitherto unattractive pursuit converted into a science, the principles of which are definite and the results conclusive. — *North American Review.*

The grand idea of the work is happily expressed by the author, where he calls it the *geographical march of history*. Faith, science, learning, poetry, taste, in a word, genius, have liberally contributed to the production of the work under review. Sometimes we feel as if we were studying a treatise on the exact sciences; at others, it strikes the ear like an epic poem. Now it reads like history, and now it sounds like prophecy. It will find readers in whatever language it may be published. — *Christian Examiner.*

The work is one of high merit, exhibiting a wide range of knowledge, great research, and a philosophical spirit of investigation. Its perusal will well repay the most learned in such subjects, and give new views to all of man's relation to the globe he inhabits. — *Silliman's Journal.*

COMPARATIVE PHYSICAL AND HISTORICAL GEOGRAPHY; or, the Study of the Earth and its Inhabitants. A series of graduated courses for the use of Schools. By ARNOLD GUYOT, author of " Earth and Man," etc.

The series hereby announced will consist of three courses, adapted to the capacity of three different ages and periods of study. The first is intended for primary schools and for children of from seven to ten years. The second is adapted for higher schools, and for young persons of from ten to fifteen years. The third is to be used as a scientific manual in Academies and Colleges.

Each course will be divided into two parts, one on purely Physical Geography, the other for Ethnography, Statistics, Political and Historical Geography. Each part will be illustrated by a colored Physical and Political Atlas, prepared expressly for this purpose, delineating, with the greatest care, the configuration of the surface, and the other physical phenomena alluded to in the corresponding work, the distribution of the races of men, and the political divisions into states, &c., &c.

The two parts of the first or preparatory course are now in a forward state of preparation, and will be issued at an early day.

GUYOT'S MURAL MAPS; a Series of elegant Colored Maps, projected on a large scale, for the Recitation Room, consisting of a Map of the World, North and South America, Europe, Asia, Africa, &c., exhibiting the Physical Phenomena of the Globe, etc. By Prof. ARNOLD GUYOT. Price, mounted, 10,00 each.

  MAP OF THE WORLD, — Now ready.
  MAP OF NORTH AMERICA, — Now ready.
  MAP OF SOUTH AMERICA, — Nearly ready.
  MAP OF GEOGRAPHICAL ELEMENTS, — Now ready.
  ☞ *Other Maps of the Series are in preparation.*

VALUABLE SCIENTIFIC WORKS.

PRINCIPLES OF ZOOLOGY: touching the Structure, Development, Distribution, and Natural Arrangement of the Races of Animals, living and extinct. With numerous Illustrations. For the Use of Schools and Colleges. Part I., COMPARATIVE PHYSIOLOGY. By LOUIS AGASSIZ and AUGUSTUS A. GOULD. Revised Edition. 12mo, cloth, 1,00.

This work places us in possession of information half a century in advance of all our elementary works on this subject. . . No work of the same dimensions has ever appeared in the English language containing so much new and valuable information on the subject of which it treats. — PROF. JAMES HALL.

A work emanating from so high a source hardly requires commendation to give it currency. The volume is prepared for the *student* in zoological science; it is simple and elementary in its style, full in its illustrations, comprehensive in its range, yet well condensed, and brought into the narrow compass requisite for the purpose intended. — *Silliman's Journal.*

The work may safely be recommended as the best book of the kind in our language. — *Christian Examiner.*

It is not a mere book, but a work — a real work, in the form of a book. Zoology is an interesting science, and is here treated with a masterly hand. The history, anatomical structure, the nature and habits of numberless animals, are described in clear and plain language, and illustrated with innumerable engravings. It is a work adapted to colleges and schools, and no young man should be without it. — *Scientific American.*

PRINCIPLES OF ZOOLOGY, PART II. Systematic Zoology, in which the Principles of Classification are applied, and the principal Groups of Animals are briefly characterized. With numerous Illustrations. 12mo, *in preparation.*

THE ELEMENTS OF GEOLOGY; adapted to Schools and Colleges, with numerous Illustrations. By J. R. LOOMIS, late Professor of Chemistry and Geology in Waterville College. 12mo, cloth, 1,00.

After a thorough examination of the work, we feel convinced that in all the requirements of a text book of natural science, it is surpassed by no work before the American public. In this opinion we believe the great body of experienced teachers will concur. The work will be found equally well adapted to the wants of those who have given little or no attention to the science in early life, and are desirous to become acquainted with its terms and principles, with the least consumption of time and labor. We hope that every teacher among our readers will examine the work and put the justness of our remarks to the test of his judgment and experience. — M. B. ANDERSON, *Pres. of Rochester University.*

This is just such a work as is needed for our schools. It contains a systematic statement of the principles of Geology, without entering into the minuteness of detail, which, though interesting to the mature student, confuses the learner. It very wisely, also, avoids those controverted points which mingle geology with questions of biblical criticism. We see no reason why it should not take its place as a text book in all the schools in the land. — *N. Y. Observer.*

This volume merits the attention of teachers, who, if we mistake not, will find it better adapted to their purpose than any other similar work of which we have knowledge. It embodies a statement of the principles of Geology sufficiently full for the ordinary purposes of instruction, with the leading facts from which they are deduced. It embraces the latest results of the science, and indicates the debatable points of theoretical geology. The plan of the work is simple and clear, and the style in which it is written is both compact and lucid. We have special pleasure in welcoming its appearance. — *Watchman and Reflector.*

This volume seems to be just the book now required on geology. It will acquire rapidly a circulation, and will do much to popularize and universally diffuse a knowledge of geological truths. — *Albany Journal.*

It gives a clear and scientific, yet simple, analysis of the main features of the science. It seems, in language and illustration, admirably adapted for use as a text book in common schools and academies; while it is vastly better than any thing which was used in college in our time. In all these capacities we particularly and cordially recommend it. — *Congregationalist, Boston.* D

CHAMBERS'S WORKS.

CHAMBERS'S CYCLOPEDIA OF ENGLISH LITERATURE. A
Selection of the choicest productions of English Authors, from the earliest to the present time. Connected by a Critical and Biographical History. Forming two large imperial octavo volumes of 1400 pages, double column letter-press; with upwards of 300 elegant Illustrations. Edited by ROBERT CHAMBERS, embossed cloth, 5,00.

This work embraces about one thousand authors, chronologically arranged and classed as Poets, Historians, Dramatists, Philosophers, Metaphysicians, Divines, etc., with choice selections from their writings, connected by a Biographical, Historical, and Critical Narrative; thus presenting a complete view of English literature from the earliest to the present time. Let the reader open where he will, he cannot fail to find matter for profit and delight. The selections are gems — infinite riches in a little room; in the language of another, "A WHOLE ENGLISH LIBRARY FUSED DOWN INTO ONE CHEAP BOOK!"

FROM W. H. PRESCOTT, AUTHOR OF "FERDINAND AND ISABELLA." The plan of the work is very judicious. . . It will put the reader in a proper point of view for surveying the whole ground over which he is travelling. . . . Such readers cannot fail to profit largely by the labors of the critic who has the talent and taste to separate what is really beautiful and worthy of their study from what is superfluous.

I concur in the foregoing opinion of Mr. Prescott. — EDWARD EVERETT.

A popular work, indispensable to the library of a student of English literature. — DR. WAYLAND.

We hail with peculiar pleasure the appearance of this work. — *North American Review.*

It has been fitly described as "*a whole English library fused down into one cheap book.*" The Boston edition combines neatness with cheapness, engraved portraits being given, over and above the illustrations of the English copy. — *N. Y. Commercial Advertiser.*

Welcome, more than welcome. It was our good fortune some months ago to obtain a glance at this work, and we have ever since looked with earnestness for its appearance in an American edition. — *N. Y. Recorder.*

☞ The American edition of this valuable work is enriched by the addition of fine steel and mezzotint engravings of the heads of SHAKSPEARE, ADDISON, BYRON; a full length portrait of DR. JOHNSON, and a beautiful scenic representation of OLIVER GOLDSMITH and DR. JOHNSON. These important and elegant additions, together with superior paper and binding, render the American far superior to the English edition. The circulation of this most valuable and popular work has been truly enormous, and its sale in this country still continues unabated.

CHAMBERS'S MISCELLANY OF USEFUL AND ENTERTAINING KNOWLEDGE. Edited by WILLIAM CHAMBERS. With Elegant Illustrative Engravings. Ten volumes, 16mo, cloth, 7,00.

This work has been highly recommended by distinguished individuals, as admirably adapted to Family, Sabbath, and District School Libraries.

It would be difficult to find any miscellany superior or even equal to it: it richly deserves the epithets "useful and entertaining," and I would recommend it very strongly as extremely well adapted to form parts of a library for the young, or of a social or circulating library in town or country. — GEORGE B. EMERSON, ESQ., CHAIRMAN BOSTON SCHOOL BOOK COMMITTEE.

I am gratified to have an opportunity to be instrumental in circulating "Chambers's Miscellany" among the schools for which I am superintendent. — J. J. CLUTE, *Town. Sup. of Castleton, N. Y.*

I am fully satisfied that it is one of the best series in our common school libraries now in circulation. — S. T. HANCE, *Town Sup. of Macedon, Wayne Co., N. Y.*

The trustees have examined the "Miscellany," and are well pleased with it. I have engaged the books to every district that has library money. — MILES CHAFFEE, *Town Sup. of Concord, N. Y.*

I am not acquainted with any similar collection in the English language that can compare with it for purposes of instruction or amusement. I should rejoice to see that set of books in every house in our country. — REV. JOHN O. CHOULES, D. D.

The information contained in this work is surprisingly great; and for the fireside, and the young, particularly, it cannot fail to prove a most valuable and entertaining companion. — *N. Y. Evangelist.*

It is an admirable compilation, distinguished by the good taste which has been shown in all the publications of the Messrs. Chambers. It unites the useful and entertaining. — *N. Y. Com. Adv.*

E

CHAMBERS'S WORKS.

CHAMBERS'S HOME BOOK AND POCKET MISCELLANY. Containing a Choice Selection of Interesting and Instructive Reading for the Old and the Young. Six vols. 16mo, cloth, 3,00.

This work is considered fully equal, if not superior, to either of the Chambers's other works in interest, and, like them, contains a vast fund of valuable information. Following somewhat the plan of the "Miscellany,' it is admirably adapted to the school or the family library, furnishing ample variety for every class of readers, both old and young.

We do not know how it is possible to publish so much good reading matter at such a low price. We speak a good word for the literary excellence of the stories in this work; we hope our people will introduce it into all their families, in order to drive away the miserable flashy-trashy stuff so often found in the hands of our young people of both sexes. — *Scientific American.*

Both an entertaining and instructive work, as it is certainly a very cheap one. — *Puritan Recorder.*

It cannot but have an extensive circulation. — *Albany Express.*

Excellent stories from one of the best sources in the world. Of all the series of cheap books, this promises to be the best. — *Bangor Mercury.*

If any person wishes to read for amusement or profit, to kill time or improve it, get "Chambers's Home Book." — *Chicago Times.*

The Chambers are confessedly the best caterers for popular and useful reading in the world. — *Willis's Home Journal.*

A very entertaining, instructive, and popular work. — *N. Y. Commercial.*

The articles are of that attractive sort which suits us in moods of indolence, when we would linger half way between wakefulness and sleep. They require just thought and activity enough to keep our feet from the land of Nod, without forcing us to run, walk, or even stand. — *Eclectic, Portland.*

The reading contained in these books is of a miscellaneous character, calculated to have the very best effect upon the minds of young readers. While the contents are very far from being puerile, they are not too heavy, but most admirably calculated for the object intended. — *Evening Gazette.*

Coming from the source they do, we need not say that the articles are of the highest literary excellence. We predict for the work a large sale and a host of admirers. — *East Boston Ledger.*

It is just the thing to amuse a leisure hour, and at the same time combines *instruction* with amusement. — *Dover Inquirer.*

Messrs. Chambers, of Edinburgh, have become famous wherever the English language is spoken and read, for their interesting and instructive publications. We have never yet met with any thing which bore the sanction of their names, whose moral tendency was in the least degree questionable. They combine *instruction* with *amusement*, and throughout they breathe a spirit of the purest morality. — *Chicago Tribune.*

CHAMBERS'S REPOSITORY OF INSTRUCTIVE AND AMUSING PAPERS. With Illustrations. An entirely New Series, and containing Original Articles. 16mo, cloth, per vol. 50 cents.

The Messrs. Chambers have recently commenced the publication of this work, under the title of "CHAMBERS'S REPOSITORY OF INSTRUCTIVE AND AMUSING TRACTS," in the form of penny weekly sheets, similar in style, literary character, &c., to the "Miscellany," which has maintained an enormous circulation of more than *eighty thousand copies in England*, and has already reached nearly the same sale in this country.

Arrangements have been made by the American publishers, by which they will issue the work simultaneously with the English edition, in two monthly, handsomely bound, 16mo. volumes, of 260 pages each, to continue until the whole series is completed. Each volume complete in itself, and will be sold in sets or single volumes.

☞ Commendatory Letters, Reviews, Notices, &c., of each of Chambers's works, sufficient to make a good sized duodecimo volume, have been received by the publishers, but room here will only allow giving a specimen of the vast multitude at hand. They are all popular, and contain valuable instructive and entertaining reading — such as should be found in every family, school, and college library.

VALUABLE WORK.

CYCLOPÆDIA OF ANECDOTES OF LITERATURE AND THE
FINE ARTS. Containing a copious and choice selection of Anecdotes of the various forms of Literature, of the Arts, of Architecture, Engravings, Music, Poetry, Painting, and Sculpture, and of the most celebrated Literary Characters and Artists of different Countries and Ages, &c. By KAZLITT ARVINE, A. M., Author of "Cyclopædia of Moral and Religious Anecdotes." With numerous illustrations. 725 pages octavo, cloth, 3,00.

This is unquestionably the choicest collection of anecdotes ever published. It contains *three thousand and forty Anecdotes*, many of them articles of interest, containing reading matter equal to half a dozen pages of a common 12mo. volume; and such is the wonderful variety, that it will be found an almost inexhaustible fund of interest for every class of readers. The elaborate classification and indexes must commend it, especially to public speakers, to the various classes of *literary* and *scientific men*, to *artists, mechanics, and others*, as a DICTIONARY, *for reference*, in relation to facts on the numberless subjects and characters introduced. There are also more than *one hundred and fifty fine Illustrations*.

We know of no work which in the same space comprises so much valuable information in a form so entertaining, and so well adapted to make an indelible impression upon the mind. It must become a standard work, and be ranked among the few books which are indispensable to every complete library. — *N. Y. Chronicle.*

Here is a perfect repository of the most choice and approved specimens of this species of information, selected with the greatest care from all sources, ancient and modern. The work is replete with such entertainment as is adapted to all grades of readers, the most or least intellectual. — *Methodist Quarterly Magazine.*

One of the most complete things of the kind ever given to the public. There is scarcely a paragraph in the whole book which will not interest some one deeply; for, while men of letters, argument, and art cannot afford to do without its immense fund of sound maxims, pungent wit, apt illustrations, and brilliant examples, the merchant, mechanic and laborer will find it one of the choicest companions of the hours of relaxation. "Whatever be the mood of one's mind, and however limited the time for reading, in the almost endless variety and great brevity of the articles he can find something to suit his feelings, which he can begin and end at once. It may also be made the very life of the social circle, containing pleasant reading for all ages, at all times and seasons. — *Buffalo Commercial Advertiser.*

A well spring of entertainment, to be drawn from at any moment, comprising the choicest anecdotes of distinguished men, from the remotest period to the present time. — *Bangor Whig.*

A magnificent collection of anecdotes touching literature and the fine arts. — *Albany Spectator.*

This work, which is the most extensive and comprehensive collection of anecdotes ever published, cannot fail to become highly popular. — *Salem Gazette.*

A publication of which there is little danger of speaking in too flattering terms; a perfect Thesaurus of rare and curious information, carefully selected and methodically arranged. A jewel of a book to lie on one's table, to snatch up in those brief moments of leisure that could not be very profitably turned to account by recourse to any connected work in any department of literature. — *Troy Budget.*

No family ought to be without it, for it is at once cheap, valuable, and very interesting; containing matter compiled from all kinds of books, from all quarters of the globe, from all ages of the world, and in relation to every corporeal matter at all worthy of being remarked or remembered. No work has been issued from the press for a number of years for which there was such a manifest want, and we are certain it only needs to be known to meet with an immense sale. — *New Jersey Union.*

A well-pointed anecdote is often useful to illustrate an argument, and a memory well stored with personal incidents enables the possessor to entertain lively and agreeable conversation. — *N. Y. Com.*

A rich treasury of thought, and wit, and learning, illustrating the characteristics and peculiarities of many of the most distinguished names in the history of literature and the arts. — *Phil. Chris. Obs.*

The range of topics is very wide, relating to nature, religion, science, and art; furnishing apposite illustrations for the preacher, the orator, the Sabbath school teacher, and the instructors of our common schools, academies, and colleges. It must prove a valuable work for the fireside, as well as for the library, as it is calculated to please and edify all classes. — *Zanesville Ch. Register.*

This is one of the most entertaining works for desultory reading we have seen, and will no doubt have a very extensive circulation. As a most entertaining table book, we hardly know of any thing at once so instructive and amusing. — *N. Y. Ch. Intelligencer.* G

IMPORTANT WORK.

KITTO'S POPULAR CYCLOPÆDIA OF BIBLICAL LITERATURE.

Condensed from the larger work. By the Author, JOHN KITTO, D. D., Author of " Pictorial Bible," " History of Palestine," " Scripture Daily Readings," &c. Assisted by JAMES TAYLOR, D. D., of Glasgow. With *over five hundred Illustrations*. One volume octavo, 812 pp., cloth, 3,00.

THE POPULAR BIBLICAL CYCLOPÆDIA OF LITERATURE is designed to furnish a DICTIONARY OF THE BIBLE, embodying the products of the best and most recent researches in biblical literature, in which the scholars of Europe and America have been engaged. The work, the result of immense labor and research, and enriched by the contributions of writers of distinguished eminence in the various departments of sacred literature, has been, by universal consent, pronounced the best work of its class extant, and the one best suited to the advanced knowledge of the present day in all the studies connected with theological science. It is not only intended for *ministers* and *theological students*, but is also particularly adapted to *parents, Sabbath school teachers, and the great body of the religious public*. The *illustrations*, amounting to *more than three hundred*, are of the very highest order.

A condensed view of the various branches of Biblical Science comprehended in the work.

1. BIBLICAL CRITICISM, — Embracing the History of the Bible Languages ; Canon of Scripture ; Literary History and Peculiarities of the Sacred Books ; Formation and History of Scripture Texts.
2. HISTORY, — Proper Names of Persons ; Biographical Sketches of prominent Characters ; Detailed Accounts of important Events recorded in Scripture ; Chronology and Genealogy of Scripture.
3. GEOGRAPHY, — Names of Places ; Description of Scenery ; Boundaries and Mutual Relations of the Countries mentioned in Scripture, so far as necessary to illustrate the Sacred Text.
4. ARCHÆOLOGY, — Manners and Customs of the Jews and other nations mentioned in Scripture ; their Sacred Institutions, Military Affairs, Political Arrangements, Literary and Scientific Pursuits.
5. PHYSICAL SCIENCE, — Scripture Cosmogony and Astronomy, Zoology, Mineralogy, Botany, Meteorology.

In addition to numerous flattering notices and reviews, personal letters from *more than fifty of the most distinguished Ministers and Laymen of different religious denominations in the country* have been received, highly commending this work as admirably adapted to ministers, Sabbath school teachers, heads of families, and *all* Bible students.

The following extract of a letter is a fair specimen of individual letters received from *each* of the gentlemen whose names are given below :—

" I have examined it with special and unalloyed satisfaction. It has the rare merit of being all that it professes to be, and very few, I am sure, who may consult it will deny that, in richness and fullness of detail, it surpasses their expectation. Many ministers will find it a valuable auxiliary ; but its chief excellence is, that it furnishes just the facilities which are needed by the thousands in families and Sabbath schools, who are engaged in the important business of biblical education. It is in itself a library of reliable information."

W. B. Sprague, D. D., Pastor of Second Presbyterian Church, Albany, N. Y.
J. J. Carruthers, D. D., Pastor of Second Parish Congregational Church, Portland, Me.
Joel Hawes, D. D., Pastor of First Congregational Church, Hartford, Ct.
Daniel Sharp, D. D., late Pastor of Third Baptist Church, Boston.
N. L. Frothingham, D. D., late Pastor of First Congregational Church, (Unitarian,) Boston.
Ephraim Peabody, D. D., Pastor of Stone Chapel Congregational Church, (Unitarian,) Boston.
A. L. Stone, Pastor of Park Street Congregational Church, Boston.
John S. Stone, D. D., Rector of Christ Church, (Episcopal,) Brooklyn, N. Y.
J. B. Waterbury, D. D., Pastor of Bowdoin Street Church, (Congregational,) Boston.
Baron Stow, D. D., Pastor of Rowe Street Baptist Church, Boston.
Thomas H. Skinner, D. D., Pastor of Carmine Presbyterian Church, New York.
Samuel W. Worcester, D. D., Pastor of the Tabernacle Church, (Congregational,) Salem.
Horace Bushnell, D. D., Pastor of Third Congregational Church, Hartford, Ct.
Right Reverend J. M. Wainwright, D. D., Trinity Church, (Episcopal.) New York.
Gardner Spring, D. D., Pastor of the Brick Church Chapel Presbyterian Church, New York.
W. T. Dwight, D. D., Pastor of Third Congregational Church, Portland, Me.
E. N. Kirk, Pastor of Mount Vernon Congregational Church, Boston.
Prof. George Bush, author of " Notes on the Scriptures," New York.
Howard Malcom, D. D., author of " Bible Dictionary," and Pres. of Lewisburg University.
Henry J. Ripley, D. D., author of " Notes on the Scriptures," and Prof. in Newton Theol. Ins.
N. Porter, Prof. in Yale College, New Haven, Ct.
Jared Sparks, Edward Everett, Theodore Frelinghuysen, Robert C. Winthrop, John McLean, Simon Greenleaf, Thomas S. Williams, — and a large number of others of like character and standing of the above, whose names cannot here appear.

H

MIALL'S WORKS.

FOOTSTEPS OF OUR FOREFATHERS; what they Suffered and what they Sought. Describing Localities and portraying Personages and Events conspicuous in the Struggles for Religious Liberty. By JAMES G. MIALL, author of "Memorials of Early Christianity," etc. Containing thirty-six fine Illustrations. 12mo, 1,00.

An exceedingly entertaining work. It is full of strong points. The reader soon catches the fire and zeal of those sterling men whom we have so long admired, and ere he is aware becomes so deeply enlisted in their cause that he finds it difficult to lay aside the book till finished. — *Ch. Parlor Mag.*

A book to stir one's spirit to activity and self-sacrifice in the work of God. It portrays the character, the deeds, the sufferings, and the success of those heroic non-conformists who stood up for the truth against tyranny. It is a book worthy of a large sale. — *Zion's Herald.*

A work absorbingly interesting, and very instructive. — *Western Lit. Magazine.*

The title of this book attracted our attention; its contents have held us fast to its pages to the very close. Its story is of principles and sufferings with which every American who prizes his birthright, and would know how it has been secured, should be familiar. It embraces graphic sketches of localities and scenes, of personages and events, illustrative of the grand struggle for religious liberty. It is fascinating in style, and reliable for substance. It is full of antiquarian lore, and abounds in charming local descriptions. Most earnestly do we recommend it. — *Watchman and Reflector.*

The events narrated and scenes described by the author give us interesting and impressive views of the great sacrifices made by the noble sufferers for the priceless boon of spiritual freedom, which American citizens claim as their birthright. — *Ch. Observer.*

This volume is devoted to biographical notices of those noble minds who made the grand discoveries of civil and religious liberty in England, and who counted not their lives dear, so that the Bible and the freedom of conscience should descend upon their children's children. The anecdotes of these men and their times are full of interest, and are drawn from the most authentic sources. — *Nat. Intel.*

This is a most captivating book, and one that the reader is compelled to finish if he once begins it. We really wish that every family in our land could have a copy. It has kept us perfectly enchained from beginning to end. — *Newport Observer.*

MEMORIALS OF EARLY CHRISTIANITY; Presenting, in a graphic, compact, and popular Form, Memorable Events of Early Ecclesiastical History, etc. By JAMES G MIALL, author of "Footsteps of our Forefathers," etc. With numerous elegant Illustrations. 12mo, cloth, 1,00.

☞ This, like the "Footsteps of our Forefathers," will be found a work of uncommon interest.

We thank Mr. Miall for this volume, which our publishers have reprinted in quite handsome style. There are plain truths plainly told in this volume about ancient Christianity and the practices of the Christians of ante-Nicene times which we could wish *churchmen* would lay to heart and profit by. — *Episcopal Register.*

It is well written, *more* interesting than a *romance*, and yet full of instruction and warning for the present generation. — *Hartford Times.*

A work of no ordinary value as a faithful exponent of early church history, and we can most cheerfully commend it to all. Every Sabbath school should be supplied with copies of it. — *Ch. Secretary.*

Mr. Miall is a Congregational minister in England, and a popular writer of unusual power. He has the power of graphic delineation, and has given us pictures of early Christianity which have the charm of life and reality. We regard the volume as one of unusual interest and value, and our readers are assured that its glowing pages will excite their admiration. — *N. Y. Recorder.*

This is an extremely interesting work, embodying classic and ecclesiastic lore, and calculated to do much good by bringing the church of *to-day* into closer acquaintanceship and sympathy with the church of the early past. — *Congregationalist.*

A very successful attempt to *popularize* the history of the church during the first three centuries. The *results* of extended research are offered to the general reader in a style of *uncommon interest*. The mass of readers know far too little on church history. — *Watchman and Reflector.*

We have in this volume, embodied in a lucid and attractive form, some of the most important facts of early ecclesiastical history, in illustration of the original purity and power of Christian faith. It is a work of labor, and labor very successfully applied. — *Puritan Recorder.*

A volume of thrilling interest. It takes the reader through a very important period of secular and ecclesiastical history. We are glad to see this work. It cannot fail of doing good. — *Western Lit. Messenger.*

Yy

DR. GRANT AND THE MOUNTAIN NESTORIANS.
BY THE REV. THOMAS LAURIE.

This volume possesses uncommon interest and value, furnishing a large amount of information concerning the origin, history, character, and condition of the Nestorian church. It gives the church the history of a remarkable man — a genuine moral hero — and unfolds to her vision a graphic picture of the perils, toils, and success of her laborers in foreign lands. — *Zion's Herald.*

Dr. Grant was a courageous, hard-working, self-sacrificing Christian, doing with his might whatever his hands found to do. The author has performed his labor with the highest credit, and has given to the public a memoir of very great value. The large and beautiful map, the portrait of Dr. Grant, and the numerous illustrations, add great attractions to this work. — *Western Lit. Gazette.*

A well-written and deeply-interesting biography of an American missionary, who was celebrated for his zealous efforts to spread the Gospel. Those who are fond of books of travel, or who feel an interest in the missionary cause, should read this succinct and graphic narrative. — *Yankee Blade.*

A work of great interest. Dr. Grant was one of the noblest of men, as well as one of the most devoted of missionaries, and his field of labor situated in the most romantic portion of Asia, and rich in the historic associations of many centuries. Aside from religious considerations, this volume is eminently readable and important as it throws much light upon the physical and political condition of the Nestorians, and other Oriental nations. — *N. Y. Commercial.*

This volume is at once a memoir of the life and missionary labors of Dr. Grant, and a historic and geographical sketch of the interesting people and country among whom he labored. It must be apparent that such a publication possesses more intrinsic interest and [value than any ordinary biographical sketch. — *Boston Atlas.*

This volume will be found full of interest to all lovers of missionary enterprise in one of the most important fields in the eastern world. Aside from the information respecting the progress and incidents of this enterprise, the work presents very accurate details of the condition of the country, manners and customs of the people, and other matters of general interest. — *Bangor Mercury.*

The volume contains a portrait, a beautiful map, eleven illustrations, and a full index. It is a very excellent memoir of a *remarkable man*, being faithfully a memoir of Dr. Grant, yet, in connection with his own history and travels, it makes us acquainted with the homes and character of an interesting people, and their romantic scenery. It is written with admirable simplicity and descriptive beauty, narrating the most thrilling and adventurous scenes with great effect. — *Vermont Chronicle.*

This is a beautiful volume in its exterior and its typographical execution, but more valuable for its contents. The name of Dr. Grant is widely known, and honored by all. Its appearance will be hailed with much delight, and its perusal afford great satisfaction. It has value, not merely as a memorial of a faithful and devoted missionary, but it possesses interest as a contribution to our geographical knowledge and information of a people that has excited so much attention, and enlisted such general sympathy among Christians. — *Evangelical Review.*

A work of much instruction and interest. — *Scientific American.*

The work of Mr. Laurie is both an account of this people, and a biography of Dr. Grant — the faithful missionary apostle among them. In this case, the two themes of descriptive history and biography have been very properly and judiciously blended. Mr. Laurie has executed his task admirably, and we cannot refrain from saying that the illustrations are in the very finest style of wood engraving. Many steel engravings are much inferior to those in point of beauty and finish. Altogether, the work is of *surpassing* interest. — *Dover Star.*

Dr. Grant will be remembered as long as there is a heart in this country to feel for the heathen world. The present memoir is not only intensely interesting, on account of the heroic man, the strange, wild, sublime religion, and the wonderful people with which it makes us familiar, but it is a valuable addition to our missionary and general knowledge. It is full of the most thrilling incidents — perils in mountain-passes, encounters with robbers, descriptions of torrents, tempests, and avalanches; remarkable characters and scenery enough for a score of romances. And yet it is pervaded everywhere by a spirit of ardent, self-denying devotion to Christ, which triumphs over privation and peril — a faith in God, and a love for souls, which Persian snows and Koordish banditti cannot destroy, or even divert. — *Cincinnati Ch. Herald.*

A very full and minute account of the Nestorians, that very singular people. The life of such a man as Dr. Grant was really necessary. He was a missionary physician, and in it we see the wisdom of the Saviour manifested in combining his healing mercy to the bodies of men when he would benefit their souls. — *Presbyterian Banner.*

The readers of the second series of Layard's "Nineveh" will doubtless remember the eulogistic reference made by the writer to Dr. Grant of the American Mission among the Mountain Nestorians. The Dr. Grant thus approvingly alluded to is the gentleman whose interesting biography and whose moving adventures in the East are narrated in this well-written volume; and which addresses itself, with many claims, to the notice and patronage of the public. — *London Ch. and State Gazette.*

THE PREACHER AND THE KING;
OR, BOURDALOUE IN THE COURT OF LOUIS XIV.

Being an Account of that distinguished Era. Translated from the French of L. BUNGENER. Paris, fourteenth edition. With an Introduction, by the REV. GEORGE POTTS, D. D., New York. 12mo, cloth, 1,25.

It combines *substantial history with the highest charm of romance;* the most rigid philosophical criticism with a thorough analysis of human character and faithful representation of the spirit and manners of the age to which it relates. We regard the book as a valuable contribution to the cause not merely of general literature, but especially of pulpit eloquence. Its attractions are so various that it can hardly fail to find readers of almost every description. — *Puritan Recorder.*

A very delightful book. It is full of interest, and equally replete with sound thought and profitable sentiment. — *N. Y. Commercial.*

It is a volume at once curious, instructive, and fascinating. The interviews of Bourdaloue, and Claude, and those of Bossuet, Fenelon, and others, are remarkably attractive, and of finished taste. Other high personages of France are brought in to figure in the narrative, while rhetorical rules are exemplified in a manner altogether new. Its extensive sale in France is evidence enough of its extraordinary merit and its peculiarly attractive qualities. — *Ch. Advocate.*

It is full of life and animation, and conveys a graphic idea of the state of morals and religion in the Augustan age of French literature. — *N. P. Recorder.*

This book will attract by its novelty, and prove particularly engaging to those interested in the pulpit eloquence of an age characterized by the flagrant wickedness of Louis XIV. The author has exhibited singular skill in weaving into his narrative sketches of the remarkable men who flourished at that period, with original and striking remarks on the subject of preaching. — *Presbyterian.*

Its historical and biographical portions are valuable; its comments excellent, and its effect pure and benignant. A work which we recommend to all, as possessing rare interest. — *Buffalo Morn. Exp.*

A book of rare interest, not only for the singular ability with which it is written, but for the graphic account which it gives of the state of pulpit eloquence during the celebrated era of which it treats. It is perhaps the best biography extant of the distinguished and eloquent preacher, who above all others most pleased the king; while it also furnishes many interesting particulars in the lives of his professional contemporaries. We content ourself with warmly commending it. — *Savannah Journal.*

The author is a minister of the Reformed Church. In the forms of narrative and conversations, he portrays the features and character of that remarkable age, and illustrates the claims and duties of the sacred office, and the important ends to be secured by the eloquence of the pulpit. — *Phil. Ch. Obs.*

A book which unfolds to us the private conversation, the interior life and habits of study of such men as Claude, Bossuet, Bourdaloue, Massillon, and Bridaine, cannot but be a precious gift to the American church and ministers. It is a book full of historical facts of great value, sparkling with gems of thought, polished scholarship, and genuine piety. — *Cin. Ch. Advocate.*

This volume presents a phase of French life with which we have never met in any other work. The author is a minister of the Reformed Church in Paris, where his work has been received with unexampled popularity, having already gone through *fourteen* editions. The writer has studied not only the divinity and general literature of the age of Louis XIV., but also the memories of that period, until he is able to reproduce a life-like picture of society at the Court of the Grand Monarch. — *Alb. Trans.*

A work which we recommend to all, as possessing rare interest. — *Buffalo Ev. Express.*

In form it is descriptive and dramatic, presenting the reader with animated conversations between some of the most famous preachers and philosophers of the Augustan age of France. The work will be read with interest by all intelligent men; but it will be of especial service to the ministry, who cannot afford to be ignorant of the facts and suggestions of this instructive volume. — *N. Y. Ch. Intel.*

The work is very fascinating, and the lesson under its spangled robe is of the gravest moment to every pulpit and every age. — *Ch. Intelligencer.*

THE PRIEST AND THE HUGUENOT; or Persecution in the Age

of Louis XV. Part I., A Sermon at Court; Part II., A Sermon in the City; Part III., A Sermon in the Desert. Translated from the French of L. BUNGENER, author of "The Preacher and the King." 2 vols. 12mo, cloth. ☞ *A new Work.*

☞ This is truly a masterly production, full of interest, and may be set down as one of the greatest Protestant works of the age. **Ff**

PHILIP DODDRIDGE.
HIS LIFE AND LABORS.

A Centenary Memorial. By JOHN STOUHTON, D. D., author of "Spiritual Heroes," &c., and an INTRODUCTORY CHAPTER by REV. JAMES G. MIALL, author of "Footsteps of our Forefathers," &c. With beautiful Illuminated Title Page, Frontispiece, etc. 16mo, cloth, 60 cts.

Since the flood of biographies, memoirs, personal recollections, &c., with which the press teems at present, it is refreshing to get hold of a book like this. — *Presbyterian Witness.*

This is a clear, concise and interesting memoir of a man whose works and praise have been, for more than a century, in the churches on both sides of the Atlantic. The thousands who have read his "Rise and Progress of Religion," will want to know more of the author; and this volume is adapted to meet that want. — *Ch. Messenger.*

The sketch is drawn with remarkable literary skill, and the volume is one to be read with high satisfaction and profit. — *N. Y. Mirror.*

There are numerous readers who will rejoice in a volume that throws fresh light on the ministerial career and the writings of Dr. Doddridge. His great reputation as a religious author is chiefly based upon the celebrated work entitled, "The Rise and Progress of Religion in the soul," but he was no mean poet, and some of his hymns are unsurpassed. — *N. Y. Commercial.*

This works merits a place among the best Christian biographies of our times. — *Phil. Ch. Obs.*

We think nobody can read the book without feeling fresh admiration for Dr. Doddridge's character, and without being impressed with the conviction, that he was one of the finest models of the benevolent spirit of Christianity with which the world has been blessed since the days of the Apostle John. — *Puritan Recorder.*

THE LIFE AND CORRESPONDENCE OF JOHN FOSTER.

Author of "Decission of Character." Essays, etc. Edited by J. E. RYLAND, with notices of MR. FOSTER, as a Preacher and Companion. By JOHN SHEPPARD. A new edition, *two volumes in one*, 700 pages. 12mo, cloth, $1,25.

In simplicity of language, in majesty of conception, in the eloquence of that conciseness which conveys in a short sentence more meaning than the mind dares at once admit; his writings are unmatched. — *North British Review.*

It is with no ordinary expectations and gratification and delight that we have taken up the Biography and Correspondence of the author of the 'Essays on Decision of Character,' etc. The memoir of such a man as John Foster, must, of necessity, possess very peculiar attractions. A man whose writings have been perused with admiration wherever the English language is spoken or understood; whose calm, transparent and impressive thoughts have, in their acquaintance and contact, cut out new channels of thought in ten thousand other minds; whose dignified and sober views of life, religion, and immortality are adapted to shed so hallowed a spirit over all who become familiar with them. Mr. Ryland, the editor of the memorials, is favorably known on both sides of the water by his literary offerings; and in compilation of these volumes he has exercised a discriminating judgment, a blameless taste, and sound discretion.

We are glad to find ourselves in possession of so much additional matter from the well-nigh inspired pen of this great master in English composition. — *Christian Review.*

A book rich in every way — in good sense, vivacity, suggestiveness, liberality, and piety. — *Mirror.*

The letters which principally compose this volume, bears strongly the impress of his own original mind, and is often characterized by a depth and power of thought rarely met with even in professedly elaborate disquisitions. — *Albany Argus.*

Mr. Foster was one of the most admirable writers of England. His life is full of instruction, and will prove of great value to those young ministers whose labors are attended with poor success. The fame and influence of Foster will live as long as talent, learning, and piety shall be respected on the earth. We commend, therefore, most heartily, the work before us to the public. We commend it to the scholar, and assure him that in the correspondence of Mr. Foster, he will find letters of rare literary worth, and much to improve his taste and his mind. We sincerely hope that all our clergymen will procure this book, and read it — read it often. We know of no work which will do more for their literary culture. — *N. Y. Ch. Messenger.*

John Foster was one of the strongest writers of his age. — *Christian Register.*

This work must constitute the choice book of the season, in the department of correspondence and biography. We all wish to know what he was as a friend, a husband, a father, and as a practical exponent of what is enshrined in the immortal productions of his pen. All will rejoice in the opportunity of adding this treasure to their libraries. — *Watchman and Reflector.*

DR. WILLIAMS'S WORKS.

RELIGIOUS PROGRESS; Discourses on the Development of the Christian Character. By WILLIAM R. WILLIAMS, D. D. Third ed 12mo, cl., 85c.

This work is from the pen of one of the brightest lights of the American pulpit. We scarcely know of any living writer who has a finer command of powerful thought and glowing, impressive language than he. The volume will advance, if possible, the author's reputation. — DR. SPRAGUE, *Alb. Atlas.*

This book is a rare phenomena in these days. It is a rich exposition of Scripture, with a fund of practical religious wisdom, conveyed in a style so strong and massive as to remind one of the English writers of two centuries ago; and yet it abounds in fresh illustrations drawn from every (even the latest opened) field of science and of literature. — *Methodist Quarterly.*

His power of apt and forcible illustration is without a parallel among modern writers. The mute pages spring into life beneath the magic of his radiant imagination. But this is never at the expense of solidity of thought or strength of argument. It is seldom, indeed, that a mind of so much poetical invention yields such a willing homage to the logical element. — *Harper's Monthly Miscellany.*

With warm and glowing language, Dr. Williams exhibits and enforces the truth; every page radiant with "thoughts that burn," leave their indelible impression upon the mind. — *N. Y. Com. Adv.*

The strength and compactness of argumentation, the correctness and beauty of style, and the importance of the animating idea of the discourses, are worthy of the high reputation of Dr. Williams, and place them among the most finished homiletic productions of the day. — *N. Y. Evangelist.*

Dr. Williams has no superior among American divines in profound and exact learning, and brilliancy of style. He seems familiar with the literature of the world, and lays his vast resources under contribution to illustrate and adorn every theme which he investigates. We wish the volume could be placed in every religious family in the country. — *Phil. Ch. Chronicle.*

LECTURES ON THE LORD'S PRAYER. Third ed. 32mo, cl., 85c.

We observe the writer's characteristic fulness and richness of language, felicity and beauty of illustration, justness of discrimination and thought. — *Watchman and Reflector.*

Dr. Williams is one of the most interesting and accomplished writers in this country. We welcome this volume as a valuable contribution to our religious literature — *Ch. Witness.*

In reading, we resolved to mark the passages which we most admired, but soon found that we should be obliged to mark nearly all of them. — *Ch. Secretary.*

It bears in every page the mark of an elegant writer and an accomplished scholar, an acute reasoner and a cogent moralist. Some passages are so decidedly eloquent that we instinctively find ourselves looking round as if upon an audience, and ready to join them with audible applause — *Ch. Inquirer.*

We are constantly reminded, in reading his eloquent pages, of the old English writers, whose vigorous thought, and gorgeous imagery, and varied learning, have made their writings an inexhaustible mine for the scholars of the present day. — *Ch. Observer.*

Their breadth of view, strength of logic, and stirring eloquence place them among the very best homiletical efforts of the age. Every page is full of suggestion as well as eloquence. — *Ch. Parlor Mag.*

MISCELLANIES. New, improved edition. (*Price reduced.*) 12mo, 1,25.

☞ This work, which has been heretofore published in octavo form at 1,75 per copy, is published by the present proprietors in one handsome 12mo volume, at the low price of 1,25.

A volume which is absolutely necessary to the completeness of a library. — *N. Y. Weekly Review.*

Dr. Williams is a profound scholar and a brilliant writer. — *N. Y. Evangelist.*

He often rises to the sphere of a glowing and impressive eloquence, because no other form of language can do justice to his thoughts and emotions. So, too, the exuberance of literary illustration, with which he clothes the driest speculative discussions, is not brought in for the sake of effect, but as the natural expression of a mind teeming with the "spoils of time" and the treasures of study in almost every department of learning. — *N. Y. Tribune.*

From the pen of one of the most able and accomplished authors of the age. — *Bap. Memorial.*

We are glad to see this volume. We wish such men abounded in every sect. — *Ch. Register.*

One of the richest volumes that has been given to the public for many years. — *N. Y. Bap. Reg.*

The author's mind is cast in no common mould. A delightful volume. — *Meth. Prot.* **Bb**

LEASANT PAGES FOR YOUNG PEOPLE;

OR, BOOK OF HOME EDUCATION AND ENTERTAINMENT.

S. PROUT NEWCOMBE. With numerous Illustrations. 16mo, 75 cts.

This work is designed for the pleasure and profit of young people; and, as the title indicates, nded as an aid to Home Education. The great variety of subjects presented, consisting of Moral ons, Natural History, History, Travels, Physical Geography, Object Lessons, Drawing and Per- tive, Music, Poetry, etc., and withal, so skilfully treated as to make truth simple and attractive, lers it an admirable family book for winter evenings and summer days.

very excellent book for children. History, philosophy, science, stories, and descriptions of games all mingled together, and he who does not like the compound must be hard to please. — *Post.*

easant pages, containing information on a great variety of subjects. Ten minutes a day on this active volume would soon make the boy quite a philosopher. We doubt whether most boys could onfined to the ten minutes. Curiosity would read on by the hour. Such books have a charming uence in the family. Here we have science and art made plain and captivating. The lessons in wing and perspective alone are worth the price of the volume. And then a thousand questions ch the intelligent young mind raises are here most pleasantly and plainly answered. — *Parlor Mag.*

his is indeed a home book of endless amusement. — *Boston Atlas.*

his is an admirable book of home education. We commend it to every family. — *Albany Spec.*

work admirably adapted to the instruction and amusement of the young. — *Albany Register.*

pleasant book, full of all sorts of information upon all sorts of subjects. — *Providence Journal.*

ne of the most delightful works for young people we have ever met with. Few persons, young or could examine its pages without gaining a better knowledge of a useful kind, or without being in- sted by the pleasant and attractive manner in which it is written. It is one of the most successful ibinations of the pleasant with the useful to be found. — *Daily Advertiser.*

his is a book of not only "pleasant pages," but of singularly *instructive* pages for young people. n people not so very young might be pleased and profited by its perusal. — *South Boston Gazette.*

presents much solid information, and opens before the young new fields of observation. The ngsters will clap their hands with joy. — *American.*

here is a great deal of valuable information communicated in a very simple and easy way. While full of useful instruction to children it is also suggestive to those who are called to conduct their cation. — *Puritan Recorder.*

e like this book: it is well fitted for its place in the family library, and the fireside companion of young. Children like facts; when these are so forth in a pleasant way, the interest is greater than on ever awakens, unless the fiction is made to appear like truth. — *Godey's Ladies' Book.*

IE GUIDING STAR; or, The Bible God's Message. By LOUISA AYSON HOPKINS. With Frontispiece. 16mo, cloth, 50 cts.

lthough written more especially for young persons, its argumentation is so cogent that it may be l with profit by adult sceptics. — *N. Y. Commercial.*

his is an excellent little work to put into the hands of youth. It is written in conversational style, l opens up most beautifully, and with great simplicity, the great leading evidences that the Bible tains God's message to man. Those seeking after truth will find it worthy of frequent perusal, and se grounded in the truth, yet wanting in peculiar arguments with which to meet the cavils of infi- s, will find it a champion of which they need not be ashamed. — DR. SPRAGUE, *in Albany Spec*

his is a happy presentation of the argument in behalf of Christianity, in the form of a dialogue ween a mother and her children. We cordially commend the work to parents, children, and Sab- h schools. — *Congregationalist.*

his volume should be in the hands of every youthful reader, and we doubt not that adult persons uld find much in it that is not only interesting, but instructive. — *Phil. Ch. Chronicle.*

he popular author of this book has conferred a favor on the public, for which she deserves some- g more than thanks. — *Ch. Secretary.*

ne of the most valuable books for youth that we have seen. It required no ordinary capacity, re- rch, and labor, to prepare it in its present shape. — *Cong. Journal and Messenger.*

his is a book of more than common excellence. While reading it, how often have we wished that the youth of our land might become familiar with its contents. — *Ch. Mirror.* **X**

NATIONAL SERIES OF AMERICAN HISTORIES.
BY REV. JOSEPH BANVARD.

PLYMOUTH AND THE PILGRIMS; or, Incidents of Adventures the History of the First Settlers. With Illustrations. 16mo, cloth, 60 cts.

The book, when once taken up, will not be laid down without regret until it is finished. — *Cour*

An exceedingly interesting volume. The incidents are well chosen, and are described in that rect, simple, and sprightly manner, for which Mr. Banvard is so justly esteemed, and which eminen qualifies him to be a writer for the young. — *Am. Traveller.*

It is written in a terse and vigorous style, and is well adapted for popular reading, and particula to entertain and instruct the youthful mind. — *Mercantile Journal.*

Every New Englander, no matter where he resides, should own this book. — *Scientific American*

This is a beautifully executed and extremely interesting volume. It is written in a plain, but v orous style, particularly adapted to young readers, though it may be read with interest by the ol ones. — *Ch. Freeman.*

Highly attractive in style and instructive in matter, and well calculated to engage the attention young persons. — *N. Y. Com. Adv.*

NOVELTIES OF THE NEW WORLD; an Account of the Adventur and Discoveries of the First Explorers of North America. Being the second volume BANVARD'S SERIES OF AMERICAN HISTORIES. With numerous Illustrations. 6

If Mr. Banvard completes the series as he has begun, he will supply an important desideratum the young -- a series of books which will serve as valuable introductions and enticements to more tended historical reading. — *Am. Travller.*

We have seen the boys bend over these pages, unwilling to leave them, either for play or sleep; a when finished, inquiring anxiously when the next would come. — *Watchman and Reflector.*

It has all the interest of a romance. — *Portland Transcript.*

Written in a felicitous style, which is neither too childish for adults, nor yet too difficult of comp hension for children. They will delight as well as instruct. — *Mercantile Journal.*

Some of the most interesting scenes and events in the New World are here brought together and vested with a charm that is irresistible by old as well as young. — *Ch. Intelligencer.*

The book is beautifully printed; the subject is handled in a masterly manner. — *Olive Branch.*

ROMANCE OF AMERICAN HISTORY; or, an Account of the Ear Settlement of North Carolina and Virginia, embracing a Narrative of the tragic Incide connected with the Spanish Settlement at St. Augustine, the French Colonies at I anoke, and the English Plantation at Jamestown; the Captivity of Captain John Smi and the interesting Adventures of the youthful Pocahontas. Being the third volume BANVARD'S SERIES OF AMERICAN HISTORIES. With numerous Illustrations. 6

It has all the interest of romance, and the additional interest of veritable history. — *Puritan Rec*

It is a most pleasing and instructive book. — *Home Journal.*

As interesting as a novel, and a thousand times more profitable reading. — *Lit. Messenger.*

Every library should be furnished with this National Series of American Histories. — *N. E. Farm*

Admirably fitted for fireside, family reading, and calculated to interest young persons. — *Travel*

This is the third volume of Mr. Banvard's attractive series of books founded on the early history our country; and it will make a most valuable addition to all family libraries. — *Arthur's Gazette.*

No more interesting and instructive reading can be put into the hands of the young. — *Port. Tro*

☞ Other volumes of this popular series are in course of preparation. The series will embrace most interesting and important events which have occurred in the United States since the settlem of the country. They will be adapted to the popular mind, and especially to the youth of our cou try, and will contain numerous fine engravings. There will be twelve or more 16mo. volumes, about 300 pages. Each volume to be complete in itself; and yet, when all are published, they will gether form a regular SERIES OF AMERICAN HISTORIES. **Y**

VALUABLE WORKS FOR THE YOUNG.
BY REV. HARVEY NEWCOMB.

HOW TO BE A MAN; a Book for Boys, containing Useful Hints on the Formation of Character. Eleventh thousand. Cloth, gilt, 50 cts.

"My design in writing has been to contribute something towards forming the character of those who to be our future electors, legislators, governors, judges, ministers, lawyers, and physicians, — after the best model. It is intended for boys — or, if you please, for *young* gentlemen, in early youth, from nine or ten to fifteen or sixteen years of age." — *Preface.*

We consider "How to be a Man" an inimitable little volume, and we desire that it be widely circulated. It should be put into the hands of every youth in the land. — *Tennessee Baptist.*

HOW TO BE A LADY; a Book for Girls, containing Useful Hints on the Formation of Character. Twelfth thousand. Cloth, gilt, 50 cts.

"Having daughters of his own, and having been many years employed in writing for the young, hopes to be able to offer some good advice, in an entertaining way, for girls or misses, between the ages of eight and fifteen. His object is, to assist them in forming their characters upon the best model; that they may become well-bred, intelligent, refined, and good; and then they will be real *ladies*, in the highest sense." — *Preface.*

Parents will consult, we are sure, the best interests of their daughters, for time and eternity, in making them acquainted with this attractive and most useful volume. — *N. Y. Evangelist.*

The following Notices apply to both the above Volumes.

It would be better for the next generation, in more particulars than we can stop to enumerate, if every youth would "read, learn, and inwardly digest" the contents of these volumes. — *N. Y. Com.*

These volumes contain much matter which is truly valuable, and will be a safe mentor to those young persons who will read the volumes and conform to the precepts contained therein. — *Mer. Jour.*

They contain wise and important counsels and cautions, adapted to the young, and made entertaining by the interesting style and illustrations of the author. They are fine mirrors, in which are reflected the prominent lineaments of the *Christian young gentleman and young lady*. The books will furnish elegant and most profitable presents for the young. — *American Pulpit.*

Mr. Newcomb's books are excellent. They contain useful hints on the formation of character, whereunto the young would do well to take heed. We are pleased to commend them. — *N. Y. Obs.*

They are books well calculated to do good. — *Phil. Ch. Chronicle.*

Designed for boys and girls, we advise all to read and listen to their suggestions. — *Jour. and Mes.*

They contain common-sense, practical hints on the formation of character and habits, and are suited to the improvement of youth in this country. — *Mothers' Journal.*

ANECDOTES FOR BOYS; Entertaining Anecdotes and Narratives, Illustrative of Principles and Character. Seventh thousand. 18mo, cloth, gilt, 42 cts.

ANECDOTES FOR GIRLS; Entertaining Anecdotes and Narratives, Illustrative of Principles and Character. Seventh thousand. 18mo, cloth, gilt, 42 cts.

There is a charm about these two beautiful volumes not to be mistaken. They are deeply interesting and instructive, without being fictitious. The anecdotes are many, short, and spirited, with a moral drawn from each, adapted to every age, condition, and duty of life. We commend them to families and schools. — *Albany Spectator.*

These anecdotes, which are always such as illustrate moral lessons, are selected from a wide range, and carefully prepared. — *N. Y. Recorder.*

Works of great value, for a truth or principle is sooner instilled into the youthful heart by an anecdote than in any other way. They are well selected, and will form an acceptable present for the holidays. — *Evening Gazette.*

Nothing has a greater interest for a youthful mind than a well-told story, and no medium of conveying moral instructions so attractive or so successful. The influence of all such stories is far more powerful when the child is assured that they are *true*. These volumes are made up of a series of anecdotes, every one of which inculcates some excellent moral lesson. We cannot too strongly recommend them to parents. — *Western Continent, Baltimore.*

VALUABLE WORKS FOR THE YOUNG

YOUNG AMERICANS ABROAD; or, Vacation in Europe: the Res[ults] of a Tour through Great Britain, France, Holland, Belgium, Germany, and Switzer[land]. By JOHN OVERTON CHOULES, D. D., and his PUPILS. With Elegant Illustra[tions]. 16mo, cloth, 75 cts.

This is a highly entertaining work, embracing more real information, such as every one wish[es to] know about Europe, than any other book of travels ever published.

Three intelligent lads, who knew how to use their eyes, were so fortunate as to accompany their [father] on a short European tour; and, from a carefully-kept journal, they wrote out, from time to time[, a] series of letters to a favorite companion in study, at home, their impressions of the most remar[kable] places *en route*. The pencillings are genuine and unaffected, and in all respects form an inter[esting] and instructive record of travel. For readers of their own age, from twelve to sixteen years, [the] fresh, intelligent reminiscences of other lands have unusual attraction, and we cordially commer[d this] work to their attention. — *Sartain's Magazine.*

Admirably calculated to gratify and interest all young readers. — *Transcript.*

One of the most attractive, instructive, and delightful books of the age. — *Southern Lit. Gazett[e.]*

Boys, here is a book that will suit you exactly. It is a series of letters from certain boys trave[lling] in Europe to their classmates in this country. You will be much more interested in it thar [you] would be in reading the travels of *men* over the same country. It will improve your knowled[ge to] read this book, and amuse you during long winter nights. — *Methodist Prot.*

We have been struck with the unaffected good taste, and the accuracy of the details, of this book; indeed, it is worth much more than many a larger and more pretentious volume, for giv[ing a] daguerreotype of things abroad. — *Congregationalist.*

A beautiful book for young people, unlike any thing of the kind we have ever seen. — *Phil. Ch[ron.]*

One of the most interesting books that can be put into the hands of the young. — *Olive Branch*

One of the best books of foreign travel for youth to be found in the whole range of American li[tera]ture. — *Buffalo Morning Express.*

THE ISLAND HOME; or, the Young Castaways. By CHRISTOPH[ER] ROMAUNT, ESQ. With Elegant Illustrations. 16mo, cloth, 75 cts.

The best and prettiest book for boys that we have lately seen. — *Boston Post.*

A stirring and unique work. It will interest the *juvenile men* vastly. — *Olive Branch.*

A delightful fiction, purporting to narrate the adventures of six boys who put to sea in an open [boat] and were drifted to a desert island, where they lived in the manner of Robinson Crusoe. — *N. Y. [...]*

The book is one of great interest, and one which will be a treat to any boy who may succeed in [per]suading his father to purchase it for him. — *Home Circle.*

Every young mind will pore over its pages with almost enchanted interest. — *Transcript.*

A modern Robinson Crusoe story, without the dreary solitude of that famous hero. It is calcu[lated] to amuse and instruct the young reader in no ordinary degree. — *Southern Lit. Gazette.*

A story that bids fair to rival the far-famed Robinson Crusoe in the estimation of youthdom. [You will] become as much interested in the Max, Johnny, Arthur, and the rest of the goodly company, as i[n the] Swiss Family Robinson. — *Sartain's Magazine.*

THE AMERICAN STATESMAN; or, Illustrations of the Life [and] Character of DANIEL WEBSTER, for the Entertainment and Instruction of Amer[ican] Youth. By the REV. JOSEPH BANVARD, author of "Plymouth and the Pilgri[ms,]" "Novelties of the New World," "Romance of American History," etc. With ele[gant] Illustrations. 16mo, cloth, 75 cts.

☞ A work of great interest, presenting a sketch of the most striking and important events w[hich] occurred in the history of the distinguished statesman, Daniel Webster, avoiding entirely all poin[ts of] a *political* character; holding up to view, for the admiration and emulation of American youth, [all] his commendable traits of character. It is just such a work as every American patriot would [wish] his children to read and reflect upon.

PILGRIMAGE TO EGYPT;

EMBRACING A DIARY OF EXPLORATIONS ON THE NILE,

[WI]TH OBSERVATIONS, illustrative of the Manners, Customs, and [In]stitutions of the People, and of the present condition of the Antiquities and Ruins. By V. C. SMITH, M. D., Editor of the Boston Medical and Surgical Journal. With numerous elegant Engravings. Third edition. 1,25.

[Th]ere is a lifelike interest in the narratives and descriptions of Dr. Smith's pen, which takes you [gen]tly along with the traveller, so that when he closes a chapter you feel that you have reached [an in]n, where you will rest for a while; and then, with a refreshed mind, you will be ready to move [a]gain, in a journey full of fresh and instructive incidents and explorations. — *Ch. Witness.*

[Ev]ery page of the volume is entertaining and instructive, and even those who are well read in [Egy]ptian manners, customs, and scenery, cannot fail to find something new and novel upon those [some]what hackneyed topics. — *Mercantile Journal.*

[On]e of the most agreeable books of travel which have been published for a long time. — *Daily Adv.*

[It] is readable, attractive, and interesting, because familiar and companionable. You seem to be [trave]lling with him, and seeing the things which he sees. — *Bunker Hill Aurora.*

[Th]e author is a keen observer, and describes what he observes with a graphic pen. The volume [abou]nds in vivid descriptions of the manners, customs, and institutions of the people visited, the [pres]ent condition of the ancient ruins, accompanied by a large number of illustrations. — *Courier.*

[W]e see what Egypt was; we see what Egypt is; and with prophetic endowment we see what it is [t]o be. It is a charming book, not written for antiquarians and the learned, but for the *million*, and [th]e million it will be read. — *Congregationalist.*

[Th]e reader may be sure of entertainment in such a land, under the guidance of such an observer as [S]mith, and will be surprised, when he has accompanied him through the tour, at the vivid im[press]ion which he retains of persons, and places, and incidents. The illustrations are capitally drawn, add greatly to the value of the book, which is a handsome volume in every respect, as are all [w]orks which issue from the house of Gould and Lincoln. — *Salem Gazette.*

[Th]is is really one of the most entertaining books upon Egypt that we have met with. It is an easy simple narration of all sorts of strange matters and things, as they came under the eye of an at[tenti]ve and intelligent observer. — *Albany Argus.*

[Dr]. Smith is one of the sprightliest authors in America, and this work is worthy of his pen. He is [parti]cularly happy in presenting the comical and grotesque side of objects. — *Commonwealth.*

[Th]e sketches of people and manners are marvellously lifelike, and if the book is not a little gossipy, [i]t is not by any means wanting in substantial information and patient research. — *Ch. Inquirer.*

[On]e of the most complete and perfect books of the kind ever published, introducing entire new [thing]s and scenes, that have been overlooked by other writers. The style is admirable and attractive, [and] abundantly interesting to insure it a general circulation. — *Diadem.*

[Re]ader, take this book and go with him; it is like making the voyage yourself. Dr. Smith writes in [ver]y pleasing style. No one will fall to sleep over the book. We admire the man's wit; it breaks [o]ccasionally like flashes of lightning on a dark sky, and makes every thing look pleasantly. Of [th]e books we have read on Egypt, we prefer this. It goes ahead of Stephens's. Reader, obtain a [copy] for yourself. — *Trumpet.*

[Th]is volume is neither a re-hash of guide books, nor a condensed mensuration of heights and dis[tance]s from works on Egyptian antiquities. It contains the daily observations of a most intelligent [trave]ller, whose descriptions bring to the reader's eye the scenes he witnessed. We have read many [book]s on Egypt, some of them full of science and learning, and some of wit and frolic, but *none which [furn]ished so clear an idea of Egypt as it is,* — of its ruins as they now are, and of its people as they [now] live and move. The style, always dignified, is not unfrequently playful, and the reader is borne [on] from page to page, with the feeling that he is in good company. — *Watchman and Reflector.*

[The] geological remarks upon the Nile and its valley, its information upon agriculture and the me[chan]ic arts, amusements, education, domestic life and economy, and especially upon the diseases of [the c]ountry, are new and important. — *Congregationalist.*

[SC]RIPTURE NATURAL HISTORY;

containing a descriptive account [of] Quadrupeds, Birds, Fishes, Insects, Reptiles, Serpents, Plants, Trees, Minerals, Gems, [an]d Precious Stones, mentioned in the Bible. By WILLIAM CARPENTER, London; [wi]th Improvements, by REV. GORHAM D. ABBOTT. Illustrated by numerous Engrav[ing]s. Also, Sketches of Palestine. 12mo, cloth, 1,00.

HUGH MILLER'S WORKS.

MY FIRST IMPRESSIONS
OF ENGLAND AND ITS PEOPLE

By Hugh Miller, author of "Old Red Sandstone," "Footprints of Creator," etc., with a fine likeness of the author. 12mo, cloth, 1,00.

Let not the careless reader imagine, from the title of this book, that it is a common book of tra on the contrary, it is a very remarkable one, both in design, spirit, and execution. The facts reco and the views advanced in this book, are so fresh, vivid, and natural, that we cannot but comme as a treasure, both of information and entertainment. It will greatly enhance the author's reput in this country as it already has in England. — *Willis's Home Journal.*

This is a noble book, worthy of the author of the Footprints of the Creator and the Old Red S stone, because it is seasoned with the same power of vivid description, the same minuteness of o vation, and soundness of criticism, and the same genial piety. We have read it with deep inte and with ardent admiration of the author's temper and genius. It is almost impossible to lay the down, even to attend to more pressing matters. It is, without compliment or hyperbole, a mos lightful volume. — *N. Y. Commercial.*

It abounds with graphic sketches of scenery and character, is full of genius, eloquence, and obse tion, and is well calculated to arrest the attention of the thoughtful and inquiring. — *Phil. Inquir*

This is a most amusing and instructive book, by a master hand. — *Democratic Review.*

The author of this work proved himself, in the Footprints of the Creator, one of the most ori thinkers and powerful writers of the age. In the volume before us he adds new laurels to his rep tion. Whoever wishes to understand the character of the present race of Englishmen, as contradi guished from past generations; to comprehend the workings of political, social, and religious agit in the minds, not of the nobility or gentry, but of the *people*, will discover that, in this volume, h found a treasure. — *Peterson's Magazine.*

His eyes were open to see, and his ears to hear, every thing; and, as the result of what he saw heard in "merrie" England, he has made one of the most spirited and attractive volumes of tr and observations that we have met with these many days. — *Traveller.*

It is with the feeling with which one grasps the hand of an old friend that we greet to our home heart the author of the Old Red Sandstone and Footprints of the Creator. Hugh Miller is one o most agreeable, entertaining, and instructive writers of the age; and, having been so delighted him before, we open the First Impressions, and enter upon its perusal with a keen intellectual a tite. We know of no work in England so full of adaptedness to the age as this. It opens up clea view the condition of its various classes, sheds new light into its social, moral, and religious his not forgetting its geological peculiarities, and draws conclusions of great value. — *Albany Spectat*

We commend the volume to our readers as one of more than ordinary value and interest, from pen of a writer who thinks for himself, and looks at mankind and at nature through his own tacles. — *Transcript.*

The author, one of the most remarkable men of the age, arranged for this journey into Eng expectng to "lodge in humble cottages, and wear a humble dress, and see what was to be see humble men only, — society without its mask." Such an observer might be expected to bring to a thousand things unknown, or partially known before; and abundantly does he fulfil this exp tion. It is one of the most absorbing books of the time. — *Portland Ch. Mirror.*

NEW WORK.
MY SCHOOLS AND SCHOOLMASTERS;
OR THE STORY OF MY EDUCATION

By Hugh Miller author of "Footprints of the Creator," "Old Sandstone," "First Impressions of England," etc. 12mo, cloth

This is a personal narrative of a deeply interesting and instructive character, concerning one o most remarkable men of the age. No one who purchases this book will have occasion to regret it word for it!

Made in the USA
Middletown, DE
11 November 2014